Mastering Databricks Lakehouse Platform

Perform Data Warehousing, Data Engineering, Machine Learning, DevOps, and BI into a Single Platform

Sagar Lad

Anjani Kumar

www.bpbonline.com

Group Product Manager: Marianne Conor

Publishing Product Manager: Eva Brawn

Senior Editor: Connell

Content Development Editor: Melissa Monroe

Technical Editor: Anne Stokes

Copy Editor: Joe Austin

Language Support Editor: Justin Baldwin

Project Coordinator: Tyler Horan

Proofreader: Khloe Styles

Indexer: V. Krishnamurthy

Production Designer: Malcolm D'Souza

Marketing Coordinator: Kristen Kramer

First published: August 2022

Published by BPB Online
WeWork, 119 Marylebone Road
London NW1 5PU

UK | UAE | INDIA | SINGAPORE

ISBN 978-93-55511-393

www.bpbonline.com

Dedicated to

My sisters ***Mohini Lad*** *and* ***Jigna Mistry*** *whose constant warmth and companionship I couldn't repay even with a lifetime of dog treats*

About the Authors

- **Sagar Lad** is a Technical Solution Architect with a leading multinational software company and has deep expertise in implementing Data & Analytics solutions for large enterprises using Cloud and Artificial Intelligence. He is an experienced Azure Platform evangelist with strong focus on driving cloud adoption for enterprise organizations using Microsoft Cloud Solutions & Offerings with 8+ Years of IT experience. He loves blogging and is an active blogger on medium,linkedin and C# Corner developer community. He was awarded the C# Corner MVP in September 2021, for his contributions to the developer community.

  Certifications to his credit – **https://www.credly.com/users/sagar-lad**

  Twitter: @AzureSagar(**https://twitter.com/AzureSagar**)

  Medium: **https://medium.com/@sagu94271**

- **Anjani Kumar** is the MD and Founder of MultiCloud4u which is one of the fastest DIgital transformation startups extensively using Data Driven solutions.

  As a technologist Anjani is a multifaceted Enterprise and Data Solution Architect and have consulted 100 of top fortune 500 clients for setting up large data warehouse and digital business transformations correctly while working with publicis.Sapient, Royal Bank Of Scotland, Microsoft, AMEX and multiple other clients such as Unilever, Citi Bank, Brown Advisory, Nissan, Sprint, Bata, Philips, Jera Americas and many more.He runs a global knowledge sharing platform called 5thir www.5thir.com

  LinkedIn Profile:

  https://www.linkedin.com/in/anjanikkumar/

About the Reviewer

- **Ilse Epskamp** is an IT Engineer with 7+ years of IT experience in the banking industry. With a strong focus on automation, she designs and develops sustainable data solutions on the Azure platform. Ilse is experienced in building automated workflows for loading, validating, transforming and ingesting data using various Azure Offerings and programming languages such as Python, as well as handling CI/CD deployment and code management with Azure DevOps. She has an educational background in the field of Artificial Intelligence and Data Science Management, is Azure certified, and enjoys expanding her technical knowledge by trainings and hands-on projects. She is a mother of two girls, living in Alkmaar, The Netherlands.

  LinkedIn:

  https://www.linkedin.com/in/ilse-epskamp

Acknowledgement

I would like to thank the entire BPB team for giving us this opportunity to author this book and guiding throughout the journey, and trusting us with this assignment.

I would like to thank the editing team for editing this book and making the manuscript look neat and perfect.

Preface

You build your data platform and then configure the databases to build data infrasture and data pipelines. Setting up the data pipeline or ETL pipeline is time-consuming. We then use various tools like Informatica etc to build ETL pipelines. All these activities take a lot of time and effort. You may also end up with issues while setting up the environment and may have to spend much effort to fix these issues, which is in no way related to your application. You must ensure that the data pipelines are up and running always and fix all hardware and hosting environment software failures that may bring the hosted application down. To sum up, you end up with a huge amount of capital and operational expenditure and effort.

Alternatively, you can build your data solutions using databricks lakehouse platform which is more stable,efficient and cheaper. You then create and schedule data pipelines with a click of button and pricing will be pay as per use. This approach would save you hardware capital cost and operational cost to some extent.

When we use Databicks Lakehouse Platform,underlying platform manages the configurations and administration task. You can focus on building your data and AI solutions using the Databricks Lakehouse platform with integration to Azure Data Factory,Power BI, Tableau etc. It has in-built feature of high availability, reliability, fault tolerance, scaling, and many more for this services.

The book starts with basic concepts of databricks lakehouse platform. We get an understanding of the real-world problems to implement data and analytics solution using Delta Lake. Then we explore about change data feed offerings and take a look at all necessary Storage Services required to store data. We get an understanding of Azure Data Factory,Databricks and its benefits. We then deep dive into detailed Architecture and devops ci/cd implementation for your data platform.

DevOps is an essential aspect of any application development process. The next chapter deals with how to create Continuous Integration and Continuous Delivery pipelines using Azure DevOps. Here we get to learn how to create generic one click pipeline to deploy your data solutions to multiple environments.

Code Bundle and Coloured Images

Please follow the link to download the
Code Bundle and the *Coloured Images* of the book:

https://rebrand.ly/n69e01o

The code bundle for the book is also hosted on GitHub at **https://github.com/bpbpublications/Mastering-Databricks-Lakehouse-Platform**. In case there's an update to the code, it will be updated on the existing GitHub repository.

We have code bundles from our rich catalogue of books and videos available at **https://github.com/bpbpublications**. Check them out!

Errata

We take immense pride in our work at BPB Publications and follow best practices to ensure the accuracy of our content to provide with an indulging reading experience to our subscribers. Our readers are our mirrors, and we use their inputs to reflect and improve upon human errors, if any, that may have occurred during the publishing processes involved. To let us maintain the quality and help us reach out to any readers who might be having difficulties due to any unforeseen errors, please write to us at :

errata@bpbonline.com

Your support, suggestions and feedbacks are highly appreciated by the BPB Publications' Family.

Piracy

If you come across any illegal copies of our works in any form on the internet, we would be grateful if you would provide us with the location address or website name. Please contact us at **business@bpbonline.com** with a link to the material.

If you are interested in becoming an author

If there is a topic that you have expertise in, and you are interested in either writing or contributing to a book, please visit **www.bpbonline.com**. We have worked with thousands of developers and tech professionals, just like you, to help them share their insights with the global tech community. You can make a general application, apply for a specific hot topic that we are recruiting an author for, or submit your own idea.

Reviews

Please leave a review. Once you have read and used this book, why not leave a review on the site that you purchased it from? Potential readers can then see and use your unbiased opinion to make purchase decisions. We at BPB can understand what you think about our products, and our authors can see your feedback on their book. Thank you!

For more information about BPB, please visit **www.bpbonline.com**.

Table of Contents

CHAPTER 1
Getting Started with Databricks Platform

Enterprise data-driven organizations struggle today to build and maintain their data solutions due to data silos, which causes major issues with maintaining the single source of truth. **Databricks Lakehouse** platform simplifies the architecture that allows different teams like data science, data engineering, and data analysts to collaborate to build data solutions without creating any silos.

In this chapter, we will start exploring the foundation of Databricks architecture, and the usage of Databricks Lakehouse platform for Data Science and Engineering and Databricks SQL.

Structure

In this chapter, we will cover the following aspects of Databricks platform:

- Introduction to Databricks
- Databricks platform architecture
- Databricks for Data Engineering and Data Science
- Databricks SQL
- Databricks components: **workspace**, **interface**, **data management**, **computation**, **model management**, **access management**, **notebook**

Objectives

After studying this chapter, you will understand why Databricks is required, who can use it, and how it can be helpful to the data teams to interpret big data.

Introduction to Databricks

> **Data is the new oil for 21st Century.**
>
> *– By Dr James Bellini*

Nowadays, most organizations are adapting to **Data Driven Decision Making (DDDM)** approach for decision-making. They are spending millions to interpret the data that is ubiquitously available around the organization sphere.

Semantically, DDDM is the process of making decisions based on actual data.

Organizations periodically generate high volumes of data across multiple platforms within several applications that are available for the decision makers in *structured, semi-structured,* and *unstructured* format, which is also known as **big data**. Earlier, making sense out of this data was tedious and time-consuming yet ineffective as compared to recent times as they don't come handy in real-time. However, recent advancement in technology has empowered us to get effective results faster with the help of cluster computing using big data processing tools.

There are many solutions available for big data processing; out of all these solutions, **Apache Spark** (*released in May 2014*) became very popular in a short period of time. It is very fast, flexible, and developer-friendly, which were the reasons for its popularity.

Organizations started configuring their own on-premise dedicated clusters to process their big data workloads using Apache Spark. But the main difficulties with this setup was infra scalability, maintenance, and security.

As we know, managing organizational data never comes easy because data grows rapidly and scales frequently. And data centers were facing challenges with regard to maintenance, security as well as scalability.

In recent years, organizations started moving to cloud, as cloud technology became popular and more reliable. Cloud technology gives rise to many SaaS products pertaining to big data. Among all these products, Databricks is the industry leading cloud data platform for big data processing and machine learning.

Databricks is an *Apache Spark* based cloud *unified analytics platform* that can perform large-scale big data processing and machine learning workloads with ease. Databricks was started in the year *2013* by the original creators of Apache Spark.

Databricks provides a user-friendly programmable and interactive notebook environment where **Data Engineers/Analysts**, **Machine Learning Engineers**, and **Data Scientists** can work collaboratively as the platform supports R, Python, SQL, and Scala languages. Databricks notebooks are so flexible that they can have code, documentation/text, data visualization in real time, and so on at one place. These notebooks can also be version controlled. All the code will be executed on Databricks spark clusters.

Databricks platform comes with all the batteries included, like cluster management, auto-scaling, platform administration, data and infra security management, and so on.

What can we do with Databricks?

Now, let us explore how different personas can work with the Databricks Lakehouse platform to work on the data solutions:

- **As a Data Engineer**: We can build data lakes/data warehouses and perform data processing at scale. For example, Data Engineers read data from `adls` in databricks, apply transformation logic with a notebook, and output as new file to `adls.`
- **As a Data Analyst**: We can perform analytics and visualization for business decisions over the data at scale. For example, data analysts can create visualization reports on the top of a data lake prepared by the data engineers.
- **As a Data Scientist/ML Engineer**: We can build machine learning/deep learning pipelines and process petabytes of data for predictive analytics. For example, data scientists can build machine learning models to predict business insights, and so on.

Databricks is integrated with AWS, Azure, and GCP cloud providers, so it can be used within these cloud providers as a service (or) it is also available as a standalone cloud solution.

Databricks architecture

Databricks is designed in a very flexible manner; it is compatible with multiple cloud vendors such as AWS, Azure, and GCP, and so on.

Underlying operations are highly abstract; customers can focus on their Data Engineering and Data Science-related tasks.

Databricks operates with two main components:

- Control plane

- Data plane

In the next section, we will discuss in detail about the control pane and data pane.

Control plane

It has a web application that acts as an interface for creating and managing interactive notebooks, cluster management, jobs, and queries for Databricks SQL.

Details of all the subcomponents of the control plane will be explained as follows:

- **Notebooks**: These are web-based interface that contains executable code, powered visualizations, and narrative texts. They are ideally used for ETLs, machine learning, and much more.
- **Cluster management**: Most of the tasks related to provisioning and maintaining of clusters is done by Databricks cluster manager on its own based on user inputs on certain parameters like quantification of worker nodes, specification of memory, and runtime version of spark as well as auto scaling.
- **Jobs**: These are scheduled or immediate executable tasks to run a notebook on Databricks cluster. These are a non-interactive way to run a notebook containing executable code or visualizations.
- **Queries**: Databricks SQL is a web-based query editor, which can be used to execute SQL queries and also helps in visualizing data.

Data plane

It resides in the client's cloud (ideally, it is compatible with AWS, Azure, and GCP). Data plane is the only way to connect control plane with customers' data. Data plane contains clusters, and it is the place where the data is processed. Using Databricks connectors, we can also connect to multiple external sources and ingest from streaming data sources.

Now, let's understand the Databricks Lakehouse platform architecture and its components in detail:

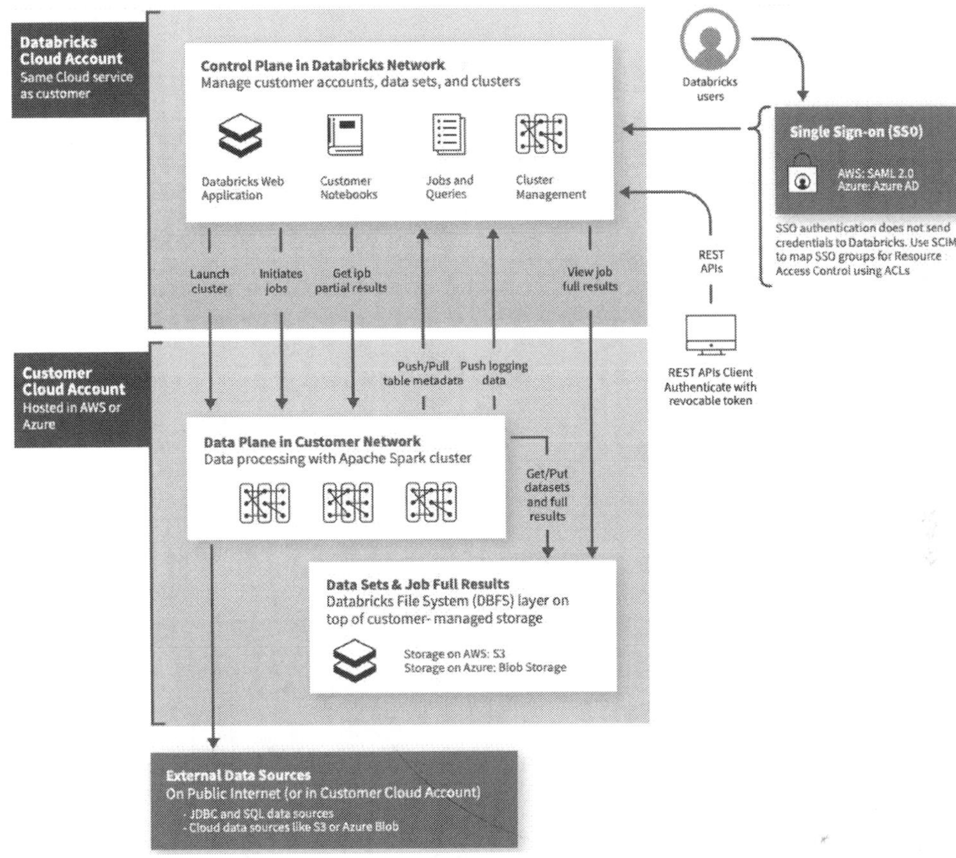

Figure 1.1: *Databricks Lakehouse architecture*

[Photo credits]: ***https://docs.databricks.com/getting-started/overview.html***

How does it work?

In order to understand Databricks better, we will consider a scenario where a data engineer wants to perform an ETL operation over the data that resides over AWS S3 and writes the results back to AWS S3.

Prerequisite

Both S3 and Databricks are already residing on the client's AWS account:

- After signing in to Databricks web application that is inside the control plane, we will go to the cluster manager and create a simple cluster with minimal configuration. Control plane uses AWS APIs to create a Databricks cluster, which is made of new AWS EC2 instances residing in the data plane.

- Once the cluster is provisioned, the Data Engineer creates ETL code in a notebook and runs it.
- Upon execution, Cluster Manager sends the code to the cluster to execute this code, which, in turn, extracts data from AWS S3, transforms it, and writes the results back to AWS S3.
- Later, cluster will report status and any output back to the cluster manager.

If you have observed the preceding flow mentioned, a data engineer has to only manage their code for getting the desired outcome. Everything with regards to infra, networking, scaling, and all the underlying process has been taken care of.

Databricks for Data Engineers and Data Scientists

Many of us have been engineering data their entire career. Since the last few years, the term *data engineering* has become a buzz word for moving and transforming voluminous data from multiple sources in a variety of formats.

- **Data Engineering** is used to refer to the tasks (ETL or ELT tasks) done by engineers on huge data.
- **Data Science** is a process of extracting actionable insights and knowledge from huge volumes of structured and unstructured data by applying mathematical models. Before working on such a huge amount of data, the data must undergo data wrangling (cleaning and unifying of complex datasets).

Data engineers make sure that high quality data is indeed available for the data scientists or BI Analysts for them to work with it.

Ever since we have all the processing capabilities available over cloud along with storage like object storage, the data movement is transformed from **Extract Transform and Load** (**ETL**) to **Extract, Load, and Transform** (**ELT**). With this change, the data transformation became more complex because data can now come from anywhere and any format. So now, set-based transformation may not always be helpful. Databricks come with a powerful feature for such complex scenarios as it supports multiple languages and multiple connectors with various sources. It supports languages such as **Python**, **Scala**, **R**, and **SQL**, which means developers can write their code in these languages simultaneously to process data, which was not possible earlier. Additionally, it can handle streaming and graph data with connectors from different sources.

Organizations do many data analytics projects with data warehouses. Here, enterprise data warehouses are built to store data in various formats. Before placing data inside these warehouses, there is a lot of processing that needs to be done to ensure that data is correctly delimited, has no in-text line feed along with checking for other migration related issues. Here, in Databricks transformations can be built using Python (for non-set-based string parsing) and SQL (for relational data) in the same transform code.

Even though data engineering is not something that came into picture recently, it has become more complex and integrated with non-relation data over the period, which requires us to use *non-relational tools* to our toolset. It has become an initial and critical step not only for data warehousing but also for machine learning and AI related activities, making Databricks the most famous tool for the community.

If you want to start with the free trial of Databricks instance, register for the Databricks Community Edition. When you open the Databricks front page, Databricks UI for **`Data Science & Engineering`** as follows:

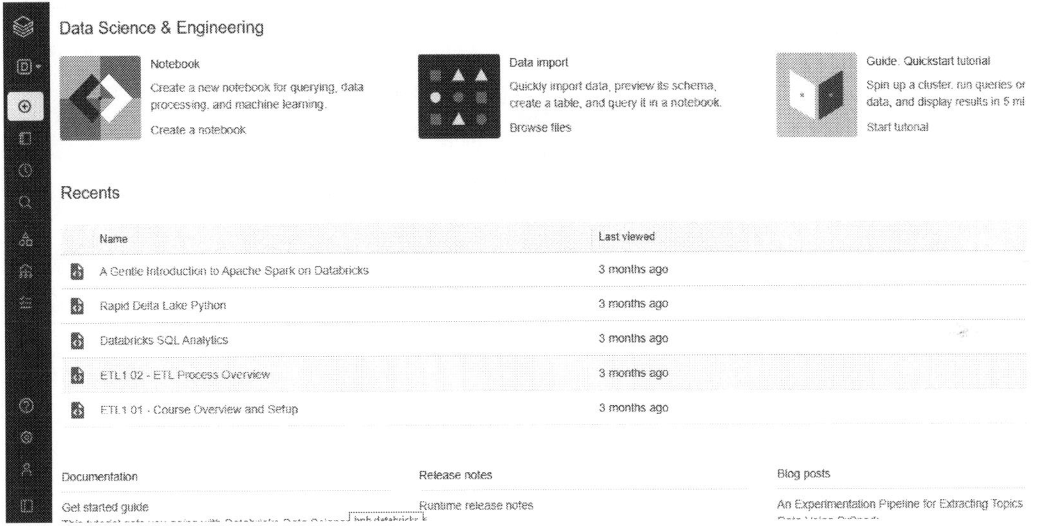

Figure 1.2*: Databricks for Data Science and Data Engineering*

As highlighted below, from the side bar, you can select the persona to use from the Databricks platform: **`Data Science & Engineering`**, **`Machine Learning`**:

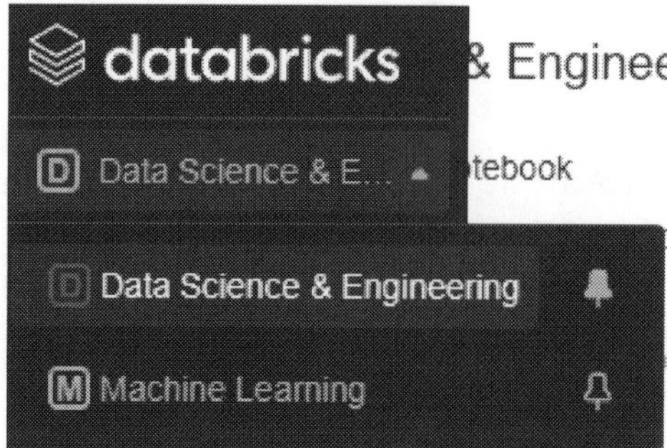

***Figure 1.3**: Databricks - Data Science and Engineering*

You can click on the **`Help`** button if you need any help to work with the Databricks Lakehouse platform:

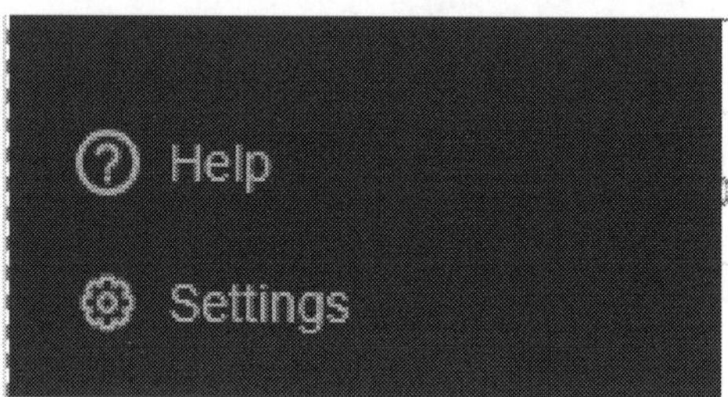

***Figure 1.4**: Databricks settings*

Before we start working with Data Science and Engineering workloads on Databricks Lakehouse platform, we need to understand the fundamental concepts to use the Databricks workspace efficiently:

- **Workspace**: Environment for accessing all the Databricks assets.
- **Interface**: Graphical interface to work with Databricks platform.
- **Data management**: Store data to perform analytics and build machine learning models.
- **Computation management**: Computations used to run jobs and notebooks in Databricks.
- **Machine learning**: To perform machine learning-related activities.
- **Authentication and authorization**: Manage authentication and authorization of the Databricks Lakehouse platform.

Databricks SQL

Databricks SQL is an integrated query execution tool for running *ad-hoc queries* and creating a dashboard on the data that is stored on Data Lake.

Databricks SQL contains two main components:

- SQL endpoint
- Query

They are explained as follows:

- **SQL endpoint:** SQL Endpoint is a serverless compute service. For executing SQL queries, we will use SQL endpoints for computation that will help us run SQL commands on data objects within the Databricks environment.

  Classic SQL endpoint (default SQL endpoint) uses the computational resources in AWS Cloud.

  We can also create Databricks managed SQL endpoints, called **Serverless SQL endpoints,** that utilize compute resources in Databrick cloud accounts. Using serverless endpoints simplifies SQL endpoint management and accelerates launch times.

- **Query:** This component is available as part of the Databricks SQL interface. Imagine this as creating a notebook. When you click on notebook, it will prompt you to create a new notebook by attaching it to a cluster. Similarly, when you select query, it will open a SQL editor that will prompt to select a SQL endpoint (a serverless compute) which needs to be attached to the SQL editor and can run *ad hoc queries.*

Features of Databricks SQL

Following are the features:

- Enables customers to work with the multi-cloud lake house architecture which is cheaper and faster compared to the conventional data warehouse and / or Data Lake architecture.

- Use SQL queries on the Data Lake house with the data warehousing capabilities and performance:

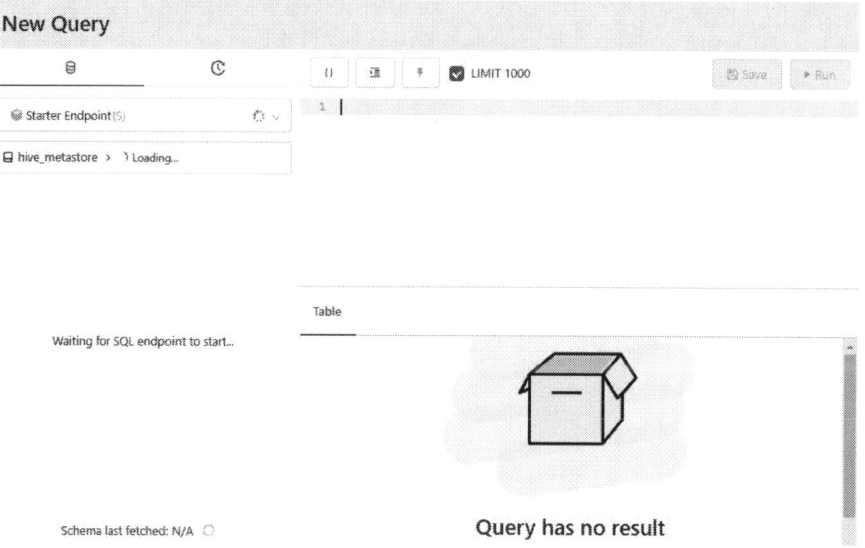

Figure 1.5: Databricks SQL query execution

- Less complex administration and configurations to set up SQL analytics for Databricks platform.

  Databricks platform itself determines the instance types and configurations to reduce the cost and improve the performance of the SQL queries.

  Databricks SQL has in-built features to easily manage user access, data, and resources including monitoring, query history, and fine-grained access management:

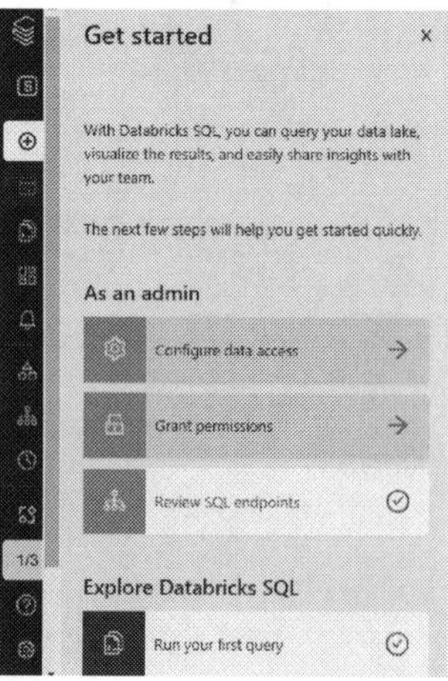

Figure 1.6: Databricks SQL - homepage

- Use preferred BI tool to perform analytics on the top of data available in the Databricks Lakehouse platform:

Partner Connect helps you connect your Azure Databricks workspace to selected partner solutions within minutes. If you do not have an account with a partner, Partner Connect helps you create a trial account with them.

You can also connect your workspace to additional partner solutions that are not listed here. Learn more

Data ingestion

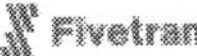

Fivetran automated data integration adapts as schemas and APIs change, ensuring reliable data access and simplified analysis with ready-to-query schemas.

Rivery

Rivery provides a cloud-native ELT+ platform that accelerates the entire Databricks workflow through data ingestion, transformation, orchestration, and reverse ETL.

Coming soon

BLITZZ

Blitzz unlocks the value of transactional and operational data with real-time, distributed CDC that has built-in heterogeneous schema management, HA, and auto-scaling.

Data preparation and transformation

Prophecy

Prophecy is a low code product to visually build Apache Spark workflows backed by code on Git and includes metadata search, lineage, and scheduling.

Coming soon

dbt Labs

dbt lets teams collaborate on data transformation workflows, following engineering best practices like modularity, testing, and version control.

Machine learning

Labelbox is a training data platform used to create training data from images, video, audio, text, and tiled imagery. Train your AI models and run data science workloads in Databricks.

BI and visualization

 Microsoft Power BI

Quickly find meaningful insights within your data and easily build rich, visual analytic reports.

Tableau helps people see and understand data with the world's broadest and deepest analytics platform.

***Figure 1.7**: Databricks SQL - connectors*

- Efficient data discovery, access using SQL queries, and quickly share new insights with the visualization capabilities:

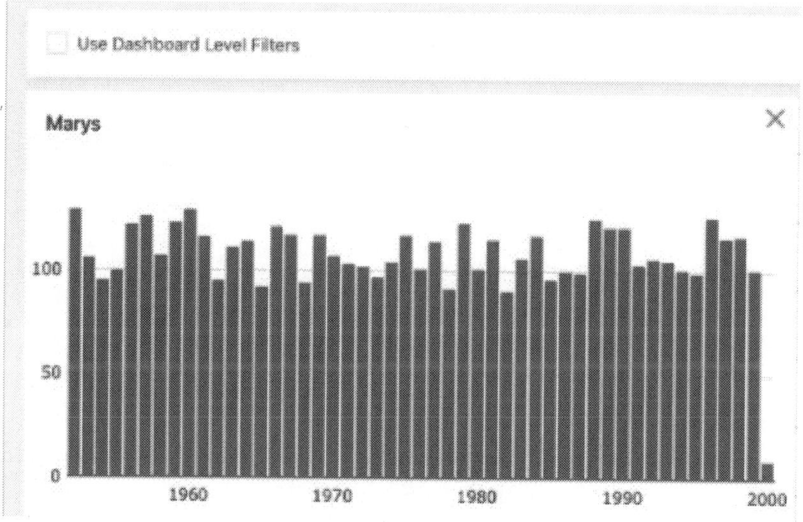

Figure 1.8: Databricks SQL - dashboards

SQL endpoints for Databricks SQL

SQL endpoint is a computation resource that enables end users to execute the SQL commands.

Open Databricks SQL and select **SQL Endpoints** from the left pane highlighted, as follows:

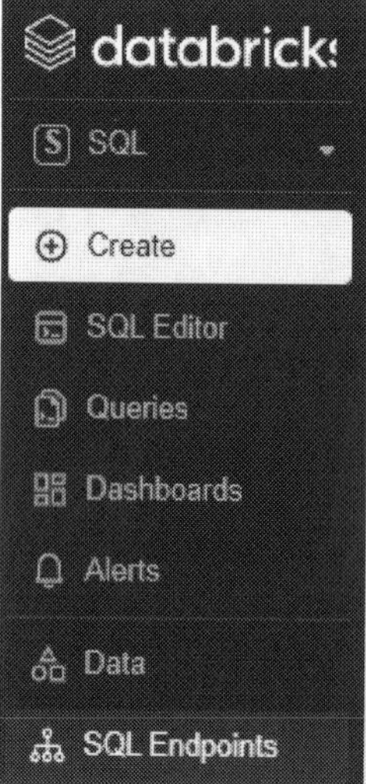

Figure 1.9: Databricks SQL - SQL endpoints

By default, Databricks SQL has an in-built endpoint named **`Starter Endpoint` to run SQL queries on the** Databricks platform:

***Figure 1.10**: Databricks SQL - SQL endpoints lists*

If you click on the SQL endpoint, we can see more configuration information about the endpoint.

- **Overview**

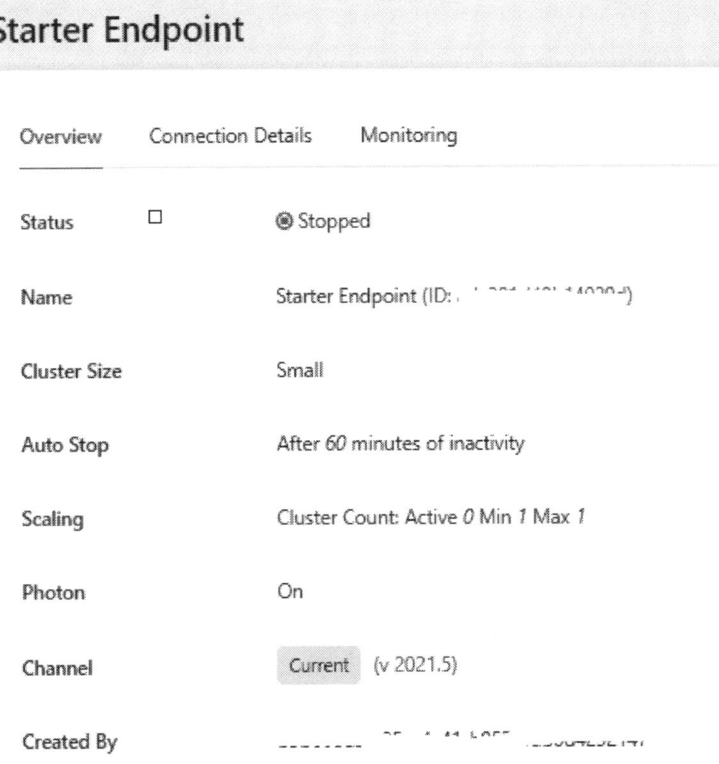

***Figure 1.11**: Databricks SQL endpoints overview page*

- **Connection details**

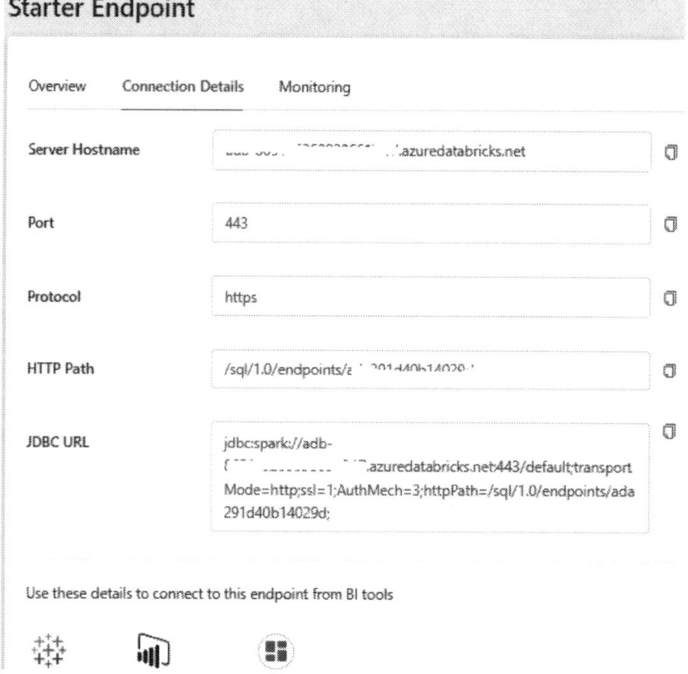

***Figure 1.12**: Databricks SQL endpoints connection details*

- **Monitoring**

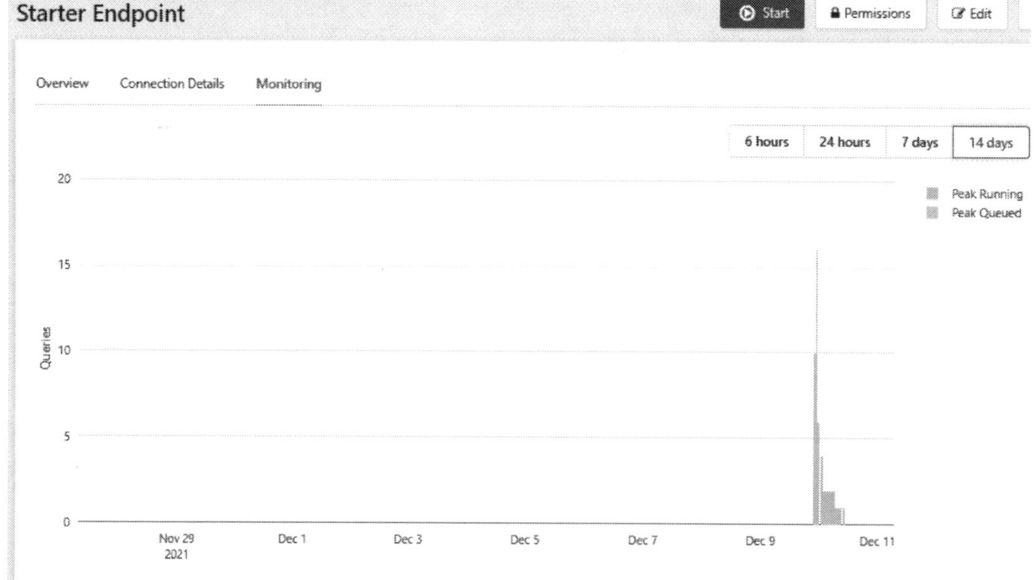

***Figure 1.13**: Databricks SQL endpoints monitoring*

1. If you want to create a new SQL endpoint, click on the **`Create SQL Endpoint`** button:

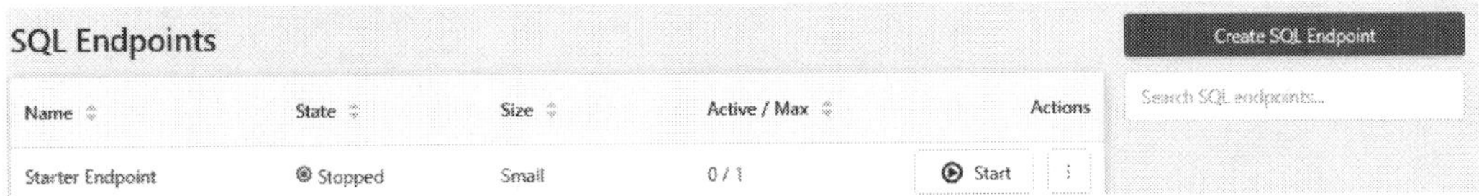

Figure 1.14: Databricks SQL endpoints

Here, we have to provide the following information to create the SQL endpoints:

- **`Name`**: Provide SQL endpoint name.
- **`Cluster Size`**: Provide the cluster size.
- **`Auto Stop`**: Provide the auto termination time.
- **`Scaling`**: Provide minimum and maximum clusters for auto scaling:

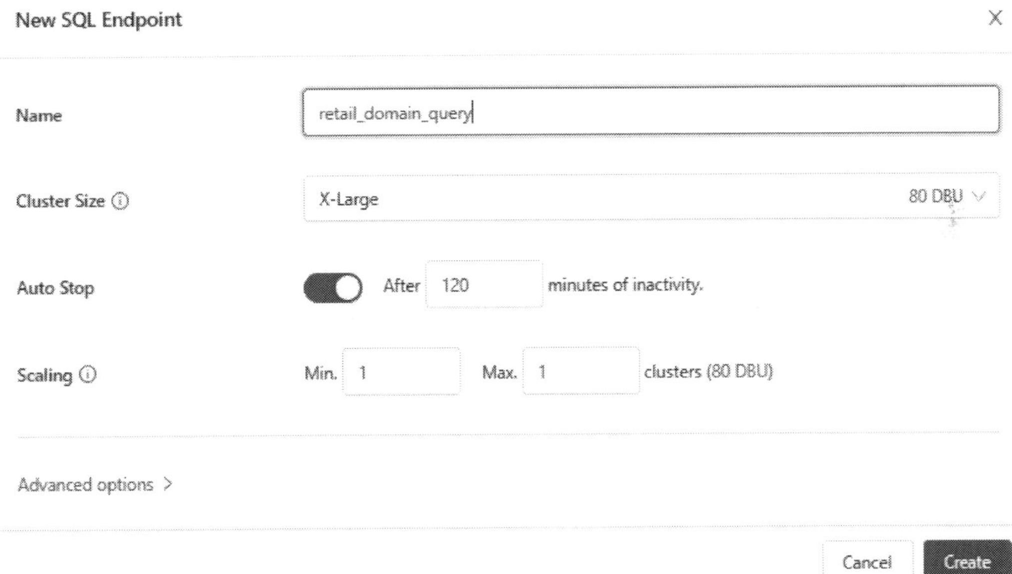

Figure 1.15: Create Databricks SQL endpoints

2. Now, click on **Advanced options** to configure additional information:

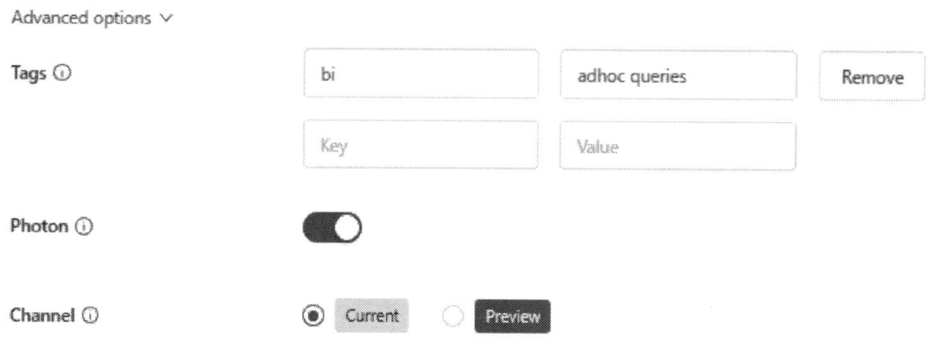

Figure 1.16: Create Databricks SQL endpoints - Advanced options

3. Now, as soon as you click on the **Create** button, you will get a pop-up box to manage the permissions for the created SQL endpoints:

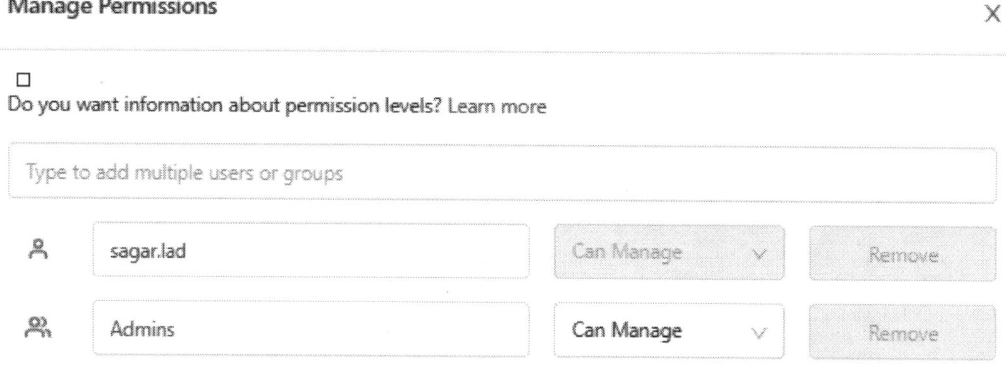

Figure 1.17: Create Databricks SQL endpoints - Manage Permissions

4. Now, a new SQL endpoint has been created successfully:

retail_domain_query

Overview   Connection Details   Monitoring

Status	Running
Name	retail_domain_query (ID:)
Cluster Size	X-Large
Auto Stop	After 120 minutes of inactivity
Scaling	Cluster Count: Active 1 Min 1 Max 1
Photon	On
Channel	Current (v 2021.5)
Tags	bi adhoc queries
Created By	sagar.lad

Figure 1.18: Databricks SQL endpoints created

5. From the list of SQL endpoints, we can start and stop the SQL endpoints based on our requirement:

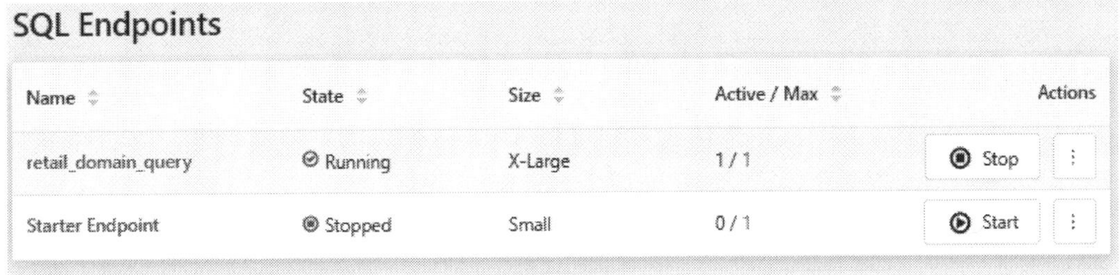

Figure 1.19: Start/stop Databricks SQL endpoints

6. It is also possible to edit the SQL endpoint configurations once it is created. Click on the *dotted* button and use the **Edit** option to edit the configurations:

***Figure 1.20**: Edit Databricks SQL endpoints*

7. If you want to configure and administer the SQL endpoints, click on the **Settings** page from the homepage and select **SQL Admin Console,** as shown in the following screenshot:

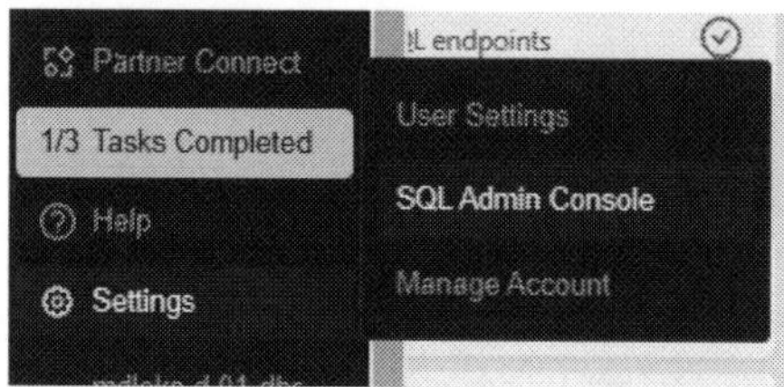

***Figure 1.21**: Databricks SQL endpoints - SQL Admin Console*

Here, we can configure the **General settings** highlighted, as follows:

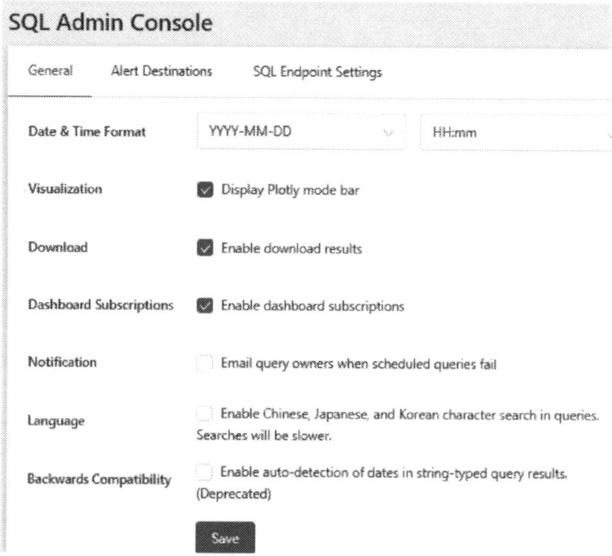

***Figure 1.22**: Databricks SQL Admin Console - General*

8. We can also configure alerts with multiple channels for proactive monitoring and respond swiftly in case of failure:

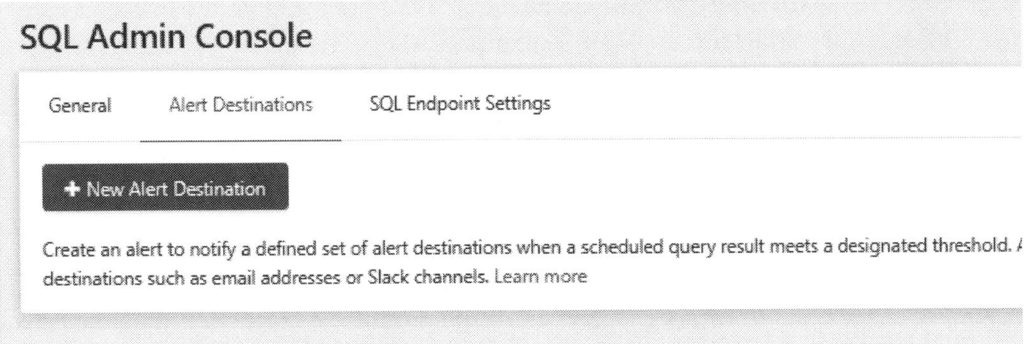

***Figure 1.23**: Databricks SQL Admin Console - Alerts*

9. We can also configure data security options to manage the storage access with the meta store properties to the service principal:

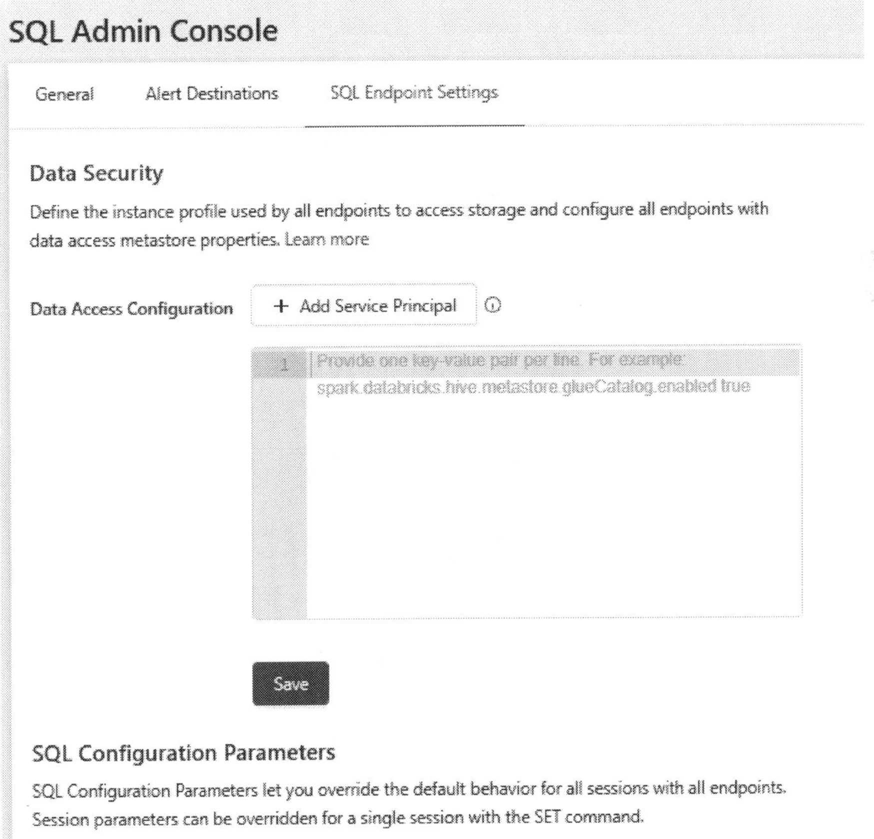

***Figure 1.24**: Databricks SQL Admin Console - Settings*

Databricks components

So far, we have discussed about Databricks and their architecture. Moving on, we will deep dive into the core components of Databricks, which we can refer to as building blocks of Databricks. These components give a *360 degree view* about Databricks and their capabilities.

Workspace

Workspace is an environment that contains all the Databricks assets/objects like notebooks, libraries, and ML experiments organized into folders. A single user can have access to multiple Databricks workspaces like **dev**, **staging**, and **prod** environments. These workspaces can be accessed via Databricks UI, Databricks API, and Databricks CLI.

Databricks assets/objects can be either shared with all the users or a specific user within the workspace. If these objects needed to be *user specific,* then it needs to be created/placed under `Users` folder. If these objects need to be shared across multiple users in the same workspace, these objects must be placed/created under the `Shared` folder:

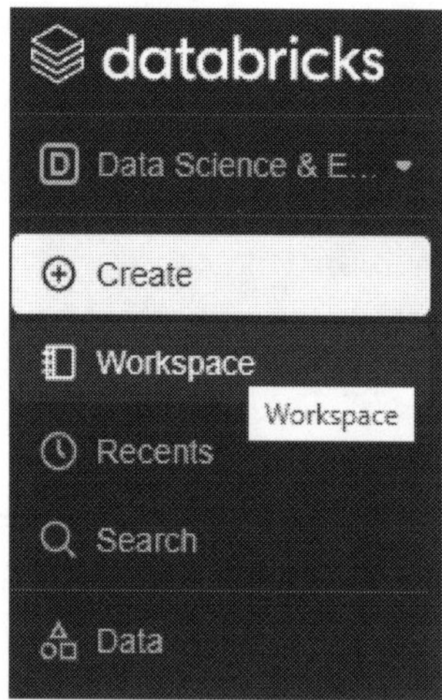

***Figure 1.25**: Databricks workspace*

Databricks assets/objects are as follows:

- Notebooks
- Libraries
- Folder
- MLflow experiments

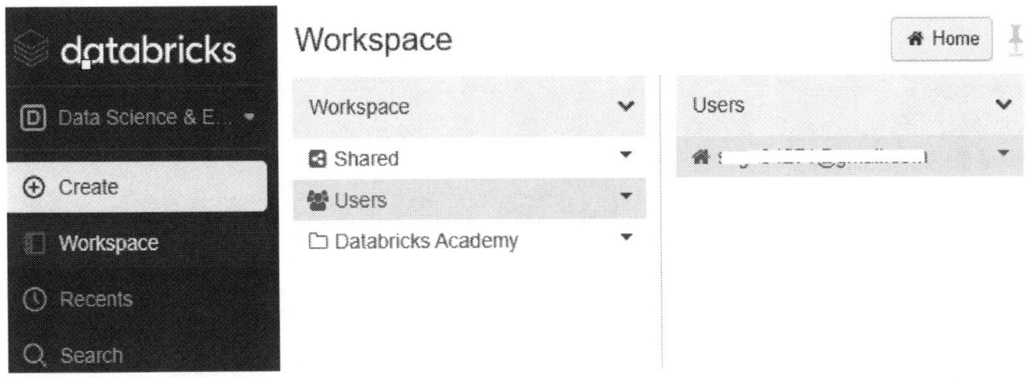

Figure 1.26: Databricks workspace overview

Notebooks

A **notebook** is a web-based programmable document (or) interface. These documents contain runnable cells (commands) that can operate on files, tables, visualizations, and narrative texts. All these cells are executed in a series, and to refer to the output of the previous cell in the current cell, the previous cell needs to be executed first:

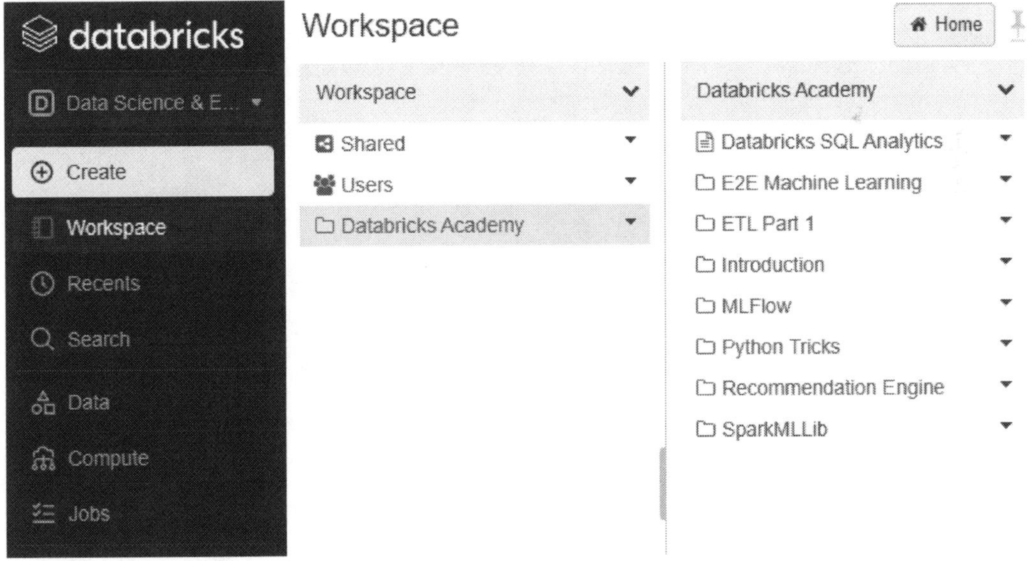

Figure 1.27: Databricks workspace folders

The following image represents three different notebook cells that contain visualization, narrative text, and code (top to bottom):

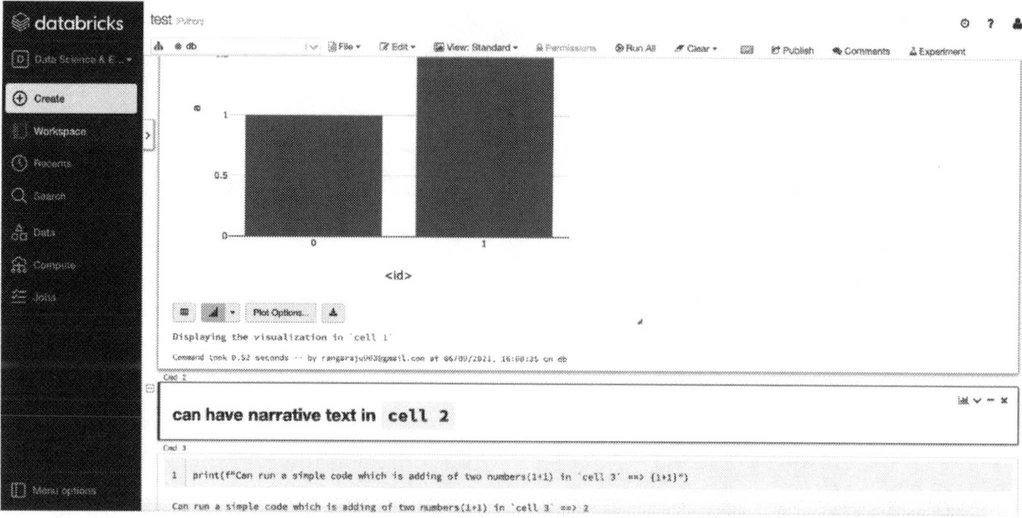

Figure 1.28: Databricks workspace notebooks

Libraries

A **library** is a Databricks notebook (or) file containing code that is built locally. These libraries can be imported as well as used in other **notebooks** (interactive way) or **jobs** (non-interactive way). These libraries can also be uploaded directly to the cluster; this way, all these libraries will be available to the notebooks that use the particular cluster:

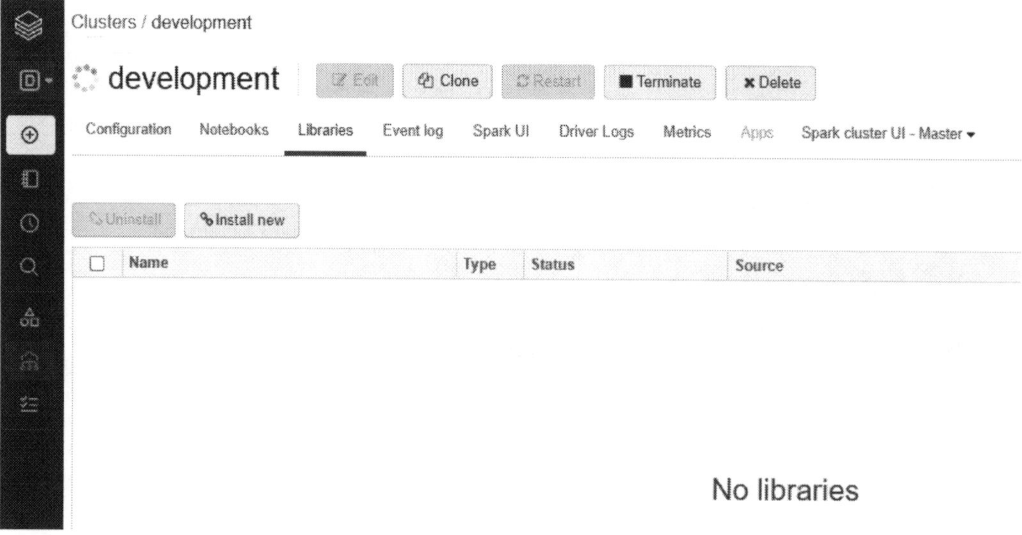

Figure 1.29: Databricks cluster libraries

Folder

It is a virtual location to store your files or documents:

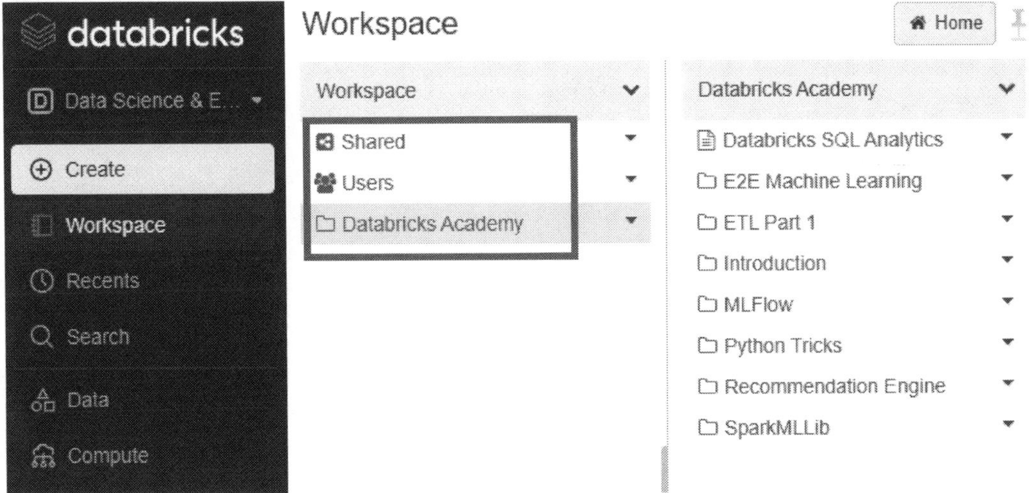

Figure 1.30: Databricks workspace folder structure

MLflow experiment

Imagine MLflow **Experiment** as a folder that contains multiple model training runs as status files. Each MLflow model training run contains the status of execution of ML code and its metadata, artifacts information, and so on:

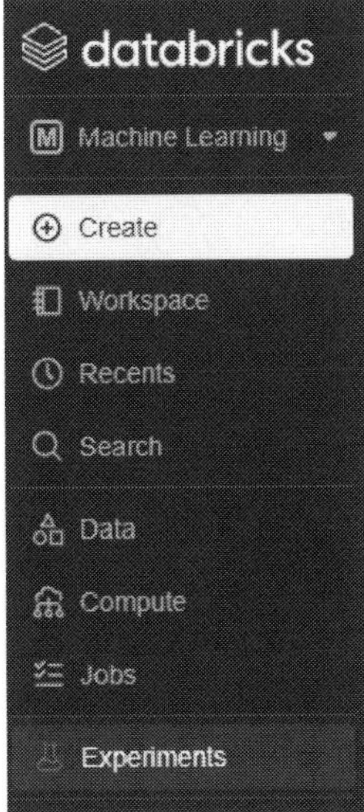

Figure 1.31: Machine learning experiments

From the MLflow Experiment perspective, we can visualize and search all these runs and compare them with other experiment runs. We can also download artifacts and metadata of each model training run from the experiment. Overall, MLflow Experiment lets you organize all the MLflow model training runs:

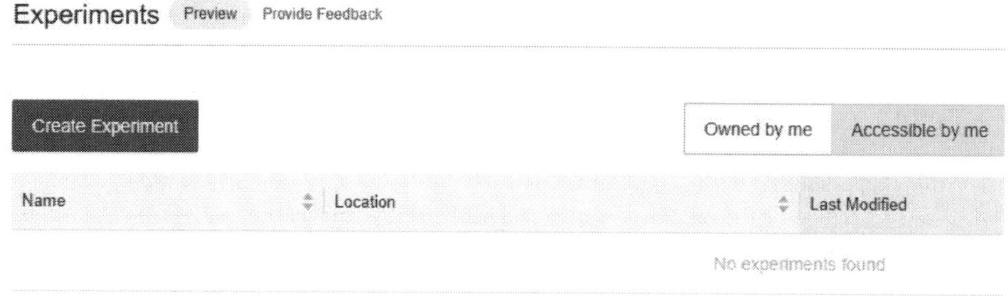

***Figure 1.32**: Machine learning experiments overview*

Interface

It is a way to interact with the Databricks services. Databricks supports three interfaces.

Databricks UI

It is a simple web-based graphical user interface. Here, we will interact with all the Databricks computational resources and workspaces. This is usually recommended while working on interactive data processing or machine learning. The following is Databricks web-based GUI; it is very simple to navigate among different Databricks options:

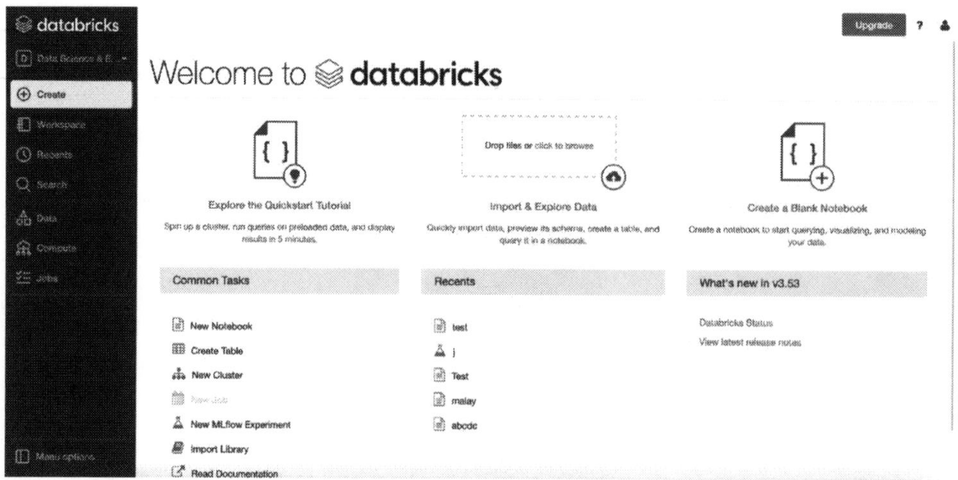

***Figure 1.33**: Databricks overview*

Databricks API

Databricks services can be triggered using Databricks supported REST API. It has two versions of **API REST API 1.2** and **REST API 2.0**. Out of these versions, **REST API 2.0** is the latest version and supports the latest functionality:

APIs

- Account API 2.0
- Clusters API 2.0
- Cluster Policies API 2.0
- DBFS API 2.0
- Global Init Scripts API 2.0
- Groups API 2.0
- Instance Pools API 2.0
- Instance Profiles API 2.0
- IP Access List API 2.0
- Jobs API 2.1
- Libraries API 2.0
- MLflow API 2.0
- Permissions API 2.0
- Repos API 2.0
- SCIM API 2.0
- Secrets API 2.0
- Token API 2.0
- Token Management API 2.0
- Workspace API 2.0

Figure 1.34

Refer to the following link for better insights into the API:

https://docs.databricks.com/dev-tools/api/latest/index.html

Databricks CLI

It is an open-source CLI built on top of Databricks API. This tool is entirely built using Python.

Data management

In this section, we will talk about the components that hold different types of data, which will be used while performing data engineering and machine learning processes.

DBFS

Databricks File System (**DBFS**) is a distributed file system, which is the same as **Hadoop Distributed File System** (**HDFS**). DBFS is built on top of cloud provider's object storage. For example, if a Databricks is being accessed from AWS, DBFS will, by default, use **S3** as its object storage. The same holds for **Azure Blob** in Azure and **GCS** in GCP. DBFS can contain images, data files, and libraries, and so on. DBFS also allows mounting of different storages with DBFS as folders. The data in DBFS is accessible by the clusters; this data is persisted even after the cluster is terminated:

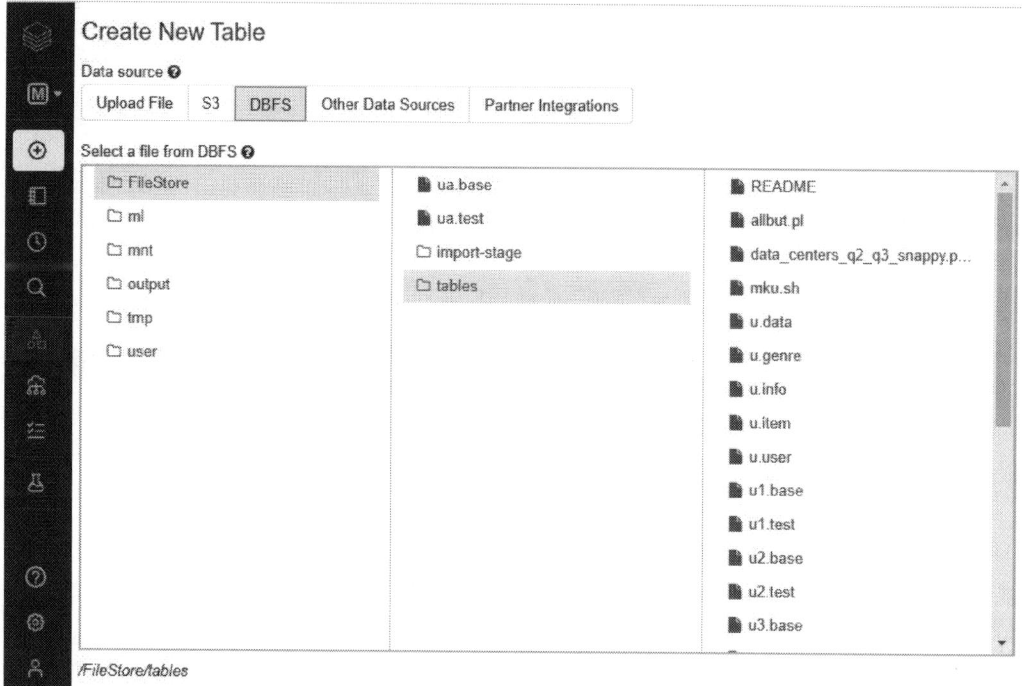

Figure 1.35: Create new table

Tables

Tables are representation of data in a structured format of rows and columns. They can be queried using Apache Spark SQL and Apache Spark APIs:

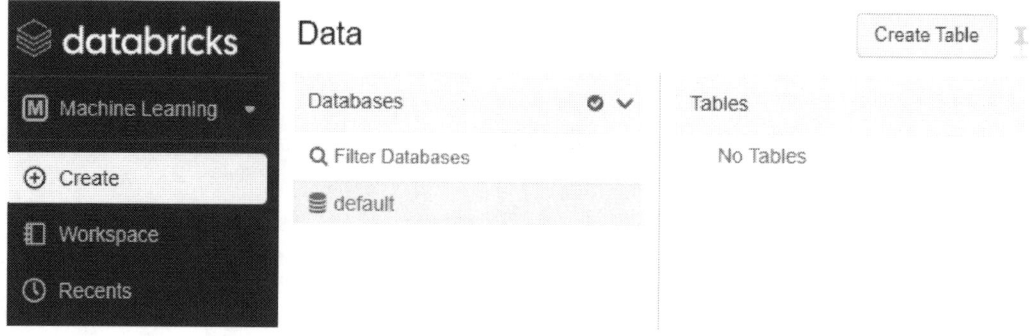

Figure 1.36: Create table option

Database

Logical grouping of all the tables.

Metastore

Metastore holds the metadata related to all data stored in Databricks, such as tables. Metastore contains the partition information and the serializers/deserializers to be used while accessing the data, and so on. It has two main functionalities: **data abstraction** and **data discovery**.

Without the metastore, whenever a user tries to access the data in a table, they should provide the table format, loaders, and the corresponding files where the data is stored. With data abstraction, all the preceding information is stored in metastore and is being used whenever data is read/written. Data discovery helps the user to discover and explore relevant data from the data warehouse. Databricks has a built-in central hive metastore, but it can also support using external hive metastore instance and **AWS Glue** data catalog.

Computation management

In this section, we will talk about different computation concepts.

Cluster

It is a computation resource on which notebooks or jobs are executed:

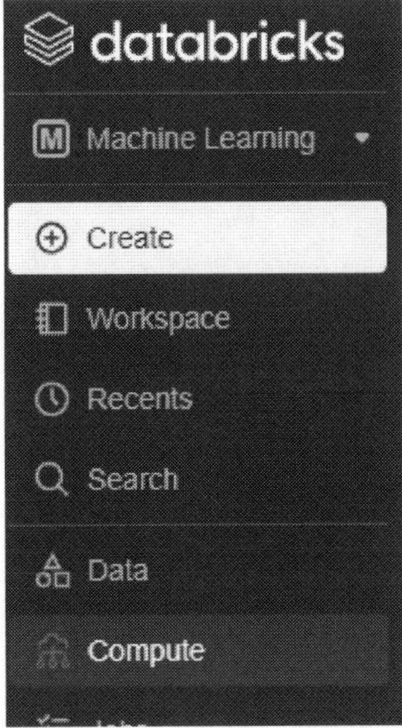

***Figure 1.37**: Databricks Compute*

While creating a cluster, it will require some properties to be set. Databricks provides two types of clusters: **`All-purpose clusters`** and **`Job clusters`**:

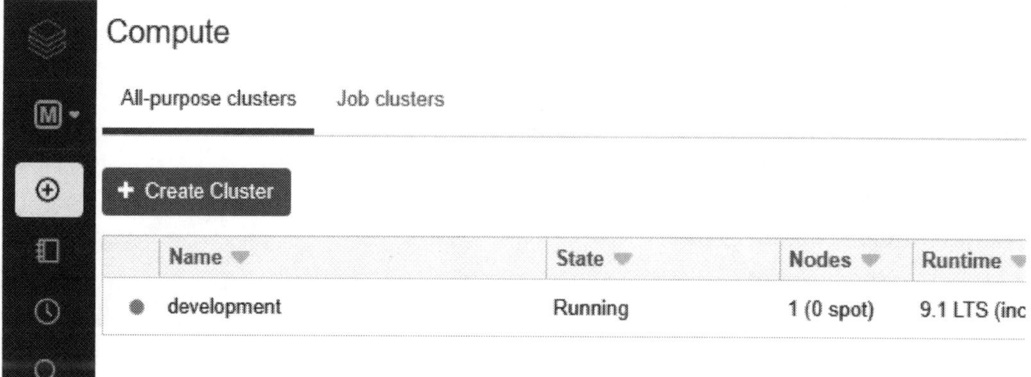

Figure 1.38: Databricks compute clusters

All-purpose cluster

It can be created using Databricks UI, Databricks API, and Databricks CLI. This cluster is majorly used for interactive processing of the data. This type of cluster can be shared across multiple users for collaboratively computing the notebooks. These clusters can be manually restarted or terminated.

Job cluster

The Databricks job scheduler creates a job cluster automatically whenever any data processing job is triggered. These clusters terminate automatically once the job is completed. These clusters are not accessible by user, and hence, cannot be used for interactive data processing:

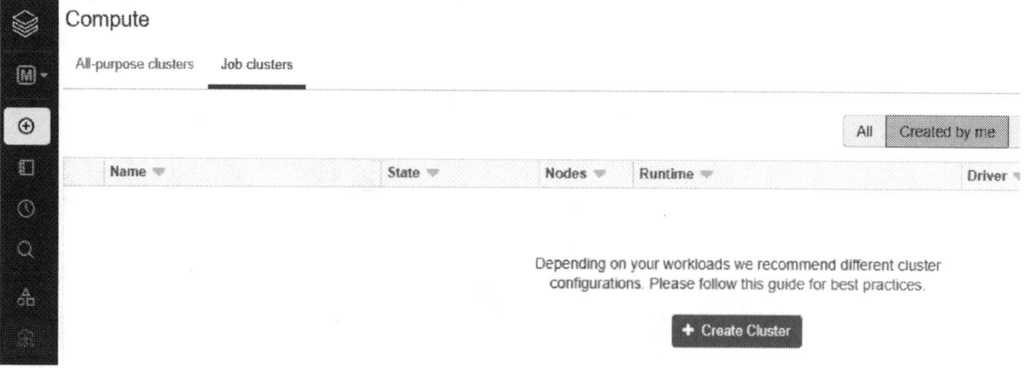

Figure 1.39: Databricks job clusters

Pools

A **pool** is, essentially, a group of warm computing instances that a cluster can pull from while it's spinning up or scaling up. To utilize the pool instances, a cluster needs to be attached with the pool; once it is attached, based on the availability, cluster will allocate driver and worker nodes from the pool. If there is any additional demand from a cluster for more resources, the pool will try to expand by allocating new instances. Once the cluster is terminated, all the resources or instances that were used will be returned to pool and will be used by other attached clusters.

Databricks does not charge for the computing instances which are idle, but the instance provider does charge for it.

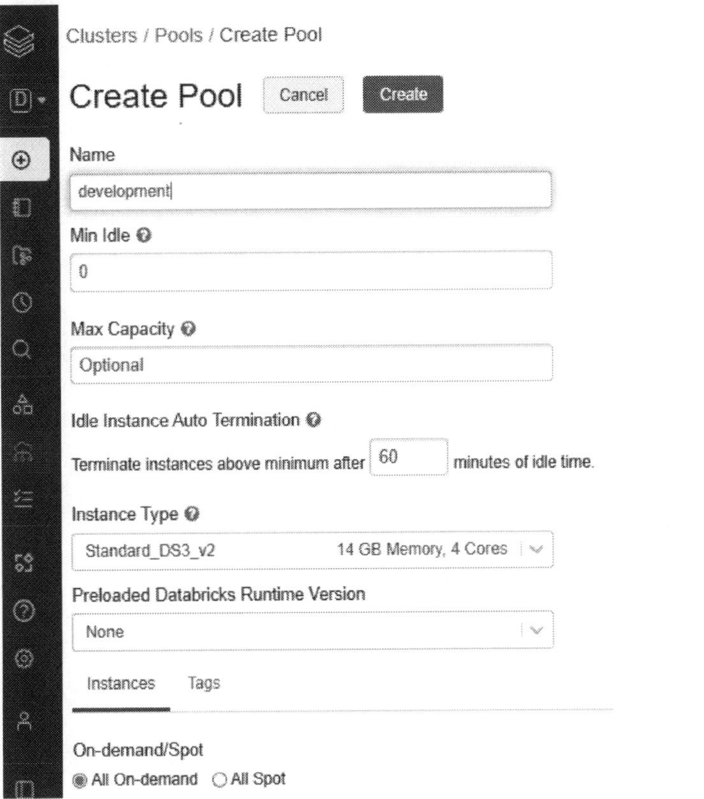

***Figure 1.40**: Cluster pools*

Databricks runtime

It is an environment in which a set of software components, including Apache Spark, is available and running on the clusters. Databricks runtime is fully managed by Databricks. Databricks constantly updates the runtime, which, in turn, improves the usability, performance, and security of big data processing or advanced analytics in Databricks environment. There are multiple types of runtime offered by Databricks:

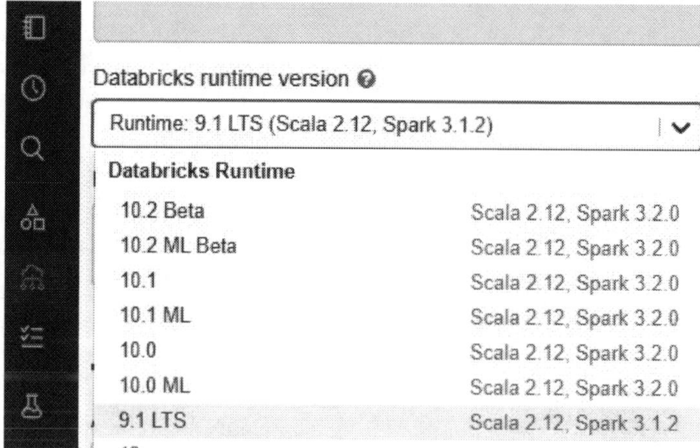

Figure 1.41: *Databricks runtime*

Databricks runtime

This runtime consists of Apache Spark and other components like:

- Delta Lake, a next gen storage layer built on Apache Spark that offers ACID transactions
- Installed Python, Scala, Java, and R libraries
- GPU libraries for GPU enabled clusters:

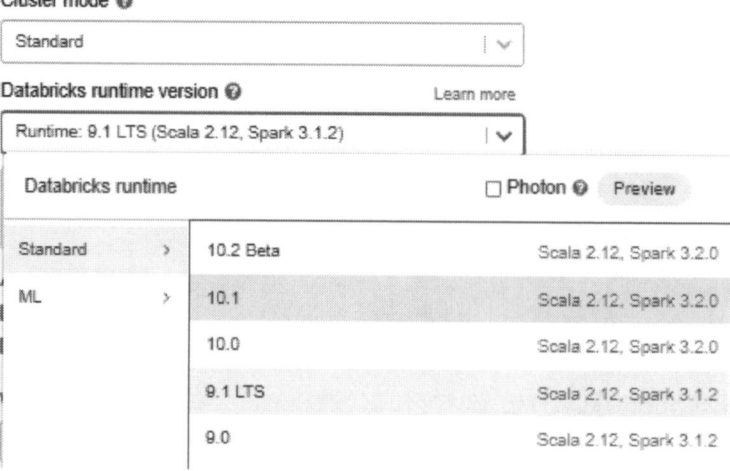

Figure 1.42: *Databricks Runtime - Standard*

Databricks runtime for machine learning

This runtime consists of all the components from Databricks runtime and all the popular machine learning libraries like **`pytorch`**, **`tensorflow`**, **`keras`**, and **`XGBoost`**. This runtime also ensures the proper library compatibility. Using this runtime speeds up the cluster creation process:

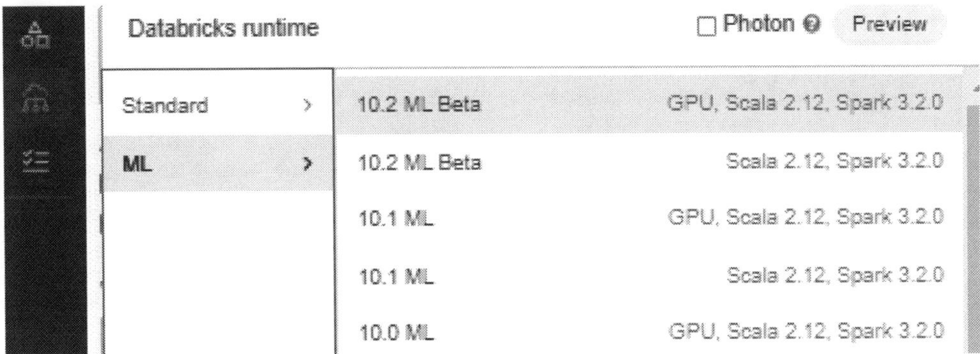

***Figure 1.43**: Databricks runtime - ML*

Photon

Photon is native vectorized query engine. It is written using C++. Photon engine is compatible with all Apache Spark API and Spark SQL. Vectorized way of data processing helps in efficiently utilizing the CPU of the underlying hardware as this runtime is a part of high-performance runtime.

There are some limitations of this runtime:

- Does not support spark structured streaming.
- Does not support Spark UDF's.
- This runtime is not recommended while querying small amounts of data.
- Window and sort functions are not supported by photon high performance runtime.

From the cost optimization perspective, this runtime reduces the duration of any heavy workload drastically.

Databricks light

This runtime is only supported and used with the job cluster when you have the automated workloads, not for interactive workloads. If our data processing requires very low computation and cost efficiency, this runtime is recommended. Given the name **Databricks light**, this runtime is lightweight; it does not support some of the main Databricks features like Delta Lakes, auto scaling, various data source connectors, and BI tools.

Databricks runtime for genomics (deprecated)

It is mostly recommended to use when dealing with genomics and biomedical data. But unfortunately, this runtime is deprecated and Databricks is no longer releasing newer versions of this runtime.

Access management

The following are the concepts we need to understand with respect to Databricks access management:

User

A Databricks user is a single unique personal (or) non personal account who will be able to access the Databricks services. All Databricks users are managed by **Databricks Admin,** who belongs to the Databricks Admin group:

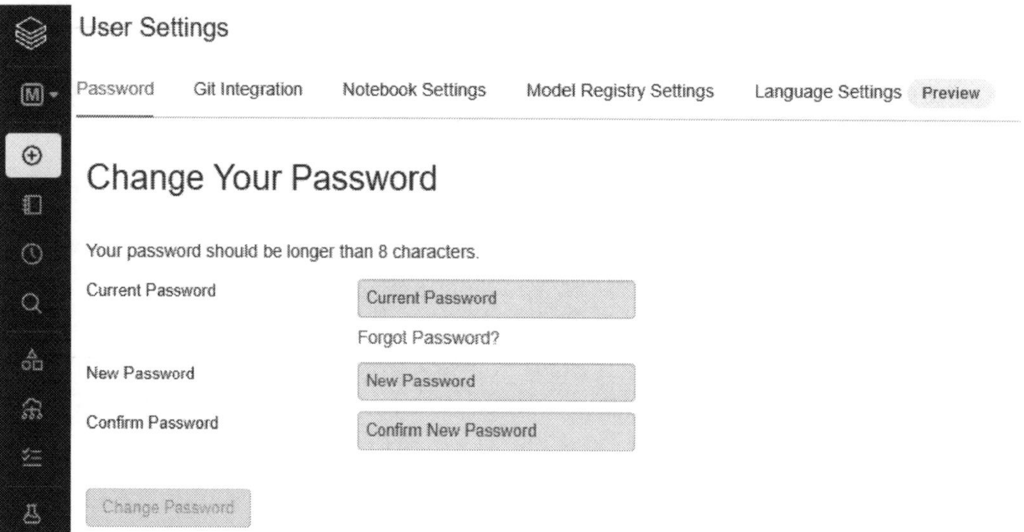

***Figure 1.44**: Databricks user settings*

Group

A **group** is used to assign the same privileges to multiple users. Users are given membership to become a part of this group, which has certain privileges (to access data objects and Databricks components) decided by the admin.

Access Control Lists (ACLs)

Access Control Lists are often referred to as **ACLs**. This ACL is used for providing permission to access Databricks components and its entities (**clusters**, **notebooks**, **folders**, **data tables**, and **jobs**, and so on).

Usually, all admins can manage these ACLs, although admins can upgrade permissions for certain users to manage ACLs.

Conclusion

Azure Data Lake Storage Gen2 is designed to create enterprise level Data Lake solutions for big data and analytics applications. Data Lake stores can efficiently manage large amounts of data. Data Lake Storage is a cost-effective solution since it is built on the top of low-cost blob storage. Data Lake Storage uses an ABFS driver that allows data access and management similar to Hadoop and optimized for big data analytics. It uses the `dfs.core.windows.net` endpoint. Data Lake Gen2 is more secure with the support of ACL and POSIX permissions.

Multiple choice questions

1. Which cloud platforms support Databricks currently?
   a. AWS, GCP, Microsoft Azure
   b. AWS, IBM Cloud, Alibaba Cloud
   c. GCP, IBM Cloud, Microsoft Azure
   d. AWS, Alibaba Cloud, Microsoft Azure

2. What are different ways to create a Databricks cluster?
   a. Databricks UI
   b. Databricks CLI
   c. Databricks API
   d. All of the above

3. Which of the following statements is not valid with regard to the Databricks platform?
   a. The Databricks platform supports only the Python programming language.
   b. The Databricks platform is used to perform ETL on data.

   c. Apache Spark original creators have built the Databricks platform.
   d. The Databricks platform supports data visualization.

4. What is the number of runtimes currently available on the Databricks platform?
   a. 2
   b. 3
   c. 4
   d. 5

5. What are the different types of clusters supported by Databricks platform?
   a. All-purpose cluster
   b. Job cluster
   c. All of the above
   d. None of the above

Answers

1. a
2. d
3. a
4. d
5. c

CHAPTER 2
Management of Databricks Platform

Databricks Lakehouse platform is a single and all-in-one platform to create your data analytics and AI solution. The all-in-one integrated Databricks Lakehouse platform simplifies the data architecture by removing the data silos that mainly separates data engineering teams, data science teams, and analytics teams. Databricks Lakehouse platform is built using the world's best open-source technologies.

In the previous chapter, we explored the foundation of Databricks architecture, the usage of Databricks Lakehouse platform for Data Science and Engineering, and Databricks SQL. In this chapter, you will learn about the Databricks Lakehouse platform.

Structure

In this chapter, we will learn the following aspects of the Databricks Lakehouse platform:

- Databricks cluster basics
- Platform architecture, security, and data protection
- Databricks data access management
- Databricks cluster usage management

- Databricks SQL Analytics Administration

Objectives

After studying this chapter, you should be able to configure, create, and deploy Databricks. We will also explore cluster/data access management and security, and we will explore the Databricks SQL Analytics Administration in detail.

Databricks cluster basics

Databricks cluster is a collection of virtual machines where we can run data analytics and AI solutions. Cluster groups a set of computers as a single computer via driver node. A Databricks cluster consists of a set of computation resources which is easy to configure to run the Data workloads.

There are two ways to execute any data solution on Databricks:

- **Databricks notebook**: We can create and combine a list of commands inside the Databricks notebook to execute those using notebooks.
- **Databricks jobs**: We can create automated Databricks jobs and schedule them to run periodically.

  Datalake house platform consists of two types of clusters:

- **All-purpose cluster**: We can use an all-purpose cluster when we want to execute interactive Databricks notebook. We can create all-purpose clusters in Databricks using CLI, UI, or REST API. All-purpose clusters can be shared by multiple users to run Databricks notebooks.
- **Job cluster**: We can use the job cluster to run scheduled and fully automated jobs faster. Job clusters will be created when the job starts and will be terminated once the job is complete.

Cluster computation resources

Now, let's explore cluster computation resources of Databricks Lakehouse platform:

Clusters

Now, let's see how to create a cluster in Databricks:

1. Create Databricks cluster using UI. Go to Databricks home page and select `Compute,` highlighted as follows:

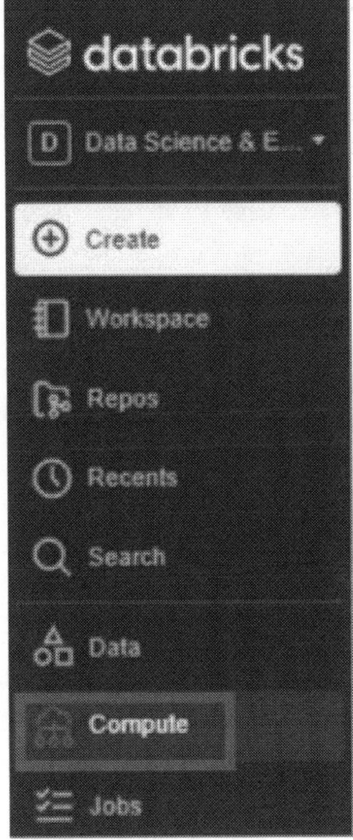

Figure 2.1: Databricks home page

2. Now, click on the **`Create Cluster`** button to create a new cluster:

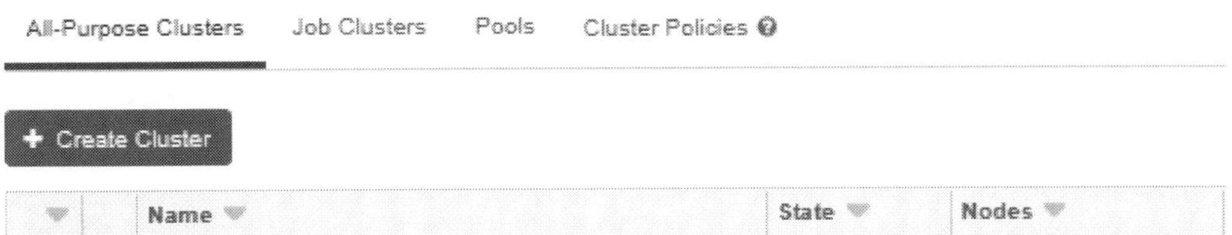

Figure 2.2: Databricks - create cluster

3. After you click on the **`Create Cluster`** button, a screen will appear where you have to provide the cluster configuration details:
   - **`Cluster Name`**: Provide cluster name.
   - **`Cluster Mode`**: **`Standard`**, **`Single Node`**, or **`High Concurrency Cluster`**.

- **`Databricks Runtime Version`**: Choose required version from standard / ML Databricks runtime.
- **`Enable autoscaling`**: Cluster will automatically scale between minimum and maximum nodes.
- **`Terminate after inactivity`**: Time in minutes to terminate cluster after inactivity.
- **`Worker Type`**: Choose worker type based on the workload.

Databricks runtime is a set of components that runs on the cluster. Databricks runtimes include Apache Spark and add components that improve usability, performance, and security.

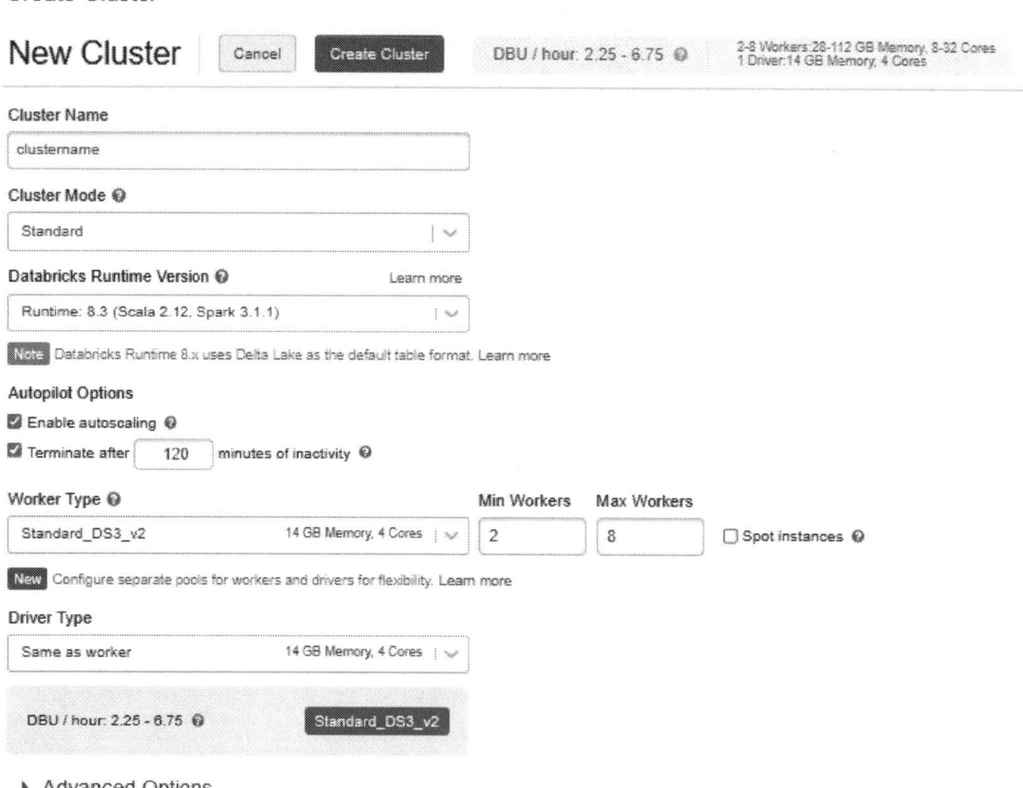

Figure 2.3: Data Bricks - cluster configuration

4. After entering the cluster configuration details, click on the **`Create Cluster`** button to create a cluster in Databricks.

Now, let's see how to edit, delete, display, start, terminate, and monitor Databricks clusters:

- **Display cluster**: As highlighted below, from the Databricks home page, select **`Compute,`** which will display all existing clusters in Databricks with details such as cluster name, state, nodes, runtime, driver, and cluster owner:

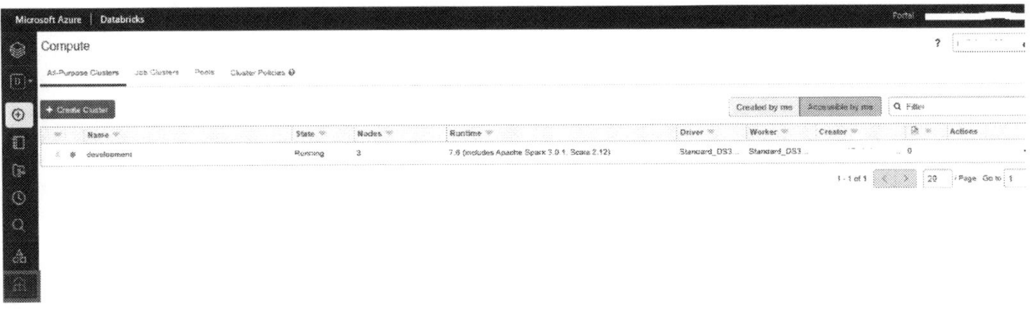

Figure 2.4: Databricks - display clusters

- **Cluster activities**: We can terminate, restart, clone, and edit cluster policies for the Databricks cluster from the **`Actions`** pane of Databricks cluster display page:

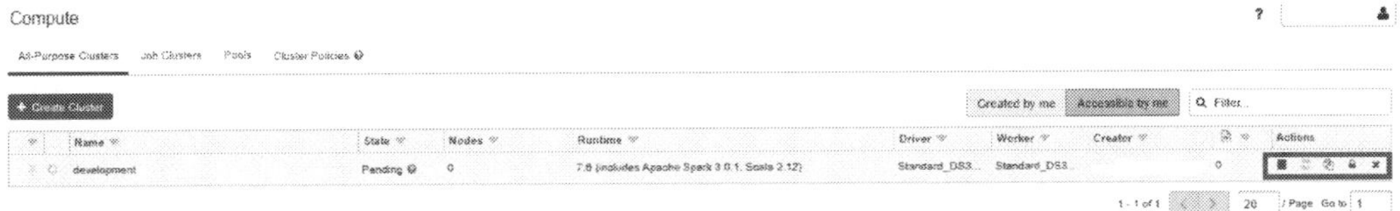

Figure 2.5: Databricks - cluster activities

Once the cluster is created, cluster definition is stored in the form of **JSON** format. Additionally, we can also JSON format definition to create a cluster in Databricks automatically using API. We can open the cluster by clicking on the cluster name. Then, the cluster configuration page will open. You can click on the **`JSON`** button to view the cluster definition in the JSON format.

Notebooks and jobs will remain attached to the cluster ever after editing the cluster. We can edit the cluster configurations even when they are in running state.

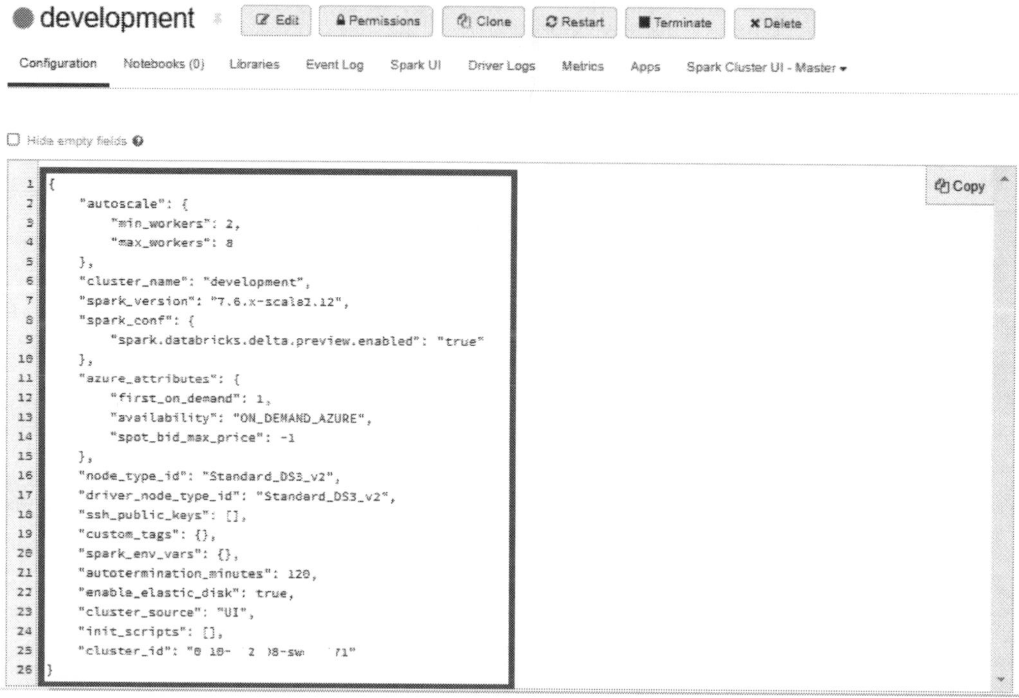

***Figure 2.6:** Databricks - cluster configuration*

Cluster governance

We can disable cluster configurations by only providing certain users permission to `Can Restart` or `Can Attach To` instead of cluster creation and managing permission. Cluster policies can be used to manage the granular level of cluster permission. Cluster admin can configure cluster policies to limit users' access to manage clusters.

We can manage the following after enabling cluster policies in Databricks:

- Limit Users for cluster creation permission with only allowed configuration settings
- Limit only certain users to create cluster in Databricks
- Setup cluster cost threshold to reduce cluster cost

From the *Display Cluster* page of Databricks, using the **`Cluster Policies`** tab, we can create a cluster policy:

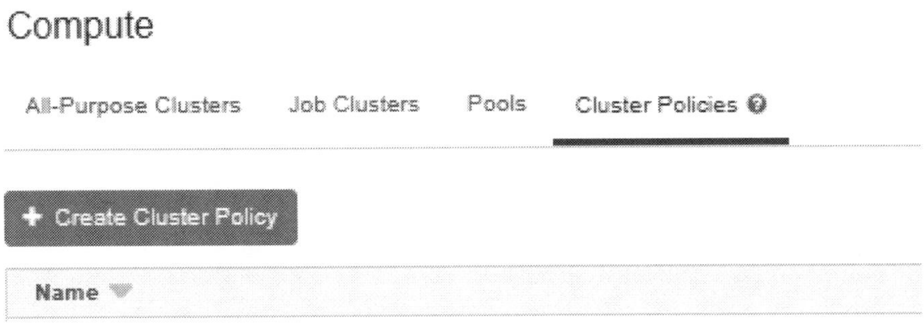

***Figure 2.7**: Databricks - cluster policy creation*

You can define cluster policy in the JSON format. For example, highlighted as in the following image, we have created a cluster policy that only allows users to create only cluster with Databricks runtime environment **`7.3.x-scala2.12`** and since the hidden flag is set to **`true`**, attribute will be hidden from the Databricks UI.

Use of cluster policies in Databricks has the following benefits:

- Enforced governed and standard cluster configurations.
- Avoid excess use of resources.
- Save cost and ensure accurate chargeback using tagging.
- Facilitate faster data processing by providing users with pre-configured cluster for certain type of workloads:

***Figure 2.8**: Databricks cluster policy created - fixed cluster size*

Implementing a cluster policy will completely change the user experience while working with Databricks. High-level steps to implement the cluster policies can be as follows:

- Inform all users about cluster policy changes and inform them to test the cluster configurations for their workload.
- Implement a soft roll out.
- Incrementally incorporate more policies across the organization in *Agile* fashion.
- Finalize implementation across the organization.

Advantage of phased roll out is that users will slowly and gradually get familiar with new cluster policies and avoid the disruption of the existing workload. Let's check a few general use cases for the cluster policy implementation:

- **Cluster policies for Data Science workloads**
    - Auto scaling
    - Auto termination after 20 minutes
    - Fix cluster size
    - Disable additional cluster creation
    - Enable minimum-maximum range for worker nodes
- **Data analysis policies**
    - T-shirt size based on the query requirements
    - Enable auto termination after certain minutes
    - Shared pool access
    - Single node policy
    - Job only policy for higher environments

Platform architecture, security, and data protection

Now, let's explore the platform architecture along with its security and data protection.

Platform architecture

Databricks is a unified analytics platform that joins the forces of Data Analytics, Data Science, and Data Engineering teams to decipher world's challenging data and AI solutions:

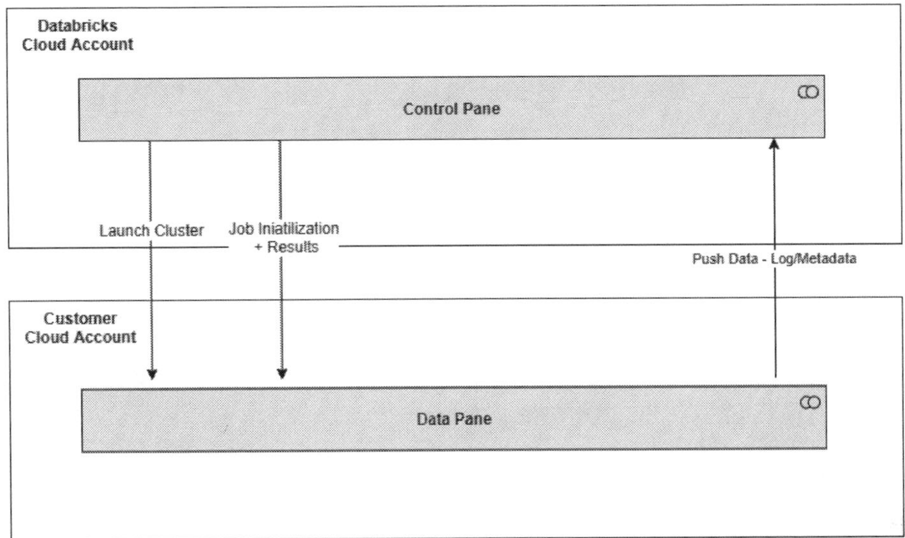

Figure 2.9: Databricks architecture

Before we start exploring the features of Databricks platform and its way of working, let's explore the high-level architecture of Databricks, as shown in the preceding diagram.

Multi-disciplined team can work simultaneously on Databricks platform for the application development, while backend services will be internally managed by Databricks.

Databricks has two main components:

- **Control pane**: Control pane is acting as a backend for the Databricks platform. Databricks has its own AWS account, which will serve the requests coming from the Databricks notebooks and stores the workspace configurations.
- **Data pane**: Data pane consists of the compute resources managed in the AWS account. There are two types of data pane available in the Databricks platform.
    - **Classic data pane**: Databricks uses classic data pane for notebooks, jobs, and classic Databricks SQL endpoints whose compute resources are managed in the AWS account.
    - **Serverless data pane**: When Databricks SQL has been enabled with the serverless compute, Databricks SQL compute resources are managed in the shared serverless data pane.

We can ingest the batch or streaming data from the external sources using the Databricks connectors. When we execute the Databricks notebook interactively, notebook results are stored in the control pane as well as the AWS storage account by default. But for security reasons, if required, it is also possible to store the interactive notebook result only in the customer workspace account. Databricks representatives can enable this feature on *ad-hoc basis*.

Platform security

Databricks platform provides end-to-end security, which safeguards the data, including the isolated and compliant Databrick workspaces for Data Engineers, Data Scientists, and Data Analysts.

Databricks platform has in-built integration with using **SCIM** and **SSO** for identity management to increase the platform security.

Databricks platform has in-built security accelerators to improve data security, workspace security, identity management, and compliance.

- **Data security**: Using custom VNET deployment with Databricks, Databricks control pane will manage the clusters with isolated VNET in the customer's cloud account.

  We can use the existing identity provider to illuminate the data access policies in the data lake. Databricks cluster always stores the data in an encrypted format. Databricks also has seamless integration and secure data access in AWS S3 and Azure Data Lake.

- **Databricks workspace**: We can create a customer VNET and deploy Databricks workspace in the custom VNET to restrict data access and processing within the custom VNET to comply with data governance policies and adhere to regulators. Using custom VNET with IP whitelisting can also restrict the incoming and outgoing traffic to the Databricks workspace.

  We can also enable code isolation to enable granular level of workspace access for different teams to restrict data only to authorized users. Databricks with custom VNET will make sure that traffic will not be sent over the public network.

- **Identity management**: Databricks has in-built identity management using cloud native identity providers, which has support for SAML protocol for authentication and authorization and **System for Cross Domain Identity Management** (**SCIM**).
- **Compliance**: Databricks platform has built-in controls to meet the industry standards compliance requirements.

Data Protection

Databricks platform comprises the following data protection features for data security:

- **Data encryption at rest using user and system managed keys**: Databricks platform has isolated compute and storage resources. Databricks clusters are compute resources that are impermanent in nature, which will be started when the data processing starts and terminated once the data processing is completed. Databricks storage services support data encryption, customer managed keys with key vault backed integration and file/folder level granular access.
- **Data encryption in transit**: When we execute notebooks or jobs in Databricks, all the traffic from the cluster will be redirected from the control pane to customer subscription and this traffic is always TLS encrypted. When clusters access the data, TLS protocol is used for the communication to ensure that the data encryption in transit.
- **File and folder level access control mechanism**: We can also enable file- and folder-level granular access management while working with Databricks platform. For example, while working with Azure Databricks, we can enable the **`ADLS passthrough`** option. When this option is enabled, authentication automatically takes place in **Azure Data Lake Storage** using the **Azure Active Directory Identity**, by which we logged in to the Azure Databricks workspace. We can read and write data to ADLS without configuring service principal credentials or any other additional configurations. User access

management will be managed based on ACLs applied at the file or folder level:

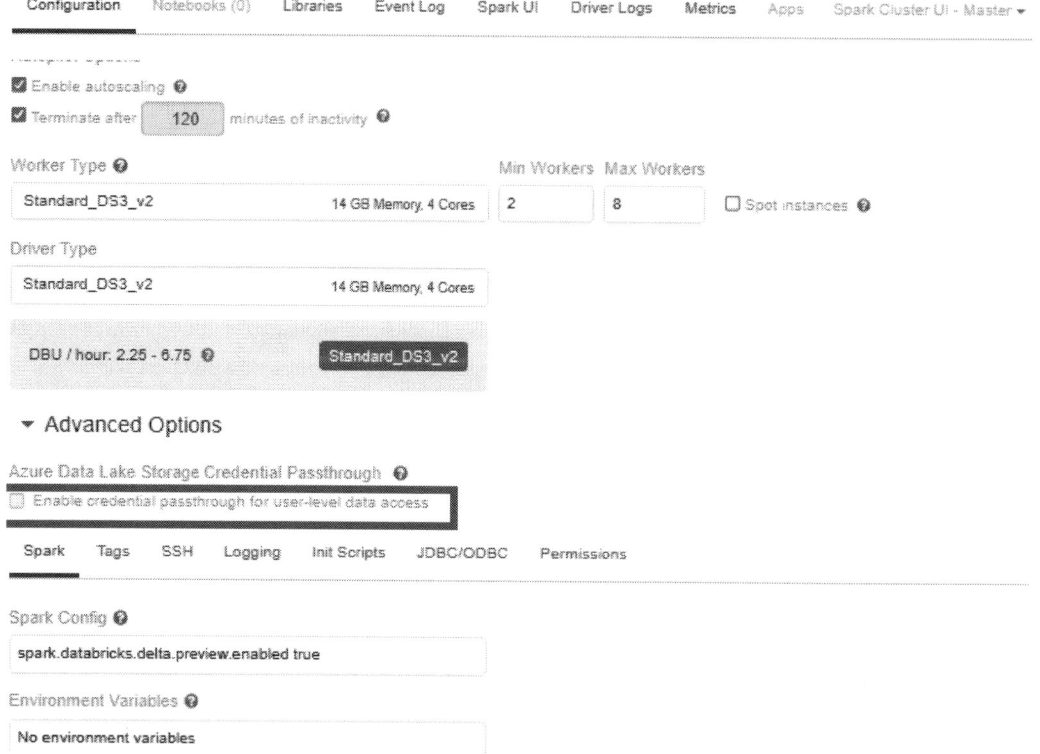

***Figure 2.10**: Databricks cluster - credential passthrough*

As shown in the preceding screenshot, we can configure Databricks cluster with credential passthrough while creating the cluster.

- **Access control tables**: When table access control is enabled in the Databricks workspace, we can programmatically grant and revoke access to the data while working with Databricks notebook in **SQL**, **Python**, and **pyspark**. By default, all the users in the Databricks workspace can access the data stored in the cluster managed table. Once the table access control is enabled, users can access restricted data objects based on the assigned permissions.

  We can create view-based access control model using the following privileges:

  - `SELECT`: Read access to an object.
  - `CREATE`: Create an object.
  - `MODIFY`: Add/delete/modify data to/from an object.

- **`READ_METADATA`**: View an object and its metadata.
- **`CREATE_NAMED_FUNCTION`**: Create a UDF in an existing catalog or database.
- **`ALL PRIVILEGES`**: Gives all privileges.

We can apply these privileges to the following classes of objects:

- **`CATALOG`**: Control permission for the data catalog.
- **`DATABASE`**: Controls access to a database.
- **`TABLE`**: Controls access to a managed/external table.
- **`VIEW`**: Controls access to SQL views.
- **`FUNCTION`**: Controls access to function.
- **`ANONYMOUS FUNCTION`**: Controls access to anonymous functions.
- **`ANY FILE`**: Controls access to the underlying file system.

- **Secret management with Databricks**: While working with the Databricks platform, we have to work with confidential information to configure and access data from various storage accounts. We can securely access secrets using the **Databricks backed** or **key-vault backed**. Databricks secrets will be stored securely. If someone tries to display the output of the secret in the notebook, then it will be automatically replaced by **`[REDACTED]`**.

  For example, we can create secret score in Azure Databricks from the portal using the URL, as shown in following screenshot:

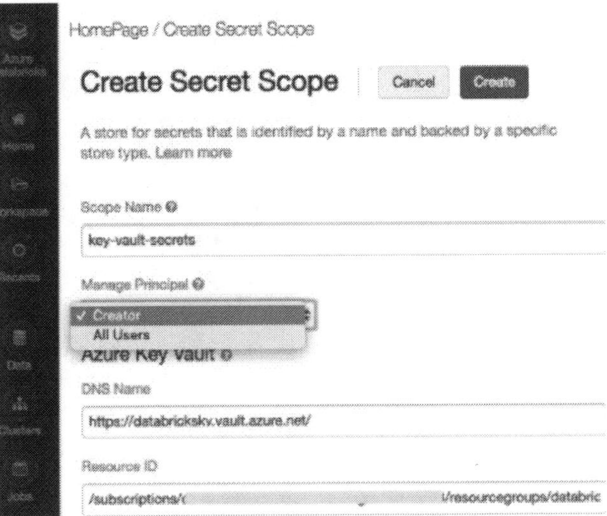

Figure 2.11: Databricks secret scope

Best recommended practice while working with the Databricks platform is to use Databricks secret scope to refer confidential secrets from the secret scope.

Databricks data access management

In this section, we will walk through the points to consider for data governance while working with the Databricks platform and best practices to be used to implement them to build an enterprise solution using Databricks.

Need of data governance with Databricks platform

Data governance consists of a collection of policies and practices to manage sensitive data securely for the enterprise organization. We can increase data security by providing the data teams more visibility and control of the user data and protecting the same from unauthorized users by configuring the required rules to meet the regulatory requirements:

Figure 2.12: Data governance

Data access management challenges

While building any data solutions for enterprise organizations, security teams, and platform administrators have to make sure that data is accessed in a secure manner and governed as per the regulatory bodies. Regulatory bodies all over the world have defined the way to capture and store the data.

Let's go through the challenges when considering the security and availability of the data while working with the cloud:

- Support of **Access Control List** (**ACL**) for the data stored in the cloud.
- Audit logging of the data access on cloud platform.
- Scalability of the security and monitoring solutions with growing data.
- Proactive monitoring of data access policies.
- Identify gaps in data governance solution.

Databricks managed data governance solution

Now, let's take a look at Databricks managed data governance solution:

- ACL to manage fine-grained access to data. Databricks has cloud backbone state-of-the-art AWS security to simplify users and secure access to the data lake.
- Databricks has cluster policies to control access to the compute resources.
- Databricks has REST API to automate provisioning and permission management.
- Robus audit logging to audit and track workspace operations.
- AWS Cloud Native Databricks workspace can provide data access information across the deployment account using **AWS CloudTrail** and **CloudWatch**.

Now, let's explore in detail the setting up the data governance solution using the in-built Databricks features:

- **Access control setup**: We can set up fine-grained access to data storage using the access control list. Using **`Instance Profile`**, we can secure data access on S3 bucket. We can select the instance profile when we launch a cluster in Databricks:

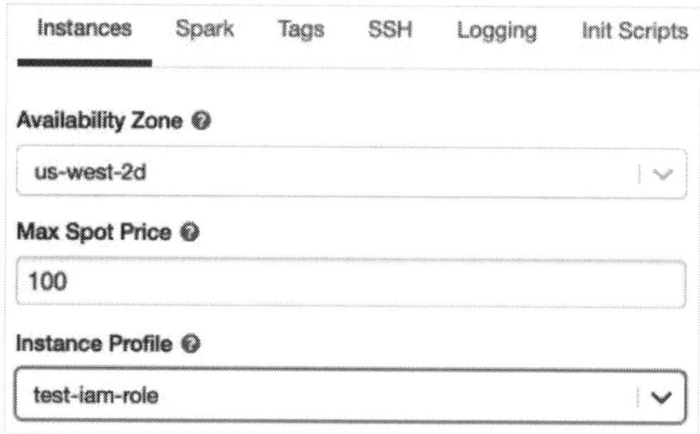

Figure 2.13: Databricks cluster instance profile

Once the Databricks cluster is created, make sure that only authorized users have access to attach the notebooks using the cluster permission setting:

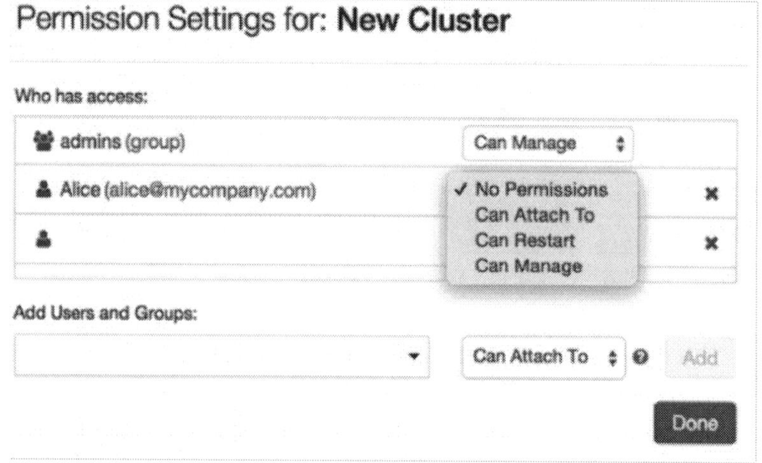

Figure 2.14: Databricks cluster permission settings

- **Table access control**: Table access control is used in Databricks to grant, deny, and revoke access to the data using the Spark SQL API. We can also manage a granular level of access to table objects like databases, tables, views, and functions.

  For example, Data Analysts want to create regulatory reporting reports using sensitive information. You only restrict access to sensitive data to certain data analysts and disable access to other users in the group. We can achieve the same by implementing the table access control:

```
%sql
GRANT select on table dbo.piidata TO sagar.lad
```

Figure 2.15: Databricks table access control - GRANT access

Similarly, we can deny access to all user **`sagar.lad`** using the following command:

```
%sql
DENY ALL PRIVILEGES on table dbo.piidata TO sagar.lad
```

Figure 2.16: Databricks table access control - DENY access

It is also possible to define fine-grained access control to specific tables or views.

- **Credential passthrough**: Databricks has the **credential passthrough** feature, which allows users to authenticate automatically to external storage services like AWS S3 or Azure Data Lake Storage Gen2 using the same identity by which a user logged in to the Databricks workspace. It is not a *compulsory* option, but if you want to enable it, you can do so while creating the cluster in Databricks.

Credential passthrough for high concurrency cluster

Figure 2.17: Databricks cluster - credential passthrough high concurrency cluster

Credential passthrough for standard cluster

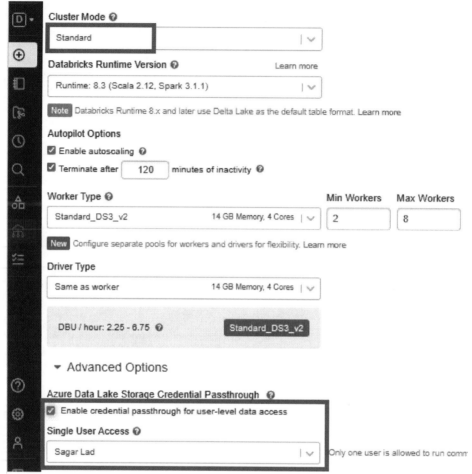

***Figure 2.18**: Databricks cluster - credential passthrough standard cluster*

Consider the scenario where the Data Engineering team wants to read and write data to Data Lake Storage Gen2. The first step is to create a high concurrency cluster in Databricks and attach an instance profile that has the required permission to Data Lake Storage Gen2 and provide cluster permission to the data engineering team. Now, suppose we want the **adls gen2** container only to be accessed by certain members of the data engineering team to write data to container and want other users to only have read access. Traditionally, we can create multiple clusters and add respective users to restrict access as per the requirements. However, it is not a cost-effective and sustainable solution as we can't create and manage multiple clusters for different requirements across the enterprise organizations. We can cater to such requirements using the credential passthrough feature of the Databricks.

- **Audit access**: Auditing and managing the data access is a mandatory step to create a data governed solution using Databricks platform. Databricks has a rich set of in-built audit events to log the user activities in Databricks and enable proactive monitoring of all the activities in the Databricks platform. Databricks provides two types of audit logs:
  - Workspace level audit logs
  - Account level audit logs

  Depending on the cloud provider (AWS/Azure/GCP), we can configure and enable audit logs for the Databricks workspace. Once configured, audit logging delivers audit logs to **`s3 bucket/adls gen2`** within *72 hours.*

  We can also extend the audit logs to monitor the storage for more granular level of access details. This will enable us to few of the answers required by the regulators:
  - *What data has been accessed and by whom?*
  - Unauthorized attempt to read/write/delete data
  - Aggregate or retire data sources from the Databricks platform

  Databricks and **Immuta** also have collaborative solutions to create an end to end data governance solution with data security. Main focus areas for this solution are fine-grained security and ease of data discovery to share data securely. The following are a few specific features of end-to-end data governance solution built by Databricks and Immuta:
  - **Fine grained access control**: Solution has powerful data masking and anonymization techniques to generate masked data on the fly. This feature will enable data to be accessed by more and more users to bring business insights and also regulatory complaint.

- o **Self-service data catalog**: Data discovery is made easier for all the Databricks data using the self-service data catalog:

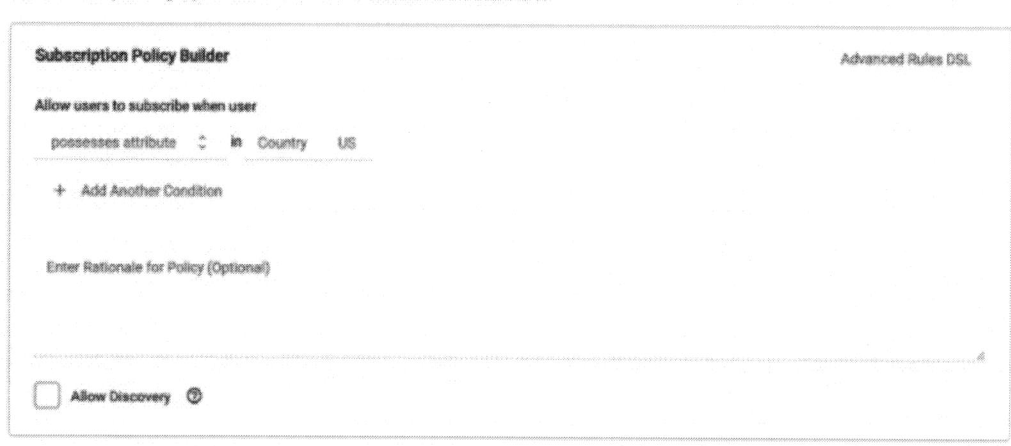

Figure 2.19: Self-service data catalog

- **No code policies for every regulation**: Policy creation and authoring doesn't force any developers to write any code. Policies can be created by simply writing the sentence. Once policies are created, they will be enforced natively by the Databricks platform:

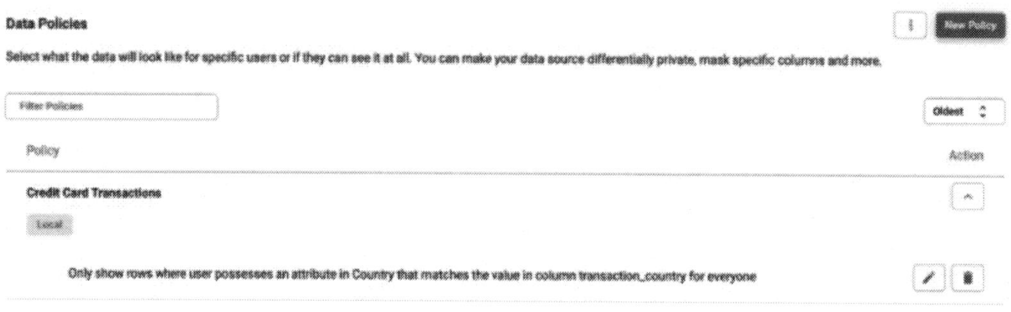

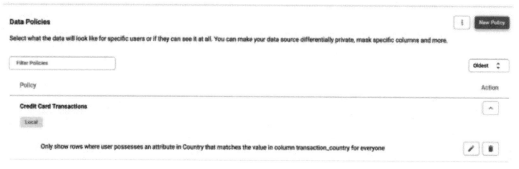

Figure 2.20: No code policy

- **Attribute based access control**: User attributes can be used to create and manage fine-grained access to the data objects.

Databricks cluster management

As we conferred about the Databricks cluster at the beginning of this chapter, Databricks cluster is a set of compute resources and configurations to run the data solutions on Databricks platform.

Databricks has multiple options to create and configure clusters with the best of performance and low cost. Let's explore cluster considerations to efficiently manage the Databricks clusters:

- **All purpose and job clusters**: All-purpose clusters can be shared by multiple users during the data exploration and development phase. Once the development is completed, it is recommended to switch to the job cluster as they will be terminated when the job ends, which will reduce the cost.
- **Cluster mode**: Databricks has standard, high concurrency, and single node cluster modes. Standard clusters are ideal for processing big data with spark. It is recommended to use a single node cluster for non-distributed workloads. High concurrency clusters are ideal when users want to share resources or run ad-hoc jobs.
- **On-demand and spot instances**: We can significantly reduce the cost by choosing spot instances instead of on-demand instances whenever possible according to the use cases:

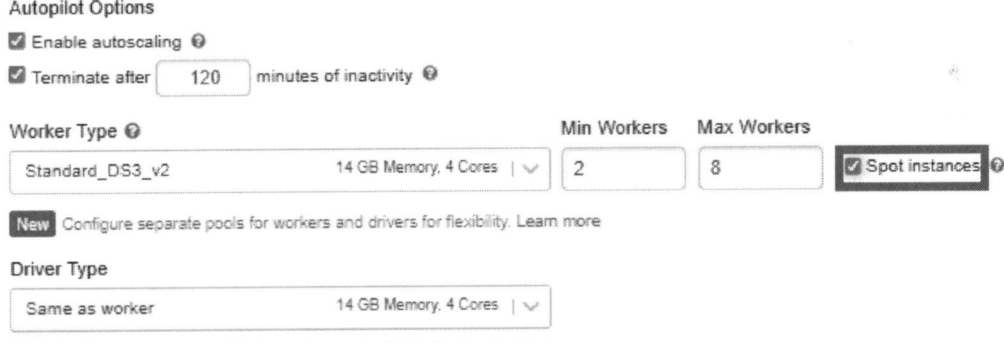

***Figure 2.21**: Databricks cluster spot instance*

- **Auto scaling**: Auto scaling feature for Databricks cluster resizes the cluster configurations automatically based on the workload. It will reduce the cost as well as increase the performance based on the workload compared to fixed-size clusters:

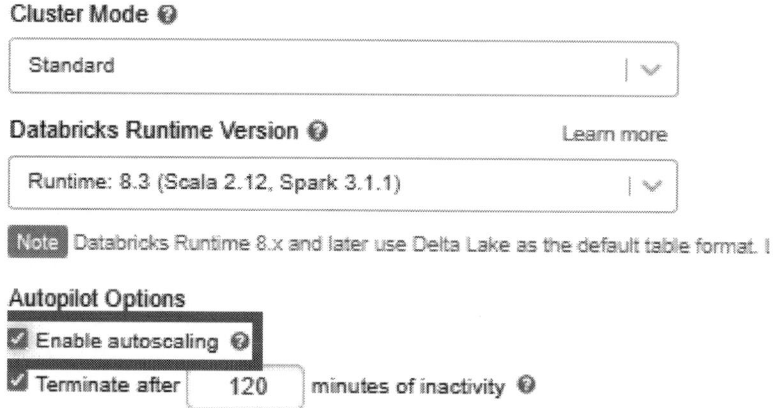

***Figure 2.22**: Databricks cluster auto scaling*

- **Cluster policies**: Databricks cluster policies ease the life of Databricks administrators to manage cluster configurations and creation in Databricks workspace. Cluster policies enforce standard cluster configuration and reduce cost by preventing excessive usage of resources and pre-configured cluster configurations for specific workloads:

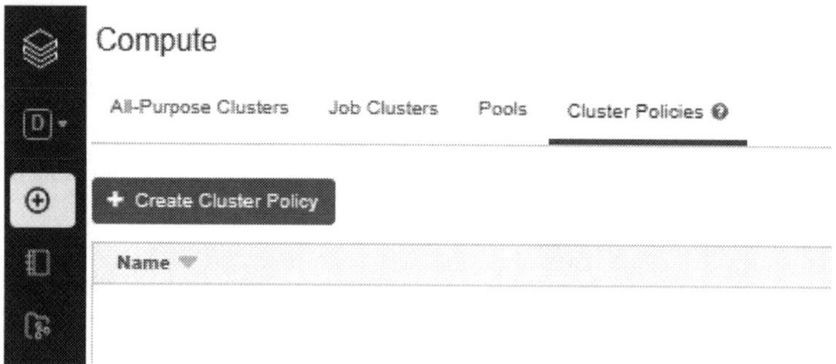

***Figure 2.23**: Databricks cluster policies*

- **Tag enforcements**: Create cluster policy to enforce tags and assign the cluster policy to make sure that tags will be created while creating the cluster using the `custom_tags.<tag-name>` attribute:

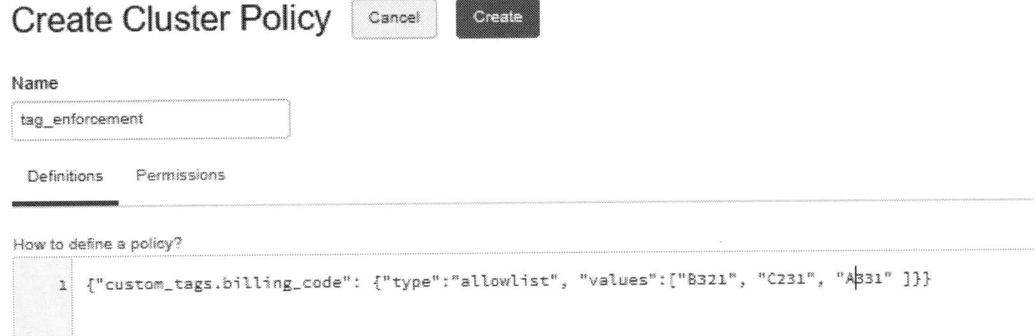

Figure 2.24: Databricks create cluster policies

Once the tag definitions are created, we can assign permissions to user, group, or service principal:

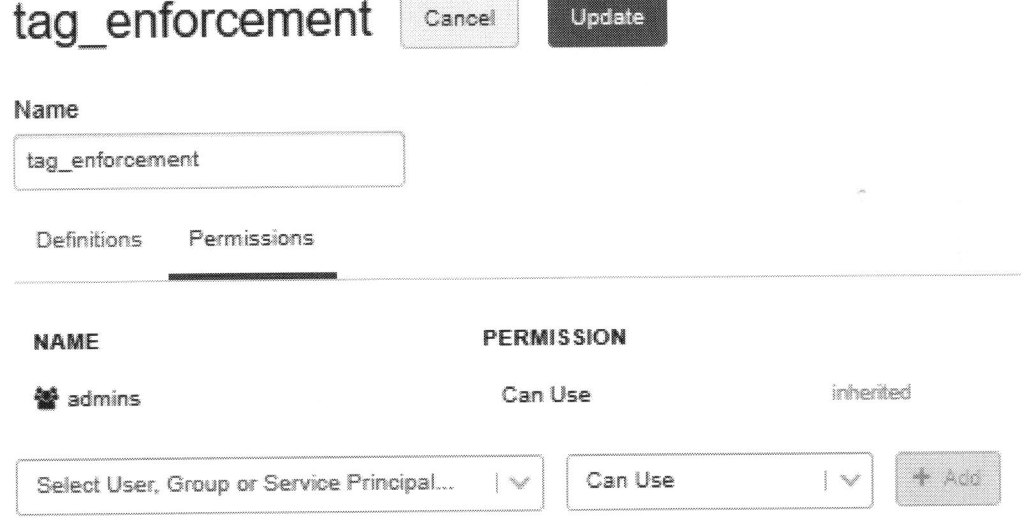

Figure 2.25: Databricks cluster policies assignment

Similarly, we can create multiple cluster policies based on use cases within Databricks to keep cluster configurations and management consistent across the Databricks workspace:

- Cluster policy to define T-Shirt sized cluster configurations.
- Cluster policy for cluster configurations based on the workload types.

- Cluster policy for cost reduction with **auto scaling, auto termination, expensive instance types**, and **worker node counts.**
- Use of instance type for cost reduction.

While creating a Databricks cluster, you also have an option to configure if you want to use spot instances to reduce the cost. If spot instances are expelled due to unavailability, on-demand instances will be deployed to replace those instances:

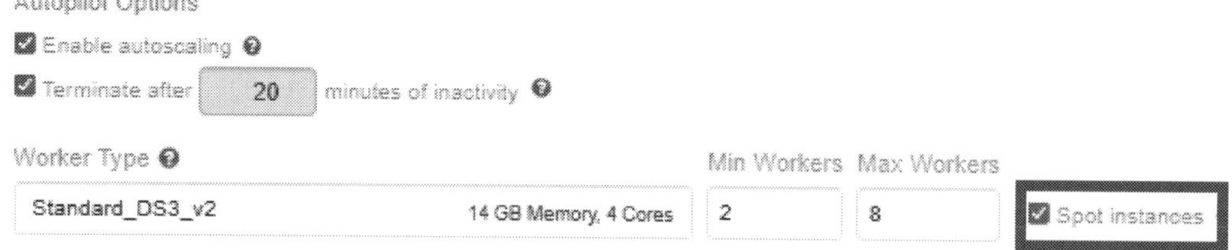

Figure 2.26: Databricks cluster - spot instances

- **Cluster tags**: Enforcing cluster tags for Databricks workspace helps enterprise organizations to monitor the cost of cloud resources. Cluster tags can be specified in the form of *key-value pairs* during the cluster creation.

  By default, Databricks applies the following tags for each cluster:

  - `Vendor`
  - `Creator`
  - `ClusterName`
  - `ClusterId`
  - `RunName` (only applicable for job cluster)
  - `JobId` (only applicable for job cluster)
  - `SqlEndpointId` (only applicable for Databricks SQL resources)

  We can add the custom tags to Databricks cluster by referring to the *cluster configuration* page. Click on **`Advanced settings`** from the cluster configuration page and select the **`Tags`** tab. Now, we can add the key-value pair to add the tags to the Databricks cluster, highlighted as follows.

  It is also a recommended practice to enforce a few mandatory tags for each cluster creation to proactively monitor the cost for the Databricks cluster:

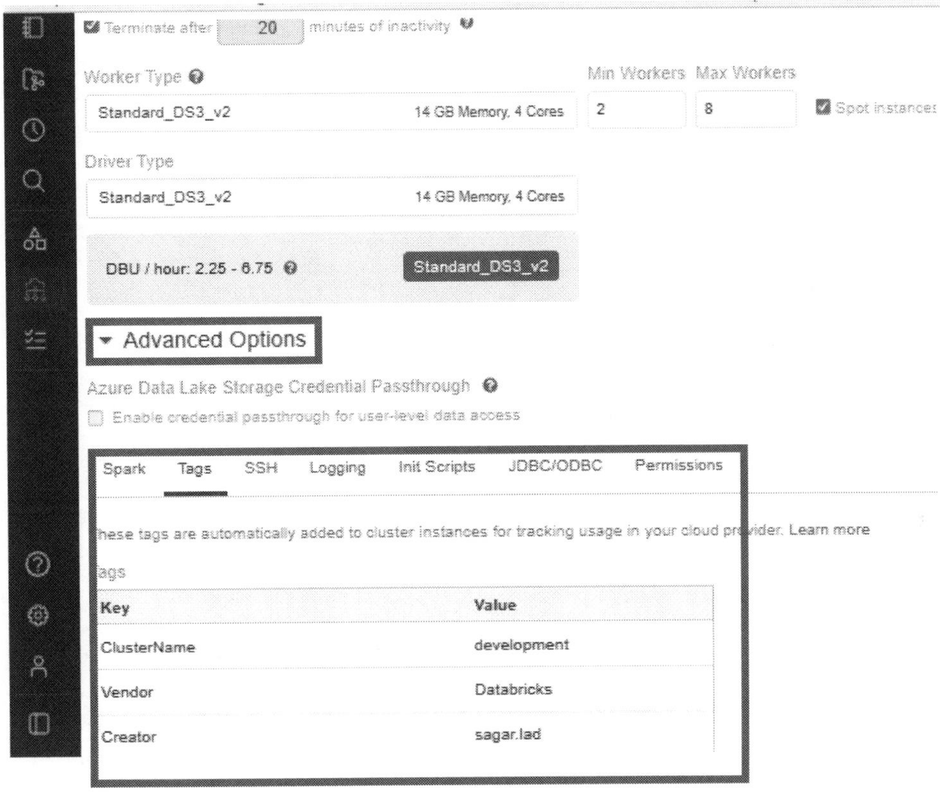

Figure 2.27: Databricks cluster - tags

- **Cluster node initialization scripts**: We can also create a shell script, which will be started automatically during the cluster initialization before the spark driver starts.

  We can use this **`init scripts`** to automate various tasks during the cluster restart process:

  - Automatically install the **`python`** package to Databricks cluster.
  - Change JVM system **`classpath.`**
  - Set environment variables and system properties to Databricks cluster.
  - Change spark configurations.

  Databricks supports two types of **init** scripts:

- **Cluster-scoped init scripts**: Scope for **cluster-scoped init scripts** is only limited to specific Databricks clusters that are configured. It is more preferable to use **cluster-scoped init scripts**.

Cluster-scope init scripts can be created for both interactive and job clusters. Cluster scoped init scripts can be configured using Databricks UI, Databricks CLI, and using cluster APIs. Cluster launch also fails if the configured **init** script fails during the cluster restart process. As highlighted in the following screenshot, you can go to edit cluster, and under **`Advanced Options`**, we can configure cluster **config init** scripts:

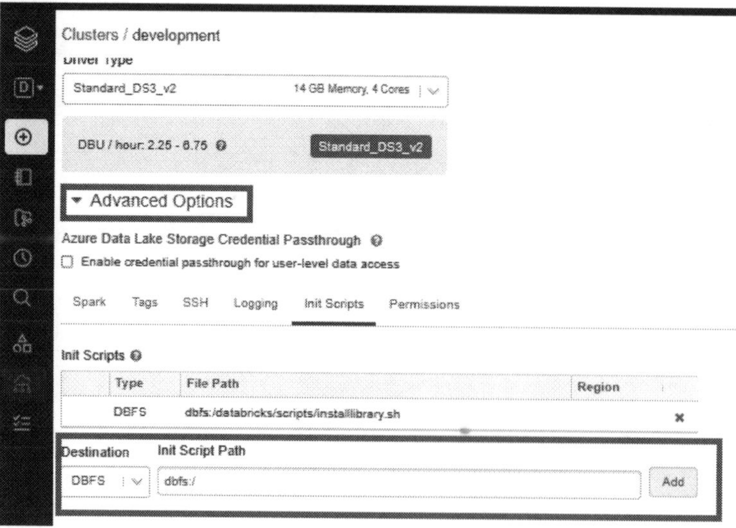

Figure 2.28: Databricks cluster config init scripts

- **Global init scripts**: Global init scripts once configured will be applicable to all the Databricks clusters. It imposes consistent cluster configurations across all Databricks clusters. Global init scripts can be created and configured only by the Databricks workspace administrator.

  Global init scripts can be created from the **`Settings -> Admin Console`** tab from the Databricks UI from the **Global init scripts**, highlighted as follows:

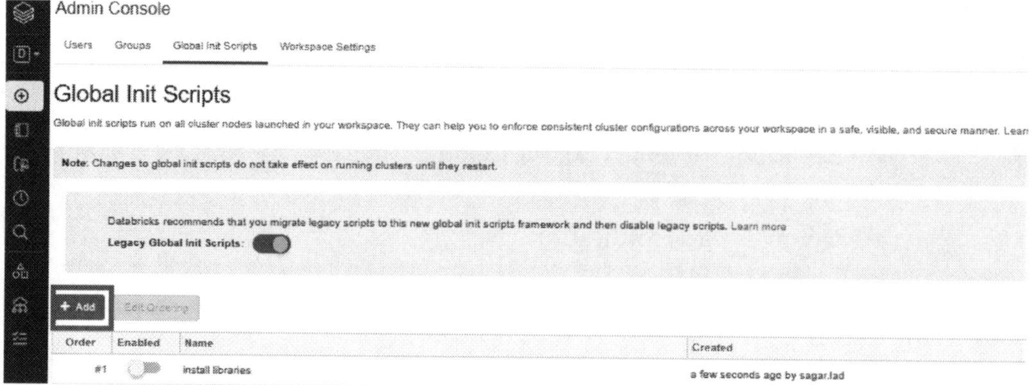

Figure 2.29: Databricks cluster config init scripts

Execution order for the init script is as follows:

- Global
- Cluster-named

init scripts can leverage the following Databricks environment variables in the script:

- **DB_CLUSTER_ID**: Cluster ID on which the script is running
- **DB_CONTAINER_IP**: Spark container private IP address
- **DB_CLUSTER_NAME**: Cluster name on which the script is running
- **DB_PYTHON_VERSION**: Cluster Python version
- **DB_IS_JOB_CLUSTER**: Check if it is a job cluster

For example, if you want to run **init** script only on specific Databricks instance types, we can use the following script:

```
echo DB_INSTANCE_TYPE
if [[ $DB_INSTANCE = "TRUE" ]]; then
    <run this part only on driver>
      else
     <run this part only on driver>
      fi
```

When we create init scripts, script details are captured in the cluster logs, and script start/stop events are also captured in the cluster event logs:

- **Garbage collection**: Working with big RAM helps us to improve the cluster performance but it also leads to delay during the garbage collection process. Such delays can be minimized by avoiding deploying the clusters with large amounts of RAMs. If we need more memory for the computation, it is recommended to deploy more cluster instances with smaller RAM sizes.
- **Cluster access control**: When the Databricks workspace is created, all users can create and edit the clusters. Databricks workspace

administrators can configure cluster access control to restrict the cluster permission at user level:

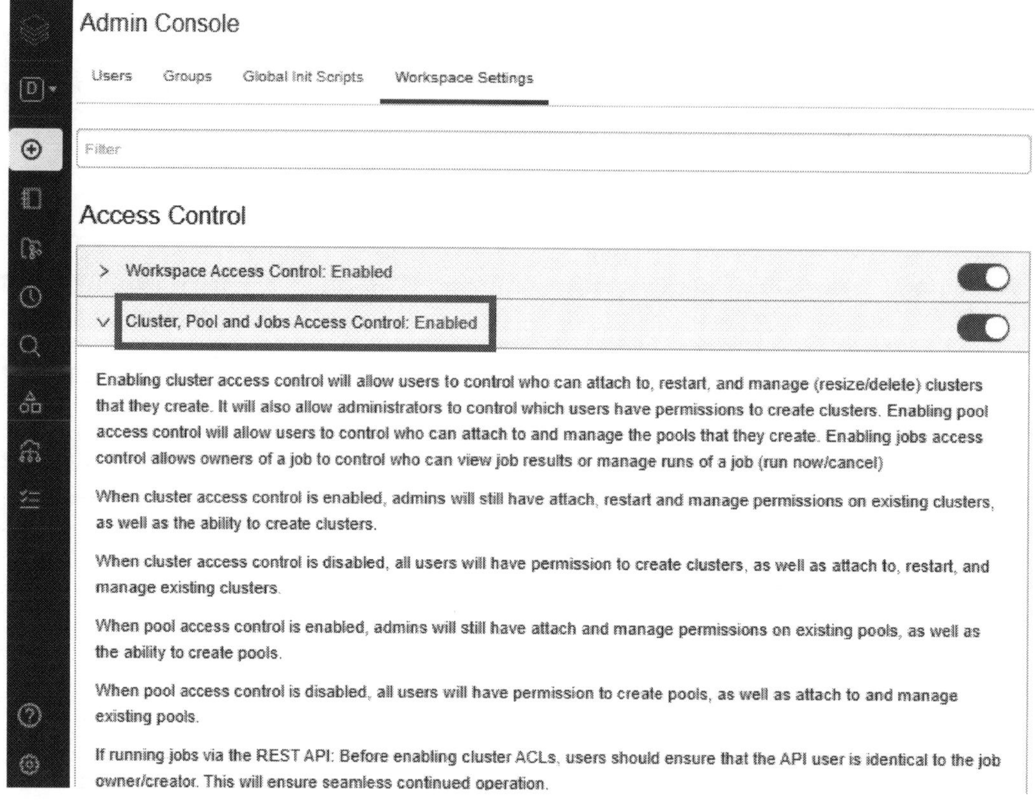

***Figure 2.30**: Databricks cluster, pool, job access control*

First, Databricks administrator has to enable the **cluster, pool, and job access control** to configure cluster access control. We can configure two types of cluster permissions:

- Cluster creation permission
- Cluster-level permission for users to attach, restart, resize, and manage the cluster

To configure cluster access control, go to computer from the Databricks workspace UI, click on **Edit cluster,** and go to **Advanced options**:

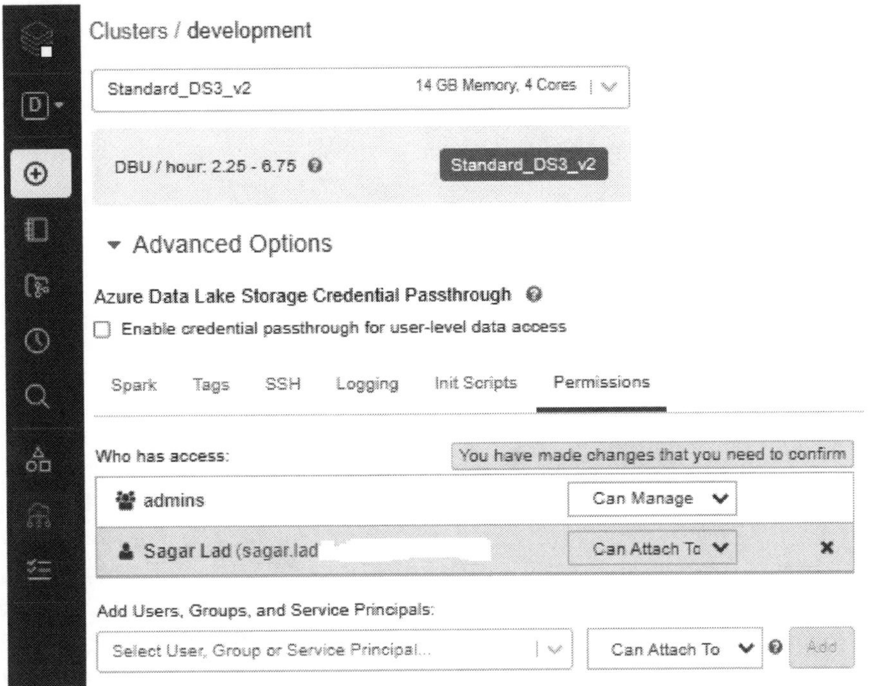

Figure 2.31: Databricks cluster access control

We can assign the following permission to users to manage the granular level of cluster permissions:

- **No Permissions**
- **Can Attach To**
- **Can Restart**
- **Can Manage**

Databricks SQL Analytics administration

Databricks SQL enables SQL users to run *ad hoc SQL queries* on data lake and create multiple visualization types to query results with different dimensions. Users can use Databricks SQL analytics from the Databricks workspace if the following requirements are met:

- Premium Databricks workspace
- E2 version of Databricks platform

- Databricks SQL access entitlement

From the Databricks workspace UI, **select persona: SQL**, as follows:

Figure 2.32: *Databricks SQL*

When we log in, the Databricks SQL page looks as follows. There are multiple options available for admins as well as Databricks SQL to run SQL queries, export available data, and import the dashboards. We can also write SQL queries using the SQL Query Editor and connect to BI tools like Tableau, Power BI, and so on. Databricks SQL also has various sample data and in-built dashboards, which we can play around with to start working with the Databricks SQL.

If you want to access cloud storage data using Databricks SQL, we have to create an instance profile. Additional instance profile and configuration is not required if we want to use Databricks-managed tables:

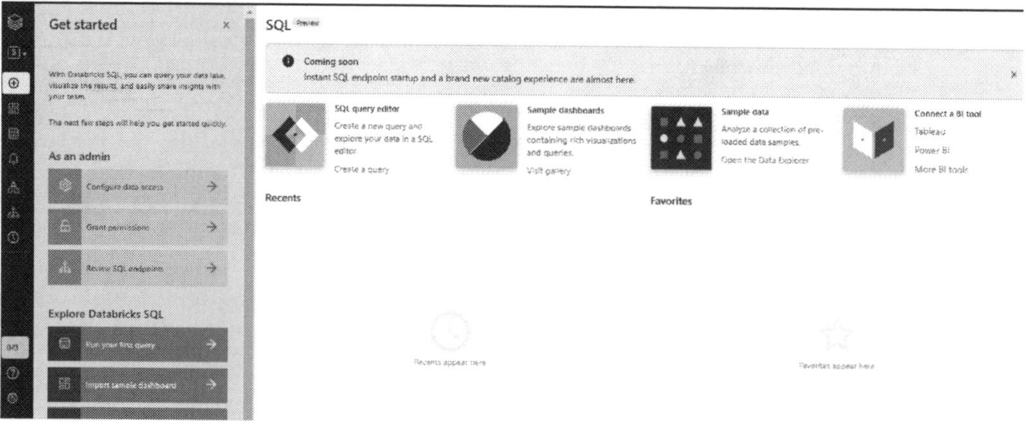

Figure 2.33: *Databricks SQL - home page*

Using access control list, we can configure permission to access Databricks SQL alerts, dashboards, data, queries, and SQL endpoints. Databricks workspace administrator can manage the following granular level of permissions for users:

- Alert access control
- Dashboard access control
- Data access control
- Query access control
- SQL endpoint access control

Databricks SQL has an in-built feature to encrypt queries as well as the query result:

- **Custom key to encrypt queries and query history**: We can use our own custom key to encrypt the Databricks SQL queries and query history. If a custom key is already configured to encrypt data for the managed services, no configuration is required. Custom encryption key only encrypts the data at rest; it doesn't encrypt the data in transit.
- **Custom key to encrypt query result:** It is also possible to encrypt the query result to avoid exposing sensitive data during the query execution with Databricks SQL. Now, let us see how to create a table with records from the Databricks dataset and allow users to access the table. We can add the users using the admin console and by clicking on the **`Add User`** button from the **`Users`** tab, as follows:

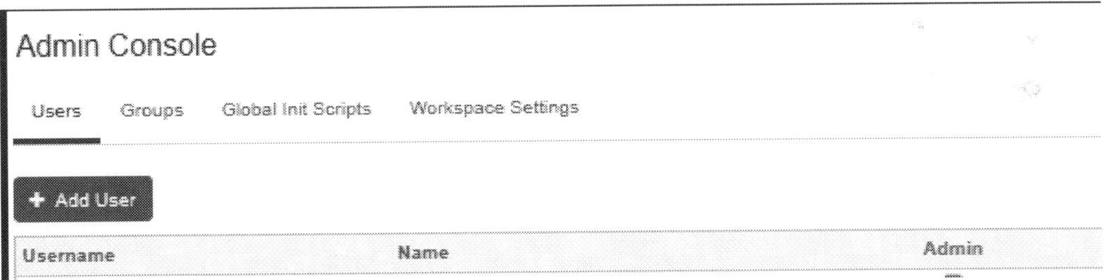

***Figure 2.34**: Databricks admin console - add users*

The next step is to create a table using the Databricks datasets. On the home page of Databricks SQL, click on the **`Create`** button and select the query:

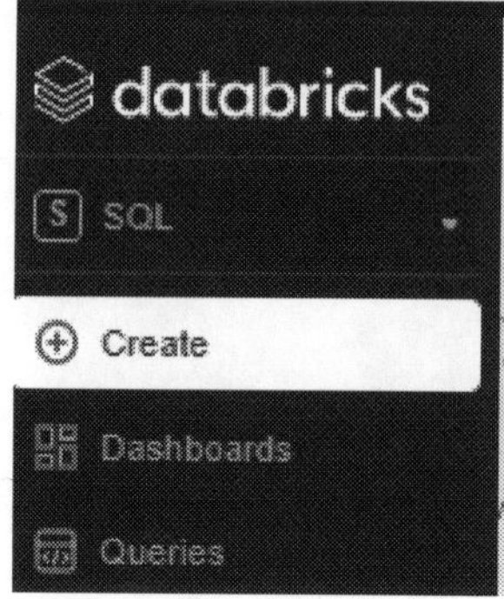

Figure 2.35: *Databricks SQL - create table*

Put the following query in the Query Editor and execute it:

```
CREATE TABLE default.people10m OPTIONS (PATH 'dbfs:/databricks-
datasets/learning-spark-v2/people/people-10m.delta')
```

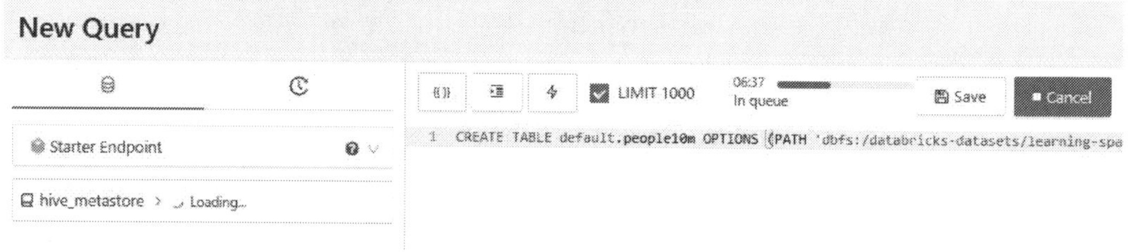

Figure 2.36: *Databricks SQL - execute query*

Once the query execution is completed, configure the access to the table using the data explorer or query editor. When you click on the button, you will be able to see the query history in the sidebar. Once the table is created, we can run the SQL query and create a visualization.

Go to the home page of Databricks SQL and execute the query to retrieve the data from the table. Once the query result appears on the screen, click on the **`Add Visualization`** button to create visualization on the query output:

birthYear	total
1,952	27
1,953	26
1,954	15
1,955	23
1,956	28

***Figure 2.37**: Databricks SQL - create visualizations*

It is also possible to save this visualization and create a dashboard out of it, which can be shared with other users.

Databricks SQL has the following components:

- **Interface**
  - o **UI**: Graphical interface to create dashboards and queries, SQL endpoints, query history, and alerts.
  - o **REST API**: Interface allows you to automate tasks on the Databricks SQL objects.
- **Data management**
  - o **Visualization**: Graphical representation of the results after query execution.
  - o **Dashboard**: Query visualization with description.
  - o **Alert**: Query notification when query threshold reaches.
- **Computation management**
  - o **Query**: Valid SQL statement for execution.
  - o **SQL endpoint**: Computation resource to execute SQL queries.
  - o **Query history**: History of executed SQL queries.

- **Authentication and authorization**
  - o **Users and groups**: Individual users and group of users who has system access.
  - o **Personal access token**: Confidential string to authenticate REST API and connect to BI Tools using the SQL endpoints.
  - o **Access control list**: Set of permissions attached to the principal that requires access to the object.
- **SQL endpoint** is a computation resource to run the SQL commands on Databricks environment. There are two types of SQL endpoints in Databricks:
  - o **Classic SQL endpoint**: Classic SQL endpoint uses the compute resources in the AWS account.
  - o **Serverless SQL endpoint**: Databricks-managed SQL endpoints are called serverless SQL endpoints that use the compute resources from the Databricks cloud account. It is much easier to manage endpoints with serverless SQL endpoints and avoid delays in the launch time.

The following are the permissions are required to create the SQL endpoint in Databricks workspace:

- Cluster creation permission in Databricks Data Science and Engineering.
- Can manage permission in Databricks SQL.

SQL endpoints can be viewed using the icon of SQL endpoints, as follows:

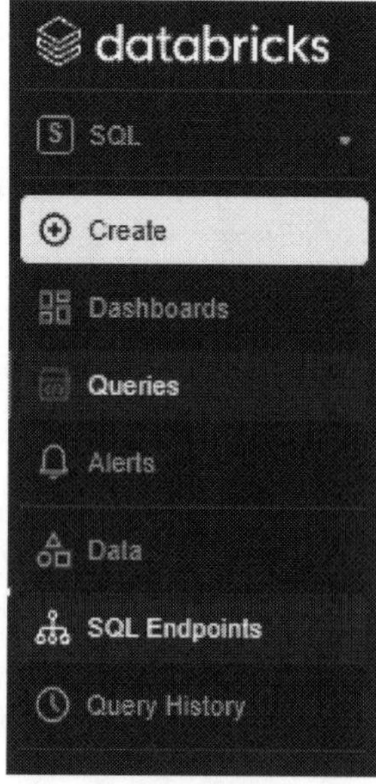

Figure 2.38: Databricks SQL endpoints

We can also create and manage alerts destinations for proactive monitoring. When the configured alerts will be invoked, it will blob of related data to configured alert destinations. Only a Databricks admin can configure and manage the alerts.

By default, alert notification will be sent to email. No additional configurations are required to get alert notifications via email. In order to configure alert destination, we can go to the **`Settings`** page and select **`User Settings`**:

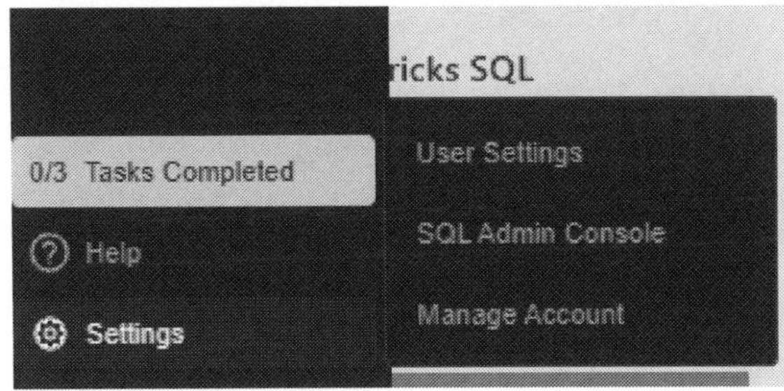

***Figure 2.39**: Databricks SQL settings*

Then, select the alert destinations:

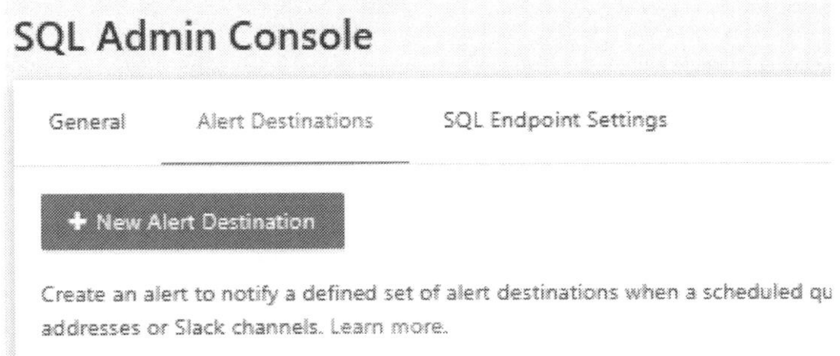

***Figure 2.40**: Databricks SQL alert destinations*

Using Databricks SQL endpoints, we can connect to business intelligence tools to create interactive visualizations and dashboards using the following tools:

- Power BI
- Tableau
- Looker
- Qlik
- TIBCO
- MicroStrategy

- ThoughtSpot
- Mode
- SQL Workbench

Databricks SQL also supports REST API to manage the queries and SQL endpoints. We can create a maximum of *30 REST API* requests for each workspace. If we make more than *30 requests*, we can get a *429 error code*.

Databricks SQL has a rich set of SQL commands, which can be used to execute SQL queries. Let's go through a few SQL commands for reference.

- **DDL statements**: Following are the data definition language commands:
    - `ALTER DATABASE`
    - `ALTER TABLE`
    - `ALTER VIEW`
    - `CREATE DATABASE`
    - `CREATE FUNCTION`
    - `CREATE TABLE`
    - `CREATE VIEW`
    - `DELETE DATABASE`
    - `DROP DATABASE`
    - `DROP TABLE`
    - `DROP FUNCTION`
    - `DROP VIEW`
- **DML statements**: Following are the data manipulation language commands:
    - `DELETE FROM`
    - `INSERT INTO`
    - `INSERT OVERWRITE`
    - `MERGE INTO`
- **Data retrieval statements**: Following are the data retrieval commands:
    - `Query`
    - `Select`
    - `Values`

- **Delta lake statements**: Following are the delta lake commands:
  - `CACHE SELECT`
  - `CONVERT TO DELTA`
  - `DESCRIBE HISTORY`
  - `GENERATE`
  - `OPTIMIZE`
  - `RESTORE`
  - `VACCUM`
- **Auxiliary statements**: Following are the list of auxiliary commands:
  - `Analyze TABLE`
  - `DESCRIBE FUNCTION`
  - `DESCRIBE TABLE`
  - `DESCRIBE DATABASE`
  - `DESCRIBE QUERY`
  - `SHOW DATABASES`
  - `SHOW FUNCTIONS`
  - `SHOW GROUPS`
  - `SHOW PARTITIONS`
  - `SHOW TABLE`
  - `SHOW TABLES`
  - `SHOW USERS`
  - `SHOW VIEWS`

Conclusion

In this chapter, we explored in detail the Databricks Lakehouse platform offerings. After understanding the architecture of Databricks Lakehouse platform, you understood the practical use cases of the Databricks Lakehouse platform. You also learned about cluster management and few best practices to configure Databricks cluster considering the cost and security. At the end, we took a quick tour of Databricks SQL offering to run interactive SQL queries on data lake and create visualization dashboards.

Multiple choice questions

1. What are the main components of Databricks Lakehouse platform architecture?
    a. Control pane
    b. Data pane
    c. Both
    d. None of the above
2. Which format is used to store cluster configurations?
    a. JSON
    b. CSV
    c. ORC
    d. All of the above
3. What are different types of cluster mode in Databricks platform?
    a. Single node
    b. Standard
    c. High concurrency
    d. All of the above
4. Is it possible to enforce consistent cluster configuration for all Databricks clusters?
    a. Yes
    b. No
5. Who can configure the global init script for Databricks workspace?
    a. All users
    b. Workspace administrators
    c. Data engineer
    d. All of the above

Answers

1. **c**
2. **a**
3. **d**
4. **a**
5. **b**

CHAPTER 3

Spark, Databricks, and Building a Data Quality Framework

Databrick is all about processing data of different kinds, be it real-time or batch-based data. Processing data has always been a challenge and is done in multiple steps, such as identifying the source and data itself, connecting the source, validating and identifying issues with the data, cleaning and restructuring, and finally, enabling it to be consumed by a consumer like a stream analytics engine, streaming solutions, database, storage or reporting tools such as **Power BI** or **QlikView**.

In the previous two chapters, we explored the foundation and basics of Databricks, Databricks architecture, usage of the Databricks Lakehouse platform for Data Science and Engineering, and Databricks SQL. In this chapter, you will learn about the evolution of Spark to Databricks, and you will process validated data securely by building an ETL pipeline in Databricks using a notebook.

Structure

In this chapter, we will cover the following aspects of the Databricks Lakehouse platform:

- Introduction to Apache Spark
- Build ETL pipeline with Databricks for streaming and batch data

- Implement policies and practices to securely manage data
- Build data quality audit framework with Databricks

Objectives

After studying this chapter, you should be able to understand Apache Spark and its evolution to Databricks, use notebooks in Databricks to build your ETL pipeline, implement data security policies, and practice with approaches and examples to build a data processing framework in Databricks that confronts the data quality audit framework.

Introduction to Apache Spark

Apache Spark has evolved as an open-source unified analytics engine for large-scale data processing. **Spark** is not a storage solution but a multi-language engine as a data processing solution for executing Data Engineering, Data Science, and Machine Learning on single-node machines or groups of machines often called **clusters**. It provides an interface for distributed programming scaled up to multiple computers dynamically to enable implicit data parallelism with high fault tolerance.

History

Back in *2009*, **Hadoop 1.0** was already out, but it was lacking a good cluster manager.

A team of researchers at *Berkeley's AMPLab* were working to mitigate this with a better cluster manager, which led to the birth of **Mesos** as a new cluster manager.

Mesos has evolved as a distributed systems kernel built using similar principles as the Linux kernel, with a different level of abstraction. The kernel in Mesos runs on every machine and provides distributed applications like **Hadoop**, **Spark**, **Kafka**, and so on with APIs for resource management and scheduling across the entire data center either on-premises or on the cloud.

Source: Apache **https://mesos.apache.org/**.

The team continued to test the power of Mesos by introducing a *New Engine* built on top of **Scala** that can perform better than map Reduce leading to the development of Spark by *Matei Zaharia* at the *University of California, Berkeley's AMPLab* (**https://en.wikipedia.org/wiki/AMPLab**).

In *2013*, the project was donated to the *Apache Software Foundation*, becoming a top-level Apache project. At the time of writing this book, the current version of **Spark is 3.2**.

Evolution to DataBricks

Databricks grew out of the *AMPLab* project at the *University of California Berkeley* with almost the same team that was involved in making Apache Spark, an open-source distributed computing framework built atop Scala. The company was founded by: *Ali Ghodsi* (**https://en.wikipedia.org/wiki/Ali_Ghodsi**), *Andy Konwinski, Arsalan Tavakoli-Shiraji, Ion Stoica* (**https://en.wikipedia.org/wiki/Ion_Stoica**), *Patrick Wendell, Reynold Xin* (**https://en.wikipedia.org/wiki/Reynold_Xin**), and *Matei Zaharia*.

Matei Zaharia now the chief technologists of Databricks originalycreated Apache Spark while a PhD candidate at the *University of California, Berkeley*, and then a professor at *Stanford University* (**https://en.wikipedia.org/wiki/Stanford_University**). Databricks team adopted and optimized Spark to be able to run as a **SaaS** platform

During the years, Databricks has worked to expand the open-source project and simplify big data and machine learning. Databricks provides a cloud-optimized platform to run Spark and ML applications on Amazon Web Services and Azure.

In *November 2017*, the company was announced as a first-party service on Microsoft Azure via the integration of Azure Databricks. The company develops **Delta Lake**, an open-source project aimed at bringing reliability to data lakes for machine learning and other data science use cases.

What happened to Apache Spark?

Spark continues to shine and currently has more than *13830* commits by *1751* contributors, making it one of the most active projects in the *Apache Software Foundation* and one of the most active open-source big data projects.

Source: GitHub **https://github.com/apache/Spark**.

Spark is supported by major vendors and companies across the globe, including *Yahoo, Conviva, Amazon, Alibaba cloud, NTT Data, EBay, Baidu*, and *DataBricks*.

Starting with Databricks, a major cloud platform has come up with a serverless version of Apache Spark:

To name a few:-

- Data Mechanics
- Data Flow by Oracle
- Alibaba Cloud Elastic MapReduce (EMR)

Features of Apache Spark

- Spark is up to *100* times faster than **Hadoop MapReduce** for large-scale data processing. It can also achieve this speed through controlled partitioning; hence, it wins on speed.
- A simple programming layer provides powerful caching and disk persistence capabilities.
- It can be deployed through multiple solutions for distributed deployment and execution, such as **Mesos**, **Hadoop** via **YARN**, or Spark's own cluster manager.
- Spark offers real-time computing and low latency because of its in-memory computation capabilities.
- Spark code can be written in multiple languages (**Java**, **Scala**, **Python**, and **R**) via its high-level APIs or via shell scripting in Scala and Python.
- It's often associated with the term **polyglot** because of its capabilities to support multiple programming languages.

The book paraphrase and translation analogy

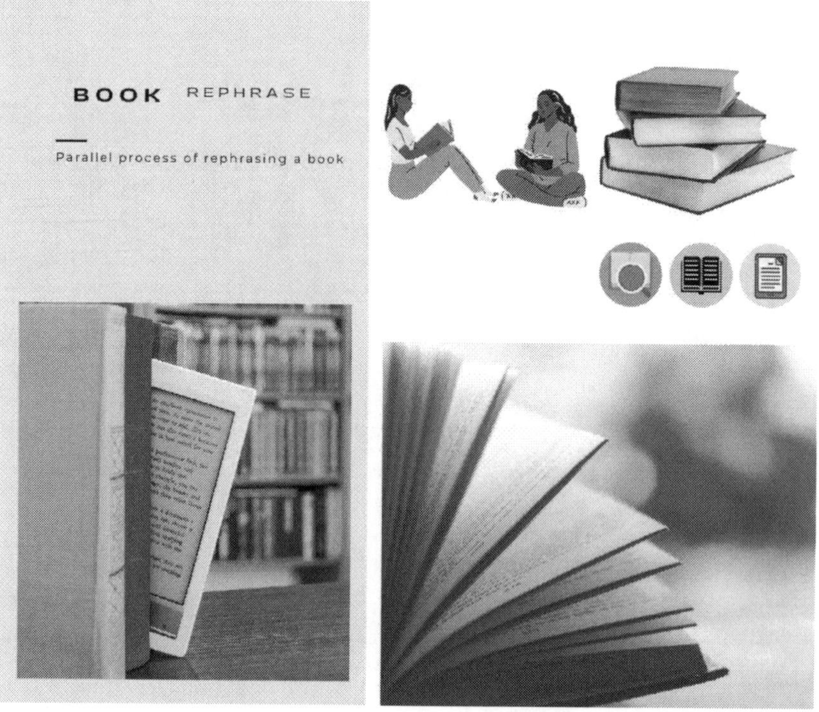

Figure 3.1*: Databricks audit: Book rephrase analogy for parallel processing*

Let's assume that *Merry* is a story freak and a voracious reader. *Merry* recently encountered an ancient menu script written in a different language, and now she wants to get that rephrased into normal English so that she can read it.

She wants to take help from a few of her friends to paraphrase and translate it. Let's call it a **Rephrase and Translate Project**.

Merry, being agile and to save time for her friends, tries to achieve maximum parallelism by breaking the manuscript into multiple portions so that everyone is able to achieve their rephrasing and translation tasks in parallel, with velocity, traceability, independence, and resiliency.

Merry is a good planner and program leader. To ensure that everything is executed perfectly, she takes the lead as the leader node and creates the best fit execution plan broken into phases or cycles based on optimal time and resources consumed. We prefer to call this **assignment phase**.

Her goal is to assign everyone a single set of non-interdependent responsibilities so that everyone can achieve their assigned portion of rephrasing and retranslation as fast as possible.

She assigns everyone a separate computer with a separate section of the novel to do the rephrasing. She creates a rephrasing and retranslation plan broken into multiple phases so that the rephrased output of one phase can be utilized in another phase in a top-down way, and no two-phase interconnects as like the *directed acyclic graphs*.

In the concluding phase of being a leader, she has to just collect all the final rephrases and collate them to conclude the final output.

Refer to the depiction as in the following diagram.

Note the term Directed Acyclic Graph (DAG).

You will notice that the flow of execution is in a single direction, and it's always reproducing a refined output, which is further linked to the next layer/phase of execution:

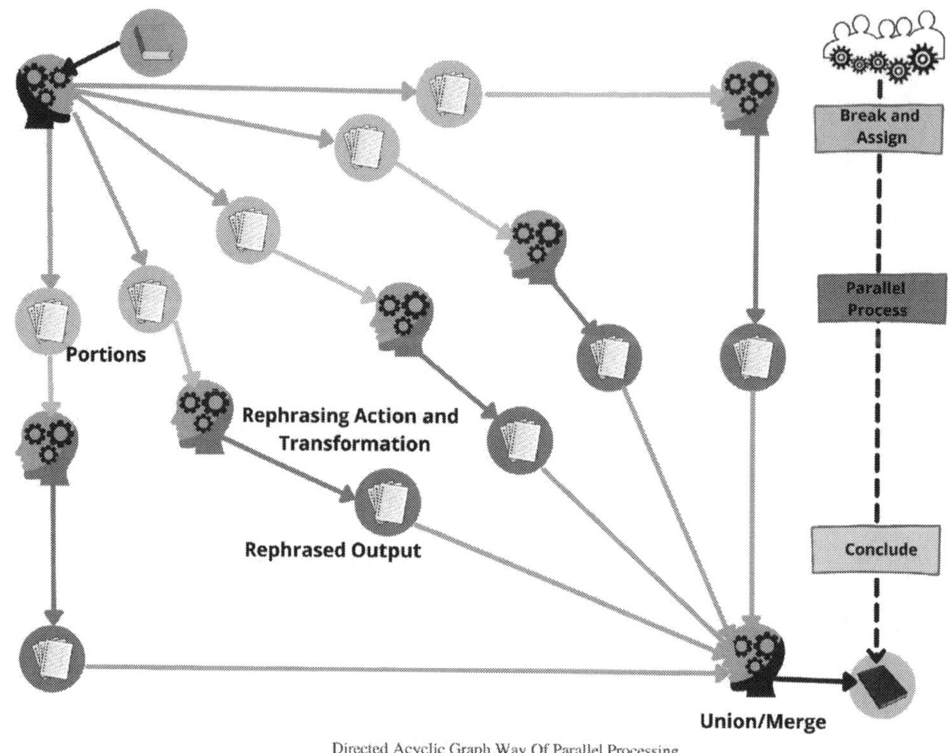

Figure 3.2*: Databricks audit: DAG*

What if Merry has to build a software to handle the parallel work?

To achieve the same output, she needs to have six computers or maybe less with independent compute containers. She can use the first machine as a **master node** and the rest as **workers**.

The master node can read the complete manuscripts into a primary dataset, create execution plans, and assign each worker machine with a portion of the manuscript to process in a specific path of execution that can have actions such as rephrasing and translation as well as spell correction and transformation such as split, filter, and merge, generating a *read-only dataset* of intermediate paraphrased and translated output, often called **Datasets** or **DataFrames**.

Datasets and DataFrames can be thought of as schematic representations of rephrased and translated content, which can be easily consumed for further processing.

She can achieve strict traceability and audit capability with instant rollback by making sure that the read-only datasets of partially rephrased and refined work are created after every transformation and any update or refinement induces the next set of datasets at the next layer.

Once the processing is done, the *6th* machine can merge all the output into one fresh dataset to create the final result.

In a more complex scenario, she can introduce the *7th* machine with a program that runs the main program to take the manuscripts for rephrasing, build execution plans, and assign resources to generate the output.

How about if one of the worker machines fails or there are thousands of other processes to be done?

Merry's program will need to have to manage more precisely in terms of using the resources on each of the machines to handle the load and handling scheduling to manage the processing of different novels. Maybe she will have to write a better program that can run on different cores on one machine, and manage the resources and handle failures among the group of worker machines to be very precisely called **clusters of nodes** or **cluster manager** or **yarn**.

You will be surprised to know that most modern distributed systems follow a similar pattern to handle parallelization and fault tolerance, and Spark is not so different but is highly optimized to handle large volumes of data.

Spark and its evolution

Spark has evolved with time, and to ease and optimize the processing, multiple components have been added so that programmers do not have to write low-level code to manage programming at the primitive RDD level, which forms the core of the Spark program.

Developers have multiple options instead of being dependent on writing low-level programs, like the established RDBMS, where the query can be written in simple SQL.

RDBMS systems has to go through a query plan cost value analysis and the one that is highly efficient and with lower cost is chosen to execute.

As Spark is more modern than the traditional OLTP system, it can understand multiple modern languages and can be compiled to be interpreted and assembled into low-level language.

When it comes to processing data, Spark has its own cost value optimization algorithm that can build highly optimized execution plans, which can be preferred based on cost value analysis, choosing the best one to process the data by generating highly efficient intermediate outputs as layers of RDDs.

Components of Apache Spark

Resilient Distributed Dataset (RDD)

RDD has been available since the beginning of Spark, and it is often considered as a fundamental data structure of Apache Spark.

RDD is *immutable* (read-only), which means that a new transformation further creates a new refined layer of RDDs.

This can be operated on many devices at the same time enabling massive parallel processing.

To understand it better , RDD can be considered as a partitioned set of unique records placed in memory on different execution units (nodes).

These nodes are spread across different machines (clusters) on which a Spark program is set up to run.

A Spark program can easily create a **Directed Acyclic Graph** during compile time to define how many layers of RDD are required after each action to compute the result; the operation on one layer of RDD generates a new lower layer of RDD.

This is the reason why Spark is considered *fault-tolerant* and *resilient*, and every operation in data is going to create a new layer of RDDs until the final results are emitted, ensuring that there is a lineage of change hierarchy available where faults can be easily rolled back and re-executed from a specific layer.

RDD enables a programmer to program in Spark at the lowest level, enabling developers to control the flow of execution and write code at the lowest level.

Cons: If the developer is not experienced enough, they can write un-optimized code, which can slow the data processing to a massive scale, especially when the file size is too large.

For example, a developer may unknowingly choose a sorting operation on entire datasets before a filter operation; consider *what will happen if the file is very large and is distributed into multiple partitions on multiple nodes?* First, a new RDD will be created after the sorting process with the same amount of data, and then, only a filtration would happen:

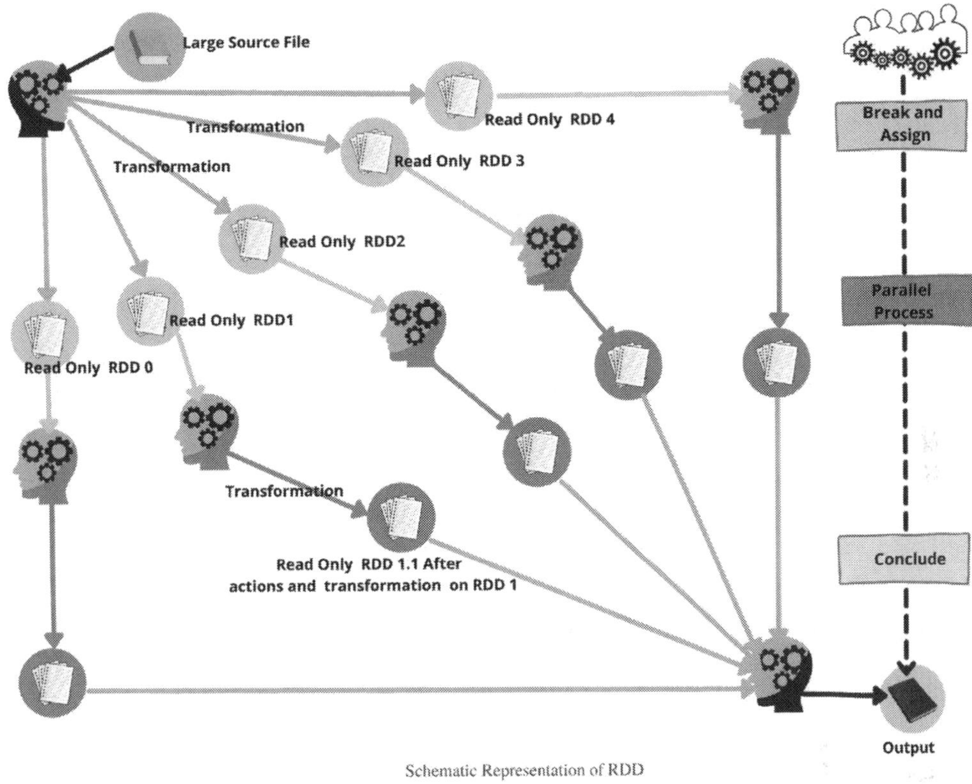

***Figure** 3.3: Databricks audit: RDD data flow*

Datasets and DataFrames

To make things simple for developers and analysts, an OLTP style query plan and selection mechanism was introduced over and above the RDD layer, called **DataFrame** and **Datasets** in Spark 2.0. This has the ability to generate different types of highly optimized code before runtime by doing a cost-value analysis, almost similar to how the database engine does for choosing a correct low-cost query plan to execute the SQL.

Datasets and DataFrames are built on top of RDD. In Spark, anything you do will go around RDD. The dataset in Spark RDDs is divided into logical partitions. If the data is logically partitioned within RDD, it is possible to send different pieces of data across different nodes of the cluster for distributed computing.

A **DataFrame** is a distributed collection of data that has a schema and is organized into rows, where each row consists of a set of columns, and each column has a name and an associated type. This is similar to tables in a relational database, but under the hood, it has much richer optimizations and is meant for highly optimized in-memory parallel processing.

Like the RDD, the DataFrame offers two types of operations: **transformations** and **actions**.

Transformations are *lazily evaluated*, and actions are *eagerly evaluated*.

A dataset is a strongly typed, immutable collection of data. Similar to a **DataFrame**, the data in a Dataset is mapped to a defined schema. It is more about *type safety* and is *object-oriented*.

Dataset has helpers, often called **encoders**. These are encoding utilities that convert data inside each object into a compressed binary format, resulting in the reduction of memory usage, reducing the number of bytes during network transfer.

As mentioned earlier Datasets and DataFrame both compile to generate RDD in a highly optimized way.

Directed Acyclic Graph (DAG)

DAG is a finite directed graph with no directed cycles. There are finitely many vertices and edges, where each edge is directed from one vertex to another.

DAG contains a finite set of vertices and edges in sequence. Every edge in DAG is directed from top to bottom in the sequence.

This is why it's great for generating multistage scheduling layers that implement stage-based scheduling. As the number of layers and depth can be more than two but *finite*, it's better and optimized than the older **Map and Reduce** programs, which run in two stages only: **Map** and **Reduce**.

How does DAG work in Spark?

The *interpreter* is the first layer, using a *Scala interpreter*, Spark interprets the code with some modifications. Spark creates an operator graph when you enter your code in the Spark console. When we call an *Action* on Spark RDD at a high level, Spark submits the operator graph to the *DAG scheduler*.

Divide the operators into stages of the task in the *DAG scheduler*. A stage contains tasks based on the partition of the input data. The DAG scheduler pipelines operators together. For example, map operators schedule in a single stage. The stages pass on to the *task scheduler*. It launches tasks through cluster manager. The dependencies of stages are unknown to the task scheduler.

The *workers* execute the task on the slave. The following diagram briefly describes the steps of how DAG works in the Spark job execution:

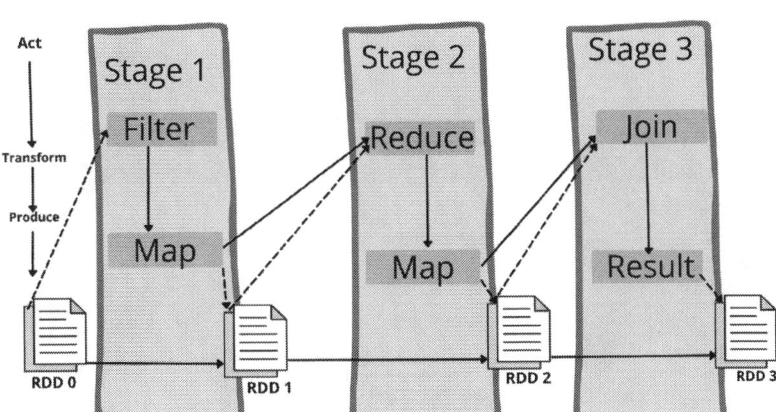

***Figure 3.4**: Databricks audit: RDD filtration*

- **Driver program**: The Apache Spark engine calls the main program of an application and creates **Spark Context**. A Spark Context consists of all the basic functionalities. RDD is created in the Spark Context.
- **Spark Driver**: It contains various other components, such as **DAG scheduler**, **task scheduler**, **backend scheduler**, and **block manager**, which are responsible for translating the user-written code into jobs that are actually executed on the cluster.
- **Cluster manager**: Cluster manager does the resource allocating work.

Execution mechanism

Spark Driver and Spark Context collectively watch over the job execution within the cluster. Spark driver works with the **cluster manager** to manage various other jobs. The cluster manager does the resource allocating work, and then the job is split into multiple smaller tasks, which are further distributed to worker nodes. Whenever an RDD is created in the Spark Context, it can be distributed across many worker nodes and can also be cached there. Worker nodes execute the tasks assigned by the cluster manager and return them to the Spark Context.

An **executor** is responsible for the execution of these tasks. The lifetime of executors is the same as that of the Spark application. If we want to increase the performance of the system, we can increase the number of workers so that the jobs can be divided into more logical portions.

Spark execution flow

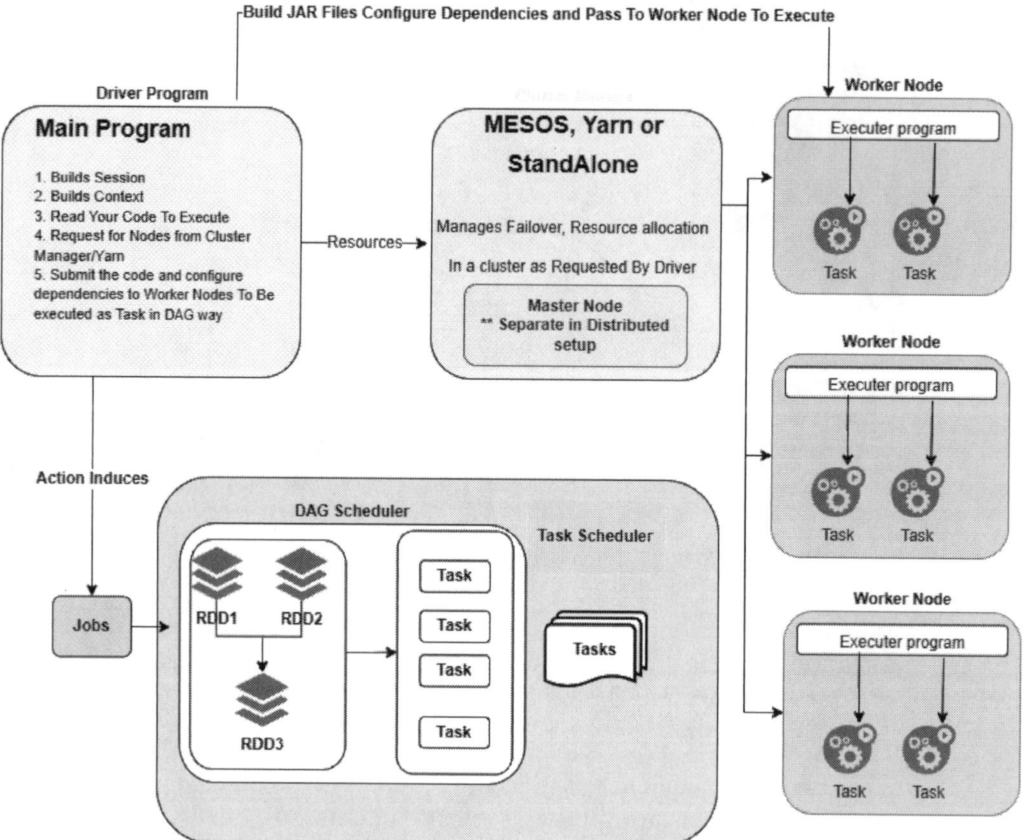

Figure 3.5: Databricks audit: Spark execution flow

Databricks is a seamless way to utilize Spark to its full potential. As it is built over Spark, it supports all the languages that Spark supports, which are **Python**, **R**, **Scala**, **Java**, and **SQL**.

Processing data using Databricks pipeline

Extract, transform, and load data by using Azure Databricks

To start with, we will use a simple use case of loading semi-structured exam data from SQL server to **Azure Data Lake Gen2** as a structured output to be consumed and queried in a variety of formats easily, giving you a varied idea of how to process data in Databricks using multiple ways.

We will be using a stand-alone instance of SQL Server table holding JSON formatted data. We will start with fetching semi-structured JSON data, filtering, and transforming it to finally generate a structured delta table to query and further process data.

To achieve it, we will be using notebooks, which is the most used and easiest way of programming with Spark-based systems and Databricks.

For programming language, we have mostly used **Scala**, considering there are easy examples available online, and they are just a Google search away. However, we have tried to put a viable balance of Scala, SQL, and Python just to make sure you understand the examples over and above the language boundaries and will be confident to code in any of these based on example available or organizational constraints.

Creating a notebook in Databricks

To create a notebook in Databricks, you can refer to the following screenshot and navigate to the **`Data Science & Engineering`** option to use the notebook feature. This also should appear in the common task section, as shown in the following screenshot.

Notebooks are the easiest and most popular way of programming for even hardcore programmers. It comes up with a single page with blocks called **cells**. Results and objects of the execution of one cell at the top are available to other cells below for consumption.

As in Databricks, there are many languages to work with. You can use the **`%{language Name}`** to let the compiler know in which language the cell (block) of the notebook is, all the variables over the cells in that language will be available for consumption below.

If you want to change the language and use it, the best way to do the intermediate transition is after you persist your data so that it can be accessed easily in the DataFrame again in the language of your choice and used further.

Once you create a notebook, use the **+** icon at the center to create a new cell and start writing your code by choosing your program of preference:

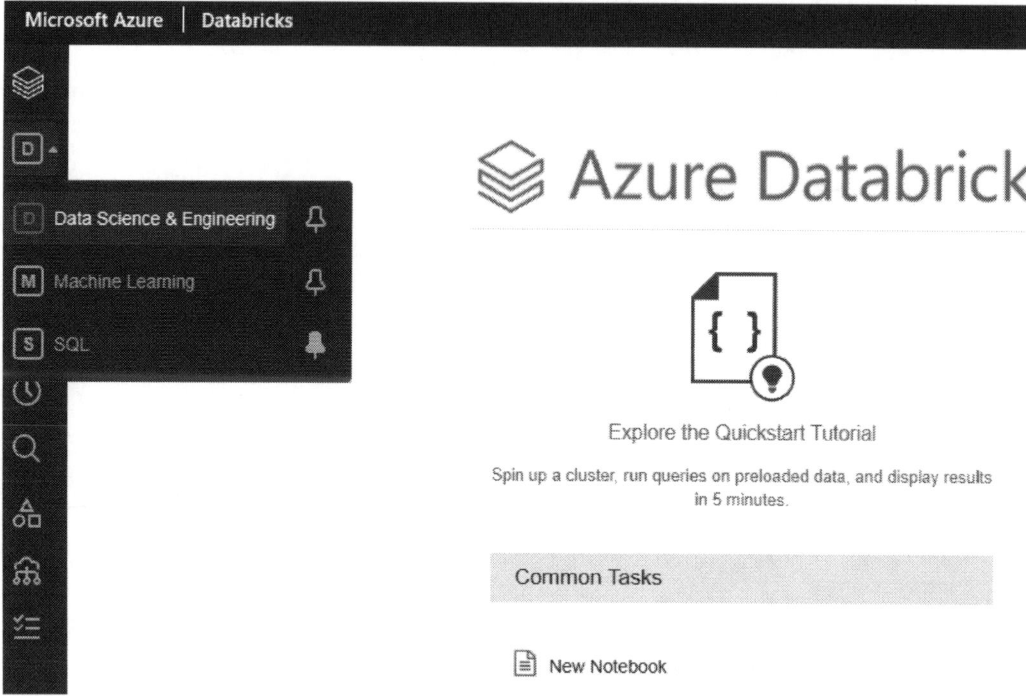

Figure 3.6*: Databricks audit: Databricks home*

In the following section, we will try to understand the data pipeline development from the lens of Databricks simple notebook-based scripts, which can be written in multiple languages, that is, Scala, Python, SQL, and Java. The beauty of notebook-based programming is that you can easily switch between these languages in different cells if you are able to persist your intermediate DataFrames to any mode of storage and data format. We will see here a simple use case of connecting to a traditional SQL database, fetching semi-structured data that holds exam results in JSON format, messaging, and transforming it through different options, including delta lakes and Databricks tables, and storing it further as **delta table**, **CSV**, and **Parquet** files.

The following flow is to help you boost your confidence in using Databricks from the flexibility of its multilingual and multi-platform capability, and it enables you to effectively choose different languages by the flexibility of examples available online vs the use case and platform and techniques for data persistence.

To fetch the exam data, the first thing we need to do is connect to the SQL server database where the exam data is stored:

Connecting with a SQL Server data source

A similar operation can be performed while connecting with different OLTP data sources.

To connect with the SQL server database, you can perform the following steps:

- Search for the connector available for a data source.
- Find if the class for the connector is available in the instance.
- Start building parameters to finally connect via the methods available.

For searching the connector availability, you can use the Databricks documentation, as follows:

https://docs.microsoft.com/en-us/azure/databricks/data/data-sources/

Check if the JDBC SQL Server driver class is already imported.

```
FilterdExamResultsInDF.createOrReplaceTempView("resultjson")
display(FilterdExamResultsInDF)
```

▸ (1) Spark Jobs

▸ FilterdExamResultsInDF: org.apache.spark.sql.DataFrame = [jsondata: string]

***Code 3.1**: Databricks audit: code example driver*

After successfully executing this command, it should give you a result that looks as follows:

```
"res0: Class[_] = class com.microsoft.sqlserver.jdbc.SQLServerDriver
Command took 6.59 seconds -- by the {user} at 1/9/2022, 9:47:40 PM on dbdemo"
```

Once you verify that the class is available, you can either comment, or remove the cell, and move on to the next step for setting up connection parameters.

```
%scala
//Setup database connection string
val Hostname = "Database Server IP Or Name"
val Port = 1433
val Database = "DataBase Name"
// Create the JDBC URL without passing in the user and password parameters.
val ConnectionUrl =
```

```
// Now Create a Properties() object to hold the parameters.
import java.util.Properties
val Properties = new Properties()
connectionProperties.put("user", s"userID")
connectionProperties.put("password", s"password")
```

***Code 3.2:** Databricks audit: Code example, setting up database connection*

It's suggested using Azure/AWS Key Vault utility rather than directly passing the parameters for safety and security reasons. Alternatively, you can use Databricks-managed secret library and tools.

Refer to this link:

docs.databricks.com/dev-tools/api/latest/secrets.html

For example, accessing a key through a Key Vault would look like this:

```
password = dbutils.secrets.get(scope="scope",key="sqlpwd")
```

This key can be passed further instead of password while setting up connection properties:

```
connectionProperties.put("password", password)
```

The next step is to assign the **`connectionProperties`** with the JDBC provider object for SQL server connectivity:

```
%scala
//Set the connection properties
val sqlprovider = "com.microsoft.sqlserver.jdbc.SQLServerDriver"
connectionProperties.setProperty("Driver", sqlprovider)
```

***Code 3.3:** Databricks audit: code example, setting up SQL provider*

Once you have your SQL connection ready, you can start querying the specific database; in this case, its table **`[oltpstore]`** from a self-hosted SQL server instance that stores semi-structured data in a structured format based on a key pair.

You would be happy to know that the following script in Scala and similar in Python is simply running a **`select * from oltpstore`**. The table in the SQL Server database and storing the output in a variable **`ExamdataFromSQLDB`**:

```
%scala
//Load the exam_data in the Exam_Data_From_SQLServer_DB variable
val ExamdataFromSQLDB = Spark.read.jdbc(jdbcUrl, "oltpstore", connec-
tionProperties)
```

***Code 3.4**: Databricks audit: Code example, setting up SQL provider*

Next is to load the data from variable to DataFrame using the **`toDF()`** function:

```
%scala
val ExamDataInDF = ExamdataFromSQLDB.toDF()
```

***Code 3.5**: Databricks audit: Load data to DataFrame*

Once you load the data into a DataFrame, you have multiple options to process and work with it. In the code, we are trying to filter from a structured schema of SQL server on column **`jsonobjecttype`**, where the value is **`CertificateRequest`**, which actually holds the exam results in JSON format. If you love SQL, the statement would translate to the following:

```
'select jsondata from oltpstore where jsonobjecttype =
'CertificateRequest'
```

Once the data is being loaded in SQL, you can create a view over the DataFrame to be able to query it like normal SQL like in *step 2* in the following code snippet:

```
%scala
// Apply filter to select exam results from all the courses
val FilterdExamResultsInDF = ExamDataInDF.filter($"jsonobjecttype" ===
"CertificateRequest").select($"jsondata")

FilterdExamResultsInDF.createOrReplaceTempView("resultjson")

display(FilterdExamResultsInDF)
```

***Code 3.6**: Databricks audit: Create view from DataFrame*

And the output is the list of JSON objects that contains exam data:

```
FilterdExamResultsInDF.createOrReplaceTempView("resultjson")
display(FilterdExamResultsInDF)
```

▸ (1) Spark Jobs

▸ FilterdExamResultsInDF: org.apache.spark.sql.DataFrame = [jsondata: string]

Table   Data Profile

	jsondata
1	{"desc1":null,"desc2":null,"desc3":null,"desc4":null,"desc5":null,"desc6":null,"requestedtime":"0001-01-01T00:00:00","returnerror":null,"certitype":null,"OrganizationGuid":"10001","TeamID":"00002","UserId":"cebc926c7714492b93692f441dd93f6b","emailId":null,"EventID":"9467ebf594f24f0bae4f572f6dfbaacc","Marks":60,"TotalMarks":100,"completiondate":"2021-03-07T20:39:46.3553812+05:30"}
2	{"desc1":null,"desc2":null,"desc3":null,"desc4":null,"desc5":null,"desc6":null,"requestedtime":"0001-01-01T00:00:00","returnerror":null,"certitype":null,"OrganizationGuid":"10001","TeamID":"00002","UserId":"cebc926c7714492b93692f441dd93f6b","emailId":"anjanihardy@gmail.com","EventID":"9467ebf594f24f0bae4f572f6dfbaacc","Marks":60,"TotalMarks":100,"completiondate":"2021-03-07T22:17:51.0855138+05:30"}
3	{"desc1":null,"desc2":null,"desc3":null,"desc4":null,"desc5":null,"desc6":null,"requestedtime":"0001-01-01T00:00:00","returnerror":null,"certitype":null,"OrganizationGuid":"10001","TeamID":"00002","UserId":"cebc926c7714492b93692f441dd93f6b","emailId":"anjanihardy@gmail.com","EventID":"9467ebf594f24f0bae4f572f6dfbaacc","Marks":60,"TotalMarks":100,"completiondate":"2021-03-07T22:21:27.0918237+05:30"}
4	{"desc1":null,"desc2":null,"desc3":null,"desc4":null,"desc5":null,"desc6":null,"requestedtime":"0001-01-01T00:00:00","returnerror":null,"certitype":null,"OrganizationGuid":"10001","TeamID":"00002","UserId":"cebc926c7714492b93692f441dd93f6b","emailId":"anjanihardy@gmail.com","EventID":"9467ebf594f24f0bae4f572f6dfbaacc","Marks":60,"TotalMarks":100

***Figure 3.7**: Databricks audit: Output*

Now, there is a new challenge: to convert this JSON data into a format that you can use for building reports, pushing it to another structured form, or doing whatever you prefer to do with it.

Well, there are different ways to achieve this from here, but one of the easiest ways that you can do is to run a SQL query using the **hive** context by passing a structured schema with the query, which enables the Spark engine to run beneath the Databricks to map and return all JSON object in a tabular form that can be easily worked on:

```
%scala
import org.apache.Spark.sql.hive.HiveContext
val sqlContext = new HiveContext(sc)

val resultjsonfilterd = sqlContext.sql("SELECT from_json(json-
data,'EventID string,OrganizationGuid string,TeamID string, UserId
string,emailId string,Marks int,TotalMarks int,completiondate Date,-
passstate string') FROM resultjson")

val resultstore = resultjsonfilterd.select("from_json(jsondata).*")
display(resultstore)
resultstore.createOrReplaceTempView("resultstore")
```

***Code 3.8**: Databricks audit: Create view from DataFrame*

Once the JSON data is reformatted, the result would show the schema in which it has been wrapped into to produce the following result:

```
from_json(jsondata):struct
EventID:string
OrganizationGuid:string
TeamID:string
UserId:string
emailId:string
Marks:integer
TotalMarks:integer
completiondate:date
passstate:string
```

***Code 3.9**: Databricks audit: Reformatting table*

EventID	OrganizationGuid	TeamID	UserId	emailId	Marks	TotalMarks	completiondate	passstate
SQL-from-the-Edge-to-the-Cloud-by-Bob-Ward	10001	00002	80a56eb55d5c4379a748634e84284072	bhaskar12ddd.tripathi@yopmail.com	100	100	2021-03-08	1
SQL-from-the-Edge-to-the-Cloud-by-Bob-Ward	10001	00002	71400aefb9494eb5ac90d9821a10d45d	bhaskar12ddd.tripathi@yopmail.com	100	100	2021-03-08	1
SQL-from-the-Edge-to-the-Cloud-by-Bob-Ward	10001	00002	71409aefb9494eb5ac90d9821a10d45d	bhaskar12ddd.tripathi@yopmail.com	100	100	2021-03-10	1
SQL-from-the-Edge-to-the-Cloud-by-Bob-Ward	10001	00002	71408aefb9494eb5ac90d9821a10d45d	bhaskar12ddd.tripathi@yopmail.com	100	100	2021-03-10	1
SQL-from-the-Edge-to-the-Cloud-by-Bob-Ward	10001	00002	71400aefb9494eb5ac90d9821a10d45d	bhaskar12ddd.tripathi@yopmail.com	100	100	2021-03-10	1
SQL-from-the-Edge-to-the-Cloud-by-Bob-Ward	10001	00002	71409aefb0404eb5ac90d0821a10d45d	bhaskar12ddd.tripathi@yopmail.com	100	100	2021-03-10	1

***Figure 3.8**: Databricks audit: Result*

Once you have the results and your stream of JSON object has been structured, you will think of using it, and some of the common work may be to push it in to another table, display it as a report via a tool like Power BI or Tableau, or save it in multiple formats, such as **CSV**, **TSV**, **Parquet**, **Excel**, or even delta table.

To do that, one most important thing that you need to do is to connect with a storage solution, be it cloud storage such as **S3 buckets**, **File Share** , **Azure Blob** storage, or something that is built for the purpose of a data warehouse, that is a **Data Lake** or **synapse**.

In an extended enterprise environment where the security, governance, and traceability are very important, one of the most accepted ways is to bind your storage source with active directory and set up mount point as per the following example.

To achieve this, you can provision an azure blob storage, enabling folder hierarchy to enable Azure Data Lake services smart capabilities.

To create a data lake storage, you can refer to this master article by Microsoft:

docs.microsoft.com/en-us/azure/storage/blobs/create-data-lake-storage-account

Once that is ready, you will have to enable it with active directory.

Alternatively, you can refer to the following link for binding your storage with active directory and **outh2.0** authentication via Databricks:

docs.databricks.com/data/data-sources/azure/adls-gen2/azure-datalake-gen2-sp-access.html

```
adlsAccountName = "dbstoragegen2mc4u"
adlsContainerName = "dbdemo"
adlsFolderName = "RAW"
mountPoint = "/mnt/raw"

# Application (Client) ID
#applicationId = dbutils.secrets.get(scope="akv-0011",key="ClientId")
 applicationId = "0b57c728-198d-4427-a4e5-f5743a607d10";
# Application (Client) Secret Key
#authenticationKey = dbutils.secrets.get(scope="akv-0011",key="Client-
Secret")
 authenticationKey =""
# Directory (Tenant) ID
tenandId = dbutils.secrets.get(scope="akv-0011",key="TenantId")

endpoint = "https://login.microsoftonline.com/" + tenandId + "/oauth2/
token"
source = "abfss://" + adlsContainerName + "@" + adlsAccountName +
".dfs.core.windows.net/" + adlsFolderName

# Connecting using Service Principal secrets and OAuth
configs = {"fs.azure.account.auth.type": "OAuth",
           "fs.azure.account.oauth.provider.type": "org.apache.hadoop.
fs.azurebfs.oauth2.ClientCredsTokenProvider",
           "fs.azure.account.oauth2.client.id": applicationId,
           "fs.azure.account.oauth2.client.secret": authenticationKey,
           "fs.azure.account.oauth2.client.endpoint": endpoint}

# Mount ADLS Storage to DBFS only if the directory is not already
mounted
if not any(mount.mountPoint == mountPoint for mount in dbutils.
fs.mounts()):
  dbutils.fs.mount(
    source = source,
    mount_point = mountPoint,
    extra_configs = configs)
```

Code 3.10: *Databricks audit: Mounting*

Alternatively, you can use direct connectivity for the understanding. For direct connectivity, you still need to create a storage account and the storage to achieve the same.

One of the more structured ways is via using the mount point, while the other way is a little easy but has security flaw if you don't access with key vault or similar secret management API for connecting with blobs use this:

```
fs.azure.account.key.<storage-account-name>.blob.core.windows.net
<storage-account-access-key>
```

For connecting with data lake, use this:

```
fs.azure.account.key.{storagename}.dfs.core.windows.net
<storage-account-access-key>
```

Similarly, there are more or less similar options for storage, like S3 and others:

```
%scala
Spark.conf.set(
  "fs.azure.account.key.{storagename}.dfs.core.windows.net", "DIt5jIt-
KHDkiaDerOP+XP4GdSbmnQkULKGJG5455sjxFG+Km2H6NrUcF5/L==")
```

Code 3.11: *Databricks audit: Mounting 2*

You will notice that the first part is the **storage account detail**, and the second part is the **access key**. The connectivity method changes based on the storage type and its provider, but it's more or less the same in terms of approach.

Additionally, ensure that you have granted a proper access request, else you may encounter an error message, as follows:

```
spark.conf.set("fs.azure.createRemoteFileSystemDuringInitialization", "true")
dbutils.fs.ls("abfss://newconatinermc4u@dbstoragegen2mc4u.dfs.core.windows.net/")
spark.conf.set("fs.azure.createRemoteFileSystemDuringInitialization", "false")
```

```
⊞Operation failed: &#34;This request is not authorized to perform this operation us
 ing this permission.&#34;, 403, PUT, https://dbstoragegen2mc4u.dfs.core.windows.ne
 t/newconatinermc4u?resource=filesystem, AuthorizationPermissionMismatch, &#34;This
 request is not authorized to perform this operation using this permission. Request
 Id:ba65e0b9-a01f-0052-183d-02a16e000000 Time:2022-01-05T14:05:01.6934064Z&#34;
```

Code 3.12: *Databricks audit: Configuration setting for read*

To read the directory, you can also use the following command:

```
%scala
dbutils.fs.ls("abfss://dbdemo@{storagename}.dfs.core.windows.net/")
```

Code 3.13: *Databricks audit: Direct data read*

Syntax and approach remain almost the same whether you are writing using Python or Scala. What changes is the way you connect to different storage and in different modes. So, it's very important to look for the latest connectivity examples on Databricks or its cloud partner documentation.

In the following example, we have tried writing in multiple formats – **CSV**, **JSON**, and **Parquet** – through different formats of data stored in DataFrames:

```
%scala

—Json

resultstore.write.json("abfss://dbdemo@{storagename}.dfs.core.windows.net/RAW/resultstore.json")

—Csv

resultstore.write.mode(SaveMode.Overwrite)
.option("header","true")
.csv("abfss://dbdemo@{storagename}.dfs.core.windows.net/RAW/resultstore.csv")

—parquet

resultstore.write.mode(SaveMode.Overwrite)
.option("header","true")
.parquet("abfss://dbdemo@{storagename}.dfs.core.windows.net/RAW/resultstore.parquet")
```

***Code 3.14**: Databricks audit: CSV and Parquet*

The next step is to convert the parquet to a table:

```
%sql
CREATE TABLE parquetresultstore
USING parquet
OPTIONS (path "abfss://dbdemo@dbstoragegen2mc4u.dfs.core.windows.net/RAW/resultstore.parquet")
```

***Code 3.15**: Databricks audit: Parquet to hive table*

In the next step, we just query the tabular data, store the results in a DataFrame, and write that into delta files. *Why delta?* To understand this better, you may have to wait for the details later in this chapter and later in this book:

```
df = Spark.sql('select * from  parquetresultstore')

df.write.format("delta").mode('overwrite').option("overwriteSchema",
"true").save("abfss://dbdemo@{storagename}.dfs.core.windows.net/RAW/
parquetresultstore.delta")

Spark.sql("CREATE TABLE IF NOT EXISTS deltaresultstore USING DELTA
LOCATION 'abfss://dbdemo@dbstoragegen2mc4u.dfs.core.windows.net/RAW/
parquetresultstore.delta'")
```

Code 3.16: *Databricks audit: Writing data*

Well, you can achieve the following steps, starting from any of the preceding examples, but we went with this to ensure that your concepts are clear.

Once you have the data in a tabular form, it becomes easy to query, filter, or do other things based on SQL.

In the next example, we are trying to filter records for the students who have passed the exam.

Now, the requests can be easily queried. One can use it for generating another set of curated output, either for populating another source or analytics as per the requirements:

```
%sql
select * from deltaresultstore where passstate = "1" and userid
!="null"
```

Code 3.17: *Databricks audit: Filtration via query*

Let's connect the operations with the basic operations of Spark and Databricks.

If you go back to what you learned at the beginning of the chapter, you will recall that any syntax that we pass through the query or command through the cells inside these notebooks is going to get converted into jobs to be submitted to the Spark engine for processing.

Let us slice and dice into the steps that each of these commands follows. The last command that we passed was to get a result from the delta table:

```
%sql
select * from deltaresultstore where passstate = "1" and userid
!="null"
```

Code 3.18: *Databricks audit: Filtration via query condition*

To produce the result as follows:

```
%sql
select * from deltaresultstore where passstate = "1" and userid !="null"
```

▸ (1) Spark Jobs

Table Data Profile

	EventID	OrganizationGuid	TeamID	UserId	emailId	Marks	TotalMarks	completiondate	passstate
1	SQL-from-the-Edge-to-the-Cloud-by-Bob-Ward	10001	00002	60a56eb55d5c4379a748834e84284072	bhaskar12ddd.tripathi@yopmail.com	100	100	2021-03-08	1
2	SQL-from-the-Edge-to-the-Cloud-by-Bob-Ward	10001	00002	71409aefb9494eb5ac90d9821a10d45d	bhaskar12ddd.tripathi@yopmail.com	100	100	2021-03-08	1
3	SQL-from-the-Edge-to-the-Cloud-by-Bob-Ward	10001	00002	71409aefb9494eb5ac90d9821a10d45d	bhaskar12ddd.tripathi@yopmail.com	100	100	2021-03-10	1
4	SQL-from-the-Edge-to-the-Cloud-by-Bob-Ward	10001	00002	71409aefb9494eb5ac90d9821a10d45d	bhaskar12ddd.tripathi@yopmail.com	100	100	2021-03-10	1
5	SQL-from-the-Edge-to-the-Cloud-by-Bob-Ward	10001	00002	71409aefb9494eb5ac90d9821a10d45d	bhaskar12ddd.tripathi@yopmail.com	100	100	2021-03-10	1
6	SQL-from-the-Edge-to-the-Cloud-by-Bob-Ward	10001	00002	71409aefb9494eb5ac90d9821a10d45d	bhaskar12ddd.tripathi@yopmail.com	100	100	2021-03-10	1
7	SQL-from-the-Edge-to-the-Cloud-by-Bob-Ward	10001	00002	71409aefb9494eb5ac90d9821a10d45d	bhaskar12ddd.tripathi@yopmail.com	100	100	2021-03-10	1

Showing all 171 rows

Shift+Enter to run

***Figure 3.9**: Databricks Audit: Exploring query output results*

Every statement that you ask Databricks and underlying Spark to execute gets submitted as a job to Spark Engine running at the core of Databricks. To navigate to the status and further details on the job submitted, you can click on the highlighted options on your notebook:

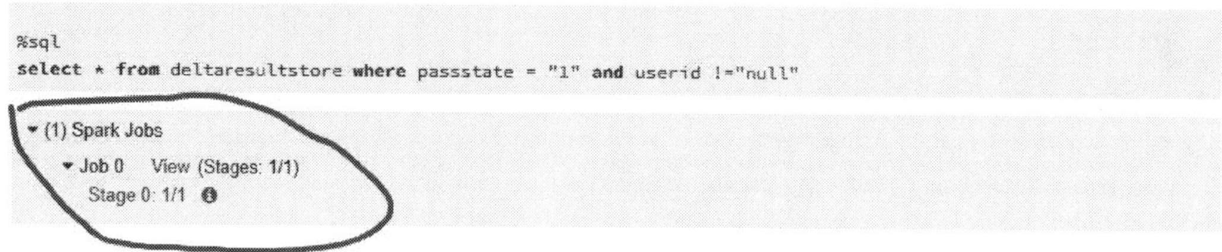

Figure 3.10

After clicking on the **`View`** option, you will get a popup with multiple options to explore:

***Figure 3.11**: Databricks audit: Jobs low-level*

Click on the **`Jobs`** option.

Once you click on it, you will be able to navigate to the event timeline and DAG visualizer.

An **event timeline** is a quick option that can be used to analyze the events and activities that happened around executing the submitted job.

Now, let's understand the DAG scheduling and the interface that Databricks give us for analysis, optimization, and understanding purposes:

Details for Job 0

Status: SUCCEEDED
Submitted: 2022/01/13 02:44:52
Duration: 9 s
Associated SQL Query: 11
Job Group: 8530833757693946044_5928176846141914169_50c62378e77a40a485da1ca84131c650
Completed Stages: 1

▸ Event Timeline
▾DAG Visualization

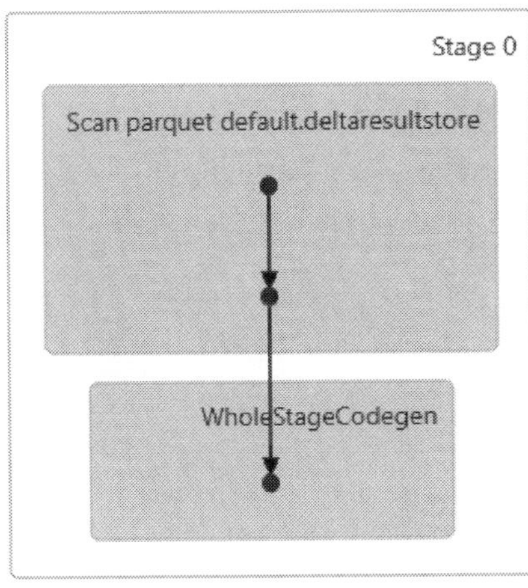

Figure 3.12: Databricks audit: DAG flow sample

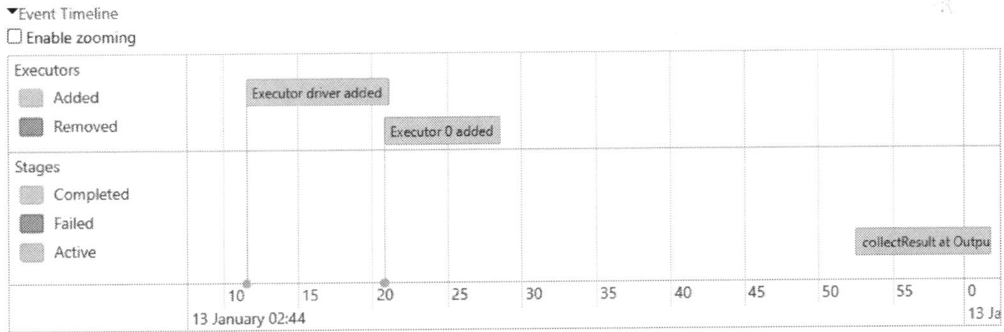

Figure 3.13: Databricks audit: Understanding DAG from Databricks low-level job interface

The blocks in *blue* are *DAG steps*; once you click on this, it will take you to different stages that the master schedules for its workers:

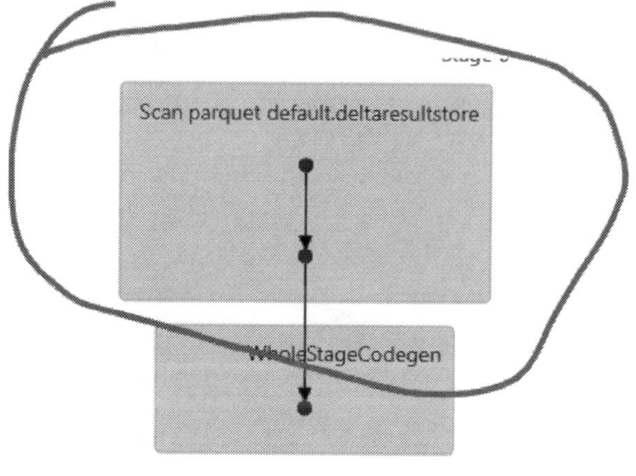

***Figure 3.14**: Databricks audit: DAG example 2*

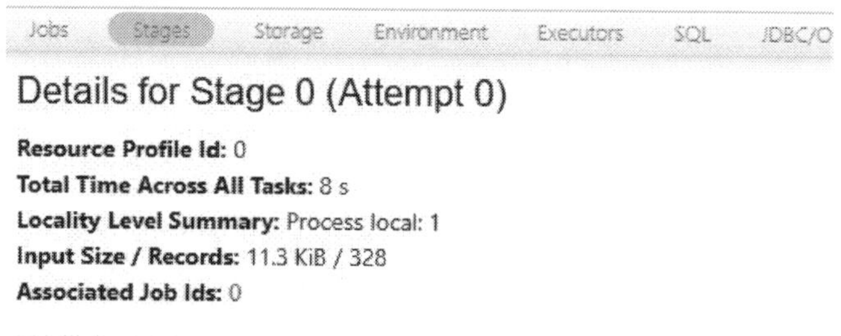

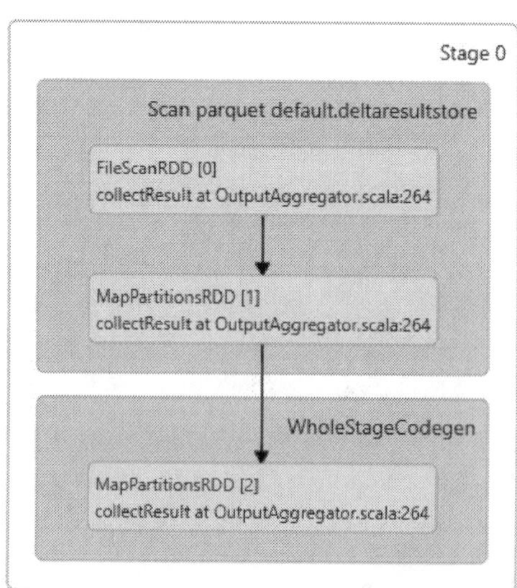

***Figure 3.15**: Databricks audit: DAG example 3*

If we expand this by using the event timeline, we can see the basic metrics around the execution. You can also add further metrics to find out more about the completed or failed job/stage.

This is more around collecting the record via scanning the delta result store for the corresponding delta table where the result is stored, which, in itself, has **ACID** capability. So, the job would need to scan the **Parquet** formatted data beneath, mapping with the transaction log to return a result at a specific state.

The **visualizer** also gives you options to show additional metrics around the job that got executed so that you can optimize your steps further as well as the compute, memory, and storage requirements. After clicking on one of the blocks, you can reach a report where it gives you the capability to analyze the execution metrics based on **scheduler delay**, **result time**, **JVM heap**, **peak storage memory**, **pool memory**, **record size aggregated**, and so on:

▾Show Additional Metrics
- ☐ Select All
- ☐ Scheduler Delay
- ☐ Task Deserialization Time
- ☐ Result Serialization Time
- ☐ Getting Result Time
- ☐ Peak Execution Memory
- ☐ Peak JVM Memory OnHeap / OffHeap
- ☐ Peak Execution Memory OnHeap / OffHeap
- ☐ Peak Storage Memory OnHeap / OffHeap
- ☐ Peak Pool Memory Direct / Mapped

▸ Event Timeline

Summary Metrics for 1 Completed Tasks

Metric	Min	25th percentile	Median	75th percentile	Max
Duration	8 s	8 s	8 s	8 s	8 s
GC Time	0.3 s	0.3 s	0.3 s	0.3 s	0.3 s
Input Size / Records	11.3 KiB / 328	11.3 KiB / 328	11.3 KiB / 328	11.3 KiB / 328	11.3 KiB / 328

Showing 1 to 3 of 3 entries

▾Aggregated Metrics by Executor

Show 20 entries Search:

Executor ID	Logs	Address	Task Time	Total Tasks	Failed Tasks	Killed Tasks	Succeeded Tasks	Excluded	Input Size / Records
0	stdout stderr	10.139.64.5:34413	9 s	1	0	0	1	false	11.3 KiB / 328

***Figure 3.16**: Databricks audit: DAG example 4*

Now, the next thing you can do is to click on **Job** again; that's where you found breaking things into multiple stages and jobs at a lower level like a directed acyclic graph, as suggested in the book analogy at the beginning of the Spark section.

One job can be completed in multiple stages, depending on how complex the operation is and how it processes. In *Spark version 2.0* and above as in this case, these jobs, and also the underlying processing, is mostly automatic. However, analyzing each of these steps gives you an opportunity to understand more about it and further optimize your operation.

While the example here is already optimized by Spark engine beneath the Databricks as we are just querying a delta lake, when you dig down to stages and cells above in the notebook where data collections and filtering from different sources are happening, you will start optimizing your data flow steps very effectively and frugally.

The **visualizer** is so easy to understand that you just have to shift between stages and jobs a couple of times, and then click on a specific stage or job to see the DAG in that stage as well as execution statistics, such as the **number of completed jobs**, **descriptions**, **conditions**, **filtration**, or any other operation performed:

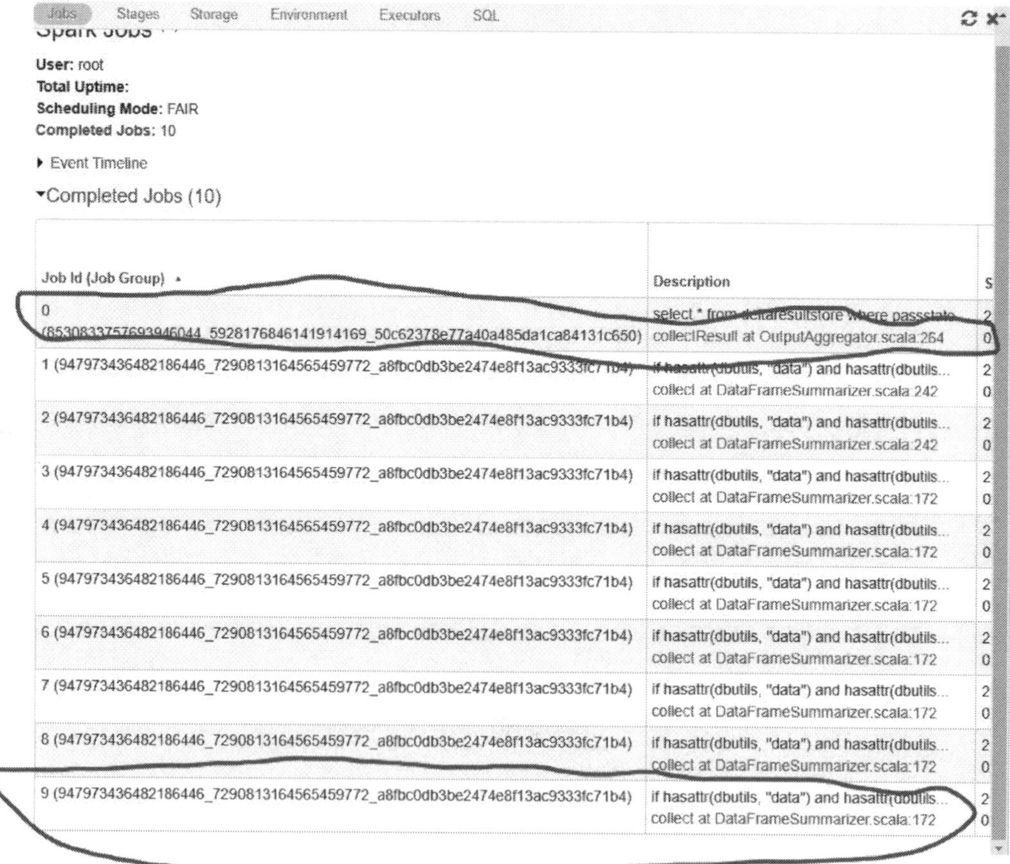

Figure 3.17: Databricks audit: The job list

The most important job is job **9** when the results from different stages are collected to finally provide you with the result. In job **9**, it's all collection and union to produce the result.

At the end stage here, we see it is doing **projection**, **shuffling**, **merging**, and **union** to complete the task. Do note the term **union** here and try finding it in one of the preceding diagrams in the same chapter; you will be able to closely correlate how human thinks and divide tasks among peers when it comes to distributed operations, and how at the end, you need to collect and merge your outputs to produce the final result.

As you will notice in the following diagram, a few stages are skipped, and that is the level of auto-optimization that Spark achieves by making sure it's not repeating an operation, which is no more required and has already been performed earlier:

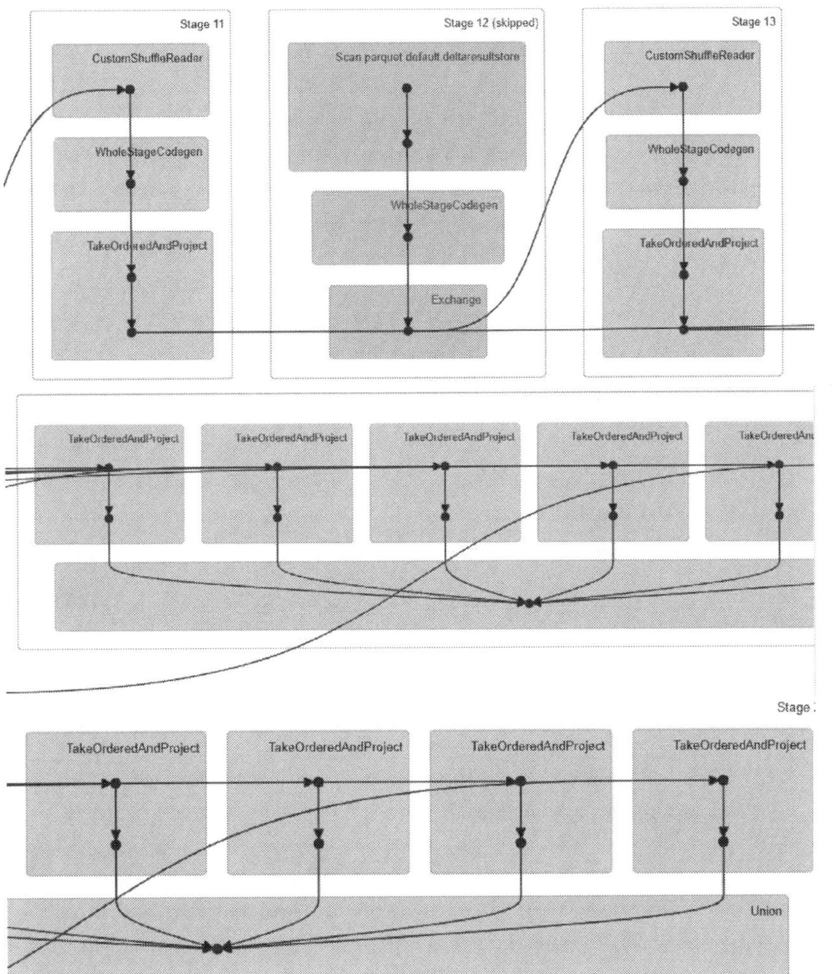

Figure 3.18: Databricks audit: Dag expanded with segregation, collection, and union

Once you visualize, it becomes easy for you to understand and build effective ETL pipelines with Databricks.

As Databricks allows your notebook to schedule, you can create multiple sets of notebooks depicting different stages before you load the data to the destination. This is also called **orchestration**, which has been detailed further in the next chapter.

Building an audit framework with Databricks

When it comes to data quality, there is always contention between what was expected versus what was provided. If you are building a warehouse, your system needs to assure you of the following:

- Validity
- Velocity
- Versioning
- Veracity

Not to be confused with **4Vs** of big data:

- **Validity** is *Are you able to effectively validate and report on data quality issues before they reach and dirty your data warehouse?*
- **Versioning** is *How fast can you accommodate schema and data changes, can you time travel with your changes, and are you compliant with regulatory requirements of making your system auditable in terms of who did what, and when can you report it. Does it have a quality to roll back.*
- **Velocity** is *How fast can you accommodate schema and data changes, or When there is a load failure or review stop, how fast can the system start populating data to the warehouse.*
- **Veracity** *is related to consistency, accuracy, quality, and trustworthiness of data which can be achieved by handling the biasedness, noise and abnormality in data flow.*

How does it help?

Building a data quality as well as general governance audit framework helps save your data lake/warehouse from the human, system, regulatory, and governance conflicts, and ensures that your data warehouse/data lake house stands strong on 4V.

Audit frameworks can be built in multiple languages, and there are several different approaches to building and implementing the same.

In this section, we will focus on Databricks and Azure Data Factory to build an audit framework using the capabilities that Databricks and Spark provide with Delta Lake.

Let's take a typical data load scenario from a *flat-file source*, where the data is being loaded from widely used file formats, such as **CSV** or **JSON**.

With the presence of technologies like delta tables and Databricks, it's no longer required to move it directly to databases or write custom code to validate and load data.

Data can now be loaded via scripts written in Databricks in landing zones and converted to Parquet or Delta format directly to enable easy operation and advance time-driven change tracking, be it a change in schema or data.

Once the data is in Delta Lake, operations like **validate**, **clean**, and **transform** can be handled easily with consistent data operations that support **Atomicity, Consistency, Isolation, and Durability** (**ACID**) as well as parallel executions.

As SQL queries can be applied easily on delta tables, validation rules can be easily written in a language that Data Engineers and Analysts understand: SQL.

Data can be loaded using scripts in Databricks, and as shown in the example in this chapter, the loaded data can be converted into a delta table where another set of scripts written in Databricks notebook can run validation logic and generate validation output with rejected data or warning messages in another delta table, or an OLTP source. This can be SQL and oracle, which can be easily fed to tools like Power BI and Tableau to generate validation reports based on the data load activity.

Based on the outcome, extra triggers can be embedded into the load to stop processing further or accommodate the schema to the incoming acceptable changes.

Some of the basic validation rules can be **Validate Column Name**, **Check Data Types**, **Validate Data Length (Boundary Value Analysis)**, and **Validate Referential Integrity**.

These all flow written in multiple notebook files under Databricks can be orchestrated to be scheduled and executed through the Azure Data Factory.

Azure Data Factory is a data-integration service based on the cloud that allows us to create data-driven workflows in the cloud for orchestrating and automating data movement and data transformation. Azure Data Factory is a data pipeline tool that can be used for data processing as well as orchestrating data movement through different sources and tools like Databricks:

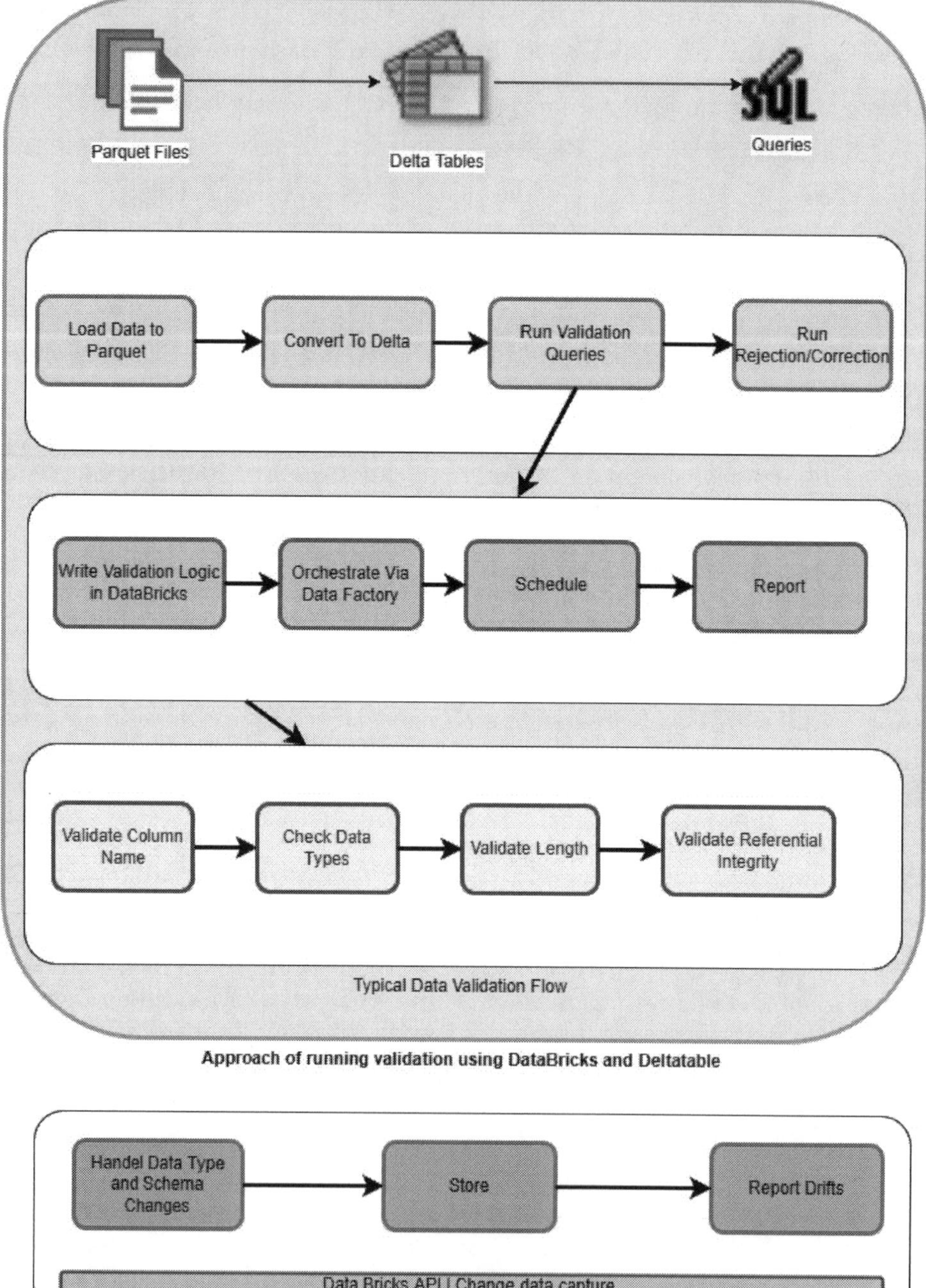

Figure 3.19: Databricks audit: Audit framework

A typical validation flow with Azure Data Factory and Databricks:

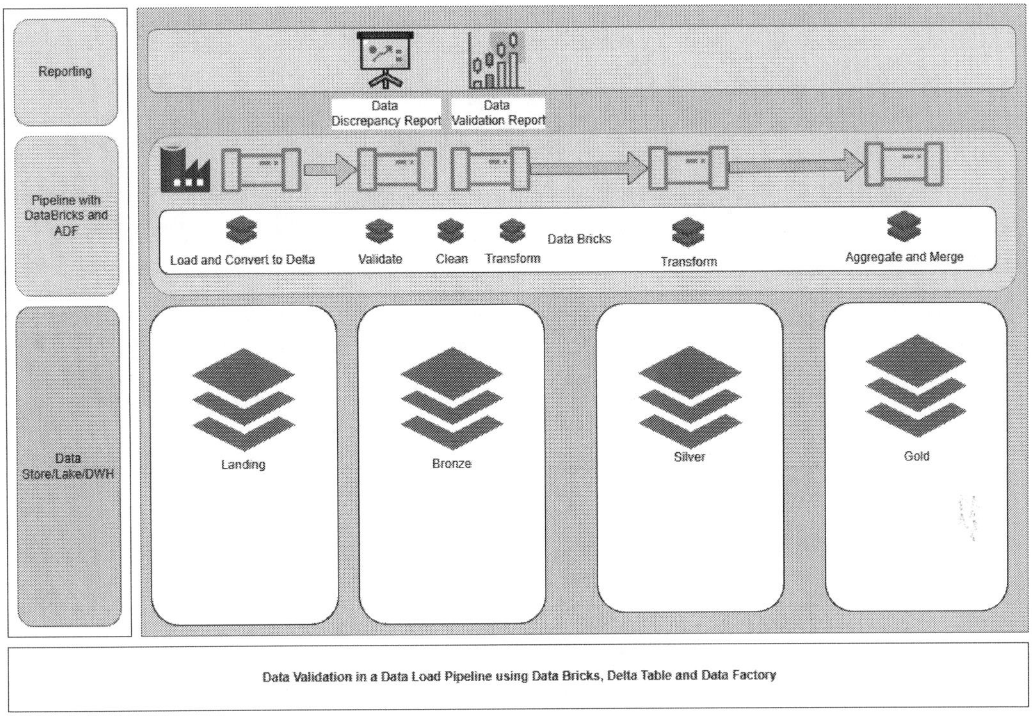

Figure 3.20: Databricks Audit: Data validation stages

Data Quality Audit Framework are not just needed for compliance and regulatory requirements but also to make sure your system is fault-tolerant and can be validated, audited, and traced to a certain point without compromising velocity.

While this can be achieved by building and extending your system to handle schema changes with DDL and DML audits to a certain extent, you also need to assure that you are able to time travel to a certain point to find out if what was there before is present or absent now.

This is not always possible without building a system that is based on transactional logs, be it a **Data Definition** or **Data Manipulation** based change. Luckily, Delta Lake seamlessly and naturally provides the feature of maintaining a history of changes via transaction logs.

Delta Lake transaction log serves as a single source of truth that is able to track all changes that users make to the table. One could compare this transaction log feature in Delta Lake as something like a source code repository that maintains all changes in an incremental form.

How does Delta Lake maintain transaction logs?

A typical way to store a delta formatted data is in **Parquet** files; consider it as one set of data with a certain schema being maintained inside one folder, and each folder has an incremental and partitioned entry of records in Parquet format and a folder that maintains the logs of changes, be it a **Data Definition** or **Data manipulation**.

Each incremental change is versioned with a unique file number and partition in a **delta log** folder associated and unique to specific datasets so that it's always easy for concurrent and consistent writing.

To simplify this, you can correlate each of these sets of data as tables in databases to be able to perform a set of unique operations, such as the following:

- **Adding file**: Used and mentioned when a data file, for example, **Parquet** files, are added
- **Removing file**: Whenever a removal happens, similar to drop or truncation
- **Updating metadata**: Whenever someone updates the table's metadata (for example, changing the table's name, schema, or partitioning)
- **Setting transaction**: Records commits
- **Commit info**rmation: Contains information around the commit

The transaction logs in Delta Lakes guarantee *atomicity* - if there is no record in the transaction log, it means that the transaction was never done.

By only recording transactions that execute fully and completely, the Delta Lake transaction log allows users to have fundamental trustworthiness on the final state of data, and being parallel, it can guarantee atomicity at a petabyte scale.

Whenever an **INSERT**, **DELETE**, **UPDATE,** or **MERGE** operation similar to what we see in the databases is performed, Delta Lake breaks that operation down into multiple actions.

As and when the change occurs in the table, those changes are recorded as ordered atomic commits in the transaction log.

Each commit is written out as a **JSON** file, starting with **`000000…..00.json`**. Additional changes to the table generate subsequent JSON files in ascending order so that the next commit is written out as **`000001.json`**, the following as **`00000….2.json`**, and so on. Each numeric JSON file that got incrementally written denotes a new version of the table.

In a real example from the operation that we did previously, you can notice the CRC and JSON files being created sequentially:

Name
[..]
_tmp_path_dir
00000000000000000000.crc
00000000000000000000.json
00000000000000000001.crc
00000000000000000001.json

***Figure 3.21**: Databricks Audit: Transaction log structure delta tables, delta lakes*

An important thing to understand is that the transaction log is the single source of truth for your **delta table**.

If we break the operations between reading and writing, in a parallel situation, we may have multiple readers reading and writing to a delta table.

So, any reader that's reading through basic operations on Delta Lakes, your delta table will take a look at the transaction log first based on commits as incremental JSON files and subsequently, the version of Parquet files, which are already mentioned in JSON files in the transaction log in sequential order.

Any modification being done in the delta table, be it adding or removing records, changing schema, and so on, is going to create a new version with the delta operations, allowing the delta table to construct the final consistent output.

Even if it is a void operation like adding a record in one transaction and deleting the same record in another transaction, which, in fact, *nullifies* the insert action it would still be recorded.

Let's say you first insert an item, The transaction would automatically be added to the transaction log, saved to disk as commit **`0000000..x.json`** (**`x`** denotes the incremental number) mentioning *add* operation with the corresponding Parquet. Later, you decide to remove those files (for example, run a **`DELETE`** from table operation), those actions would be recorded as the next commit and table version in the transaction log, as **`00000..x+1.json`** with a new Parquet file, implementing atomicity in Delta Lake.

Even though the two Parquets are no longer part of our Delta Lake table, their addition and removal are still recorded in the transaction log because those operations were performed at some point in time.

This unique feature makes sure that you can time travel to a past point. There is *atomicity* in the transaction, and the operations performed on a delta table are fully auditable.

To understand this, refer to the following **add** and **remove** operation from a single transaction log:

Add

add		
path	part-00000-fafbff58-c7a8-4476-9ac1-4e37daae548e-c000.snappy.parquet	
partitionValues		
size	5050	
modificationTime	1641470002000	
dataChange	true	
stats	{"numRecords":102,"minValues":{"UserId":"0216165492154a0c836bb1e2aa481794"," 08T08:21:59.8864153+05:3"},"maxValues": {"UserId":"fe8dc4e6d6334e79b195e15312ac2d44�","emailId":"bhaskar12ddd.tripathi 04-04T07:33:15.4817985-07:0�"},"nullCount":{"UserId":1,"emailId":1,"Marks":1,"To	
tags		
INSERTION_TIME		164
OPTIMIZE_TARGET_SIZE		268

⊟ {}**tags**

- INSERTION_TIME:1641470002000000
- OPTIMIZE_TARGET_SIZE:268435456

***Figure 3.22**: Databricks audit: Transaction log 1*

Remove

remove		
path	part-00000-0cccb520-1752-420f-9e62-621601ef8041-c000.snappy.parquet	
deletionTimestamp	1641470003579	
dataChange	true	
extendedFileMetadata	true	
partitionValues		
size	5050	
tags		
INSERTION_TIME		1641469853000000
OPTIMIZE_TARGET_SIZE		268435456

***Figure 3.23**: Databricks Audit: Transaction log 2*

Commit information

{}
{}commitInfo
- timestamp:1641470003580
- userId:3142818608021500
- userName:anjani.kumar@multicloud4u.com
- operation:WRITE
{}operationParameters
- mode:Overwrite
- partitionBy:[]
{}notebook
- notebookId:2366424665020677
- clusterId:0104-072952-v5xcytk7
- readVersion:0
- isolationLevel:WriteSerializable
- isBlindAppend:false
{}operationMetrics
- numFiles:1
- numOutputBytes:5050
- numOutputRows:102

***Figure 3.24**: Databricks Audit: Transaction log 3*

The corresponding Parquet files are being affected by the transaction:

[..]
_delta_log
part-00000-0cccb520-1752-420f-9e62-621601ef8041-c000.snappy.parquet
part-00000-fafbff58-c7a8-4476-9ac1-4e37daae548e-c000.snappy.parquet

***Figure 3.25**: Databricks Audit: Transaction log 4*

Why add and delete in the same log?

If you review the operation related to the delta table in the preceding *data flow* section, you will see that we applied overwrite, which means that the last Parquet file was overwritten, removing and adding operations subsequently.

This also matches with the **void** operation example in this section:

```
df = Spark.sql('select * from  parquetresultstore')

df.write.format("delta").mode('overwrite').option("overwriteSchema",
"true").save("abfss://dbdemo@{storagename}.dfs.core.windows.net/RAW/
parquetresultstore.delta")

Spark.sql("CREATE TABLE IF NOT EXISTS deltaresultstore USING DELTA
LOCATION 'abfss://dbdemo@dbstoragegen2mc4u.dfs.core.windows.net/RAW/
parquetresultstore.delta'")
```

Code 3.19: *Databricks Audit: Overwrite option and how it reflects in log*

Reviewing the transaction log structure

The transaction contains many pieces of information stored as strings or columns within the transaction log JSON.

Typically, this can be divided into operations, (*what was added, what was removed,* and *commit information* for that specific and atomic transaction).

If you review a simple **add** operation in the log, you can clearly see the **parquet** file that was created, for which this log has been generated, size, time, type of change, stats, and so on:

⊟ {}add
- path:part-00000-fafbff58-c7a8-4476-9ac1-4e37daae548e-c000.snappy.parquet
⊟ {}partitionValues
- size:5050
- modificationTime:1641470002000
- dataChange:true
- stats:{"numRecords":102,"minValues":{"UserId":"0216165492154a0c836bb1e2aa4
03-08T08:21:59.8864153+05:3"},"maxValues":
{"UserId":"fe8dc4e6d6334e79b195e15312ac2d44�","emailId":"bhaskar12ddd.tripa
04-04T07:33:15.4817985-07:0�"},"nullCount":{"UserId":1,"emailId":1,"Marks":1,"
⊟ {}tags
- INSERTION_TIME:1641470002000000
- OPTIMIZE_TARGET_SIZE:268435456

Figure 3.26: *Databricks Audit: Transaction log 5*

And the minimum and maximum values in the file:

numRecords		102
minValues		
UserId	0216165492154a0c836bb1e2aa481794	
emailId		
Marks	0	
TotalMarks	100	
completiondate	2021-03-08T08:21:59.8864153+05:3	
maxValues		
UserId	fe8dc4e6d6334e79b195e15312ac2d44�	
emailId	bhaskar12ddd.tripathi@yopmail.co�	
Marks	280	
TotalMarks	100	
completiondate	2021-04-04T07:33:15.4817985-07:0�	
nullCount		
UserId		1
emailId		1
Marks		1
TotalMarks		1
completiondate		1
passstate		102

***Figure 3.27**: Databricks Audit: Transaction log 6*

The metadata contains a lot of interesting information, for example:

- The type of operation that is occurring in the preceding image is **`{}add`**.
- How many files were added (**`numAddedFiles`**), removed (**`numRemovedFiles`**), output row's (**`numOutputRows`**), and output bytes (**`numOutputBytes`**).
- **`operation`** parameters, such as if this operation would append or overwrite the data within the table.
- The table version is associated with this transaction commit.
- **ClusterID** notebook identifies which Databricks cluster and notebook executed this commit, and the **userID**, **userName ID**, and **name** of the user executing the operation. add information.

Reading the transaction log via code

- Read the transaction log of a specific version:

```
>%python
```

```
log = Spark.read.json("/.../00000…2.json")
```

- The Delta transaction log commits metadata can be read using the following code snippets:

```
%python # Commit Information display(log.select("commitInfo").
where("commitInfo is not null"))
```

- The Delta transaction log adds metadata that can be read using the following code snippets:

```
%python # Commit Information
display(log.select("add").where("add is not null"))
```

Delta Lake can optimize their queries, affecting the number of files being important, especially in cases like dynamic partition pruning, as it can be read from the preceding high-level primer.

As the Delta Lake transaction log tracks the files and other metadata to ensure both atomic transactions and data reliability, it does not eagerly remove the files from the disk, even though the underlying data files from the table are removed. The **[VACUUM]** operation can be used to delete the files that are no longer needed.

For large-scale systems built on batch or streaming, Spark may create a lot of small files to maintain atomicity; this often leads to a *small-file* problem where it becomes ever more inefficient to query the **transaction log** folder (that is, **delta log subdirectory**). To handle this issue, Delta Lake creates a checkpoint file in Parquet format after it creates the *10th* commit or transaction.

Creating a transaction log after every *10th* commit helps save the entire state of the table at a point in time in native Parquet format. This makes it quick and easy for Spark to read and handle the small file problem.

Time travel

As you write into a Delta table or directory, every operation is automatically versioned. You can access the different versions of the data in two different ways:

- Delta Lake time travel allows you to safely remove data from your Delta Lake, reverse it in case there are mistakes, and track the progress through the Delta Lake transaction log.
- This not only helps in handling audibility issues but also major governance and compliance tracking in a case where it's required to delete a specific user data from everywhere and sometimes go back to a certain past state of the table to verify what was there.

Consider GDPR, *How would you avoid drowning in data requests use cases?*

Rollbacks and time travel

Rollbacks via time travel also make it easy to reset your data to a previous snapshot, either using a **timestamp** or using a **version number**.

Every table in Delta Lake is the sum total of all of the commits recorded in the Delta Lake transaction log. The transaction log can be considered as a *step-by-step guide* that details exactly how to get from the table's certain state to a required state.

This helps to recreate the state of a table at any point in time by starting with an original table and processing backwards or forward toward commits made prior to that point. This ability is known as **time travel** or **data versioning**.

Handling upstream changes

Many a times, data engineers are caught unprepared by such upstream data changes, so they struggle to reproduce to the right state. Verifying changes via navigating through **`HISTORY`** can be of great help in understanding what happened and what was instantly changed that started breaking the pipeline.

To review the historical data, you can run the **`DESCRIBE HISTORY`** command:

```
%sql DESCRIBE HISTORY deltaresultstore;
```

You can also provide the timestamp or date string as an option to the DataFrame reader using the following syntax:

```
%sql

-- Query metastore-defined Delta table by timestamp


SELECT * FROM deltaresultstore TIMESTAMP AS OF "2021-12-32"

or

SELECT * FROM deltaresultstore TIMESTAMP AS OF date_sub(current_date(),
1)
```

As every write has a version number, you can also use the version number to travel back in time:

```
%sql -- Query metastore-defined Delta table by version


SELECT COUNT(*) FROM deltaresultstore VERSION AS OF 2

SELECT COUNT(*) FROM deltaresultstore @v2 72
```

Data governance and time travel

The role of governance is to set the direction of protecting information in the form of **policies, standards**, and **guidelines**. One of the most common scenarios surrounding governance to protect people's information is the need to perform a delete request as part of any **GPDR** or **CCPA** compliance. What that means for data engineers is that you need to locate the records from your Delta Lake and delete them within the specified time period.

Users can run `DESCRIBE HISTORY` to see metadata around the changes that were made. An example of this scenario is how a company implements governance, risk, and control for Delta Lake.

Audit and compliance with Delta Lake transaction logs

As the definitive record of every change ever made to a table, the Delta Lake transaction log offer users a verifiable data lineage that is useful for governance, audit, and compliance purposes. It can also be used to trace the origin of an inadvertent change or a bug in a pipeline back to the exact action that caused it. Users can also run `DESCRIBE HISTORY` to see metadata around the changes that were made.

Conclusion

In this chapter, you learned about Spark and its transformation to Databricks, Databricks architecture, and how parallel data processing works. You learned about different ways to program with Databricks using a notebook, writing pipeline, understanding the execution matrix, and further diving into the Delta Lake and its internals. Understanding the topics covered in this chapter will bring you confidence in developing context around how data processing in Databricks works in general, building data quality audit frameworks, and getting a know-how of the internals of handling audit and compliance with features like time travel and transaction logs.

It is now easy for you to navigate to other chapters in this book as well as to learn and understand the advanced concepts of Databricks and Spark through Databricks original documentation at **https://docs.databricks.com/**.

Multiple choice questions

1. Is Apache Spark 100 times faster than Hadoop MapReduce for large-scale data processing?

   a. Yes

   b. No

2. What are the components of Apache Spark?
   a. **Resilient Distributed Dataset** (**RDD**)
   b. Data sets and data frames
   c. **Directed Acyclic Graph** (**DAG**)
   d. All of the above

3. ________________ is a seamless way by which we can use spark with its full potential?
   a. Data Frame
   b. Databricks
   c. Apache Hadoop
   d. Mapreduce

4. In Databricks, how do we make the compiler know which language the cell of the notebook is using?
   a. `@{language Name}`
   b. `%{language Name}`
   c. `${language Name}`
   d. `&{language Name}`

Answers

1. a
2. d
3. b
4. b

CHAPTER 4
Data Sharing and Orchestration with Databricks

Databricks is all about processing data of different kinds, be it real-time or batch-based data.

Processing data has always been a challenge and is performed in multiple steps, such as identifying the source and data itself, connecting the source, validating and identifying issues with the data, cleaning and restructuring, and finally, enabling it to be consumed by a consumer, such as a stream analytics engine, streaming solutions, database, storage, or reporting tools like Power BI or Qlik view.

In the last three chapters, we explored the foundation and basics of Databricks, Databricks architecture, usage of Databricks Lakehouse platform for Data Science and Engineering, and Databricks SQL. We also looked at the evolution of spark to Databricks and processing validated data securely by building an ETL pipeline in Databricks using notepad.

In this chapter, you will understand the orchestration of the workflows written in multiple notepads, which can be automated in defined steps either in parallel or in sequence.

Automation and **orchestration** are complementary to each other. **Automation** is when a machine is able to complete a task or a set of tasks embedded in the workflow without human intervention. **Orchestration** is the configuration of multiple tasks that can be executed into one set of end-to-end processes. A variety of tools exist to help data teams unlock the full benefit of orchestration with a framework through which workloads can be automated.

Orchestrating Data and Machine Learning pipelines in Databricks

Databricks makes it easy to orchestrate multiple tasks in order to easily build Data and Machine Learning workflows. Data teams can easily create and manage multi-step pipelines that transform and refine data, or they can train machine learning algorithms, saving immense time, effort, and context switching using interdependent and modular tasks consisting of notebooks, Python scripts, and other supporting languages:

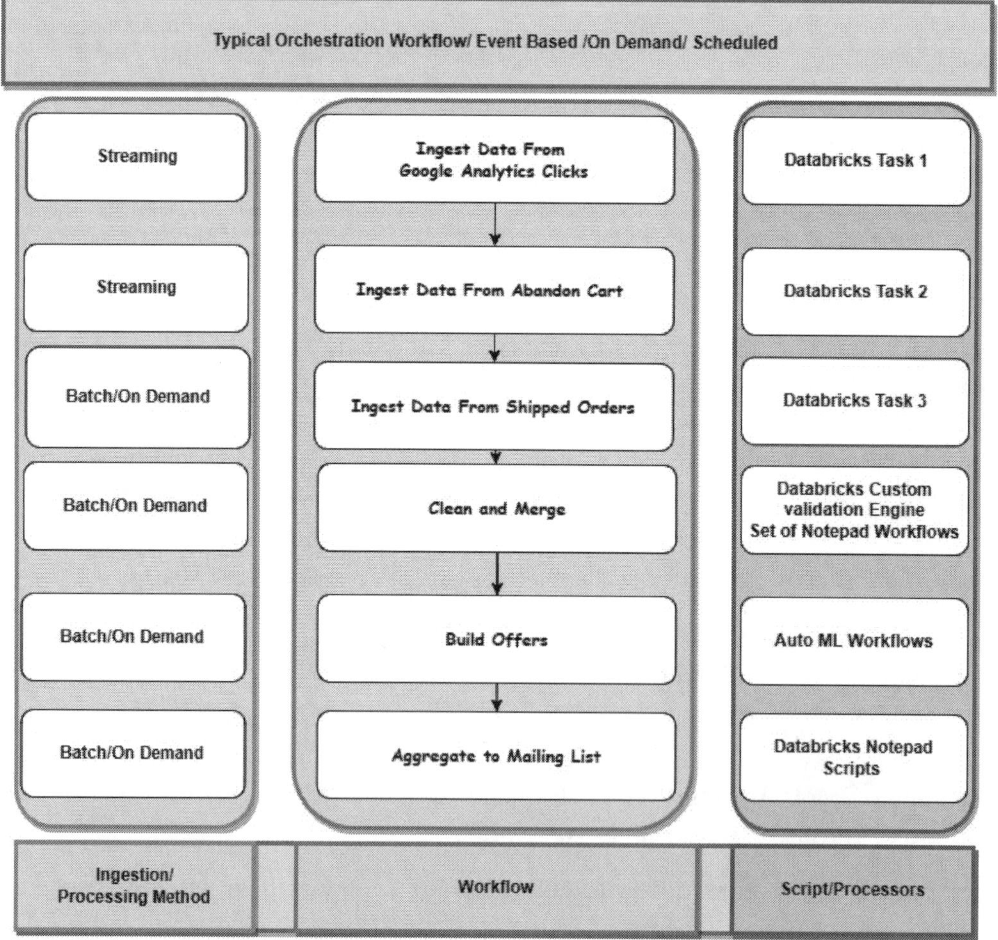

Figure 4.1: Databricks orchestration: Typical orchestration workflow

In the preceding example, you can see multiple tasks for personalized offer generation for a typical e-commerce website orchestrated and clubbed into a chain of workflow.

To orchestrate Databricks workflow and pipeline, you can use multiple cloud-based tools, such as:

- Airflow on AWS (Amazon managed apache airflow)
- Data factory on Azure
- Delta Live tables
- Interface and API provided by Databricks for job management

In this chapter, we will cover all four major options for orchestration by starting with Amazon Managed Workflow and then moving on to Data factory on Azure, Databricks job interface, and Delta Live tables.

Running Databricks tasks using Amazon Managed Airflow

Apache Airflow in Amazon can be used via Amazon **Managed Workflows for Apache Airflow** (**MWAA**).

It is a managed orchestration service for Apache Airflow. This manages the open-source Apache Airflow platform with the security, availability, and scalability of AWS. MWAA gives users additional benefits of easy integration with AWS services and a variety of third-party services via pre-existing plugins to allow customers to create complex data processing pipelines. Databricks notebook scripts can be easily configured and orchestrated through the airflow for orchestration purposes:

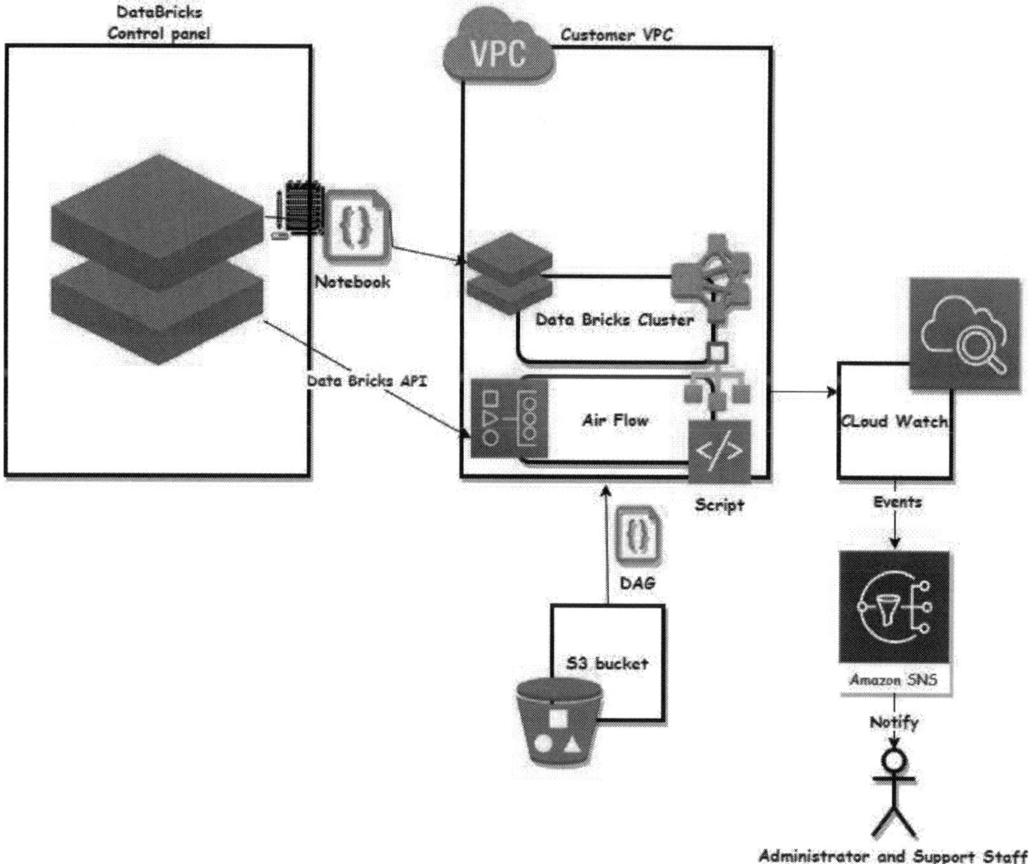

Figure 4.2: Databricks orchestration: With Airflow and Databricks API

In the preceding diagram, you will notice that the availability of API allows Amazon Managed Apache Airflow to easily execute different tasks on Databricks cluster and get instrumentation and execution status through Databricks API, which is further integrated with AWS Cloud Watch and **Simple Notification Service** (**SNS**) to notify users on different events.

Steps are as follows:

1. Create a token inside Databricks and configure the Databricks connection in MWAA:

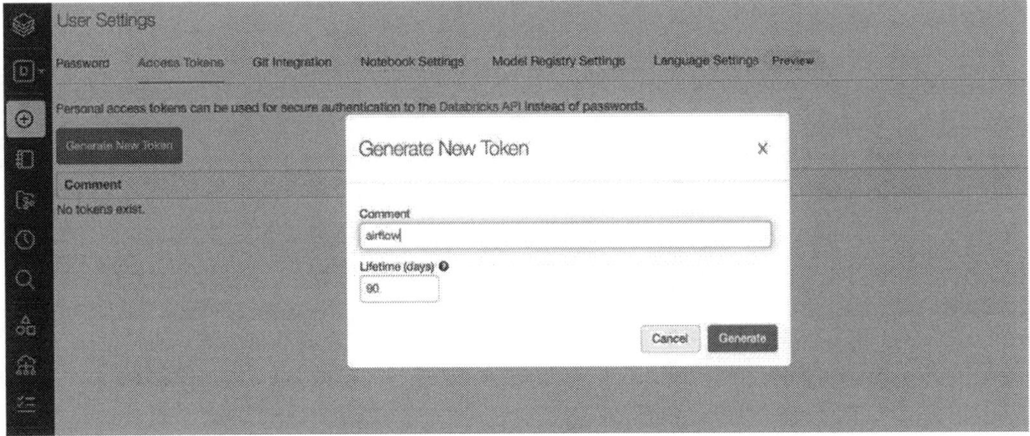

Figure 4.3: Generate token

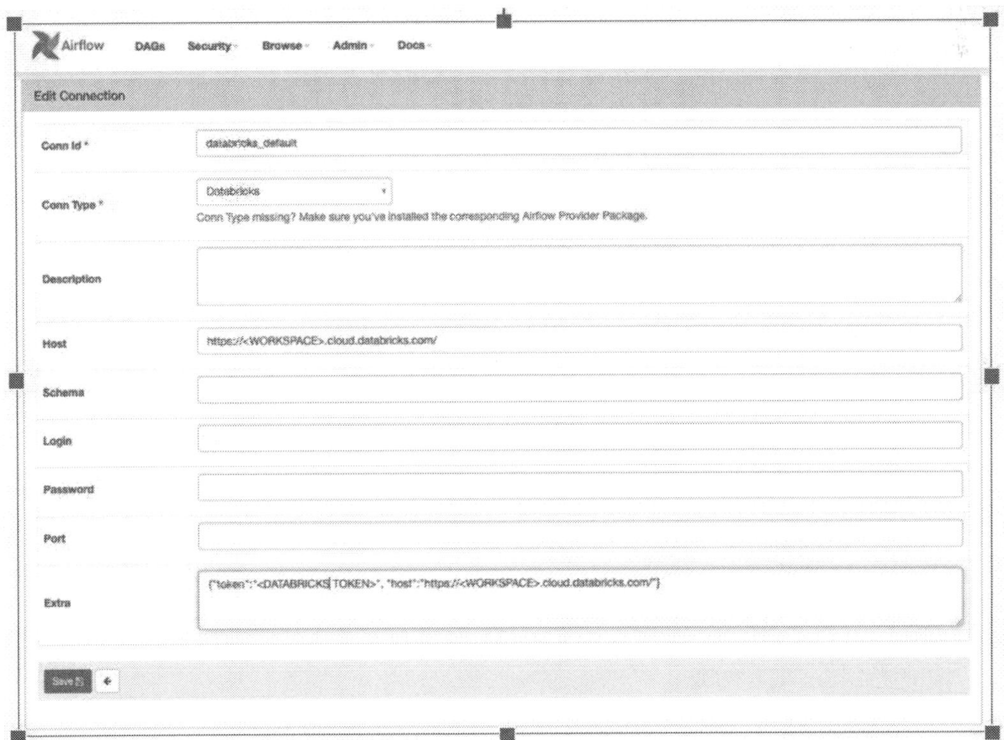

Figure 4.4: Databricks orchestration: Setup Airflow for Databricks

2. Configure the connection in MWAA. Create a notebook script and wrap it under DAG:

For example:

```
from airflow import DAG
from airflow.providers.databricks.operators.databricks import
DatabricksSubmitRunOperator, DatabricksRunNowOperator
from datetime import datetime, timedelta

#Define params for Submit Run Operator
new_cluster = {
    'spark_version': '7.3.x-scala2.12',
    'num_workers': 4,
    'node_type_id': 'Node Compute Size EC2 Instance, Large,
Medium, Micro',
     "aws_attributes": {
        "instance_profile_arn": "arn:aws:iam::XXXXXXX:instance-
profile/databricks-data-role"
    }
}

notebook_task = {
    'notebook_path': '/Users/xxxxx@XXXXX.com/user',
}

#Define params for Run Now Operator
notebook_params = {
    "Variable": Any Parameter that you need to Pass
}

default_args = {
    'owner': 'airflow',
    'depends_on_past': False,
    'email_on_failure': False,
    'email_on_retry': False,
    'retries': 1,
    'retry_delay': timedelta(minutes=5)
```

```
}

with DAG('databricks_dag',
    start_date=datetime(2022, 5, 5),
    schedule_interval='@weekely',
    catchup=False,
    default_args=default_args
    ) as dag:

    opr_submit_run = DatabricksSubmitRunOperator(
        task_id='submit_run',
        databricks_conn_id='databricks_default',
        new_cluster=new_cluster,
        notebook_task=notebook_task
    )
    opr_submit_run
```

3. Save it to an S3 bucket or a file source.
4. Link the DAG to Airflow:

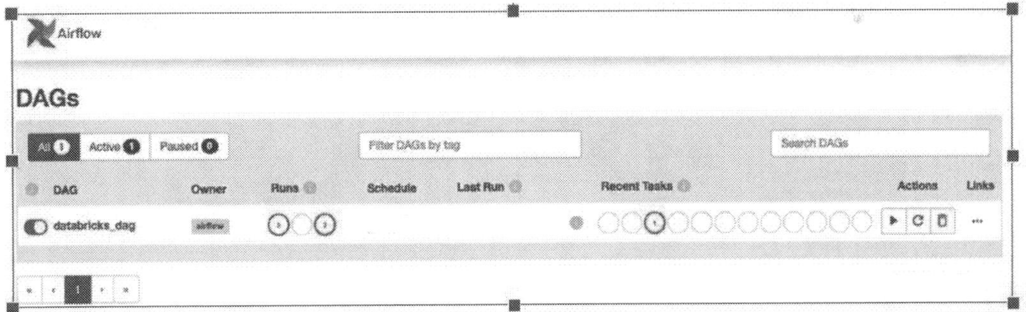

***Figure 4.5**: Databricks orchestration: Setup DAG*

5. Trigger the DAG in Airflow MWAA.

6. Once triggered, your job should show in Databricks jobs:

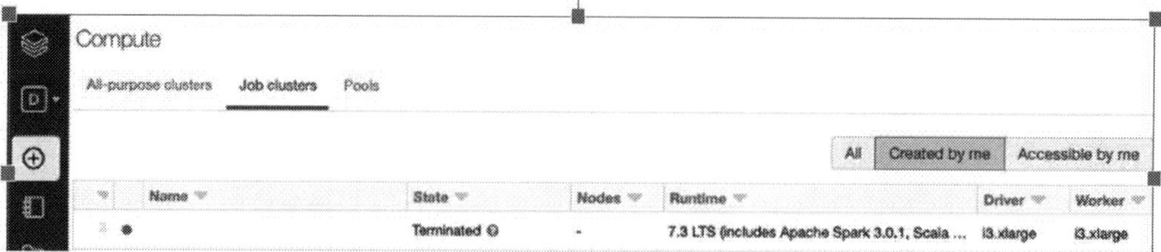

Figure 4.6: Databricks orchestration: Databricks job running log

Databricks jobs are *independent* and are an integral part of Databricks. The orchestrator tool, such as Airflow and Data Factory, creates a layer above it to provide you with the opportunity of orchestrating multiple tasks created through different tools to seamlessly integrate with Databricks jobs.

Run and orchestrate the Databricks tasks using Data Factory

In this section, we will understand the options to orchestrate and trigger Databricks tasks through **Azure Data Factory**:

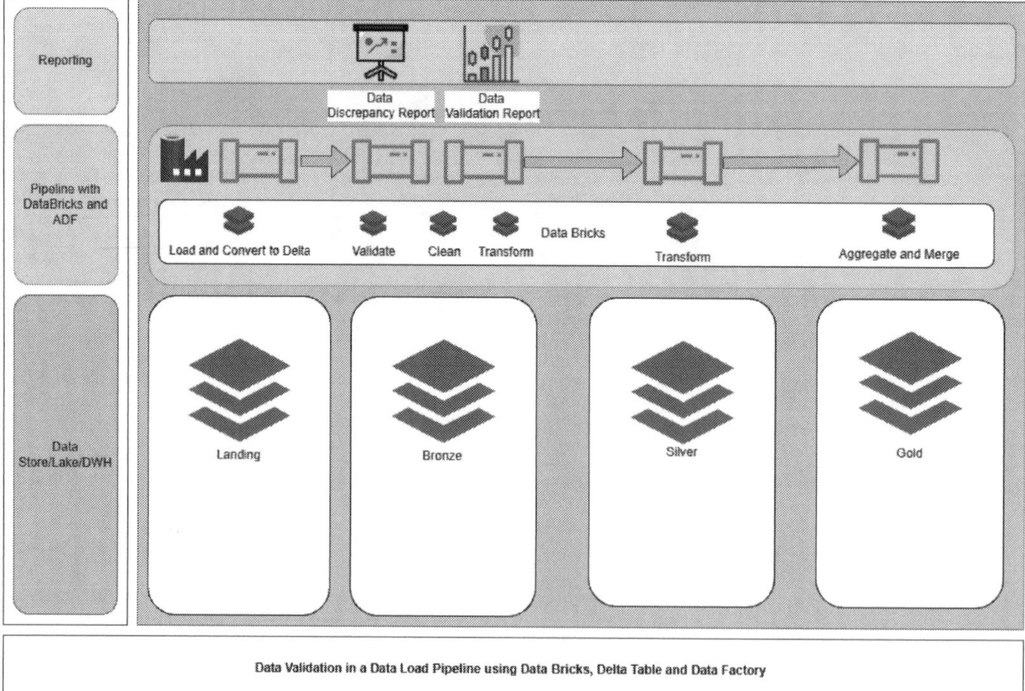

Figure 4.7: Databricks orchestration: ADF example

This is a typical example of orchestrating and executing Databricks scripts and tasks using a Data Factory workflow.

There are multiple ways to use a Data Factory for orchestration:

- Via importing the Databricks notebook and executing in the Azure Data Factory pipeline
- Via notebook or Python activity

Via importing the Databricks notebook and executing in the Azure Data Factory pipeline

The prerequisites are as follows:

- An Azure Blob storage account with a container.
- Set up a sink by noting the storage account name, container name, and access key.
- An Azure Databricks workspace.
- An access token from Azure Databricks to link it to Azure Data Factory using link service.
- Notebook import from Azure Databricks and noting the location.

Steps are as follows:

1. If you don't have a working notebook, import a notebook to Databricks for transformation; else, create a notebook, execute and test in Databricks, and further use it in the Azure Databricks pipeline for execution:

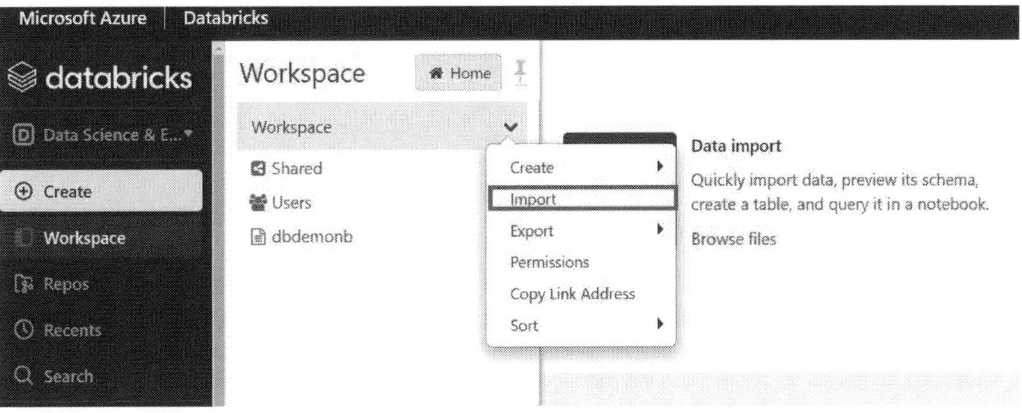

Figure 4.8: Databricks orchestration: Import notebook 1

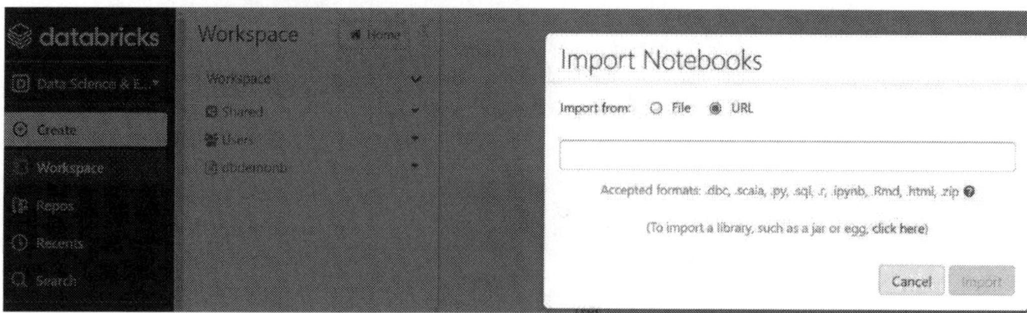

Figure 4.9: Databricks orchestration: Import notebook 2

2. To use an existing notebook, make sure you note the path; this will be required later when you set this notebook to execute in the pipeline:

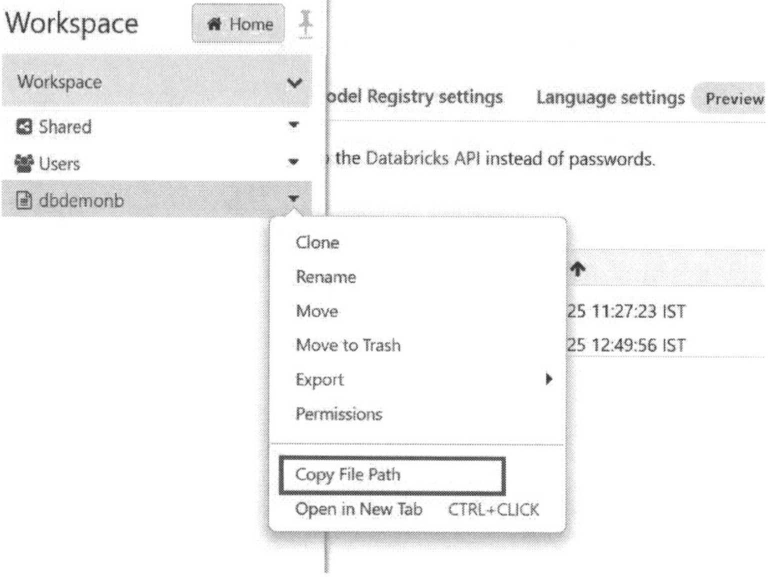

Figure 4.10: Databricks orchestration: Copy path

If you are importing the notebook from an example source, you may have to make sure that the imported notebook has all the Data Lake blob and database connectivity setup as per your environment.

Create an Azure Databricks linked service

Linked service contains the connection information for Databricks, enabling Azure Data Factory to communicate with Azure Databricks:

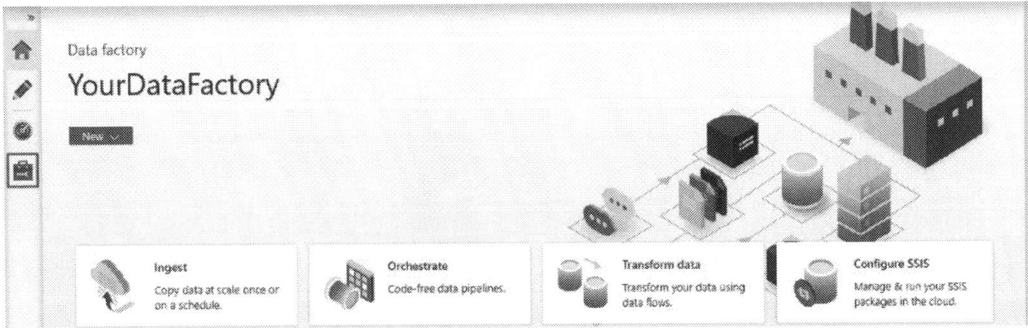

***Figure 4.11**: Databricks orchestration: Data Factory home*

Navigate to the *linked service* section and choose **`Azure Databricks`**:

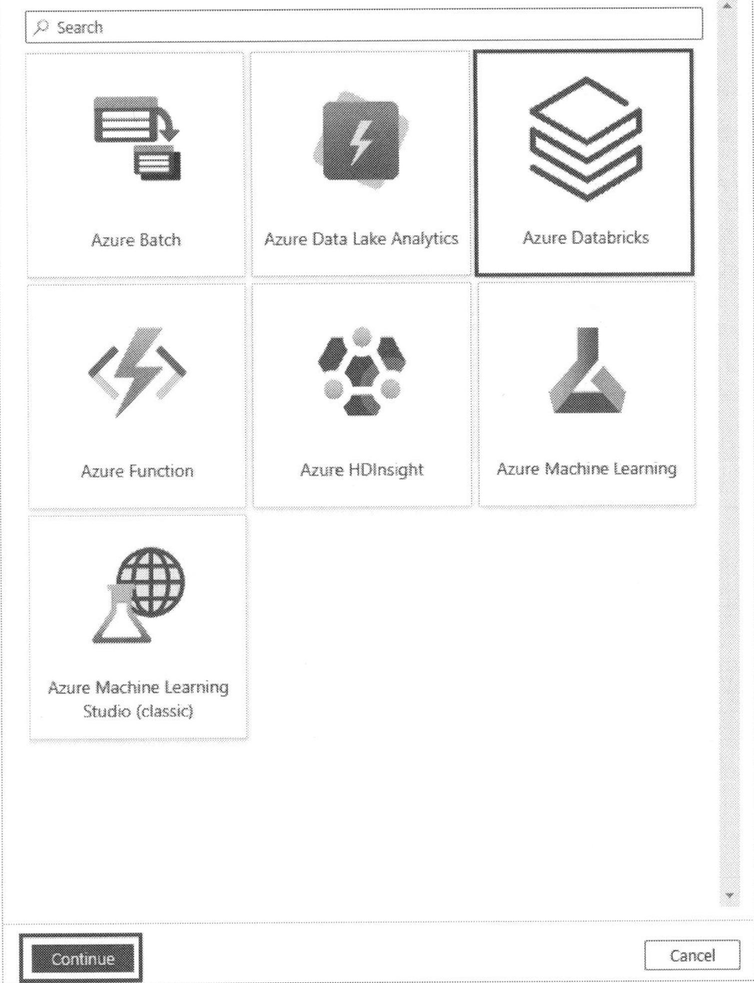

***Figure 4.12**: Databricks orchestration: Azure Databricks*

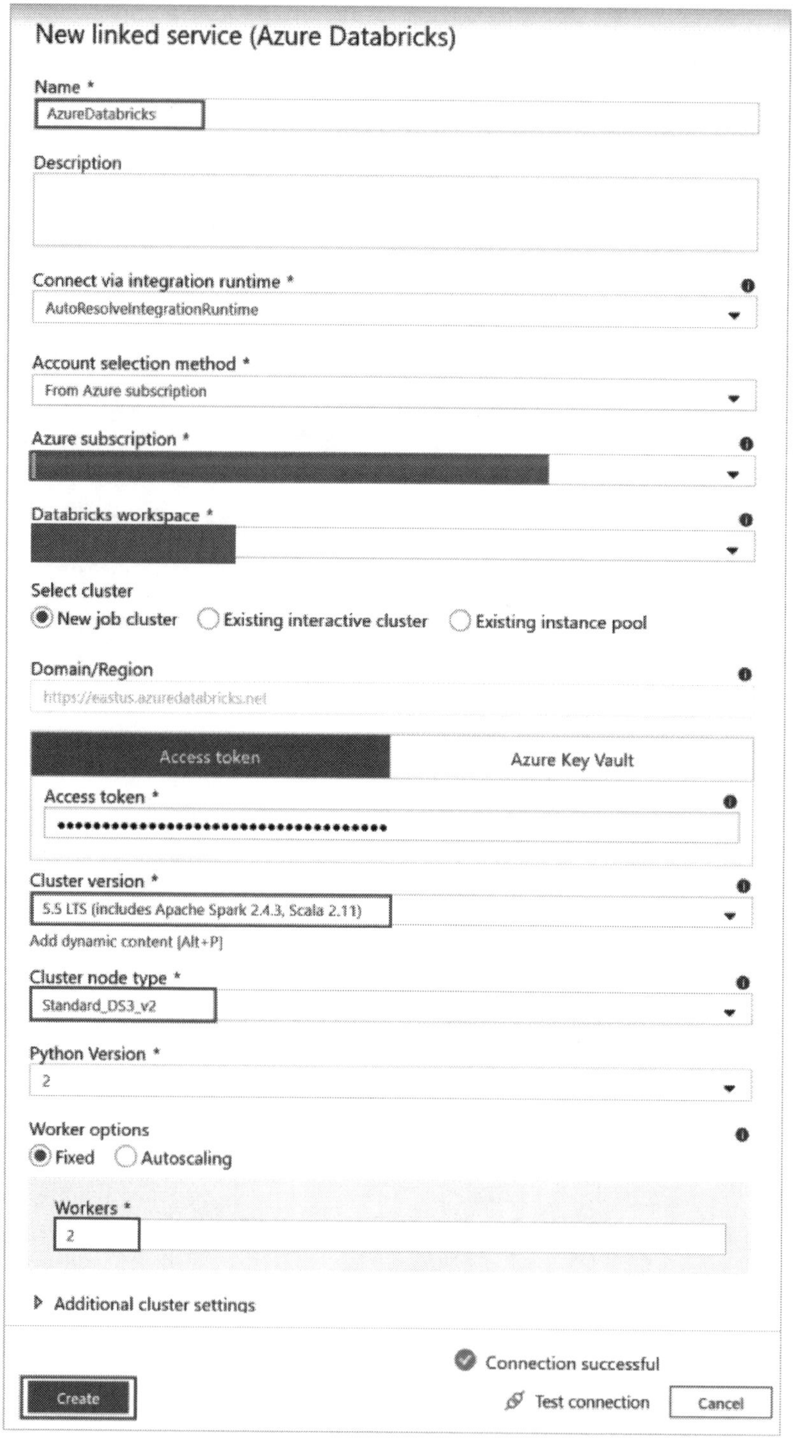

New linked service (Azure Databricks)

Name *
AzureDatabricks

Description

Connect via integration runtime *
AutoResolveIntegrationRuntime

Account selection method *
From Azure subscription

Azure subscription *

Databricks workspace *

Select cluster
New job cluster Existing interactive cluster Existing instance pool

Domain/Region
https://eastus.azuredatabricks.net

Access token Azure Key Vault

Access token *
••••••••••••••••••••••••••••••••••••••

Cluster version *
5.5 LTS (includes Apache Spark 2.4.3, Scala 2.11)
Add dynamic content [Alt+P]

Cluster node type *
Standard_DS3_v2

Python Version *
2

Worker options
Fixed Autoscaling

Workers *
2

Additional cluster settings

Connection successful

Create Test connection Cancel

***Figure 4.13**: Databricks orchestration: Setting up linked service*

Note that the access token will be the token you generated in Databricks.

Workers can be more than two based on the execution speed you want, the budget you have, and the type of load you need to run in the background.

Once the linked service is created, one can call the notebook in the pipeline to execute the Databricks task along with other data factory tasks.

The number of tasks and different linked services depends on how you are accessing the source and what type of services you are using for the same. For example, using the blob storage, **synapse** or **s3 bucket** will need a separate linked service to connect as a source or sink.

Creating your ADF pipeline

1. You can start by validating your settings:

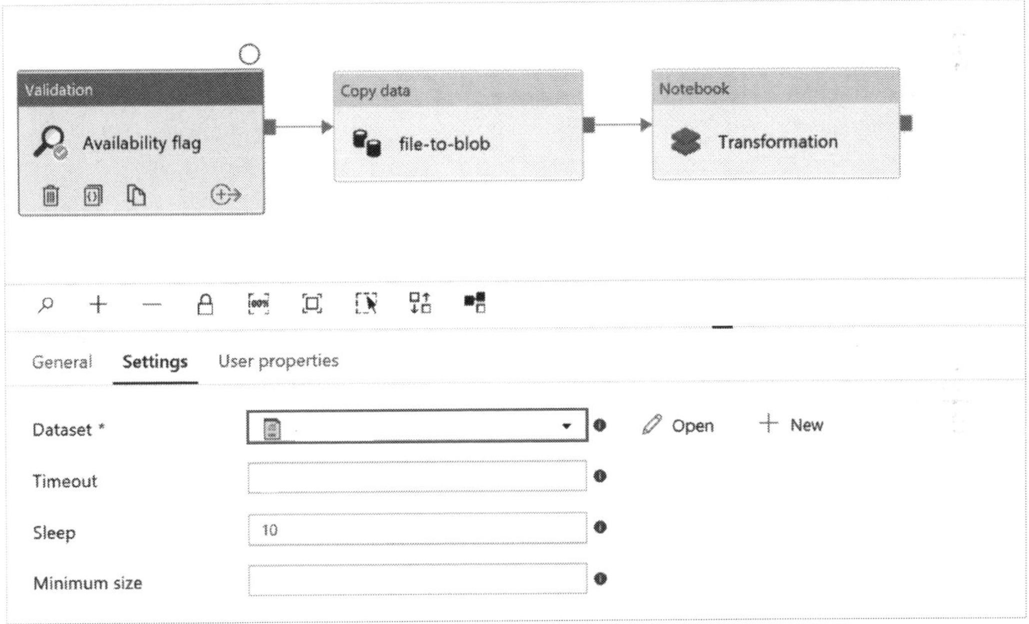

***Figure 4.14**: Databricks orchestration: ADF pipeline setup availability flag*

Setting up an availability flag at the starting of the flow will make sure all the input datasets are ready.

For a better pre-validated workflow, it's important that we set up a validation task at the beginning of the Data Factory pipeline. This will make sure all connections and resources are available before the next task in the data factory pipeline starts.

2. To find the template, choose one of the templates related to Databricks from the *template* section on your Data Factory home page:

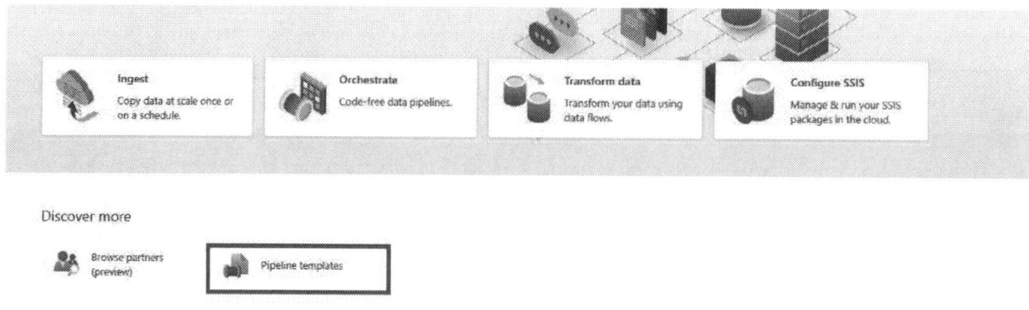

***Figure 4.15**: Databricks orchestration: Setting up linked service*

3. Now, choose any one of the Databricks templates; for example, here, we have chosen the one highlighted:

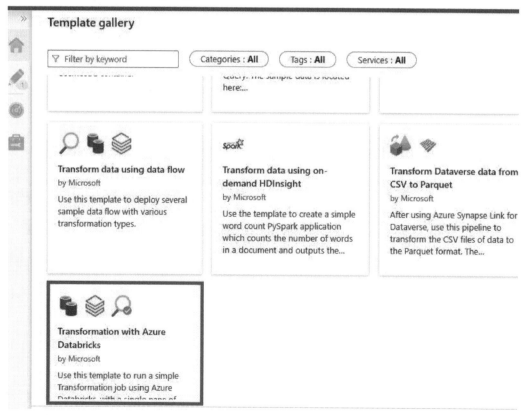

***Figure 4.16**: Databricks orchestration: Template gallery*

4. Once you set up the template, you will get the **`Linked service`** option, as follows:

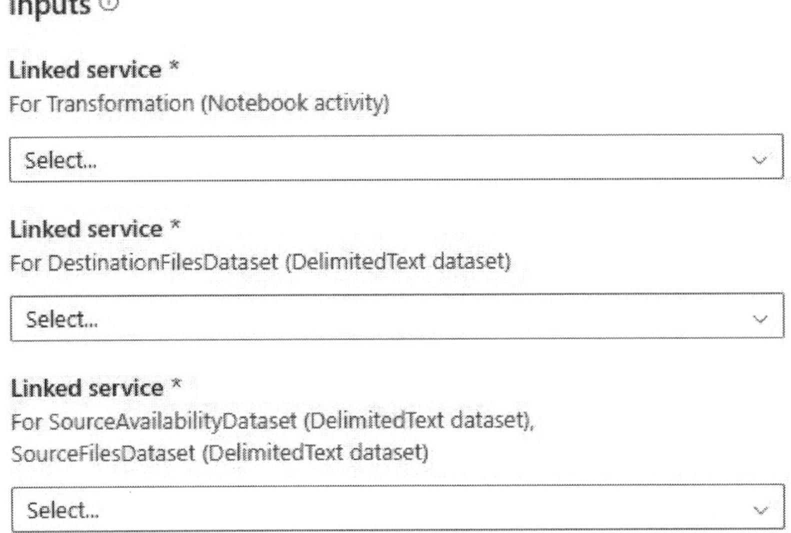

***Figure 4.17**: Databricks orchestration: Linked service*

5. Once you set up the linked service as mentioned previously, you can move to the validation steps to check the availability of source datasets:

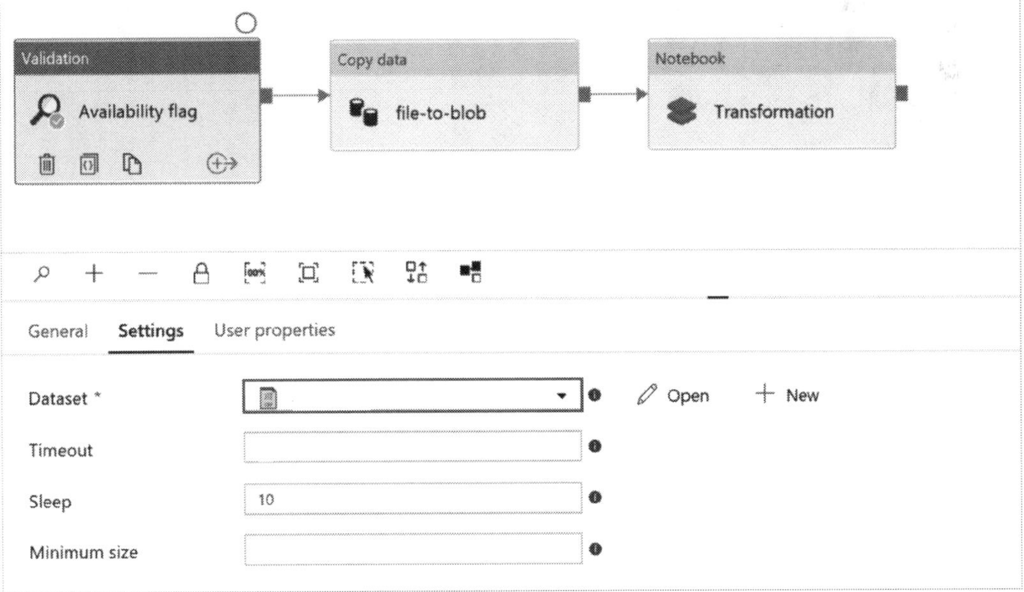

***Figure 4.18**: Databricks orchestration: Pipeline*

6. After the availability check is done, you can move to the next step of moving files to the blob:

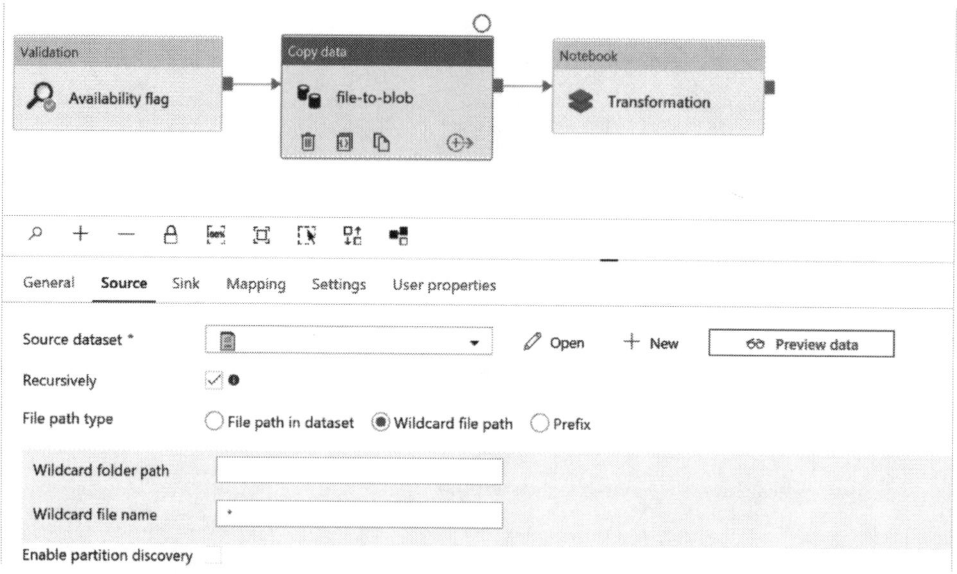

***Figure 4.19**: Databricks orchestration: Pipeline source activity*

7. Further, provide the sink settings, such as **`Sink dataset`**, as a destination, along with **`Copy behavior`**, **`Max concurrent connections`**, **`Block size (MB)`**, and so on to make the output ready to be processed by the database's transformation task in the next steps:

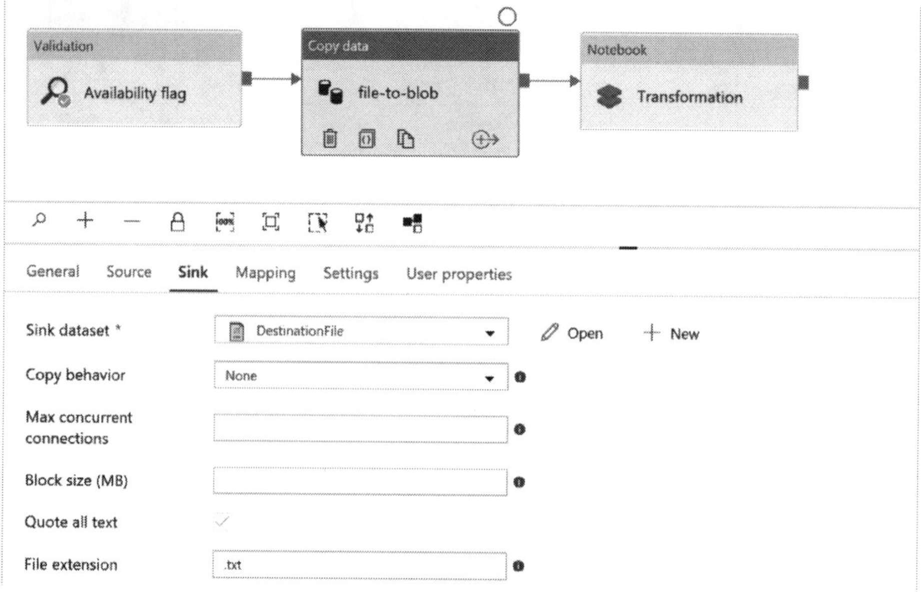

***Figure 4.20**: Databricks orchestration: Pipeline sink activity*

8. Once your source files are ready to be consumed by Databricks, the next step is to call the Databricks notepad operation to process the files for *transformation*. To make sure it runs perfectly, the first step is to connect to the Databricks linked service:

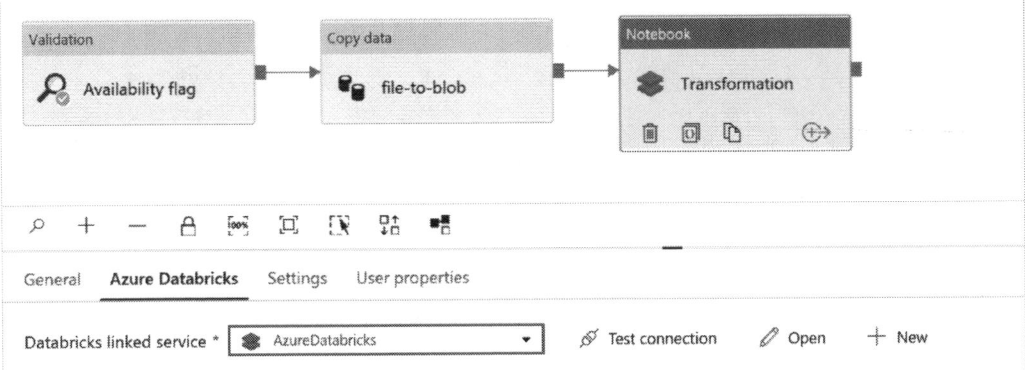

***Figure 4.21**: Databricks orchestration: Databricks task*

9. The next step is to set up the notebook path that was copied initially:

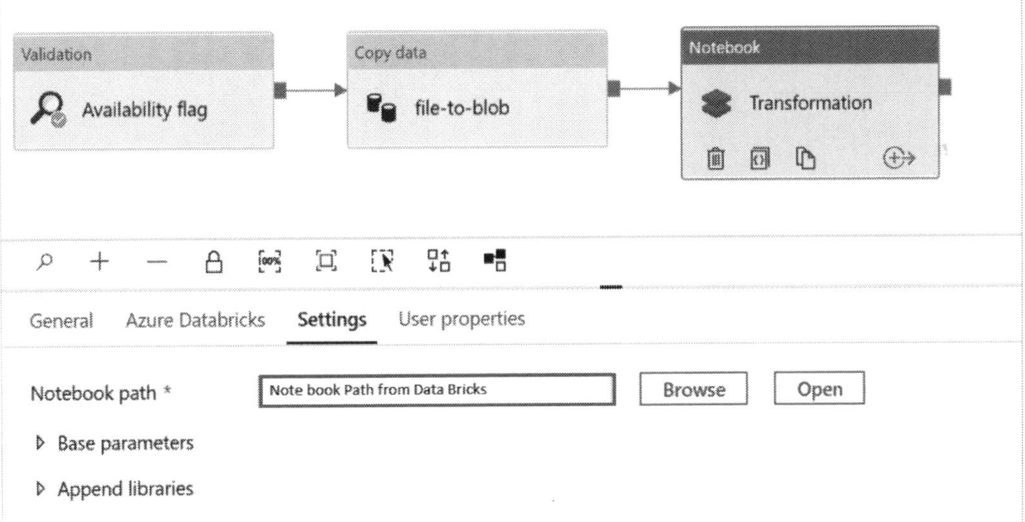

***Figure 4.22**: Databricks orchestration: Setting up path*

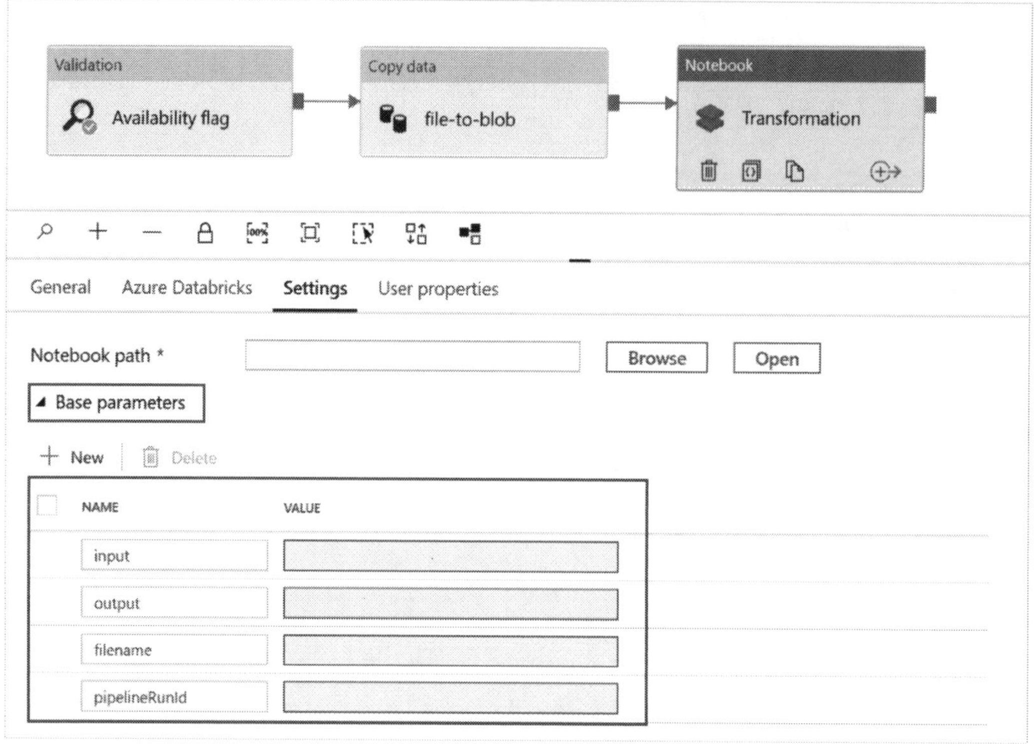

***Figure 4.23**: Databricks orchestration: Base parameters*

Make sure you set up the input path **`@pipeline().parameters.inputpath`**, output path, filename, and **`runid`** correctly:

- Notebook path is the path that you copied from the step in *Figure 4.9*.
- Input value should be **`@pipeline().parameters.inputpath`**.
- Output value should be **`@pipeline().parameters.outputpath`**.
- Filename value should be **`@pipeline().parameters.fileName`**.
- **`PipelineRunId`** value should be **`@pipeline().Runid`**.

Via notebook or Python activity

You can also run a Data Factory activity through a slightly different route, which is running via notebook or Python activity. This is almost the same as the preceding transformation task, but with an easy and specific way to execute different types of Databricks code written in notebook, low-level JAR, or Python files.

To do that, you can follow the given steps:

1. Create a Data Factory.
2. Create a Data factory linked service, as described in the earlier option in this chapter.
3. Create a pipeline that uses Databricks notebook activity:

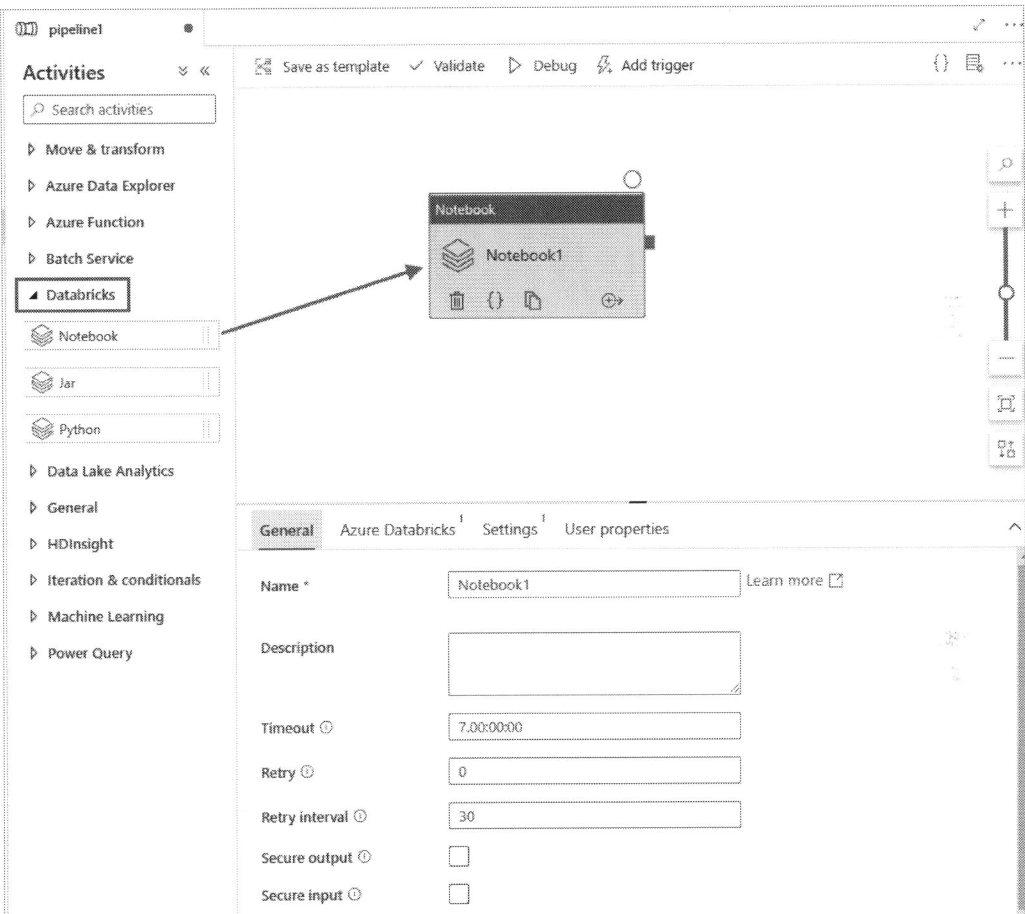

***Figure 4.24**: Databricks orchestration: Independent Databricks activity execution*

4. Once you choose to select Databricks notebook activity, you need to configure the same with proper linked service and your Databricks code or notebook path copied from the steps in *Figure 4.9*.

5. Once you are all set, you need to validate and publish the ADF activity to be further able to execute or debug it:

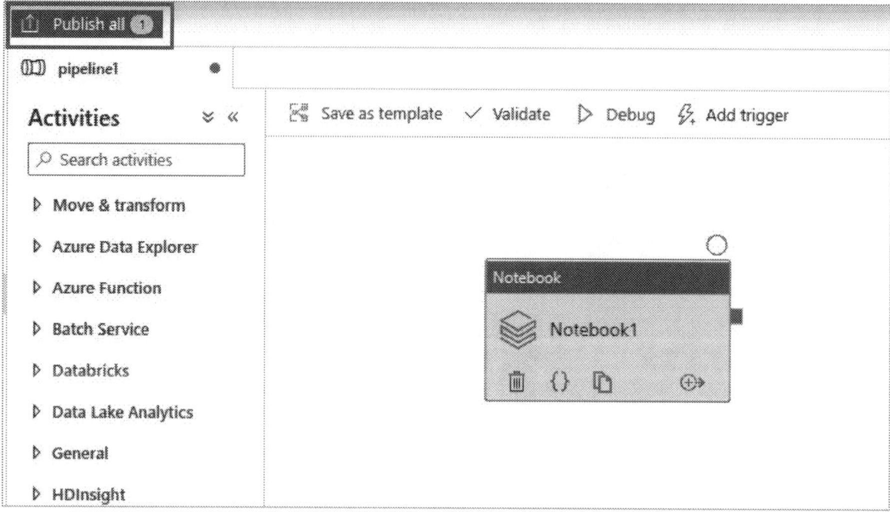

Figure 4.25: Databricks orchestration: Details task

6. The next step is to trigger a pipeline run by the following steps:

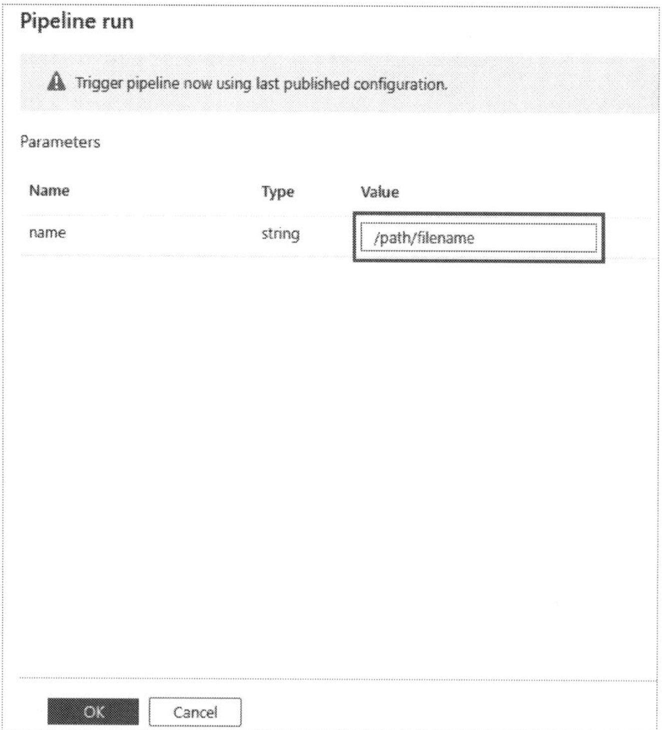

Figure 4.26: Databricks orchestration: Setup path

7. Once the pipeline is triggered, the next step is to monitor the pipeline run:

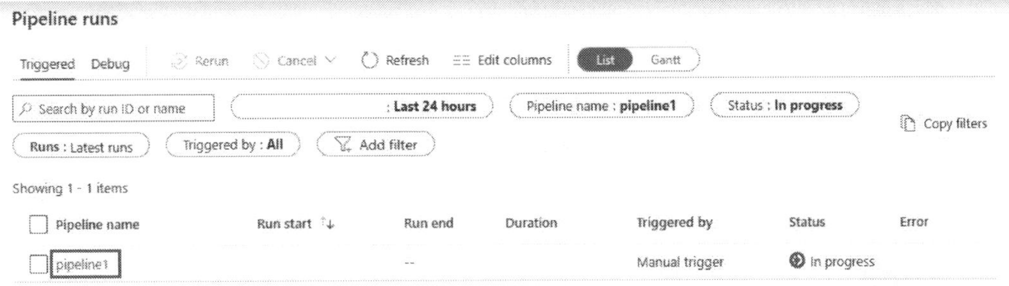

Figure 4.27: Databricks orchestration: Pipeline runs

8. All the runs can be monitored in detailed from the job and cluster section in Databricks:

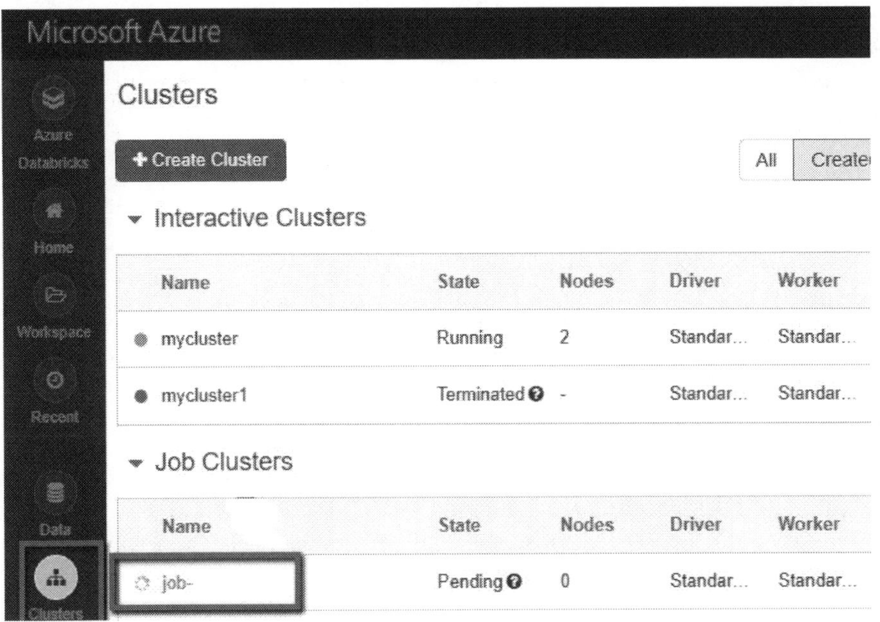

Figure 4.28: Databricks Orchestration: Cluster running status

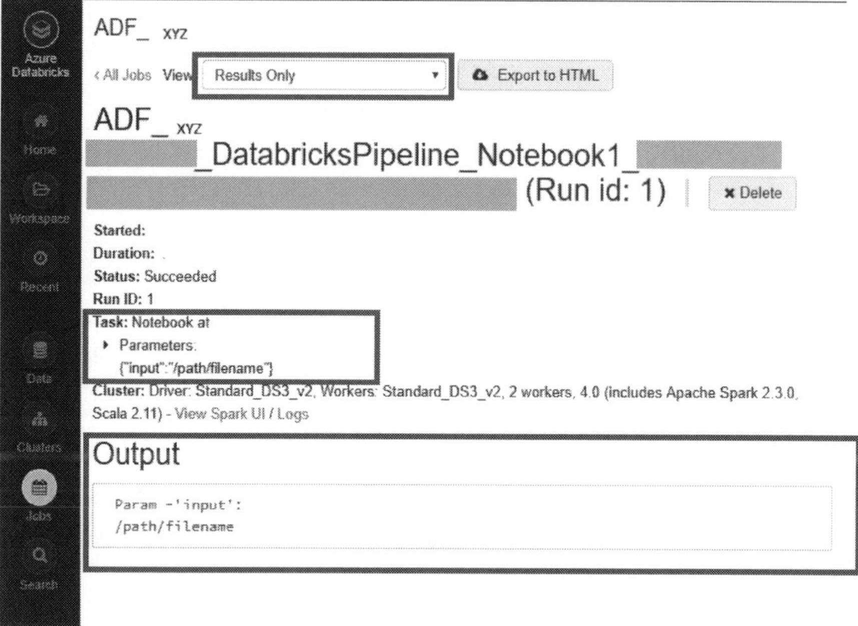

***Figure 4.29**: Databricks orchestration: Databricks jobs*

Jobs in Databricks

As job orchestration is fully integrated into Databricks, it does not require any other cloud-based tools, such as Data Factories or logic apps, to sequence and orchestrate multiple tasks.

One can even use the **jobs API** or **UI** to create and manage jobs and features, such as setting up multiple tasks either written inside Databricks, or outside Databricks, and sending email alerts for monitoring. With its powerful API-based approach, Databricks jobs can orchestrate anything that has an API (for example, pull data from Google Analytics or a third-party application or even Delta Live Tables).

If you are a beginner and don't have any specific constraints to orchestrate your pipeline outside Databricks interface, you can easily use the job interface inside Databricks for all your orchestration needs.

Jobs in Databricks get executed inside a Databricks cluster, which has *elasticity* and *scalability* on its own and runs completely under your security periphery of virtual networks. The jobs can consist of a single task or can be a large, multi-task application with complex dependencies. Once your jobs are configured properly, Databricks can manage the task orchestration, cluster management, monitoring, and error reporting for all the jobs. These jobs can run immediately *periodically* or *can be scheduled*.

The job tasks support implementation using notebooks, Delta Live Tables pipelines, or Python, Java, and Scala applications. Jobs can exhaust notebook-based segregated scripts and can consist of varied tasks, as described in *Chapter 3, Spark, Databricks, and Building a Data Quality Framework*. This can be anything from running a Python script that ingests data from cloud storage, prepares the data with a Delta Live Tables pipeline, and creates a dashboard with a notebook or handles a Data Science and Machine Learning-based use case.

The job can be created through the jobs UI, the jobs API, or the Databricks CLI. The jobs UI has detailed monitoring tools integrated that allow you to monitor, test, and troubleshoot the running and completed jobs.

To create a job, you need to click on **`Jobs`** in the sidebar.

Refer to the *Red Icon* in the following diagram. To create your jobs, you need to create tasks and associate with your scripts written in a notebook.

If you have parameters, you will have to configure as per requirements and further select the active cluster where these jobs will be executed:

1. Add a name for your job with your job name.
2. In the **`Task name`** field, enter a name for the task; for example, **`get data from sql`**.
3. In the **`Type`** drop-down, select **`Notebook`**.
4. Use the file browser to find the first notebook you created, click on the notebook name, and click on **`Confirm`**; here, it's **`DBDemo`**, which we used in *Chapter 3, Spark, Databricks, and Building a Data Quality Framework*.
5. Click on **`Create task`**.
6. Click on [+] following the task you just created to add another task.
7. In the **`Task name`** field, enter a name for the task; for example, **`filter-baby-names`**.
8. In the **`Type`** drop-down, select **`Notebook`**.
9. Use the file browser to find the second notebook you created, click on the notebook name, and click on **`Confirm`**.
10. Click on **`Add`** under **`Parameters`**. In the **`Key`** field, enter parameters in key and value format.

11. Click on **`Create task`**:

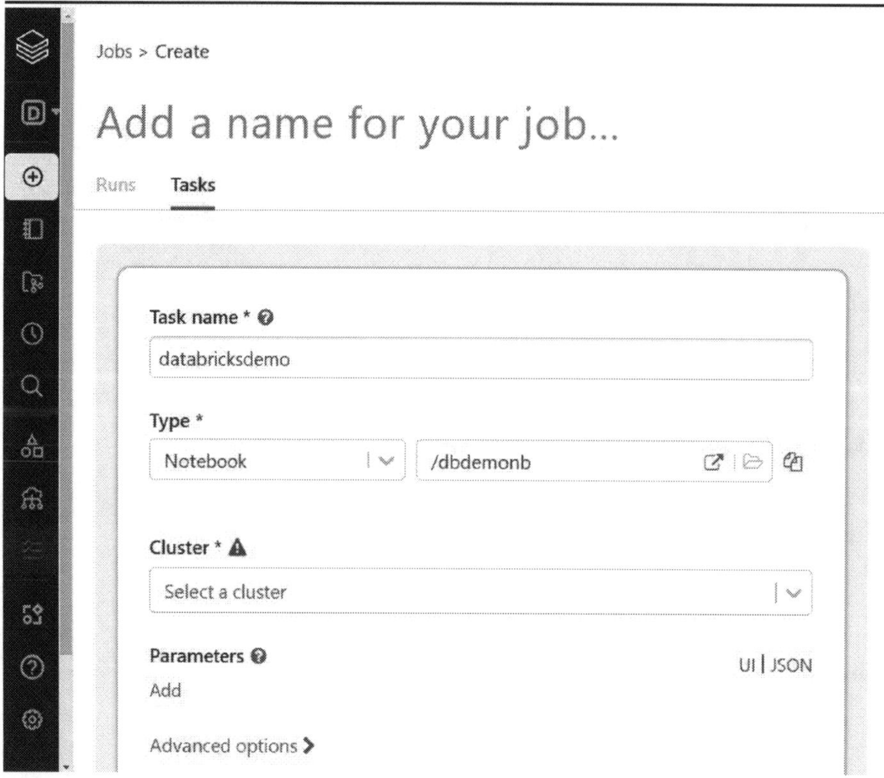

Figure 4.30: Databricks orchestration: Jobs

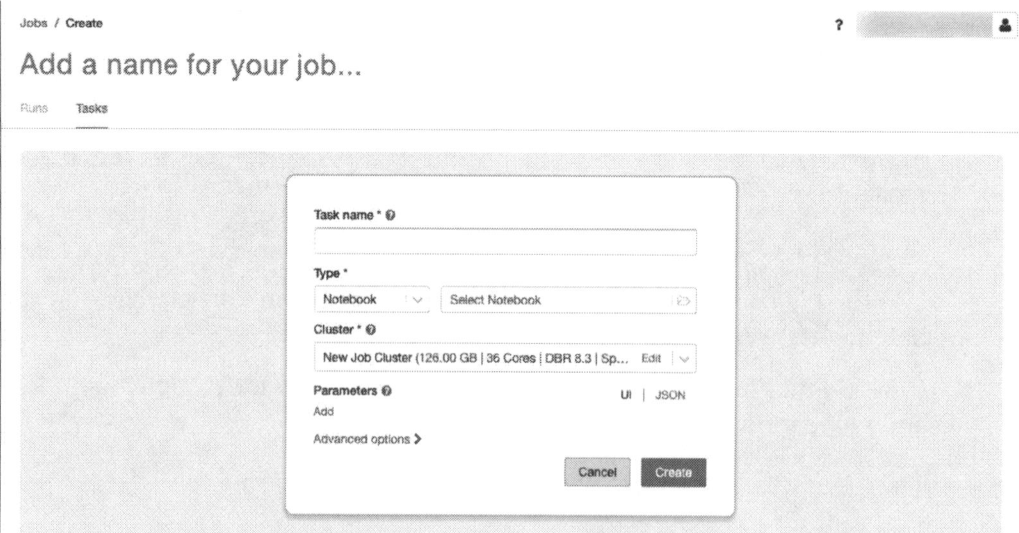

Figure 4.31 Databricks orchestration: Jobs

Run the job

To run the job immediately, click on Run Now in the upper-right corner. You can also run the job by clicking on the **Runs** tab and clicking on **Run Now** in the **Active Runs** table.

View run details

Job runs

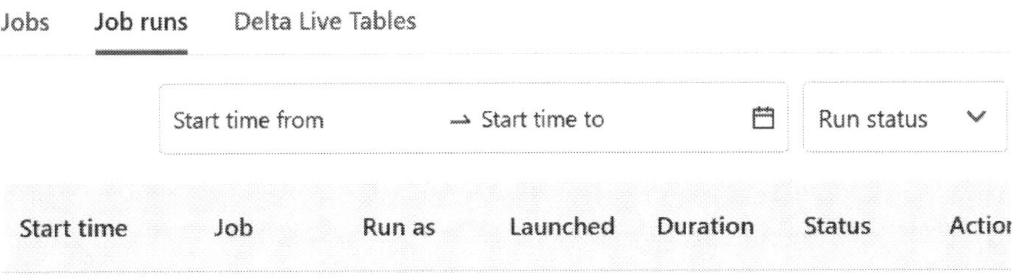

Figure 4.32: Databricks orchestration: Job runs

Databricks maintains a history of your job runs for up to *60 days*. If you need to preserve job runs, Databricks recommends that you export results before they expire:

1. Click on the **Runs** tab and click on the link for the run in the **Active Runs** table or in the **Completed Runs (past 60 days)** table.
2. Click on either task to see the output and details. For example, click on the **filter-baby-names** task to view the status and output for the filter task.

   For a job that orchestrates multiple tasks, click on a task to view task run details, including the cluster that ran the task, the job UI for the task, logs for the task, and the metrics for the task.

   Once done, you can click on the job ID value to return to the **Runs** tab for the job. Click on the job runs ID value to return to the job run details.

Task dependencies

When orchestration of multiple tasks is enabled, you can define the order of execution of tasks in a job using **Depends** in the dropdown. You can set this field to *one* or *more* tasks in the job.

Delta Live tables

To schedule a Delta Live table jobs, navigate to the *Delta Live* section. Here, you can set up a workflow based on JSON configuration and the number of notebooks you want to run in sequence or in parallel:

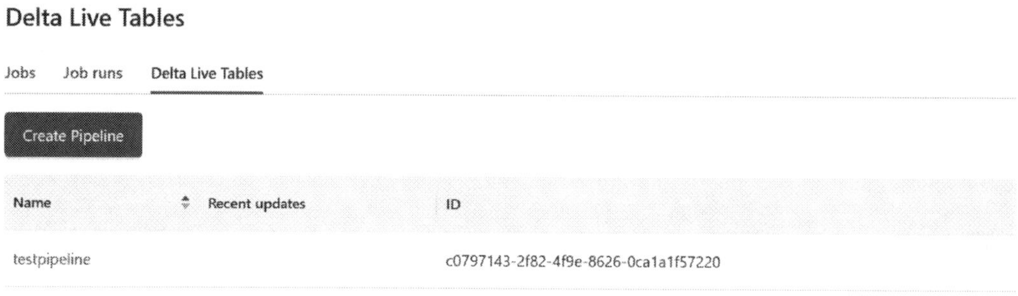

Delta Live Tables

Jobs Job runs Delta Live Tables

Create Pipeline

Name	Recent updates	ID
testpipeline		c0797143-2f82-4f9e-8626-0ca1a1f57220

***Figure 4.33**: Databricks orchestration: Delta Live tables*

As per Databricks official documentation:

Delta Live Tables (DLT) is the first ETL framework that uses a simple declarative approach to building reliable data pipelines and automatically managing your infrastructure at scale so data analysts and engineers can spend less time on tooling and focus on getting value from data. With DLT, engineers are able to treat their data as code and apply modern software engineering best practices like testing, error handling, monitoring, and documentation to deploy reliable pipelines at scale.

Delta Live table accelerates ETL development by giving you the ability to develop an environment separate from production, easily test before deployment, and deploy and manage environments using parameterization. One can conduct unit testing easily, simplifying the development, testing, deployment, operations, and monitoring of ETL pipelines.

This brings confidence in your data by delivering reliable data with built-in quality controls, testing, monitoring, and enforcement to ensure accurate and useful BI, Data Science, and ML. This helps prevent bad data from flowing into tables, tracks data quality over time, and provides tools to troubleshoot bad data with granular pipeline observability. This gives you a high-fidelity lineage diagram of your pipeline and lets you track dependencies and aggregate data quality metrics across all of your pipelines.

You can easily configure it either via JSON or using the wizard in the **`Job`** section. You can also edit the pipeline using the **`Edit Pipeline Settings`**, as follows:

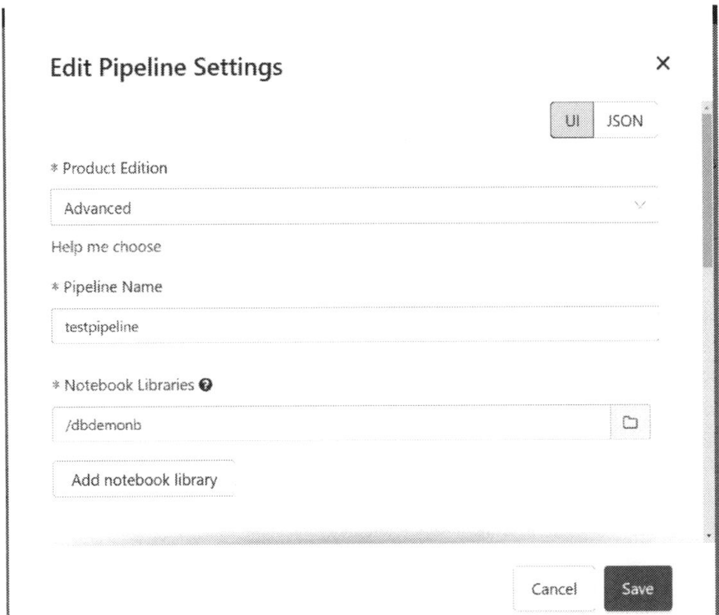

Figure 4.34*: Databricks orchestration: Pipeline settings*

Running jobs via Databricks job API

You can perform multiple type of rest-based operations:

- Create
- Runs submit
- Update
- Reset
- List
- Get
- Runs get
- Runs get output
- Runs list

They are explained as follows:

- **Create**: To create a single-task format job through the **`Create a new job operation (POST /jobs/create)`** (https://docs.databricks.com/dev-tools/api/latest/jobs.html) in the jobs API, you do not need to change existing clients.

To create a multi-task format job, use the **Tasks** field in **Job Settings** to specify settings for each task. The following example creates a job with two notebook tasks. This example is for **API 2.0** and **2.1**:

```
{
  "name": "Multi-task-job Test",
  "max_concurrent_runs": 1,
  "tasks": [
    {
      "task_key": "Pull Sql data",
      "description": "pull and prepare the data",
      "notebook_task": {
        "notebook_path": "/Users/user@databricks.com/DbDemo"
      },
      "existing_cluster_id": "cluster001",
      "timeout_seconds": 3600,
      "max_retries": 3,
      "retry_on_timeout": true
    },
    {
      "task_key": "Load Data To Delta Tables",
      "description": "Load to Delta Table",
      "notebook_task": {
        "notebook_path": "/Users/user@databricks.com/deltedemo"
      },
      "depends_on": [
        {
          "task_key": "Delta_Table_Load"
        }
      ],
      "existing_cluster_id": "cluster002",
      "timeout_seconds": 3600,
      "max_retries": 3,
      "retry_on_timeout": true
    }
  ]
}
```

- **Runs submit**: To submit a one-time run of a single-task format job with the **`Create and trigger a one-time run operation (POST/runs/submit)`** (**https://docs.databricks.com/dev-tools/api/latest/jobs.html**) in the jobs API, you do not need to change existing clients.
- **Update**: To update a single-task format job with the **`Partially update a job operation (POST /jobs/update`**) (**https://docs.databricks.com/dev-tools/api/latest/jobs.html**) in the jobs API, you do not need to change existing clients.

  To update the settings of a multi-task format job, you must use the unique **`Task key`** field to identify new task settings. See, create (**https://docs.databricks.com/data-engineering/jobs/jobs-api-updates.html#create-job**), for an example job settings specifying multiple tasks.
- **Reset**: To overwrite the settings of a single-task format job with the **`Overwrite all settings for a job operation (POST /jobs/reset)`** in the jobs API, you do not need to change existing clients.
- **List**: To **`Retrieve a list of jobs using (GET /jobs/list)`** in the jobs API. For multi-task format jobs, most settings are defined at the task level and not the job level. Cluster configuration may be set at the task or job level to modify clients to access cluster or task settings for a multi-task format job returned in the job structure:
  - Parse the **`job_id`** field for the multi-task format job.
  - Pass the **`job_id`** to get a job operation (**`GET /jobs/get`**) in the jobs API to retrieve job details.
- **Get**: To **`Get a job operation (GET /jobs/get)`** in the jobs API. Multi-task format jobs return an array of task data structures containing task settings. If you require access to task-level details, you need to modify your clients to iterate through the tasks array and extract the required fields.

These are just a few examples to help you start with job API. For a detailed understanding, you can refer to the Databricks documentation.

https://docs.databricks.com/dev-tools/api/

Conclusion

In this chapter, you learned how to orchestrate workflows written in multiple ways. You learnt about running Databricks processes written in different ways, such as notebook JAR and in multiple languages. You also learned to sequence and orchestrate dataflow and data processing tasks using cloud based tools provided by different cloud vendors such as Data Factory on Azure, and , Apache Airflow on AWS working outside but in situ with the Databricks implementation specific to that cloud vendor. This chapter have further helped you in understanding general concepts around working with Databricks native jobs and Delta Live tables. While there is still a lot of reading that you may have to do before you find yourself to be an expert on this topic, this chapter gave you a nice kickstart in working effectively with Databricks jobs.

Multiple choice questions

1. Which of the following cloud-based tool sets can be used to orchestrate Databricks workflows?
    a. Airflow on AWS (Amazon managed apache airflow)
    b. Data Factory on Azure
    c. Delta Live tables
    d. All the above
2. What are the different ways to use Data Factory for orchestration?
    a. Importing the Databricks notebook and executing in the Azure data factory pipeline
    b. Using Notebook or Python activity
    c. Import pipeline file using Azure functions
3. How jobs can be created in Databricks?
    a. Through jobs UI
    b. Through jobs API
    c. Through Azure CLI
    d. Through Databricks CLI
4. Databricks maintains a history of our job runs for up to _________ days?
    a. 30 days
    b. 50 days
    c. 60 days
    d. 100 days

Answers

1. **d**
2. **a, b**
3. **a, b, d**
4. **c**

CHAPTER 5

Simplified ETL with Delta Live Tables

Delta Live Tables is a framework that helps the data engineering teams to build reliable data pipelines to cater high quality data on the delta lake. Delta live tables simplify the ETL pipeline development with automatic testing and visibility for end-to-end pipeline monitoring.

In the last chapter, we explored how to perform data sharing from the Databricks Lakehouse platform. You also learned in detail about how to schedule and manage the jobs using the Databricks UI as well as API.

Structure

This chapter deals with Delta Live Tables components and how to use them to implement and run a Delta Live Tables pipeline. Here are the topics covered in the chapter:

- Delta Live Tables concepts
- Development workflow with Delta Live Tables
- Delta Live Table configurations

Objectives

After studying this chapter, you should be able to understand in detail the fundamentals of Delta Live Tables. We will also look at creating a development workflow to build ETL pipelines with the Delta Live Tables to simplify development testing and monitoring. Additionally, we will explore how to configure Delta Live Tables.

Delta Live Table concepts

Delta Live Table is the foundation for creating reliable, maintainable, and stable data processing pipelines with Databricks Lakehouse platform. Delta Live Table makes it easier to design the data pipelines and control the quality of data.

Delta Live Table can be used for creating simplified ETL pipelines:

- Orchestration
- Cluster management
- Monitoring
- Data quality
- Efficient error handling

Features of Delta Live Table are as follows:

- **Ease of creating data pipelines**: With the Delta Live Table, we can easily create an end-to-end data pipeline (refer to *Figure 5.1*), starting from getting data from the data source to transformation logic and storing the output to destination so that we don't have to manually integrate these stages explicitly:

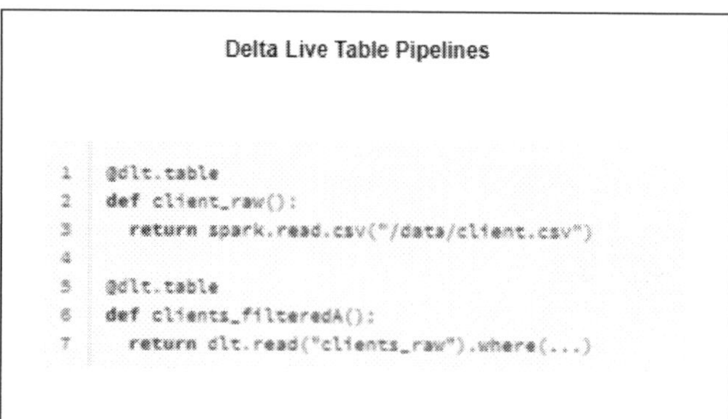

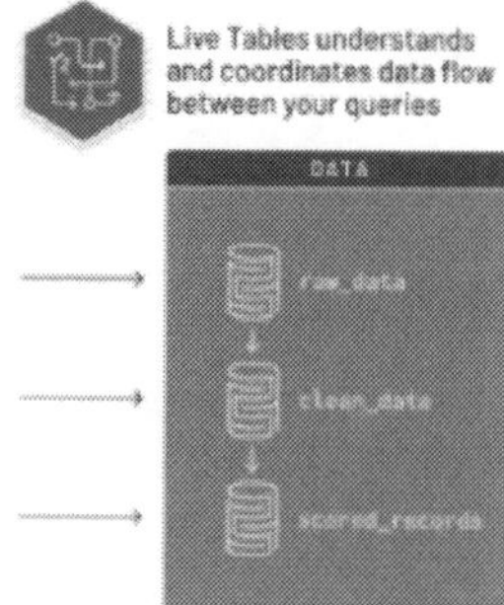

Figure 5.1: Delta Live Table pipelines

- **Automated testing:** Use of the Delta Live Table enables the use case to ensure that we are working with the quality data for BI, data science, and ML use cases for the consumers. We can also enhance and monitor the data quality trends over time to know more about how the data is evolving.
- **Ease of recovery and detailed monitoring:** We can reduce downtime by enabling automatic error handling and make faster deployment with one-click deployment:

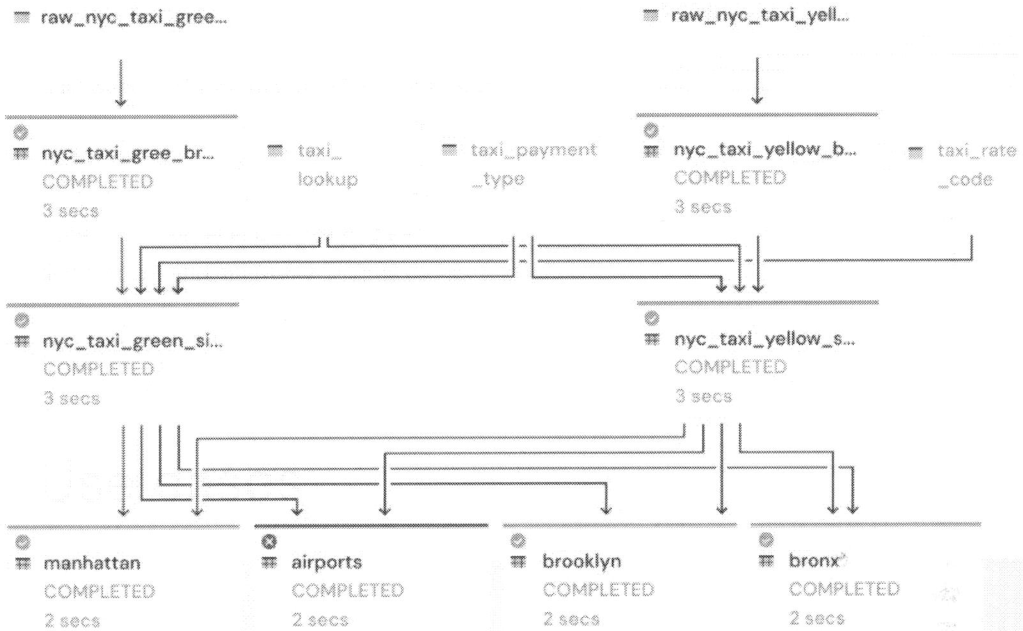

***Figure 5.2**: Ease of recovery and end-to-end monitoring*

***Image source**: https://databricks.com/product/delta-live-tables*

Components of the Delta Live Table

Let's understand the components of the Delta Live Table and how we can build them together to create a Delta Live Table pipeline:

- **Pipeline**: Pipeline is a fundamental unit of execution in the Delta Live Table. Pipeline can be considered as a **Directed Acyclic Graph** (**DAG**), which links the data from the source dataset to target datasets.

  We can create delta live tables using SQL queries or Python. We also need to configure the pipeline settings to run the pipeline, including the data quality constraints with datasets.

Pipeline subcomponents can be defined as follows:

- o **Queries**: Pipeline queries contain the actual implementation logic for the data transformations from the source dataset to the target dataset using Python or SQL.
- o **Expectations**: We can specify the data quality expectations to control the data quality of the dataset. Expectations provide flexibility to process the records even though records don't meet the criteria. We can define expectations to **retain/drop records or hold the pipeline** when the records fail.

- **Pipeline settings**: We can define the pipeline settings in the JSON format with parameters required to run the pipeline:
  - o Libraries
  - o Cloud storage location
  - o Other dependent Python packages
  - o Optional spark cluster configuration
- **Pipeline update:** Once the pipeline is created, we can start the update to run the pipeline. Update will execute these activities:
  - o Start Databricks cluster
  - o Discover all tables and views
  - o Create/update all tables and views with the most recent data
- **Datasets**: Delta Live Table pipeline has two types of datasets:
  - o **Views**: Views in the Delta Live Table are the same as temporary views in SQL. Views simplify the query by breaking down the complex queries into the simpler and smaller queries. Views exist only during the pipeline run and can't be queries interactively.
  - o **Tables**: Delta Live Table creates tables in the delta format and makes sure they are updated with the results which the query creates. If table is an incremental table, then data will be continuously ingested into the table.

    We can also create temporary tables, as follows, to prevent the publishing of tables that should not be accessed for external use:

```
SQL

CREATE TEMPORARY LIVE TABLE temp_table
AS SELECT ... ;
```

***Figure 5.3**: Temporary table*

- **Continuous and triggered pipelines**: We can create Delta Live Tables with continuous and triggered pipelines.
  - **Triggered pipelines**: It will update the table when the data is available for the Delta Live Table. It will also stop the cluster once the data update is done. Delta Live Table analyzes the dependencies between the tables. Tables will be updated by the pipeline when the dependent tables are updated.
  - **Continuous pipeline**: Continuous pipelines will update the tables continuously whenever the input data changes. The advantage of a continuous pipeline is that most recent data will be available and accessible, but it requires always running clusters.

  We can configure the execution mode flag using the **`continuous`** flag in the pipeline setting. By default, the execution mode is *triggered only*, as shown here:

```
{
  ...
  "continuous": "true",
  ...
}
```

***Figure 5.4**: Delta Live Table execution mode*

The execution mode is independent of the type of table being computed. We can also configure the update frequency for tables in order to put delay while ingesting the data to the table:

```
Python

spark_conf={"pipelines.trigger.interval", "1 hour"}
```

***Figure 5.5**: Delta Live Table trigger interval*

In order to optimize the workload while creating the pipeline, we can switch the execution mode between the **`Development` and `Production`** mode.

As shown in the following screenshot, we can switch between the **`Development`** and **`Production`** mode from the pipeline UI:

***Figure 5.6**: Delta Live Table execution mode*

- o **Development mode**: In this mode, the Delta Live Table system restarts the cluster to avoid restart overhead.

  It also disables the retry interval to detect and fix the error.

- o **Production mode**: It restarts the cluster only for specific errors.

- **Publish tables**: We can also publish the output of Delta Live Table to make it available for the query. We can specify the target settings in the Delta Live Table settings:

```
{
  ...
  "target": "prod_customer_data"
  ...
}
```

***Figure 5.7**: Delta Live Table publish tables*

When we specify the **`target`** property, it will only publish the table and the metadata associated with it. Views will not be published.

- **Pipeline implementation**: Now, we will explore Delta Live Table pipeline implementation in detail.

- **Notebooks**: We can use Databricks notebooks to implement the Delta Live Table in the pipeline. We can use a single notebook or multiple notebooks using Python or SQL.

- **Queries**: We can implement the Delta Live Table either using SQL or Python.

  In Python, we can use the **`@view`** or **`@table`** decorator to define the view or table in Python. In the following example, we are first creating the view named **`pnc_raw,`** which reads the JSON file and creates a **`filtered_data`** table:

```
@dlt.view
def pnc_raw():
  return spark.read.json("/databricks-datasets/pnc/sample/json/")

# Use the function name as the table name
@dlt.table
def filtered_data():
  return dlt.read("pnc_raw").where(...)

# Use the name parameter as the table name
@dlt.table(
  name="filtered_data")
def create_filtered_data():
  return dlt.read("pnc_raw").where(...)
```

***Figure 5.8**: Delta Live Table publish tables*

Apart from reading the data from the external files, we can access the datasets defined in the pipeline with the Delta Live Table **read()** function:

```
@dlt.table
def client_raw():
  return spark.read.csv("/data/client.csv")

@dlt.table
def clients_filteredA():
  return dlt.read("clients_raw").where(...)
```

***Figure 5.9**: Delta Live Table publish tables*

Delta Live Table internally takes care of dependency between the datasets. Delta Live table uses this dependency information to know the execution order while performing the update and tracking the lineage information in the pipeline.

It is also possible to return the dataset using the **spark.sql** expression in the query function:

```
@dlt.table
def all_customers():
  return spark.sql("SELECT * FROM LIVE.customers WHERE city = 'all'")
```

***Figure 5.10**: Delta Live Table function to select all customers*

In SQL, we can create the view or table using **`CREATE LIVE VIEW`** or **`CREATE LIVE TABLE`.** Let's understand the example by creating a view and table by using the JSON file and as an input:

```
%sql

CREATE LIVE TABLE all_raw AS SELECT * FROM json.`/databricks-datasets/nyc/sample/json/`

CREATE LIVE TABLE filtered_data AS SELECT name FROM LIVE.all_raw
```

***Figure 5.11**: Delta Live Table - create dataset*

Delta Live Table automatically detects the dependencies between the datasets defined in the pipeline and uses those dependencies to determine the execution order to record lineage.

External data sources

We can use the following external data sources to create datasets:

- Data source supported by Databricks runtime
- Any cloud storage supported files
- DBFS files

We can use the **autoloader** feature in the Databricks to read the data from the supported files. Auto loader is an efficient feature, which is extensible and supports schema inference.

Let's look at the example of auto loader to create datasets from the CSV and JSON files:

```
@dlt.table
def flights():
  return (
    spark.readStream.format("cloudFiles").option("cloudFiles.format", "csv").load("/databricks-datasets/flights/"))

@dlt.table
def flight_sales_orders():
  return (
    spark.readStream.format("cloudFiles").option("cloudFiles.format", "json").load("/databricks-datasets/flight_sales_orders/")
  )
```

***Figure 5.12**: Delta Live Table - auto loader*

Expectations

We can define expectations in the Delta Live Table to define the data quality constraints on the datasets. Expectations can be defined with the following configurations:

- Description
- Invariant

- Action to take when the record fails

We can apply the expectations to query using the Python decorators or SQL constraints in SQL query.

We can use **expect**, **expect or drop** and **expect** or **fail** with Python or SQL queries to define the data quality constraint. Decorators take a Python dictionary as an input. which is the *key-value pair* format. Here, *key* is the expectation **name,** and **value** is the expectation constraint:

i. **Keep invalid records**: If you want to keep the invalid records while defining the expectations, we can use the **`expect`** operator. Records that don't meet the expectation criteria will be added to the **`target`** dataset, including the valid records. We can see the invalid records using the following code:

   Python

   ```
   @dlt.expect("valid country", "col("country") = 'USA'")
   ```

   SQL

   ```
   CONSTRAINT valid_country EXPECT (country = 'USA')
   ```

ii. **Drop invalid records**: We can use the **`expect or drop`** operator to prevent the processing of invalid records. Records that don't meet the criteria will be dropped from the **`target`** dataset:

   Python

   ```
   @dlt.expect_or_drop("valid_account_no", "current_account_no IS NOT NULL AND current_account_name IS NOT NULL")
   ```

   SQL

   ```
   CONSTRAINT valid_account_no EXPECT (current_account_no IS NOT NULL and current_account_name IS NOT NULL) ON VIOLATION DROP ROW
   ```

iii. **Fail on Invalid Records:** When we want to halt the execution of invalid records, we can use the `expect` or `fail` operator to halt the execution immediately when the record fails the validation:

   Python

   ```
   @dlt.expect_or_fail("valid_positive_no", "count > 0")
   ```

   SQL

   ```
   CONSTRAINT valid_positive_no EXPECT (count > 0) ON VIOLATION FAIL UPDATE
   ```

When the pipeline fails due to the invalid records, we must fix the pipeline code to handle the invalid data before executing the pipeline again.

Fail expectations modify the spark query plan of the transformation to track the information to detect and report the violations.

iv. **Multiple expectations**: We can also define multiple expectations to handle the valid or invalid records to include in the target dataset:

- **expect_all**: We can use **expect_all** to specify various data quality constraints when records that don't meet the expectation criteria need to be included in the **target** dataset:

```
@dlt.expect_all({"valid_count": "count > 0", "valid_account_no": "current_account_no IS NOT NULL AND current_account_name IS NOT NULL"})
```

- **expect_all_or_drop:** We can use **expect_all_or_drop** to specify multiple data quality constraints when records that fail the validation should be dropped from the **target** dataset:

```
@dlt.expect_all_or_drop({"valid_count": "count > 0", "valid_account_no": "current_account_no IS NOT NULL AND current_account_name IS NOT NULL"})
```

- **expect_all_or_fail**: We can use **expect_all_or_fail** to specify the constraints when the record fails validation and then halt the pipeline:

```
@dlt.expect_all_or_fail({"valid_count": "count > 0", "valid_account_number": "current_account_number IS NOT NULL AND current_account_name IS NOT NULL"})
```

After understanding the fundamental concepts of Delta Live Table, let us understand the workflow of Delta Live Table pipelines to test and debug the transformation logic in the **development**, **test**, **acceptance**, and **production** environment.

We can create a generic pipeline to combine the Delta Live Table functionality with the Databricks **Repos**:

```
{
  "name": "Data Ingest to Development",
  "target": "customers_dev",
  "libraries": ["/Repos/user@databricks.com/ingestion/etl.py"],
}
```

```
{
  "name": "Data Ingest to Production",
  "target": "customers_production",
  "libraries": ["/Repos/production/ingestion/etl.py"],
}
```

We can also create parameters in the pipeline using the pipeline settings. Parameterization enables the following use cases:

- Faster testing
- Reduce the amount of data processing
- Reuse the transformation logic

For example, we can create and use pipeline variable **country** to get the value of country dynamically:

SQL

```
CREATE LIVE TABLE countries
AS SELECT * FROM all_countries WHERE country = ${mypipeline.country};
```

Python

```
@dlt.table
def countries():
  start_date = spark.conf.get("mypipeline.country")
  return read("sourceTable").where(col("date") > start_date)
```

Many applications also want to ingest the data incrementally in near real time. We can use Delta Live Table to incrementally load the data which will reduce the cost of data ingestion and make sure that the data is available for access without any delays.

Python

```
@dlt.table
def streaming_ingest_table:
  return dlt.read_stream("streaming_ingestion_table").where(...)
```

SQL

```
CREATE INCREMENTAL LIVE TABLE streaming_ingestion_table
AS SELECT * FROM STREAM(LIVE.streaming_bronze_table)
WHERE ...
```

If you want to refresh the data, then go to the *Pipeline Details* page and click on the *Refresh* button to select the **`Full Refresh`** option.

Creating Delta Live Tables using Python and SQL

Now, let us also explore in detail how to create Delta Live Tables using Python and SQL:

- **Python**

  a) Create table using Python. We have to use **`@table`** decorator to create a table:

```
import dlt

@dlt.table(
  name="<name>",
  comment="<comment>",
  spark_conf={"<key>" : "<value", "<key" : "<value>"},
  table_properties={"<key>" : "<value>", "<key>" : "<value>"},
  path="<storage-location-path>",
  partition_cols=["<partition-column>", "<partition-column>"],
  schema="schema-definition")
@dlt.expect
@dlt.expect_or_fail
@dlt.expect_or_drop
@dlt.expect_all
@dlt.expect_all_or_drop
@dlt.expect_all_or_fail
def <function-name>():
    return (<query>)
```

Figure 5.13: Delta Live Table - create table using Python

  b) **Create view:** View can be created using the **`@view`**:

```
import dlt

@dlt.view(
  name="<name>",
  comment="<comment>")
@dlt.expect
@dlt.expect_or_fail
@dlt.expect_or_drop
@dlt.expect_all
@dlt.expect_all_or_drop
@dlt.expect_all_or_fail
def <function-name>():
    return (<query>)
```

Figure 5.14: Delta Live Table - create view using Python

If we want to install the Python libraries while creating the Delta Live Table, we can use the magic command **%pip install**. Once we install the Python package, every Python notebook used in the pipeline has access to the installed libraries:

```
%pip install logger

import pandas

@dlt.table
def dataset():
    df=pd.date_range("20130101", periods=6)
    return dlt.read(..)
```

***Figure 5.15**: Delta Live Table - install Python packages*

- **SQL**

a) Create table:

```
CREATE [TEMPORARY] [INCREMENTAL] LIVE TABLE table_name
  [(
    [
    col_name1 col_type1 [ COMMENT col_comment1 ],
    col_name2 col_type2 [ COMMENT col_comment2 ],
    ...
    ]
    [
    CONSTRAINT expectation_name_1 EXPECT (expectation_expr1) [ON VIOLATION { FAIL UPDATE | DROP ROW }],
    CONSTRAINT expectation_name_2 EXPECT (expectation_expr2) [ON VIOLATION { FAIL UPDATE | DROP ROW }],
    ...
    ]
  )]
  [USING DELTA]
  [PARTITIONED BY (col_name1, col_name2, ... )]
  [LOCATION path]
  [COMMENT table_comment]
  [TBLPROPERTIES (key1 [ = ] val1, key2 [ = ] val2, ... )]
  AS select_statement
```

***Figure 5.16**: Delta Live Table - create table using SQL*

b) Create view:

```
CREATE [INCREMENTAL] LIVE VIEW view_name
  [(
    [
    col_name1 [ COMMENT col_comment1 ],
    col_name2 [ COMMENT col_comment2 ],
    ...
    ]
    [
    CONSTRAINT expectation_name_1 EXPECT (expectation_expr1) [ON VIOLATION { FAIL UPDATE | DROP ROW }],
    CONSTRAINT expectation_name_2 EXPECT (expectation_expr2) [ON VIOLATION { FAIL UPDATE | DROP ROW }],
    ...
    ]
  )]
  [COMMENT view_comment]
  AS select_statement
```

***Figure 5.17**: Delta Live Table - create view using SQL*

Delta Live Table also supports API to **create**, **edit**, **delete**, **start**, and **view** details about the pipeline.

c) Create pipeline using API:

Endpoint name: **`2.0/pipelines`**

HTTP Method: **`POST`**

When we execute the pipeline, it will create a new pipeline:

Example

The following example will create pipeline named **`Data pipeline (SQL)`**:

```
{
  "name": "Data pipeline (SQL)",
  "storage": "/Users/username/data",
  "clusters": [
    {
      "label": "default",
      "autoscale": {
        "min_workers": 1,
        "max_workers": 5
      }
    }
  ],
  "libraries": [
    {
      "notebook": {
        "path": "/Users/username/DLT Notebooks/Delta Live Tables
Data Pipelines"
      }
    }
  ],
  "continuous": false
}
```

Here, make sure to replace the **<databricks-instance>** name with the workspace name.

d) Edit pipeline:

Endpoint name: **2.0/pipelines/{pipeline_id}**

HTTP Method: **PUT**

This endpoint will allow us to edit/update the existing pipelines.

Example:

```
{
"id": "{pipeline id}",
"name": "Data Ingestion pipeline",
"storage": "/Users/username/data",
"clusters": [
  {
    "label": "default",
    "autoscale": {
      "min_workers": 1,
      "max_workers": 5
    }
  }
],
"libraries": [
  {
    "notebook": {
       "path": "/Users/username/DLT Notebooks/Delta Live Tables
Data Ingestion"
    }
  }
],
"target": "data_ingestion_data",
"continuous": false
}
```

e) Delete pipeline:

Endpoint name: **`2.0/pipelines/{pipeline_id}`**

HTTP method: **`DELETE`**

We can delete the pipeline using this endpoint.

Example:

```
curl --netrc --request DELETE \
https://<databricks-instance>/api/2.0/pipelines/{pipeline}
```

Here, we have to replace the **`databricks-instance`** with the actual Databricks workspace name.

f) Get pipeline details:

Endpoint name: **`2.0/pipelines/{pipeline_id}`**

HTTP method: **`GET`**

We can get the pipeline details using these endpoints.

Example:

Sample response of the endpoint looks as follows:


```
{
  "pipeline_id": "{pipelineid}",
  "spec": {
    "id": "{id}",
    "name": "Data Ingestion pipeline",
    "storage": "/Users/username/data",
    "clusters": [
      {
        "label": "default",
        "autoscale": {
          "min_workers": 1,
          "max_workers": 5
        }
      }
    ],
    "libraries": [
```

```
      {
        "notebook": {
            "path": "/Users/username/DLT Notebooks/Data Ingestion
Pipeline"
        }
      }
    ],
    "target": "data_ingestion",
    "continuous": false
  },
  "state": "IDLE",
  "cluster_id": "{clusterid}",
  "name": "Data Ingestion pipeline",
  "creator_user_name": "username",
  "latest_updates": [
    {
      "update_id": "{update_id}",
      "state": "COMPLETED",
      "creation_time": "2021-11-06T00:37:30.279Z"
    },
    {
      "update_id": "{update_id}",
      "state": "CANCELED",
      "creation_time": "2021-11-06T00:35:51.902Z"
    },
    {
      "update_id": "{update_id}",
      "state": "FAILED",
      "creation_time": "2021-11-06T00:33:38.565Z"
    }
  ]
}
```

g) Fetch update details:

Endpoint name: **`2.0/pipelines/{pipeline_id}/updates/{update_id}`**

HTTP method: **`GET`**

We can get all details about the pipeline update using this endpoint.

Example:

Sample response of the endpoint looks as follows:

```
{
"update": {
  "pipeline_id": "{pipelineid}",
  "update_id": "{updateid}",
  "config": {
    "id": "{id}",
    "name": "Streaming Data pipeline",
    "storage": "/Users/username/data/streaming",
    "configuration": {
      "pipelines.numStreamRetryAttempts": "5"
    },
    "clusters": [
      {
        "label": "default",
        "autoscale": {
          "min_workers": 1,
          "max_workers": 5
        }
      }
    ],
    "libraries": [
      {
        "notebook": {
          "path": "/Users/username/DLT Notebooks/Delta Live Ta-
bles Streaming Data"
```

```
            }
          }
        ],
        "target": "streaming_data",
        "filters": {},
        "email_notifications": {},
        "continuous": false,
        "development": false
      },
      "cause": "API_CALL",
      "state": "COMPLETED",
      "creation_time": 16433815050279,
      "full_refresh": true
    }
  }
```

Delta Live Table components

Let's also understand the data structure of the Delta Live Table components:

- **Notebook library**:

Field name	Type	Description
Path	STRING	Absolute notebook path

- **Pipeline library:**

Field name	Type	Description
`notebook`	Notebook library	Notebook path where the Delta Live Table definition is created

- **Pipeline settings**:

Field name	Type	Description
`id`	STRING	Unique pipeline identifier

`name`	STRING	Pipeline name
`storage`	STRING	DBFS directory
`configuration`	Map of `STRING:STRING`	Spark configuration key-value pair to run the pipeline
`clusters`	Array of pipeline clusters	Cluster to run the pipeline
`libraries`	Array of pipeline library	Notebook containing pipeline with dependent Python packages
`target`	STRING	Database name to keep the pipeline output
`development`	Boolean	Flag to check if we need to run pipeline in development or not
`continuous`	Boolean	Flag if it is a continuous pipeline

- **Pipeline state information:**

Field name	Type	Description
`state`	STRING	Pipeline status
`pipeline_id`	STRING	Pipeline identifier
`cluster_id`	STRING	Unique cluster identifier
`name`	STRING	Pipeline name
`latest_updates`	Array of `UpdateStateInfo`	Most recent update status of pipeline
`creator_user_name`	STRING	Pipeline creator name

- **Update status information:**

Field name	Type	Description
`state`	STRING	Pipeline status
`update_id`	STRING	Unique update identifier
`creation_time`	STRING	Timestamp when the update was created

Development workflow with Delta Live Table

During the traditional ETL pipeline development, we define a series of Apache Spark tasks. However, Delta Live Table manages how the data is transformed based on the target schema for each processing step.

We can create Delta Live Table pipelines using the Databricks notebook. Let us take an example to create Delta Live Table pipeline on the dataset with the following steps:

- Read the JSON file into a table
- Read the records from the table and use delta-live table expectations to create a new table that contains cleansed data
- Use records from cleaned data table to make Delta Live Table queries

Only prerequisite to start creating Delta Live Tables using the Databricks notebook is to have a cluster creation permission to start the pipeline. Delta Live Tables runtime creates a cluster before it runs the pipeline and fails if the permission doesn't exist.

Creating Delta Live Table using Databricks notebook

1. First, import the required Python packages to create Delta Live Tables in the Databricks notebooks:

```
import dlt
from pyspark.sql.functions import *
from pyspark.sql.types import *
```

2. The next step is to ingest the raw data using the delta table:

```
json_path = "/datasets/wikipedia/clickstream.json"
@dlt.create_table(
  comment="The raw wikipedia dataset for click stream"
)
```

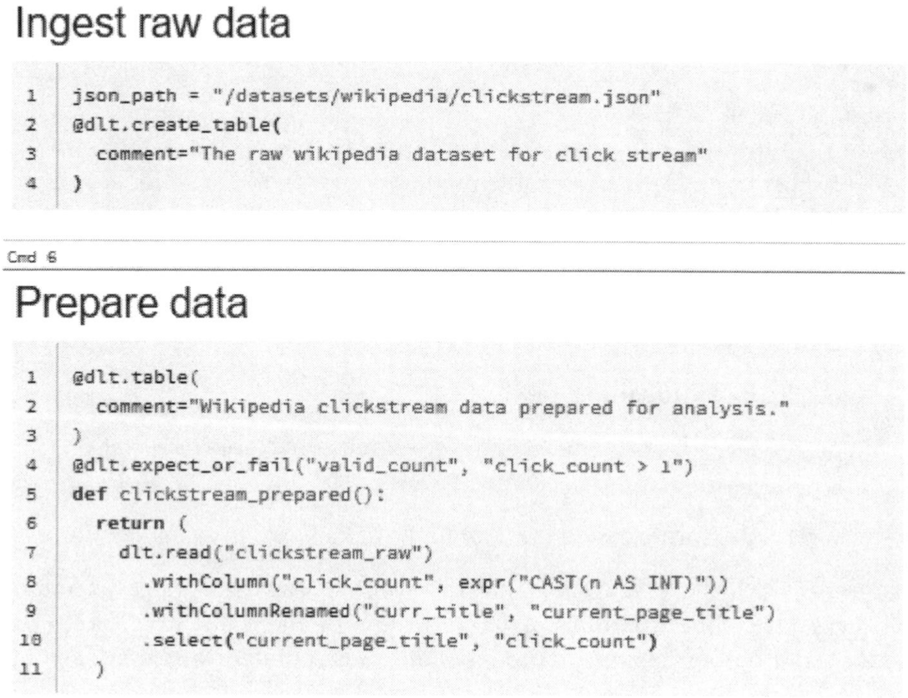

Ingest raw data

```
json_path = "/datasets/wikipedia/clickstream.json"
@dlt.create_table(
  comment="The raw wikipedia dataset for click stream"
)
```

Cmd 6

Prepare data

```
@dlt.table(
  comment="Wikipedia clickstream data prepared for analysis."
)
@dlt.expect_or_fail("valid_count", "click_count > 1")
def clickstream_prepared():
  return (
    dlt.read("clickstream_raw")
      .withColumn("click_count", expr("CAST(n AS INT)"))
      .withColumnRenamed("curr_title", "current_page_title")
      .select("current_page_title", "click_count")
  )
```

***Figure 5.18**: Databricks Delta Live Tables*

3. Once the delta table is created, prepare the data with expectations:

```
@dlt.table(
  comment="Wikipedia clickstream data prepared for analysis."
)
@dlt.expect_or_fail("valid_count", "click_count > 1")
def clickstream_prepared():
  return (
    dlt.read("clickstream_raw")
      .withColumn("click_count", expr("CAST(n AS INT)"))
      .withColumnRenamed("curr_title", "current_page_title")
      .select("current_page_title", "click_count")
  )
```

Create pipeline

1. Go to the **`Jobs`** tab from the Databricks UI and click on the **`Pipelines`** tab to create the pipeline:

***Figure 5.19**: Databricks jobs*

2. Now, select the notebook that we want to use in the pipeline:

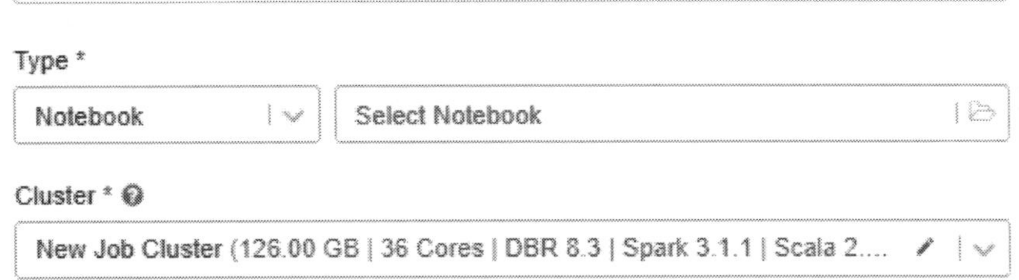

***Figure 5.20**: Databricks select notebook*

3. We need to configure the storage locations, pipeline mode (**`Triggered`** or **`Continuous`**), and minimum and maximum worker nodes for the cluster:

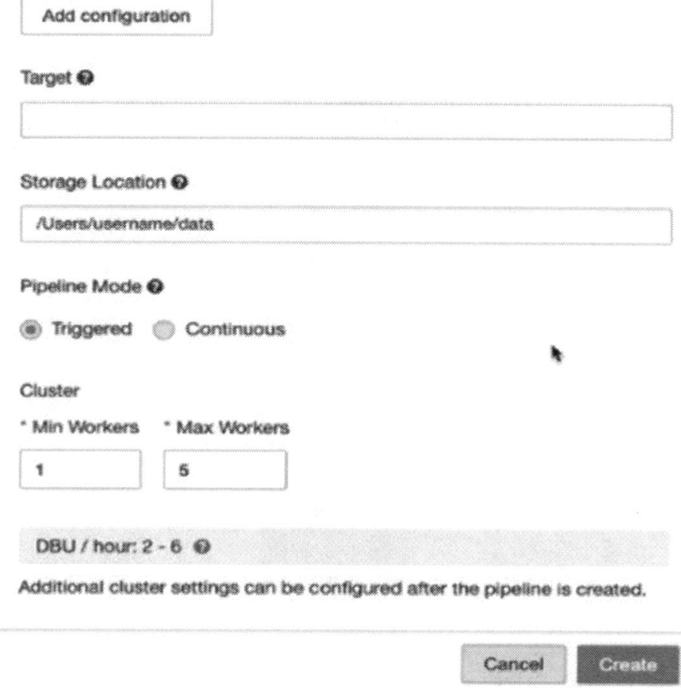

***Figure 5.21**: Databricks Delta Live Table pipeline*

4. Once all the configurations are entered, click on the **`Create` button** to create the pipeline. Once the pipeline is created, the system displays the *Pipeline details* page:

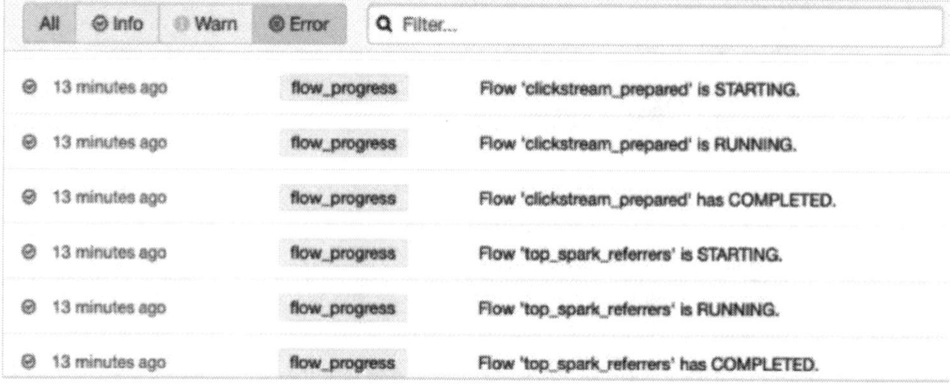

***Figure 5.22**: Databricks Pipeline details page*

5. Click on the **`Start` button** to start the pipelines. Once you click on the **`Start` button**, Databricks will start the pipeline:

***Figure 5.23**: Databricks - start pipeline*

As soon as the pipeline starts, it performs the following steps:

- Start the cluster using the cluster configurations created by the Delta Live Table
- Create table and ensure that schema is correct for the existing tables
- Update the table with the latest data
- Shut down the cluster

Once the pipeline execution is done, we can view the result of Delta Live Table pipeline processing visually in the form of graphs, schemas, and number of records processed/failed.

We need to start pipeline from the Delta Live Tables tab of the jobs' user interface. Clicking on the *Run* icon to run the pipeline will return an error.

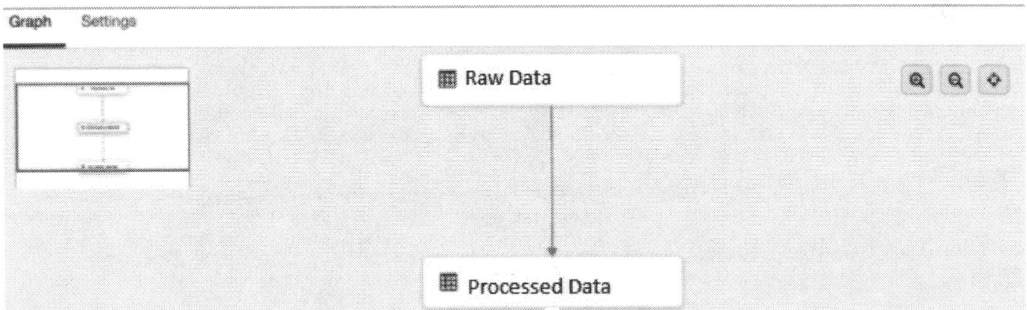

***Figure 5.24**: Delta Live Table - pipeline results*

6. Click on the dataset on the pipeline result to find the schema information about the dataset:

```
Schema
city: string
order_date: date
customer_id: string
customer_name: string
curr: string
sales: long
qantity: long
product_count: long
quantity: long
```

***Figure 5.25**: Delta Live Table - pipeline results schema*

We can also see the detailed pipeline results by clicking on the **JSON** tab:


```
    "timestamp": "2021-06-17T23:25:49.544Z",
    "message": "Flow 'clickstream_prepared' has COMPLETED.",
    "level": "INFO",
    "details": {
        "flow_progress": {
            "status": "COMPLETED",
            "metrics": {
                "num_output_rows": 22509897
            },
            "data_quality": {
                "dropped_records": 0,
                "expectations": [
                    {
                        "name": "valid_current_page_title",
                        "dataset": "clickstream_prepared",
                        "passed_records": 22509892,
                        "failed_records": 5
                    }
                ]
            }
        }
    },
    "event_type": "flow_progress"
}
```


***Figure 5.26**: Delta Live Table - pipeline results JSON format*

Once the pipeline executions are completed, it is also possible to make pipeline output available for querying. To configure data to be made available for querying, change the **target settings** to configure the database name of the table:

Edit Pipeline Settings X

```
{
    "id": "                                   ",
    "name": "DLT Wikipedia Python pipeline",
    "storage": "/Users/                                   /data",
    "libraries": [
        {
            "notebook": {
                "path":
"/Users/                               /dlt-wikipedia-python"
            }
        }
    ],
    "target": "wikipedia_analysis",
    "continuous": false
}
```

Cancel Save

Figure 5.27: Delta Live Table - query able

7. Once the configurations are done, start the pipeline; this will output the data into a table, as follows:

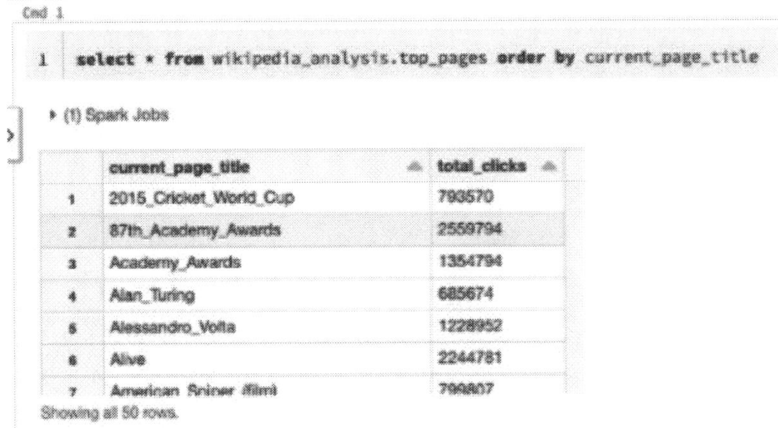

Cmd 1

```
select * from wikipedia_analysis.top_pages order by current_page_title
```

▸ (1) Spark Jobs

	current_page_title	total_clicks
1	2015_Cricket_World_Cup	793570
2	87th_Academy_Awards	2559794
3	Academy_Awards	1354794
4	Alan_Turing	685674
5	Alessandro_Volta	1228952
6	Alive	2244781
7	American_Sniper_(film)	799807

Showing all 50 rows.

Figure 5.28: Delta Live Table output table

After understanding the development flow of Delta Live Table, let's look at the use cases of Delta Live Table implementation:

- **Implement regulatory requirements**: We can capture all the information about the table for analytics and auditing purposes. We can also understand how the data flows to meet the regulatory requirements.
- **Simplified data pipeline development, deployment, and testing**: We can capture and maintain data lineage information to keep the latest data everywhere. We can query the same data in all the environments.
- **Less operational complexity with the support for both batch and streaming data**: We can build and create both batch and streaming pipelines to capture and automate the data refresh, which will save a lot of time and reduce complexity.
- Efficient in-built monitoring for data quality, logs, and real-time data updates.

Delta Live Table configurations

Delta Live Table configuration settings has a list of Databricks notebooks that implement the pipeline and parameters, which specify how to execute the pipeline in environments like development, test, acceptance, and production.

We can specify the Delta Live Table in the form of JSON, and we can also modify the settings from the Delta Live Table UI.

Now, let us explore the different Delta Live Table settings in detail:

Field name	Type	Description
`id`	string	Unique pipeline identifier
`name`	string	Pipeline name
`storage`	string	DBFS location or cloud storage for pipeline execution output
`configuration`	object	Spark cluster configurations
`Libraries`	array of objects	Array of Databricks notebook
`clusters`	array of objects	Clusters to run the pipeline
`continuous`	string	Flag to check if pipeline run continuous or not
`target`	string	Database name to persist pipeline output

***Table 5.1**: Delta Live Table settings*

We can also configure clusters used by the pipelines in the JSON format. We can specify configurations for both **default cluster** and **maintenance cluster**:

Example:

```
{
  "clusters": [
    {
      "label": "default",
      "node_type_id": "c5.4xlarge",
      "driver_node_type_id": "c5.4xlarge",
      "num_workers": 20,
      "spark_conf": {
        "spark.databricks.io.parquet.nativeReader.enabled": "false"
      },
      "aws_attributes": {
        "instance_profile_arn": "arn:aws:..."
      }
    },
    {
      "label": "maintenance",
      "aws_attributes": {
        "instance_profile_arn": "arn:aws:..."
      }
    }
  ]
}
```

We can also configure multiple notebooks in the pipeline. We have to use the libraries field to configure the pipeline with the multiple notebooks. It is flexible to add the notebooks in order since the Delta Live Table will automatically analyze the dependencies between the datasets to build the processing graph of the pipeline.

For example, the following configurations will create the pipeline, which includes the datasets defined in **notebook_1** and **notebook_2**:

```
{
  "name": "pipeline",
  "storage": "dbfs:/pipeline-examples/storage-location/example",
  "libraries": [
    { "notebook": { "path": "/notebook_1" } },
    { "notebook": { "path": "/notebook_2" } }
  ]
}
```

The following example will create configurations to trigger the pipeline implemented in **notebook_1** using DBFS for storage and run it on one note cluster:

```
{
  "name": "pipeline",
  "storage": "dbfs:/pipeline-examples/storage-location/example1",
  "clusters": [
    {
      "num_workers": 1,
      "spark_conf": {}
    }
  ],
  "libraries": [
    {
      "notebook": {
         "path": "/Users/user@databricks.com/notebook_1"
      }
    }
  ],
  "continuous": false
}
```

We can't configure the spark version for the cluster configurations. Delta Live Table clusters run with the custom version of Databricks runtime, which is updated to get the latest updates.

Conclusion

In this chapter, we explored the delta live table concepts and its features and components in detail. You also understood in detail how to create Delta Live Table pipelines using Python, SQL, and REST API. Additionally, you got an overview of how to configure different components while creating Delta Live Table pipelines.

Multiple choice questions

1. Which one of the following can be implemented using Delta Live Table?
    a. Orchestration
    b. Cluster management
    c. Monitoring
    d. All of the above
2. Can we implement automation testing using Delta Live Table?
    a. Yes
    b. No
3. What type of datasets can be used for Delta Live Tables?
    a. Tables
    b. Views
    c. Both
4. Is it possible to create Delta Live Table pipelines using REST API?
    a. Yes
    b. No
5. Can we configure storage locations while creating Delta Live Table pipelines?
    a. Yes
    b. No

Answers

1. **d**
2. **a**
3. **c**
4. **a**
5. **a**

CHAPTER 6

SCD Type 2 Implementation with Delta Lake

Databricks Lakehouse platform has a capability to enable real-time stream data processing. Structured streaming is an **Apache Spark API** by which we can expose computation on streaming data similar to the batch computation on static data.

In the last chapter, we explored how to simplify data engineering ETL pipelines using **Delta Live Tables**. In this chapter, you will learn about the real-time streaming of data using the structured streaming with *SCD Type 2 implementation* for data historization.

Structure

In this chapter, you will learn the following aspects of Databricks Lakehouse platform:

- Streaming data with structured streaming
- Change data feed

Objectives

After studying this chapter, we will be able to do end-to-end implementation of **SCD Type 2** data historization with Delta Lake and Databricks.

Streaming data with structure streaming

Working with streaming data is different from working with batch data. Apache Spark structured streaming is built on top of the **Spark SQL API** to leverage its optimization. With Spark streaming, we can process the data in near real time from the sources and output the data to the external systems:

***Figure 6.1**: Spark streaming: Input, streaming engine, sink*

Spark streaming has three major components:

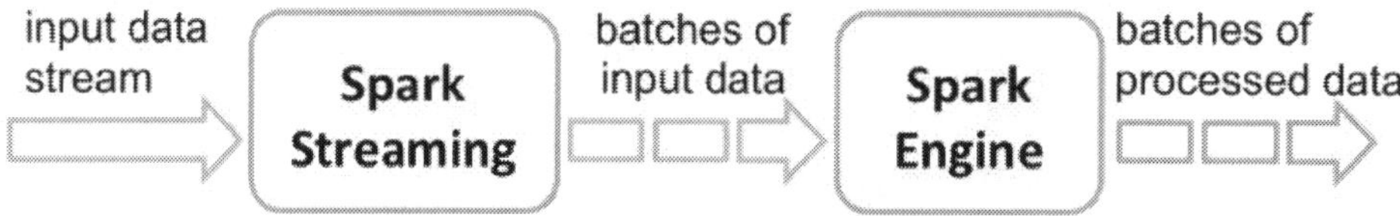

***Figure 6.2**: Spark streaming components*

- **Source input**: Input sources can be streaming **Kafka**, **Flume**, **HDFC**, and so on.
- **Streaming engine**: Streaming engines process incoming data from the various input sources.
- **Sink**: Sink takes care of storing processed data from the streaming engine like HDFS, relational database, or NO SQL database.

Let's understand spark streaming as an unbounded table where the new data will be appended when it arrives in future:

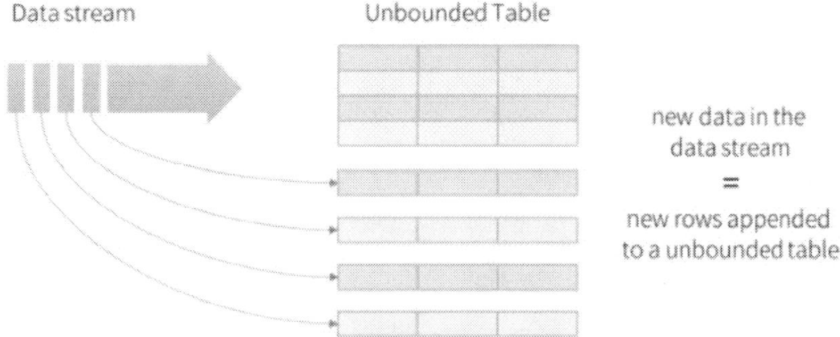

***Figure 6.3**: Streaming data as an unbounded table*

Spark will process the data in *micro batches*, which will be defined by the trigger that will process the data. Consider an example: when we define the trigger as *1 minute*, spark will create the micro batches every minute and process them accordingly. While ingesting the data based on the trigger, we can output the data in various modes:

- **Append mode**: In the append mode, Spark will only output newly processed records from the last trigger.
- **Update mode**: In this mode, Spark will output only updated rows from the last trigger. If the aggregation on streaming data is not enabled, then it will behave similar to append mode.
- **Complete mode**: In this mode, Spark will output all the rows that have been processed so far:

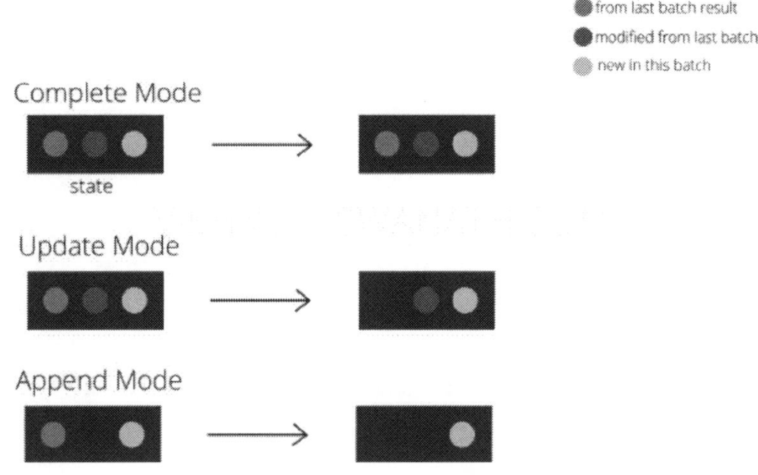

***Figure 6.4**: Streaming output modes*

Let's take an example of building the streaming application using **Spark streaming**:

1. First, list down all the files from the sample dataset path: **`/databricks-datasets/structured-streaming/events/`**.

   There are around **50** JSON files in the sample dataset. Each JSON file contains records in the form of key-value pairs.

   An example is as follows:

   ```
   {"time":1469501107,"action":"Open"}
   {"time":1469501147,"action":"Open"}
   {"time":1469501202,"action":"Open"}
   {"time":1469501219,"action":"Open"}
   ```

   ```
   %fs ls /databricks-datasets/structured-streaming/events/
   ```

path	name
dbfs:/databricks-datasets/structured-streaming/events/file-0.json	file-0.json
dbfs:/databricks-datasets/structured-streaming/events/file-1.json	file-1.json
dbfs:/databricks-datasets/structured-streaming/events/file-10.json	file-10.json
dbfs:/databricks-datasets/structured-streaming/events/file-11.json	file-11.json
dbfs:/databricks-datasets/structured-streaming/events/file-12.json	file-12.json
dbfs:/databricks-datasets/structured-streaming/events/file-13.json	file-13.json
dbfs:/databricks-datasets/structured-streaming/events/file-14.json	file-14.json

   ***Figure 6.5**: Sample dataset streaming data*

2. The next step in attempting to process the data is to query the input data interactively. In order to do that, we first need to create the DataFrame on the files and give the table name.

   Reference code is as follows:

   ```
   from pyspark.sql.types import *
   inputPath = "/databricks-datasets/structured-streaming/events/"

   # Create the schema
   jsonSchema = StructType([ StructField("time", TimestampType(),
   True), StructField("action", StringType(), True) ])

   # Create the data frame
   ```

```
InputDF = (spark.read.schema(jsonSchema).json(inputPath))
display(InputDF)
```

time	action
2016-07-28T04:19:28.000+0000	Close
2016-07-28T04:19:28.000+0000	Close
2016-07-28T04:19:29.000+0000	Open
2016-07-28T04:19:31.000+0000	Close
2016-07-28T04:19:31.000+0000	Open
2016-07-28T04:19:31.000+0000	Open
2016-07-28T04:19:32.000+0000	Close
2016-07-28T04:19:33.000+0000	Close

Figure 6.6: DataFrame output

3. Now, we can compute the number of **`open`** and **`close`** actions within the **`1 hour`** window:

```
from pyspark.sql.functions import *
# Create the DataFrame and cache it
CountsDF=(InputDF.groupBy(InputDF.action,window(InputDF.time,"1 hour")).count())
CountsDF.cache()
# Register the DataFrame
CountsDF.createOrReplaceTempView("Counts")
```

4. We can now use the SQL to query the table:

```
%sql select action, sum(count) as total_count from static_counts group by action
```

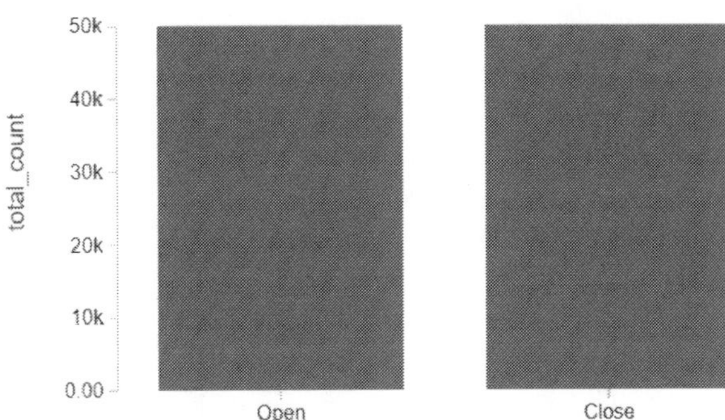

Figure 6.7: Total counts across all hours

5. After understanding the data interactively, let's convert it to the streaming query, which will continuously update the data as it comes. We need to create the streaming example by emulating the stream of data by reading one file at a time:

```
from pyspark.sql.functions import *


streamingInputDF=(spark.readStream.schema(jsonSchema).
option("maxFilesPerTrigger", 1).json(inputPath))


streamingCountsDF=(streamingInputDF.groupBy(streamingInputDF.
action, window(streamingInputDF.time, "1 hour")).count())


streamingCountsDF.isStreaming


Out[3]: True
```

From the preceding code, we can see that the DataFrame **`streamingCountsDF is a streaming`** DataFrame. We can now start the streaming computation by defining the sink:

```
spark.conf.set("spark.sql.shuffle.partitions", "2")
shuffles small

query = (
  streamingCountsDF
    .writeStream
    .format("memory")
    .queryName("counts")
    .outputMode("complete")
    .start()
)
```

▸ counts (id: [illegible]) Last updated

***Figure 6.8**: Streaming DataFrame*

6. Here, **the query** continuously picks up the files and updates the **`window`** counts:

```
%sql select action, date_format(window.end, "MMM-dd HH:mm") as time, count from
counts order by time, action
```

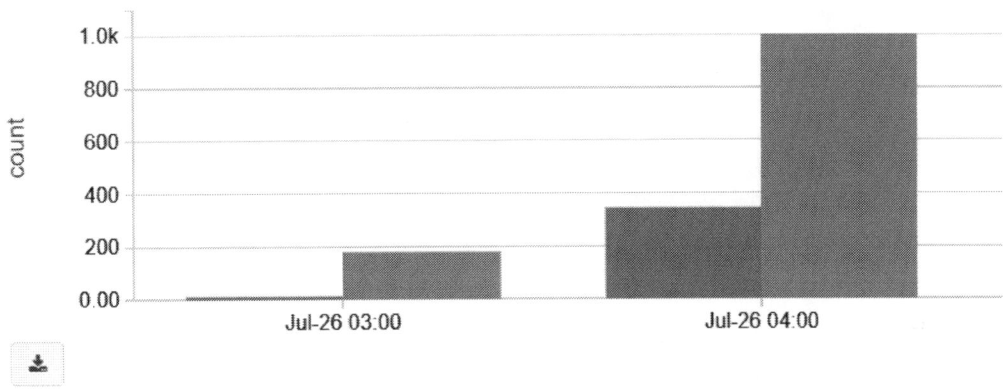

***Figure 6.9**: Streaming DataFrame visualization dashboards*

Event time is the time embedded in the data itself. Many applications want to operate in near *real time*. For example, if we want to get the number of events generated by the IOT device every minute, we want to use the time when the data was generated rather than the time when Spark received the data. Delivering end to end exactly one semantics is one of the major goals of structured streaming:

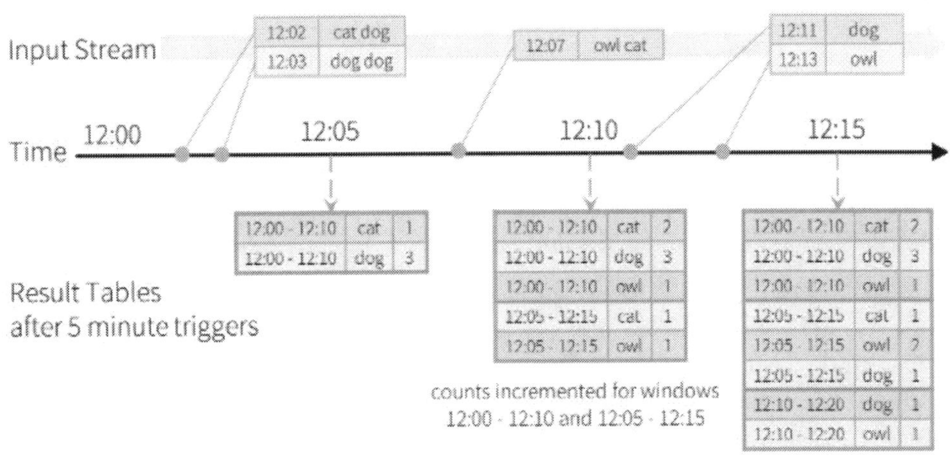

***Figure 6.10**: Windowed grouped aggregation*

Aggregation with the sliding event window is straightforward with the structure streaming, and it is very similar to the grouped aggregations. **Grouped aggregations** aggregate the value maintained for each unique value. In case of **window-based aggregations**, aggregate values are maintained for each window.

Structured streaming in Databricks has built-in support for many streaming data sources and sinks. Let's take an example of Delta Lake structured streaming with Amazon Kinesis. Here, we will use kinesis as a streaming source with Delta Lake and apache structured streaming.

Amazon Kinesis makes it easy to collect, process, and analyze real-time, streaming data so we can get timely insights and react quickly to new information. Amazon Kinesis offers key capabilities to cost-effectively process streaming data at any scale, along with the flexibility to choose the tools that best suit the requirements of your application:

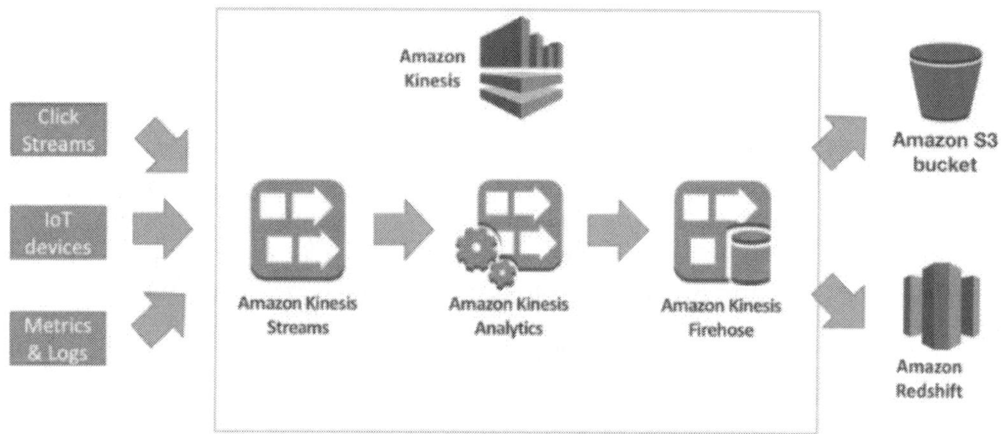

***Figure 6.11**: Amazon Kinesis*

Amazon Kinesis is also known as **KDS**. It is a popular choice for the streaming data service on AWS since it provides ease of use and serverless setup. It has individual throughput units known as **shards,** and billing is done based on shards.

Once we collect the data in KDS, we can use the deep integration of structured streaming with Delta Lake for applications such as **Log Analytics**, **Clickstream Analytics**, and **Real Time Insights**. With this structured streaming, we can continuously process the data and store it in the Delta Tables. Before we deep dive, let's look at the reference architecture diagram for the use case.

In order to understand the use case, we will first understand the Kinesis as a streaming source and key technical considerations and best practices to create a solution. Kinesis solution architecture is shown as follows:

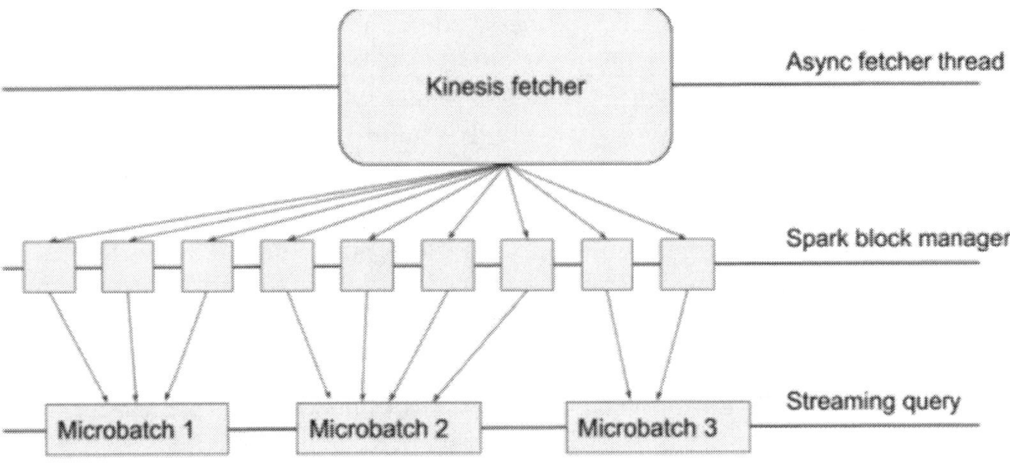

Figure 6.12: Kinesis fetcher

Databricks runtime has an out-of-the-box kinesis source. Key technical considerations and best practices of kinesis with Delta Lake is as follows:

- Databricks runtime version
- Databricks recommends using the **Databricks runtime 6.5** or above

Create Cluster

Runtime: 10.4 LTS (Scala 2.12, Spark 3.2.1)

Databricks runtime ☐ Photon Preview

Standard >	10.5 Beta	Scala 2.12, Spark 3.2.1
ML >	10.4 LTS	Scala 2.12, Spark 3.2.1
	10.3	Scala 2.12, Spark 3.2.1
	10.2	Scala 2.12, Spark 3.2.0
	10.1	Scala 2.12, Spark 3.2.0
	9.1 LTS	Scala 2.12, Spark 3.1.2
	9.0 aarch64	Graviton, Scala 2.12, Spark 3.1.2
	7.3 LTS	Scala 2.12, Spark 3.0.1
	6.4 Extended Support	Scala 2.11, Spark 2.4.5

Figure 6.13: Databricks runtime

- **Optimize prefetching**: The kinesis source executes the Spark jobs in a background thread to pre-fetch kinesis data periodically and cache it in the memory of the Spark executors. Streaming query processes the cached data after each pre-fetch step completes and makes the data available for processing.

  Default setting for the **`shardsPerTask`** configuration parameter is **`5`**. This could require a large number of CPU cores, so setting **`10`** might be a good starting point. Then, depending on the complexity of the streaming workload and data volume, we can adjust the value based on the metrics such as CPU, memory, network, and so on.

- **Enable S3 VPC endpoints**: Databricks' recommendation is to enable S3 VPC endpoints to ensure that all S3 traffic is routed on the AWS network:

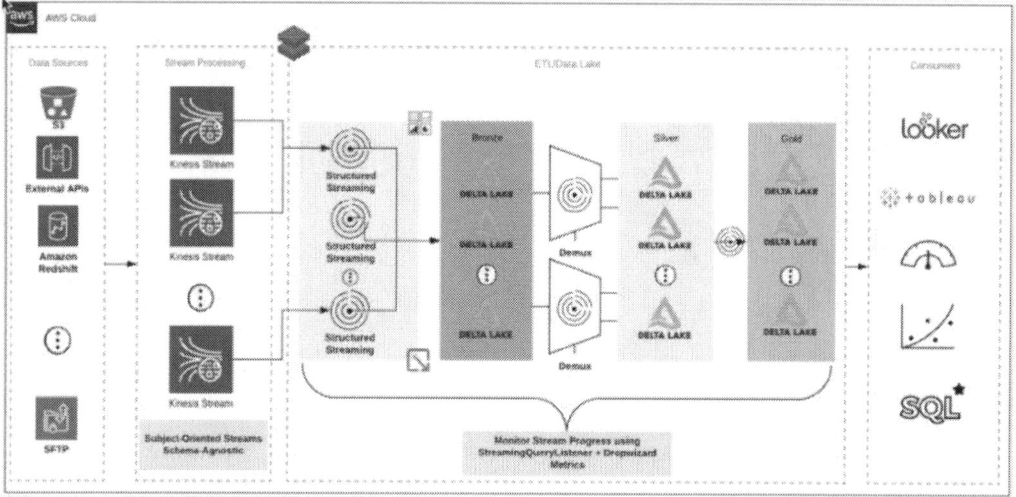

Figure 6.14: Reference architecture: Structured streaming with KDS

- **Reduce rate limit errors**: An amount of data read from kinesis can be reduced by *half* each time it encounters a rate limiting error and records events in the log. In **Databricks Runtime 6.4** and below, consistent kinesis rate limiting can lead to a stream being consumed at *1 kb/sec*.

- **Monitor streaming applications**: Databricks recommends using Spark's **Streaming Query Listener** implementation to monitor streaming applications. Observable metrics are named **arbitrary aggregate functions,** which can be defined on a DataFrame. As soon as the DataFrame execution reaches a completion point, a named event is emitted that contains the metrics for the data processed since the last completion point.

We can observe these metrics by attaching a listener to the Spark session. The listener depends on the execution mode:

- **Batch mode**: **`QueryExecutionListener`** is called when the query completes. Access the metrics using the **`QueryExecution.observedMetrics map`**:

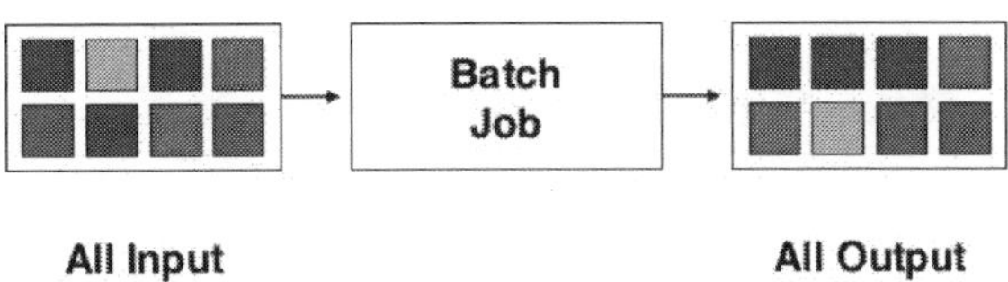

Figure 6.15: Batch processing

- **Streaming**: **`StreamingQueryListene`**r is called when the streaming query completes an *epoch*. Databricks does not support continuous execution streaming:

Figure 6.16: Spark streaming use case

Example is as follows:

```
val obs_ds = ds.observe("my_event", count(lit(1)).as("rc"),
count($"error").as("erc"))
        obs_ds.writeStream.format("...").start()

      // Monitor the metrics using a listener
      spark.streams.addListener(new StreamingQueryListener()
```

```
{
          override def onQueryProgress(event:
QueryProgressEvent): Unit = {
          event.progress.observedMetrics.get("my_event").foreach
{ row =>
          // Trigger if the number of errors exceeds 5 percent
         val num_rows = row.getAs[Long]("rc")
         val num_error_rows = row.getAs[Long]("erc")
         val ratio = num_error_rows.toDouble / num_rows
         if (ratio > 0.05) {
           // Trigger alert
         }
       }
    }
 })
```

We can also use the monitor metrics through the UI. If you are using **Databricks Runtime 7.0** or above, use the **`Streaming`** tab in the Spark UI. If you are using **Databricks Runtime 6.x**, you can use Spark's observable APIs.

- **Resharding**: Resharding is also supported by structured streaming. Increasing the number of shards is required to work with structured streaming. We don't have to switch streams or create temporary streams to balance the traffic.

Change Data Feed

Business transactions captured in the relational database are critical to the understanding of business operations. Organizations need a way to analyze the data when it is generated:

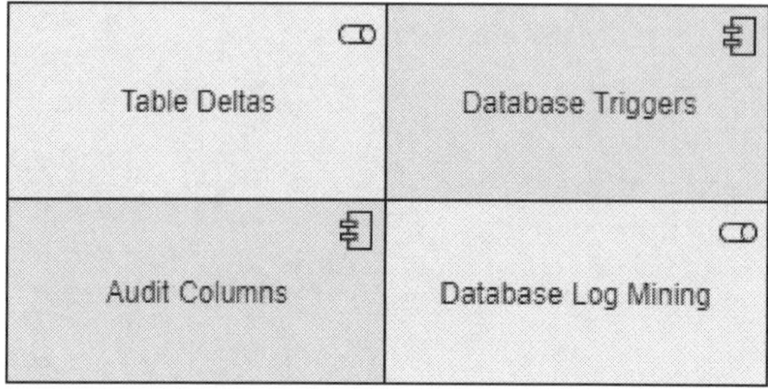

***Figure 6.17**: Change Data Feed*

Time-sensitive data is a major focus during the cloud migrations since data is constantly changing and shutting down applications. In a normal scenario, IT organizations use a batch pattern to move data once or several times a day. One disadvantage of *batch pattern* is that it introduces a delay and reduces the operational values that organizations can bring through the availability of data.

Change Data Capture (CDC) is considered to be an ideal solution to build a near real-time solution of data movement from relational databases like **Oracle**, **Azure SQL DB**, and **SQL Server** to traditional data warehouses, Data Lakes, or other databases. **Change Data Capture** is a software process that can easily recognize and track changes to data in the database. It provides a *near-real-time movement* of data by moving and processing data continuously as and when the event occurs:

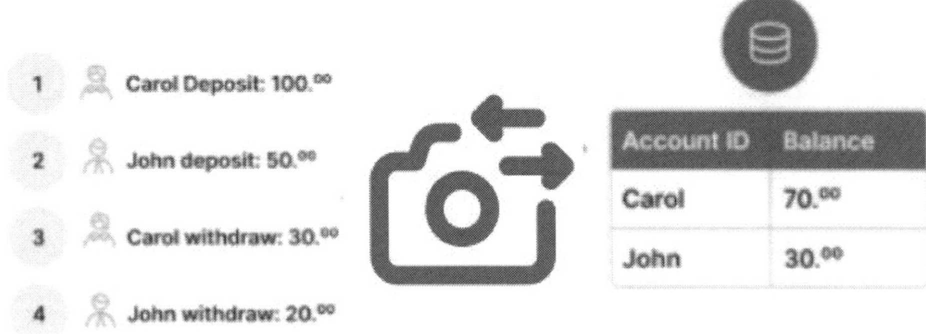

***Figure 6.18**: Change Data Capture with example*

Normally, we see change in data capture in the ingestion to analytics architecture, which is also known as the **medallion architecture**. This architecture takes raw data from the source system and refines it through bronze, silver, and gold tables. CDC and the medallion architecture provide multiple benefits to end users since only changed or added/deleted data should be processed. In addition, Databricks also has an exciting new **Change Data Feed** (CDF) feature in Delta Lake, which makes this architecture simpler to implement, and the **MERGE** operation and log versioning of Delta Lake possible:

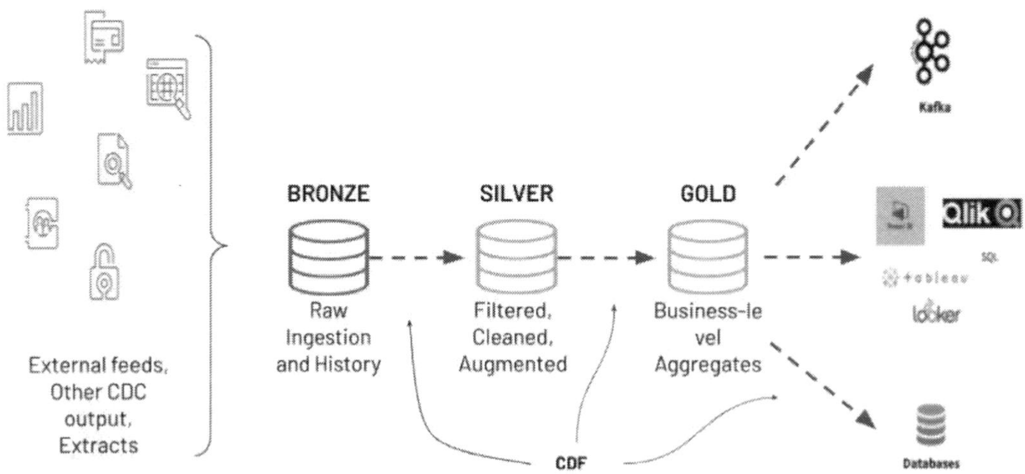

***Figure 6.19**: Change Data Feed Databricks feature*

Reference is as follows:

https://databricks.com/blog/2021/06/09/how-to-simplify-cdc-with-delta-lakes-change-data-feed.html

Many enterprise organizations use Databricks to implement the change of data capture end to end as it is simple to implement with Delta Lake as compared to other implementations and technologies. Sometimes, it is also difficult to implement CDC with the right tools. But with the Databricks CDF feature, implementation can be simpler and can easily address a few challenges related to CDC:

- **Data quality issue**: Row-level changes are very difficult to handle between various versions:

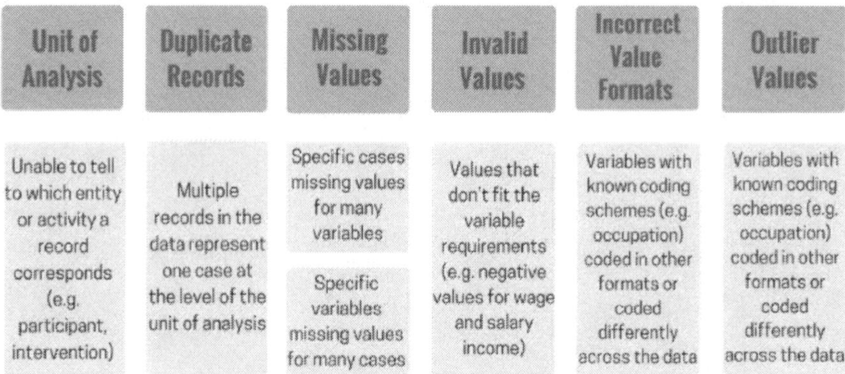

***Figure 6.20**: Common data quality issue*

- **Inefficiency**: It is inefficient to handle non-changing rows since the current version changes at the file level, and it doesn't change at the row level.

The preceding challenges will be addressed using the change data feed feature of Databricks:

- **Simplicity**: It provides an easy-to-use pattern to identify changes, which makes the code simple and easy to use.
- **Efficiency**: It makes downstream consumptions of merge, delete, and update operations efficient.

Change Data Feed captures changes only from the Delta Table and only forward looking once enabled.

With the Change Data Feed feature, the data is ingested into the `bronze` table, followed by the preprocessing in the `silver` table and finally, aggregate values in the `gold` table based on the changed data in the `silver` table.

Now, let us understand how to enable the CDF feature in Databricks:

1. To enable the CDF feature, we must first enable the feature on the said table. The following is an example of enabling CDF for the `bronze` table at table creation:

   ```
   Create Table bronze_tbl ( date string,analyst int) USING DELTA
   TBLPROPERTIES (delta.enableChangeDataFeed=true);
   ```

2. Once the Change Data Feed feature is enabled, in order to query the change data, we can use the `table_changes` operations:

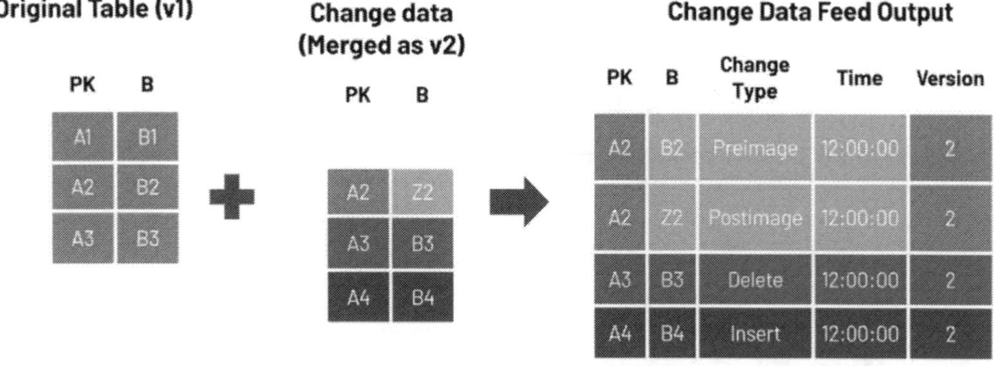

Figure 6.21: Change Data Feed: Original + merged data

The preceding example includes inserted rows, and two rows that represent pre and post images of updated rows, respectively, so that we can evaluate the differences in the changes if needed.

Let's understand the use cases of Change Data Feed implementation:

- **Silver and Gold tables**: Improve delta performance by processing only row-level changes following the **MERGE**, **UPDATE**, or **DELETE** operations to create ETL/ELT pipelines:

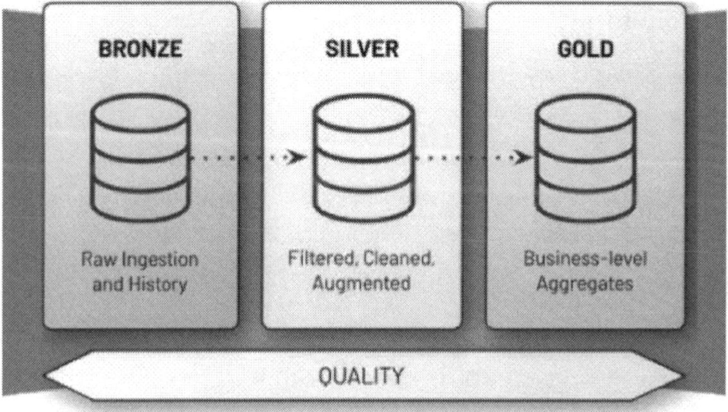

Figure 6.22: Bronze, Silver, and Gold tables

- **Materialized views**: We can create aggregated views to use in Business Intelligence and Advanced Analytics without reprocessing the underlying tables by updating them only where changes have come through instead:

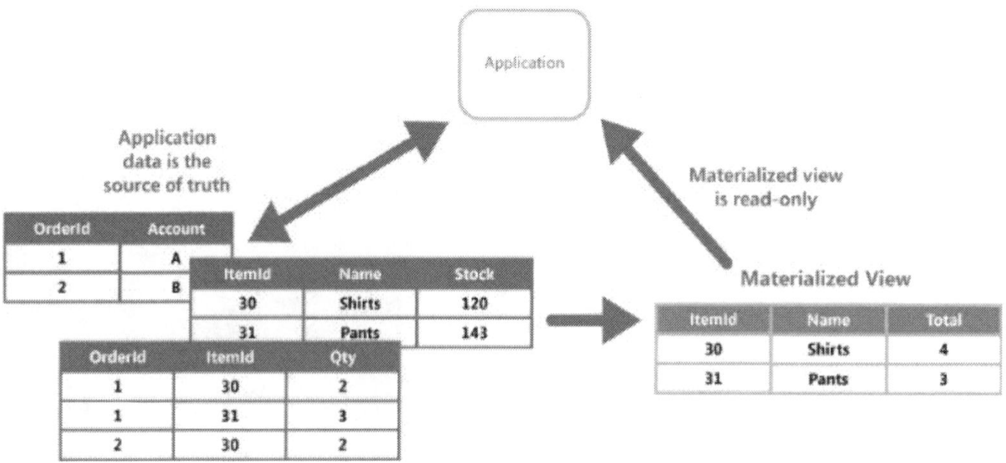

Figure 6.23: Materialized view

- **Make data available for the downstream applications**: Another use case is to send the change data feed to the downstream applications such as **Kafka** or **RDBMS,** which we can use to incrementally process in the later stage of the pipeline:

Figure 6.24: CDF as a feature to use it for downstream applications

- **Audit trail**: We can capture the Change Data Feed to view all the changes over time, including when deletes occur, what updates were made, and when new records were added.

In order to enable the change feed, we can the following configure for both existing and new tables:

- **Existing table**: First, we need to set the table property `delta.enableChangeDataFeed = true` with the `ALTER TABLE` command:

  ```
  ALTER TABLE myTable SET TBLPROPERTIES (delta.enableChangeDataFeed
  = true)
  ```

- **New table**: We need to enable table property using `delta.enableChangeDataFeed = true` in the `CREATE TABLE` command.

  Example:

  ```
  CREATE TABLE std (year INT, name STRING, age INT) TBLPROPERTIES
  (delta.enableChangeDataFeed = true)
  ```

- **All new tables**: If we want to set the change data feed for all tables, we need to configure the following property:

```
set spark.databricks.delta.properties.defaults.
enableChangeDataFeed = true;
```

We need to consider the following points before we enable the Change Data Feed.

- We can only read the table once the **Change Data Feed** option for a table is *enabled;* we can no longer write to the table using **Databricks Runtime 8.1** or below.
- Past changes to a table won't be captured with the CDF feature. Change Data Feed will be captured only once we enable the Change Data Feed.

Another use of Change Data Feed is in a **MERGE** statement. Aggregate MERGE statements can be very complex by nature, but changing the data feed feature makes the coding more simple and efficient:

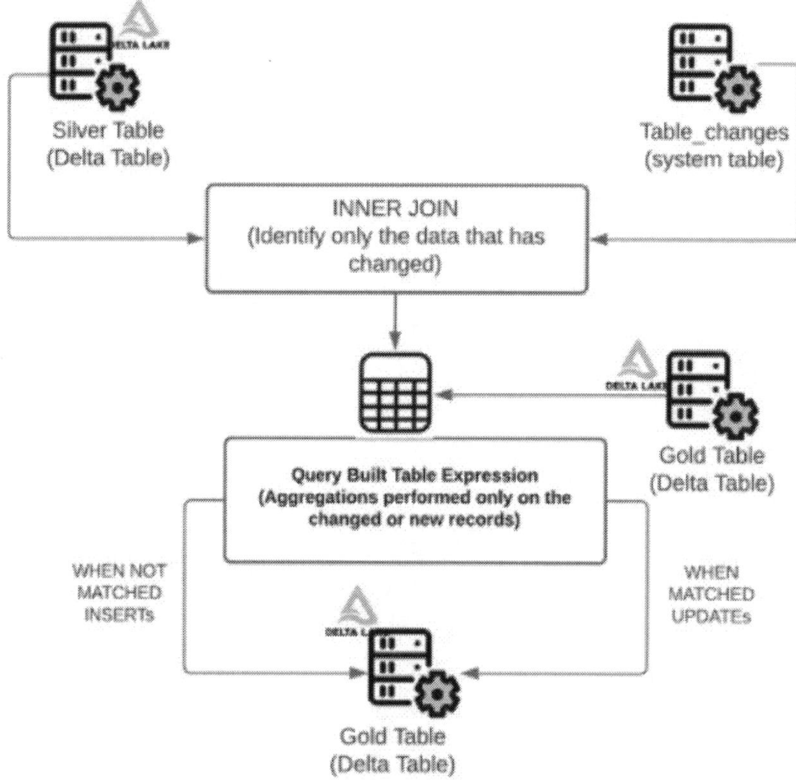

***Figure 6.25**: CDF MERGE statement*

***Reference**:*

https://databricks.com/blog/2021/06/09/how-to-simplify-cdc-with-delta-lakes-change-data-feed.html

As we can see in the preceding diagram, CDF makes it simpler for us to understand which rows have been changed as it only performs the aggregations on the data that has been changed or using the **`table_change`** operation.

Using the following query, we can understand how to use the changed data to determine dates and stock symbols that have been changed.

Example:

```
Select DISTINCT date,stock_symbol from tables_changes ('silver',2)
```

Conclusion

In this chapter, we explored the Spark streaming offering of Databricks Lakehouse platform in detail. We also learned in detail about Spark streaming use case to implement it end to end. Additionally, we understood in detail the Change Data Capture feature and how easily it can be implemented using the Change Feed Feature. So, we can enable near real-time solutions using the Spark streaming with the Databricks Lakehouse platform.

Multiple choice questions

1. What are the three main components of structured streaming?
   a. Input source
   b. Streaming engine
   c. Sink
   d. All of the above
2. Does Change Data Capture maintain the history of data?
   a. Yes
   b. No
3. What are output modes of streaming data?
   a. Append
   b. Update
   c. Complete
   d. All of the above

4. Does Databricks runtime support Amazon Kinesis as source?
    a. Yes
    b. No
5. Does Databricks have an out-of-the-box feature to capture data history?
    a. Yes
    b. No

Answers

1. **d**
2. **a**
3. **d**
4. **a**
5. **b**

CHAPTER 7
Machine Learning Model Management with Databricks

Enterprise organizations nowadays use **CI/CD pipelines** to deploy their workload to all the environments using the best practices and various DevOps tools. **MLOps** is a process of leveraging the best practices and technologies which provides scalable, centralized, and governed solutions to deploy machine learning applications in different environments. MLOps is an open-source platform for managing the end-to-end machine learning lifecycle.

In the previous chapter, we explored the **SCD Type 2** implementation using the Databricks Delta Lake. We also learned how to work with streaming data using structured streaming. In this chapter, we will explore the MLOps and MLflow with Databricks Lakehouse platform and learn in detail about the model life cycle management with MLflow.

Structure

In this chapter, we will learn end-to-end implementation of machine learning solutions using the Databricks Lakehouse platform. Here are the topics we will cover:

- Introduction to MLOps and MLflow
- Model life cycle management with MLflow

- Getting started with MLflow environment
- Feature engineering with Databricks
- Setting up MLflow project with model repository
- Train and deploy the model
- Log model metrics

Objectives

After studying this chapter, you should be able to understand the fundamentals of MLOps and MLflow functionality with Databricks Lakehouse platform. We will also explore the model lifecycle management with MLflow in detail.

Introduction to MLOps and MLflow

Organizations nowadays use the process to deploy the code automatically from the development environments to higher environments: **test**, **acceptance**, and **production** environments. Organizations have DevOps teams who develop continuous integration and continuous delivery pipelines using tools like Azure DevOps / Jenkins, and so on. Databricks Lakehouse platform has in-built integration available with DevOps tools like **Azure DevOps** or **Jenkins,** which makes the overall integration and deployment easier and faster.

For machine learning projects, most of the enterprise organizations don't have such a process in place to enable faster application deployment. Possible reasons for inefficient process are as follows:

- Data Science teams don't follow the machine learning development life cycle, like the software development life cycle followed by the developers.
- Since machine learning development and related initiatives are new to organizations, processed around machine learning are not fully integrated.
- Data Science teams don't manage the artifacts efficiently as a separate entity.
- Data Scientists use many tools that might not be as per the organization's standards.

In order to manage the Data Science workloads efficiently and address the previously mentioned problems for the Data Science workloads, we can use MLflow, an open-source platform to manage the machine learning life cycle.

While working with machine learning and Data Science projects for solving complex, real-world projects and getting business insights out of data, Data Scientists and Data Engineers have to tackle the following challenges:

- Handle large volumes of data
- Management of compute resources
- Accelerators to speed up machine learning deployment
- Rapid advances in the machine learning fields

MLOps is an engineering process to create sustainable and unified machine learning development and operations.

The following diagram shows the steps involved in the machine learning process:

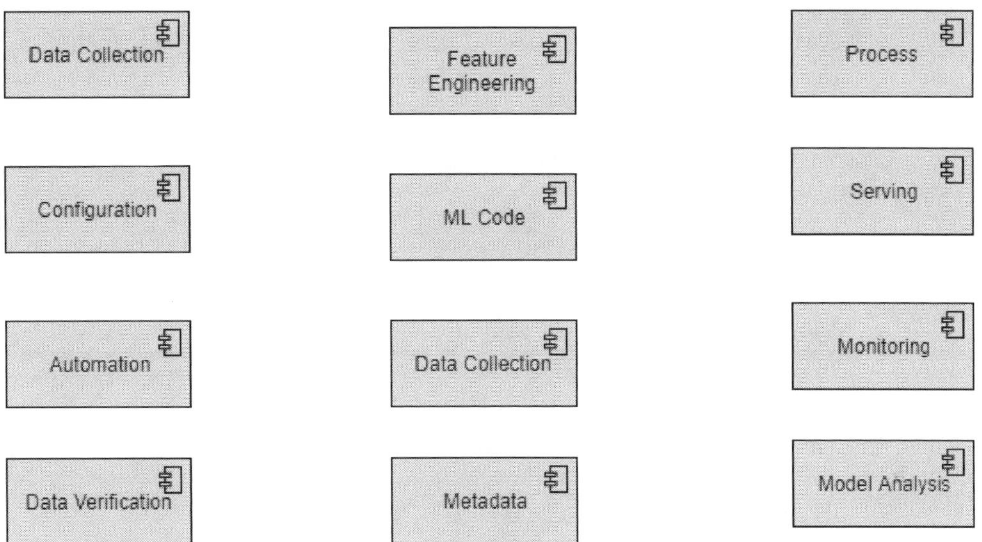

***Figure 7.1**: Elements of machine learning*

In order to decrease the time to market for the machine learning workloads, it is advised to enable continuous integration of the source control, unit testing, integration testing, and the continuous delivery of the package, but there are significant differences, as follows:

- CI pipeline focuses more on testing and validating the data, data schemes, and machine learning models.
- Continuous deployment pipeline for machine learning workload should automatically deploy the artifacts to other services.
- Continuous testing is concerned with automatically retraining and serving the machine learning model.

Typical traditional Data Science machine learning projects consist of the following steps:

- **Data extraction**: Extract relevant data from the different data sources and integrate them to create data usable for the machine learning projects.
- **Data analysis**: Perform data analytics on the top of data stored to use in the machine learning model:
    - o Understand the data.
    - o Identify the data preparation and feature engineering for the data model.
    - o **Data preparation**: Data preparation steps involve data cleansing, split data for the training and validation, and apply data transformation.
    - o **Model training**: Data Scientists create machine learning algorithms to work on the prepared data. Output of the phase is the trained machine learning model.
    - o **Model evaluation**: Machine learning model is evaluated based on the dataset to evaluate the quality of the data.
    - o **Model validation**: Model validation step is used to validate the machine learning model.
    - o **Model serving**: Once the machine learning model is valid and ready for serving, the validated model should be deployed to the target environment to serve the predictions. There are multiple ways to serve the machine learning models.
        - ▪ Micro service implementation with REST API
        - ▪ Embedded model to mobile device
        - ▪ Batch system
- **Model monitoring**: Model predictive performance should be monitored to check the performance of the model and take proactive actions:

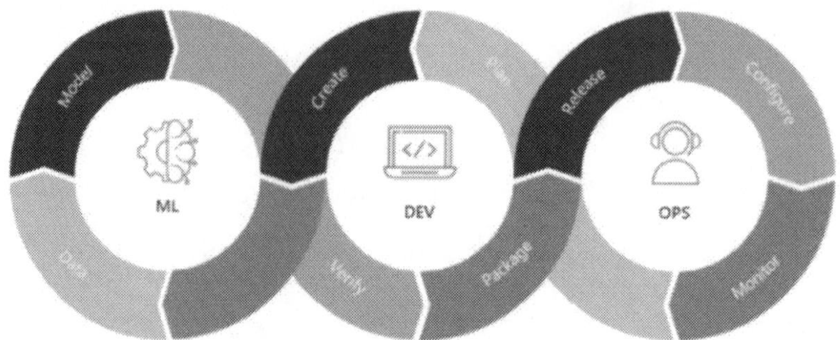

***Figure 7.2**: ML Ops life cycle*

As we can see in the pictorial representation of the ML Ops life cycle, there are multiple steps involved:

The amount of automation involved in these steps determines the maturity of the machine learning process. This automation can determine the velocity of training new models on the data.

Let's look at the steps involved in the end-to-end machine learning pipeline implementation.

At a higher level, the machine learning process involves the following steps:

- Source control
- Testing and build ML service
- ML model deployment
- Model registry
- Feature store
- Metadata store
- ML pipeline execution

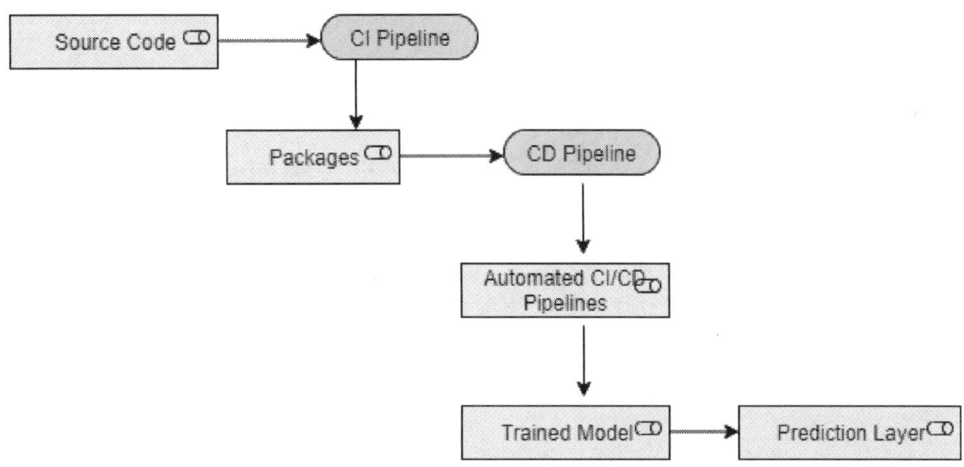

***Figure 7.3**: Automated CI/CD pipeline for machine learning process*

The preceding diagram shows the stages of an automated CI/CD pipeline:

- **Development**: Data Scientists and machine learning engineers try to develop machine learning models where the experiment's steps are orchestrated. Output of this step is the source code that will be pushed to the repository.

- **Continuous integration pipeline**: Once the source code is ready, it will be committed to the repository after creating the package and testing. Output of this stage is the package that will be deployed to the later stage.
- **Continuous delivery pipeline**: Once the CI pipeline is ready, CD pipeline will deploy the artifacts produced by the CI stage to the target environments.
- **Automated production deployment**: CI/CD pipeline will be executed automatically in the production environment based on the schedule or trigger.
- **Continuous delivery**: Once the trained model is ready, it will be deployed to the prediction service to enable service for the predictions.
- **Monitoring**: With monitoring, we can monitor the model performance based on the live data. Output of this stage is to execute the pipeline based on the model performance threshold.

Data analysis is still a manual step that will be performed by the Data Engineers/ Data Analysts based on the before the pipeline execution in the source code.

Continuous integration setup for machine learning projects

In the continuous integration pipeline setup for the machine learning projects, components are built, tested, and packaged to the source code repository. CI pipeline also has the following steps:

- Unit testing of the source code for the feature engineering implementation.
- Unit testing of the implemented functions of the machine learning models.
- Model training test coverage.
- Integration testing for the pipeline components.

Continuous delivery setup for machine learning projects

Continuous delivery pipeline enables rapid and reliable pipelines and models:

- Verify the compatibility of the model with the target infrastructure.
- Test the machine learning model endpoint with API.
- Automated model deployments to the higher environments: **test**, **acceptance**, and **production**

To enable efficient model management, Databricks uses **MLflow**, an open-source platform for the machine learning life cycle.

MLflow model registry is a centralized model store to manage the complete life cycle of the machine learning models. MLflow provides model lineage, model versioning, and stage transitions as well:

MLflow Tracking	MLflow Projects	MLflow Models	Model Registry
Record and query experiments: code, data, config, and results	Package data science code in a format to reproduce runs on any platform	Deploy machine learning models in diverse serving environments	Store, annotate, discover, and manage models in a central repository

***Figure 7.4**: MLflow*

MLflow is an open-source machine learning platform that has the following two basic features:

- **Open source**: Open-source projects that can be used by developers and end users. MLflow's open format makes it easier to share models across organizations.
- **Open user interface**: MLflow can work with any ML library, algorithm, deployment tools, or language. MLflow is based on the REST APIs and enables easy integration with various tools. We can also add existing ML code to the MLflow to share code using the ML library to share across the organization.
- MLflow has the following main components:
  - Tracking
  - Projects
  - Models
  - Repositories

  MLflow is mainly designed to work with any type of machine learning library, check the code conventions to be followed, and check the required changes to integrate with the existing source code. MLflow also makes the code reproducible and reusable by different data scientists.

  Few use cases of the MLflow can be: Data Scientists can use MLflow tracking to track the experiments locally on the machine, and large organizations can share projects, models, and results using the MLflow.

MLflow supports integration with various tools:

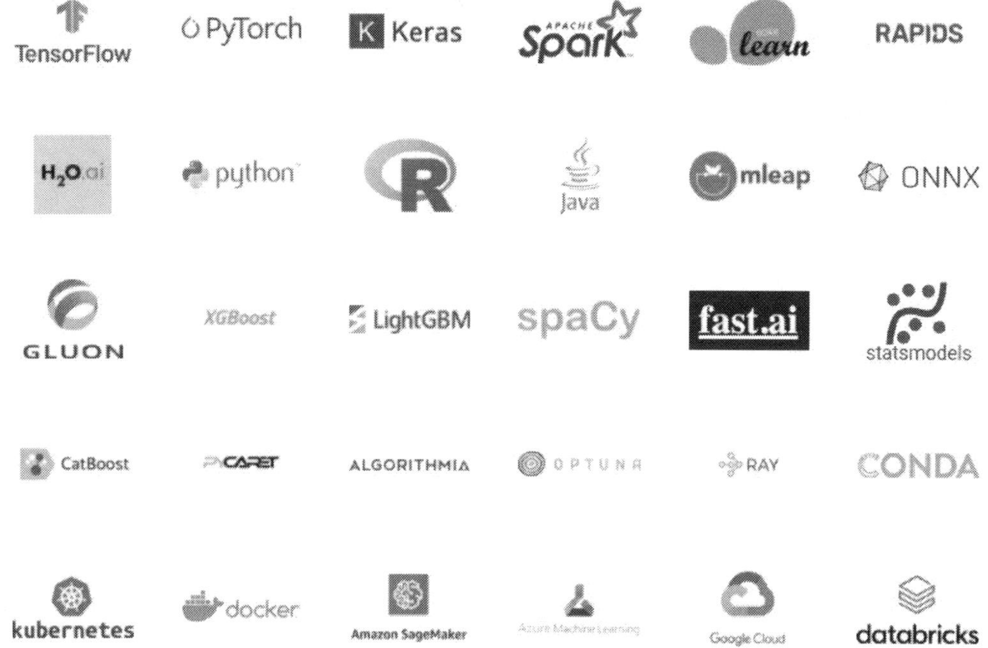

Figure 7.5: MLflow integrations

As mentioned earlier, MLflow is available as an open-source framework that has been leveraged by organizations all over the world. With MLflow, we can work with large datasets, large machine learning models, and a large number of experiments.

If you want to install MLflow, you can use the following command to install the MLflow Python package:

```
pip install mlflow
```

The following organizations all over the world are using MLflow to implement machine learning projects:

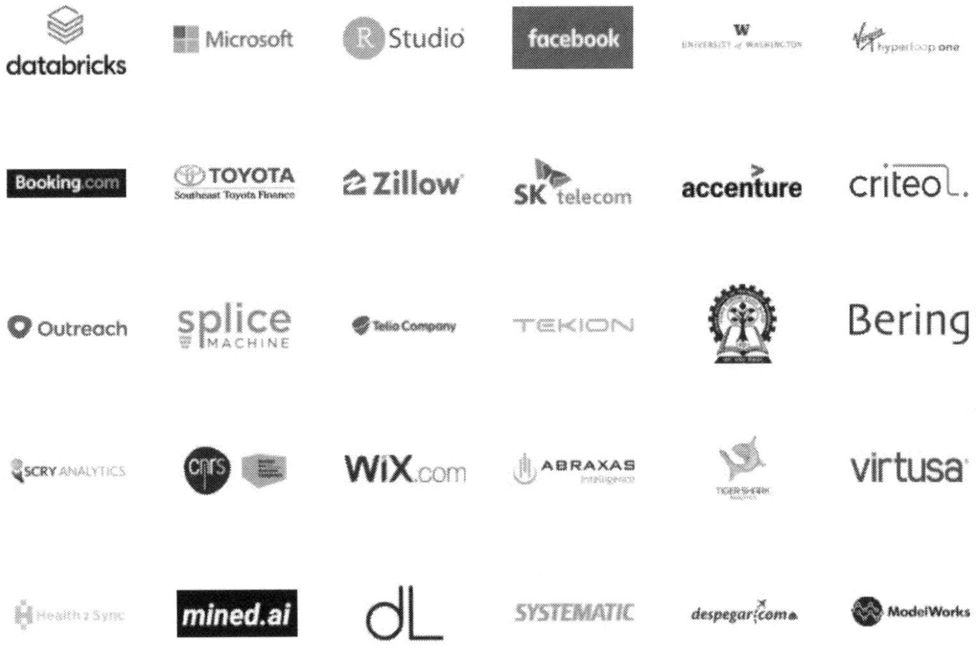

Figure 7.6*: Companies using MLflow*

Databricks also has its hosted version of the MLflow to use it with the Databricks hosted environment. Databricks hosted MLflow integrates with Databricks unified analytics platform, including notebooks, jobs, and Databricks delta, to run the existing MLflow jobs.

MLOps and MLflow are major components while working on the machine learning projects for enterprise organizations. After understanding the overview and basics of the MLOps and MLflow, we will deep dive into the model life cycle management using the MLflow.

Model life cycle management using MLflow

Databricks Lakehouse platform has a fully managed and hosted version of the MLflow, with high-level security, availability, and compatibility with the other Databricks workspace features. We can manage an end-to-end machine learning life cycle using the MLflow:

- **Tracking**: We can track machine learning experiments over time and compare the results.
- **Models**: End users can manage the machine learning models from various ML libraries on multiple platforms.
- **Projects**: We can package the machine learning project using MLflow projects so that it can be shared and used by multiple Data Scientists.
- **MLflow model registry**: We can create a centralized model store for managing the model lifecycle starting from development to production deployment, versioning, and so on.
- **Model serving**: Enables end users to host the MLflow models using the REST endpoints.

When we go to the Databricks home page UI, we can select the `Machine Learning` option, as follows:

Figure 7.7: Databricks machine learning workspace

Databricks machine learning home page has options to select notebooks, AutoML, and so on:

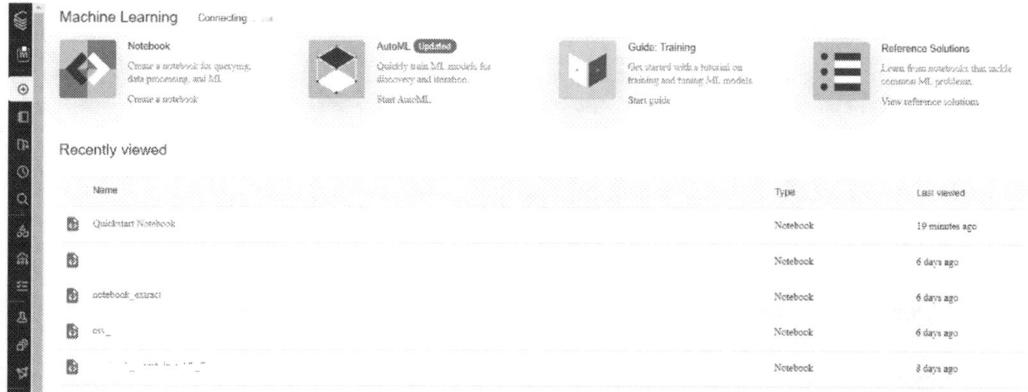

Figure 7.8: Databricks machine learning home page

Getting started with MLflow environment

MLflow provides various APIs for logging the metrics, parameters, and machine learning models to keep track of the deployed models.

MLflow installation

Databricks Lakehouse platform uses the Databricks runtime. If you use theDdatabricks runtime ML, MLfLow will be pre-installed.

If you don't use Databricks runtime, we can also install the MLflow package from the **pypi** repository.

MLflow has in-built auto logging capabilities, which will automatically log the result of the machine learning model and machine learning model score:

```
# Install MLFLow:
%pip install mlflow

```

***Figure 7.9**: Install MLflow*

Databricks runtime for machine learning is a ready-to-use environment for the Data Science and machine learning related workloads. Various machine learning libraries, like **Tensorflow**, **PyTorch**, **scikit-learn**, and **XGBoost**, are already installed on the Databricks runtime ML:

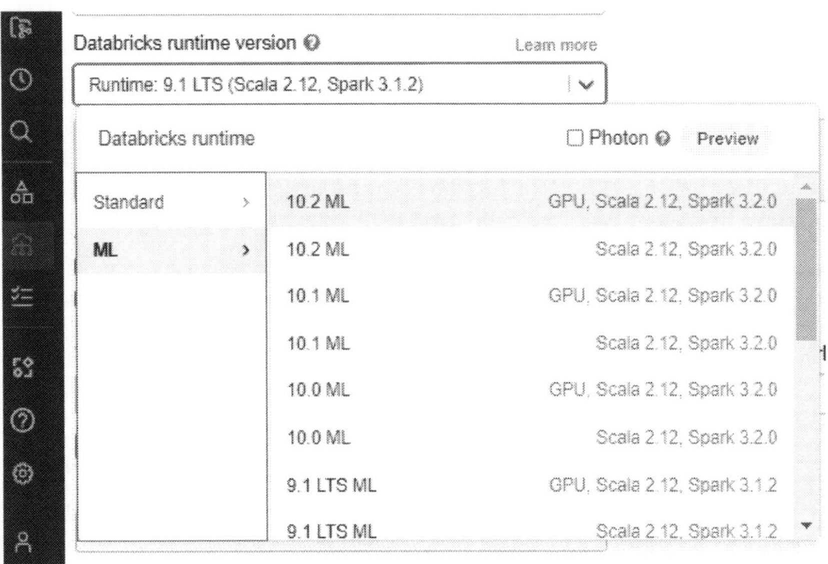

***Figure 7.10**: Databricks ML - runtime*

Once you open the Databricks *compute* option, as highlighted in the preceding screenshot, we can select from the list of Databricks runtime ML for the processing. It is also possible to create a custom environment for the Databricks cluster by adding the additional libraries.

`mlflow ui` command enables the end user to launch the web UI, as shown in the following screenshot. From the web UI, we can see experiments, compare the metrics of results with hyper parameters, and so on:

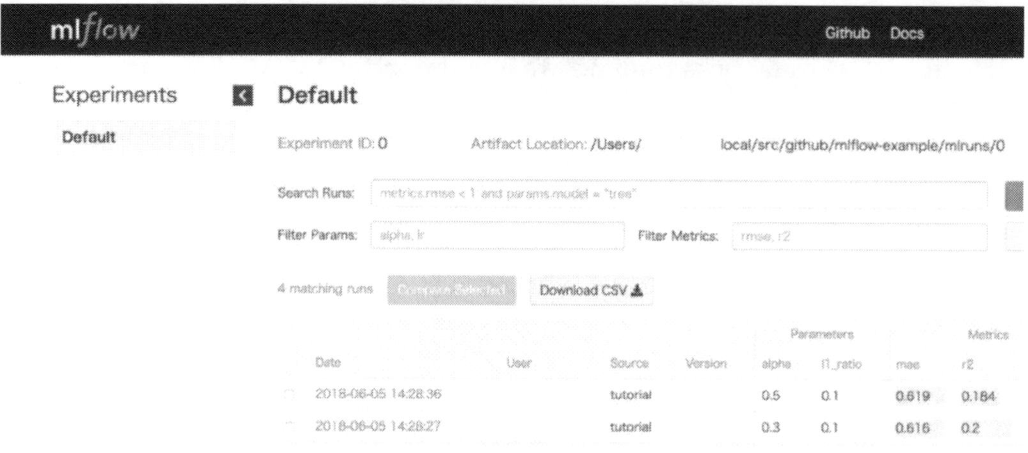

***Figure 7.11**: Databricks MLflow UI*

Feature engineering with Databricks

Machine learning algorithms use input data to run against the machine learning model to generate output. Input data is mainly in the form of structured data with columns. Machine learning algorithms require columns in certain formats to use it by the machine learning model to predict the outcome and business insights. This process of transforming the columns in a specific format so that it can be used by the machine learning model is called **feature engineering**.

With feature engineering activity, we can achieve the following:

- Prepare and transform input data to make it compatible with the machine learning model
- Optimize and improve the performance of the machine learning model

According to the survey in *Forbes*, Data Scientists spend more than *80% of time* in data preparation, which is quite a significant amount of time. This fact proves the importance of feature engineering in the overall machine learning lifecycle process:

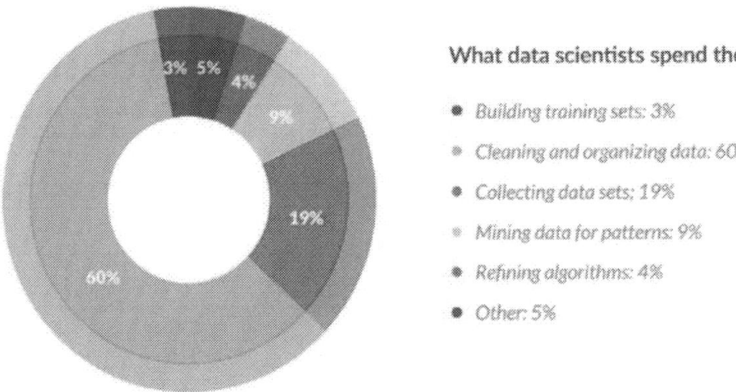

***Figure 7.12**: Data preparation*

https://www.forbes.com/sites/gilpress/2016/03/23/data-preparation-most-time-consuming-least-enjoyable-data-science-task-survey-says/?sh=539744866f63

Feature engineering is one of the most important and time-consuming steps of the machine learning process. Data Scientists and Data Analysts spend an extensive amount of time to find the different combinations of the features to improve the overall performance of the machine learning model and generate business insights reports. Bigger the size of the datasets, the more time Data Scientists and Data Analysts have to spend on feature engineering.

The major challenges of features engineering faced by Data Scientists are as follows:

- Define feature in a consistent way
- Reuse existing features
- Maintain and track features and machine learning models
- Manage the feature life cycle

The following diagram shows the overall workflow of feature engineering in the overall machine learning process. The major steps involved are as follows:

- Extract features from the raw data
- Store the features into the feature store

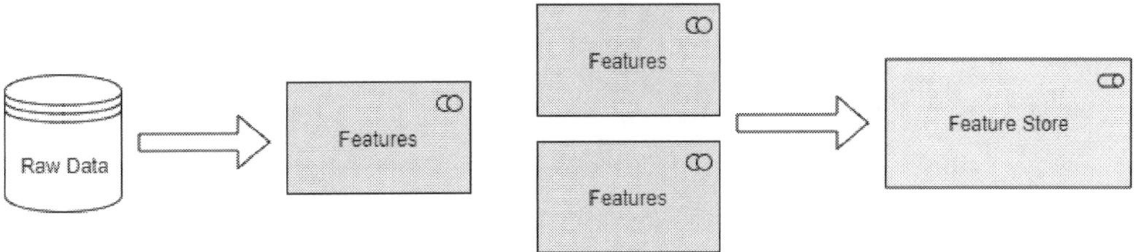

***Figure 7.13**: Feature engineering workflow*

Considering the importance of feature engineering, let's understand the basic techniques of feature engineering in Python using **pandas and numpy**.

Before we run any code, make sure you import two libraries, as follows:

```
import pandas

import numpy
```

There are various techniques to perform the feature engineering. Let's understand a few of them in detail:

- **Imputation**: Missing values in the input data is one of the most common problems for data preparation for machine learning. There are multiple causes of missing values in data, like human errors, interruptions in the technical data flow, privacy related issues, and so on:

	col1	col2	col3	col4	col5
0	2	5.0	3.0	6	NaN
1	9	NaN	9.0	0	7.0
2	19	17.0	NaN	9	NaN

mean() →

	col1	col2	col3	col4	col5
0	2.0	5.0	3.0	6.0	7.0
1	9.0	11.0	9.0	0.0	7.0
2	19.0	17.0	6.0	9.0	7.0

Mean Imputation

Figure 7.14: Data imputation - mean

Various machine learning algorithms automatically drop the rows from the dataset due to the missing values in the model training phases. Dropping the rows due to the missing values decreases the model performance. On the other hand, data privacy, manual errors, and such also lead to missing data.

For example, if we want to replace all the missing values with **0** in the dataset, then we can use the following command in the Python code:

```
data = data.fillna(0)
```

- o **Handle outliers**: We should remove outliers from the dataset to avoid influencing the final outcome of the machine learning model. Outlier handling can be handled in multiple ways and a variety of scales to produce more accurate data as an input for the machine learning model. Let's look at various methods to handle outliers with the data:

- o **Remove Outliers**: Records that have outliers will be removed using this method. However, the problem with this approach is that a majority of the records will be removed when there are outliers present for the numerical variables.

- o **Replace value for outliers**: We can also handle outliers as missing values and replace them with the suitable imputation.
- o **Capping**: We can also use an arbitrary value from a variable distribution to replace the maximum and minimum values from to handle the outliers.
- o **Discretization**: Discretization is the process of converting continuous variables, models, and functions into discrete ones. We can implement the same by constructing a series of continuous bins that spans the range of desired variables.

So, we can use one of the preceding imputation methods based on the scenario to prepare the best input data for the machine learning model.

- **Log transform**: This is one of the most widely used techniques by Data Scientists. With this method of outlier handling, it tried to turn the skewed distribution into the normal skewed distribution. In this approach, we have to get the log of the values in the column and use them to transform the actual column values:

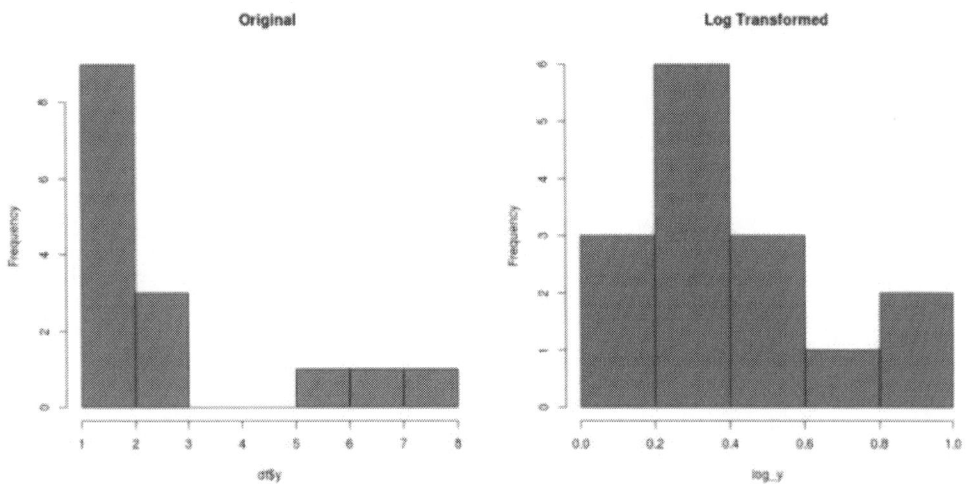

Figure 7.15: Log transform

Log transform method is mainly used to handle confusing data when the data becomes more approximate to the normal applications.

- **One-hot encoding**: One-hot encoding is a type of encoding when the element of the certain set is represented by the index in the set where one element has its index set to **1** and other elements are assigned the index in the range of *o* to *n-1*. On the other hand, in binary encoding, we only assign two values: *0* and *1*.

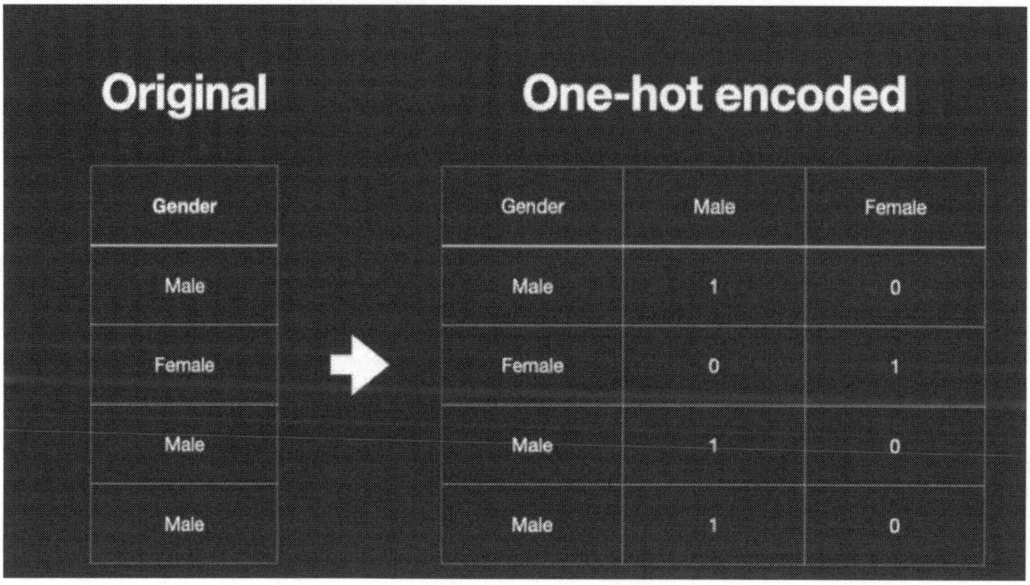

Original

Gender
Male
Female
Male
Male

One-hot encoded

Gender	Male	Female
Male	1	0
Female	0	1
Male	1	0
Male	1	0

***Figure 7.16**: One-hot encoding*

- **Scaling**: Feature scaling method is one of the most challenging but also very important feature engineering techniques while working the machine learning model. We need to scale features up or down in order to train the predictive model. Once we perform the scaling operations, continuous features become similar in terms of range.

  There two commonly used ways of scaling:

  - **Normalization**: With the normalization technique, all record values will be scaled in the range of *0* and *1* using the *min-max approach*. It has no influence on the feature distribution, but it affects the outliers due to the lower standard deviations.
  - **Standardization**: It is a process of scaling values while considering the standard deviation. If the standard deviation feature differs, the range of those features will also differ:

❑Normalization

$$X_{changed} = \frac{X - X_{min}}{X_{max} - X_{min}}$$

❑Standardization

$$X_{changed} = \frac{X - \mu}{\sigma}$$

Figure 7.17: Scaling

After understanding the overview of feature engineering, let's understand how to perform feature engineering practically.

Feature definitions are applied to raw data to generate machine learning features as a data frame and save the data frame to the feature registry using the feature store APIs. Feature definitions stored in the feature stores are version controlled and enable us to provide traceability, reproduction, and audit as needed:

```
def compute_features(data):
    features = ShopSales()
        fv_mnths = features.total_sales.multiply("i_category", ["Dance", "Rent", "Clothes"]).multiply("month_id", [202012, 202011, 202010])
    df = append_features(src_df, [features.collector], fv_mnths)

    return df

features_df = compute_features(src_df)
```

The preceding example code shows how we can create feature definitions and register those features to the feature stores.

Base feature definition

Spark API has powerful functions for Data Engineering that can be used to perform feature engineering with a wrapper to reduce the complexity and promote the reusability. Feature class provides an interface to define features with the following components:

- **_base_col**: Column or other features that are columnar expressions.
- **list of conditions**: If the expression is *True*, then logic defined **in _base_col** will be taken as the feature. Otherwise, the feature will be calculated using the **_negative_value.**
- **_negative_value**: Evaluated if **the _filter** returns *False*.
- **_agg_func**: This will define the Spark SQL functions to aggregate the base column.

Feature modularization

The most common challenge faced by data scientists while performing feature engineering is that Data Science teams are defining their own features, but those feature definitions are not well documented and easily visible and accessible by other Data Science teams for the reusability.

Due to the lack of visibility of feature sharing, it results in duplicate efforts, code and features with the same use but different logic and result. Modularizing the feature definitions can help Data Scientists to overcome the mentioned challenges.

Module is implemented as a *feature family* that we can call a collection of features. A *read-only* property is defined for each feature to provide easy access. A feature family extends an **ImmutableDictBase** class that is generic and can serve as base class for collections of features, filters, and other objects.

Feature operations

Feature can be extended to include higher-order functions, which reduces verbosity, enables reusability, and improves feature definition.

Features vectors

Feature operations can be further simplified by storing the features with the same operations in a vector. Feature vector can be created from a feature dictionary by listing feature names.

Example is as follows:

```
features = Features()
fvctr = FeatureVector.create_by_names(features, ["total_cost", "total_transactions"])
```

Features definition governance

Databricks notebooks manage and track the versions of the feature definitions that can be integrated with the GitHub repos. Automated job will run the functional and integration test against the newly created features. We can also perform the additional stress tests to determine its impact on the performance. Once all types of testing are completed and code is approved, the feature definitions will be deployed to the production environments.

MLflow tracking tracks and logs (**https://www.mlflow.org/docs/latest/tracking.html**) the code version and source data when building models from the features. `mlflow.spark.autolog()` enables and configures logging of Spark data source path, version, and format.

Features explorations

As the number of features increases, it becomes difficult to browse and find specific feature definitions. An *abstracted feature* class will help us add a description attribute for each feature.

The following image shows the overall mapping of the created machine learning features from the raw data using the process mentioned previously:

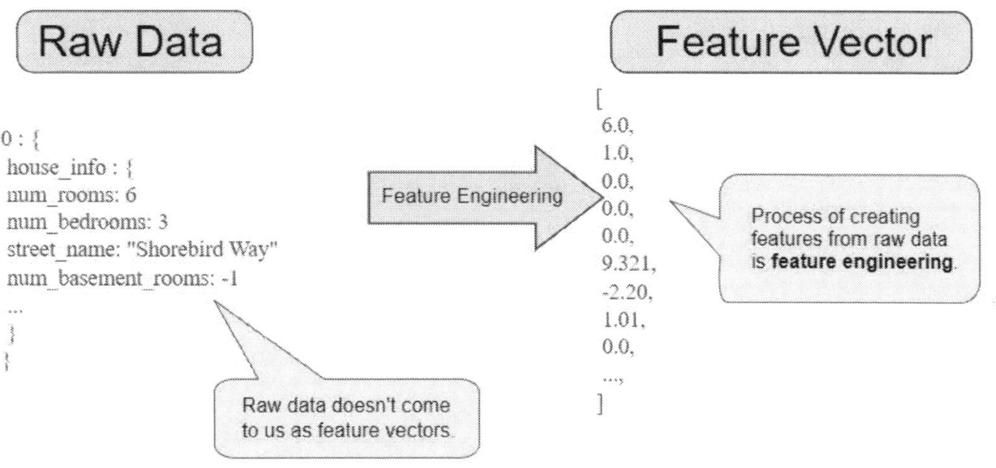

Figure 7.18*: Feature engineering mapping for raw data with ML features*

Setting up MLflow project with model repository

MLflow model registry provides a user interface and API to centrally manage machine learning models and their lifecycles.

Model registry has few concepts to describe the full life cycle of an MLflow model:

- **Model**: An MLflow model is created from the experiment logged with machine learning model flavor's using the `mlflow.<model_flavor>.log_model()` method. Once it is logged, the model will then be registered with the model registry.
- **Registered model**: We can register an MLflow model with the model registry. Registered model has a unique name, which consists of unique **names**, **versions**, **model lineage**, and **metadata**.
- **Model version**: Each registered machine learning model has one or many versions. When we add a new model to the model registry, it is added as *version 1*. Every time the new model is registered for the same model, the same model name increments the version number.
- **Model stage**: We can assign different model versions one stage at any time. MLflow has various predefined stages like **staging**, **production**, and **archived**. We can move from one stage to another easily.
- **Annotations and descriptions**: We can annotate top-level models and versions using the mark down, including the description and other relevant information:

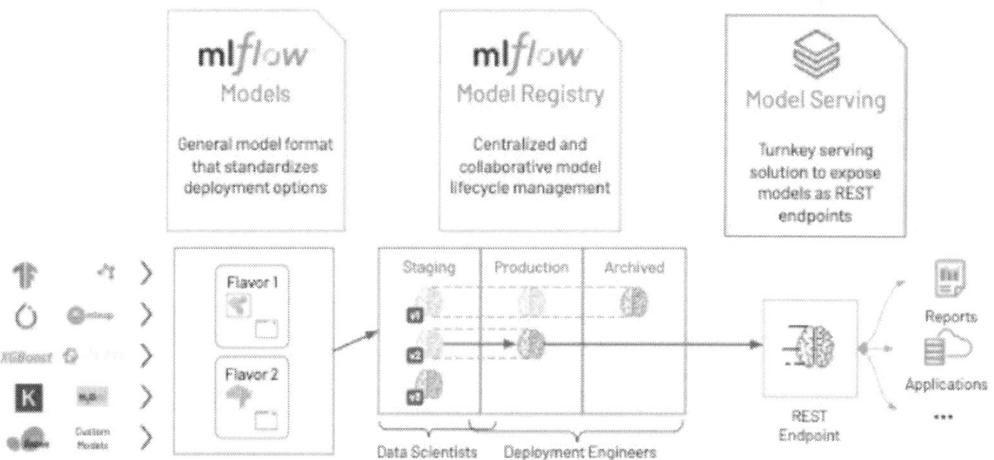

Figure 7.19: MLflow model serving with Databricks

Now, let us explore in detail how the model registry workflow works.

We must use a database backed store to access the model registry using the API or user interface if we are running our own MLflow server. Before we add a model to the model registry, we must log the same using the **`log_model`** methods. Once we log the model, we can add, modify, update, or delete the model stored in the model registry.

UI workflow

- **Register a model to MLflow model registry**

  In order to register the model, select the logged MLflow model from the `Artifacts` section from the MLflow `Run` detail page:

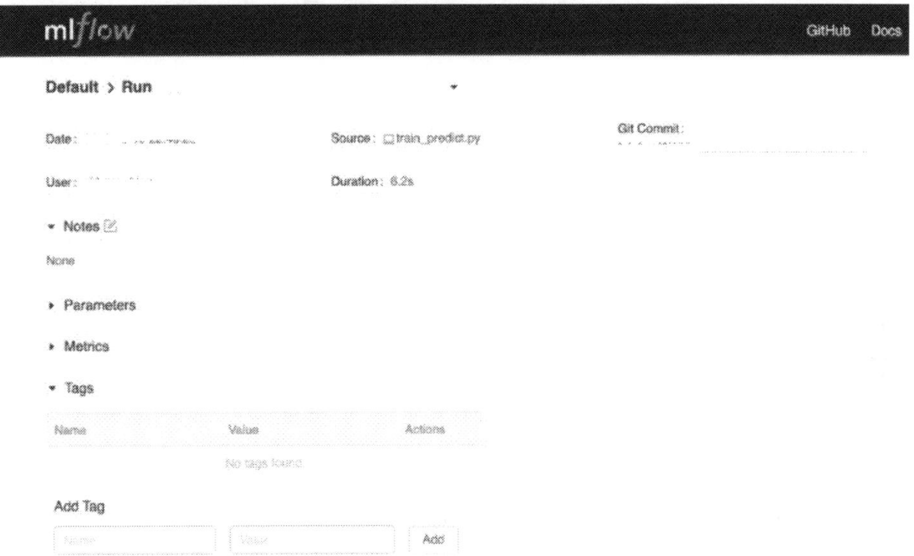

Figure 7.20: Register MLflow model

Then, click on the `Register Model` button to register the model in the MLflow model registry. Once we click on the button, a pop-up box will appear. In the `Model Name` field, provide the unique name to identify the model. Select the existing model from the dropdown in case you want to pick up the existing model:

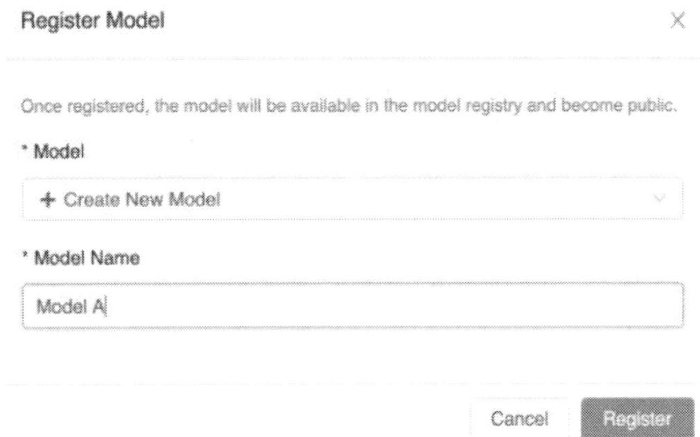

Figure 7.21: Register MLflow model

- **Use model registry**

  In order to view the model properties, navigate to the **`Registered Models`** page:

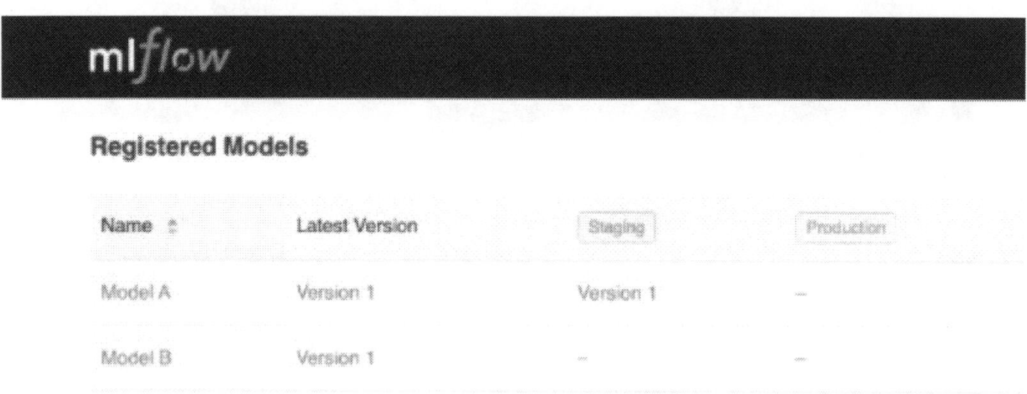

Figure 7.22: Registered MLflow models

In order to know more about the model, go to the **`Artifacts`** section of the run detail page and click on the model version in the top right to view the version created:

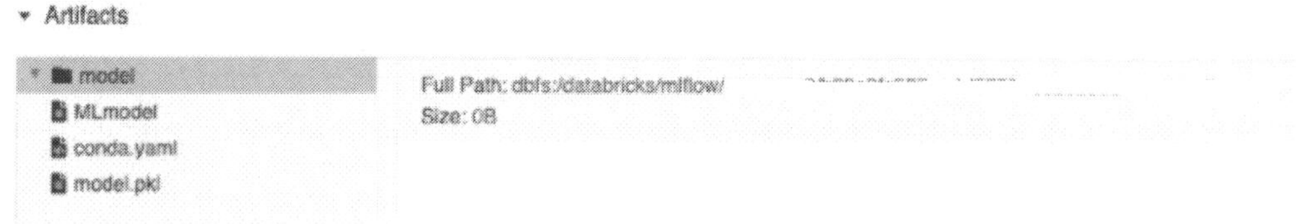

Figure 7.23: Artifacts

Each model has an *overview* page, which shows the active versions:

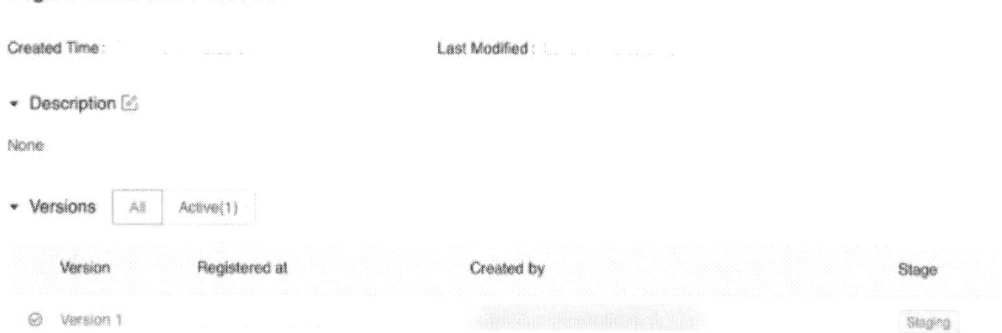

Figure 7.24: MLflow model overview

Now, click on **`Version 1`** to know more about the version details:

Registered Models > Model A > Version 1

Registered At:

Creator:

Stage: Staging

Last Modified:

Source Run: Run

Description

None

Figure 7.25: *MLflow model version details*

From the *Version details* page, we can view the model version details and the current stage of the model version. In the top left corner, there is a drop-down menu that shows how the model transitioned from one stage to another valid stage:

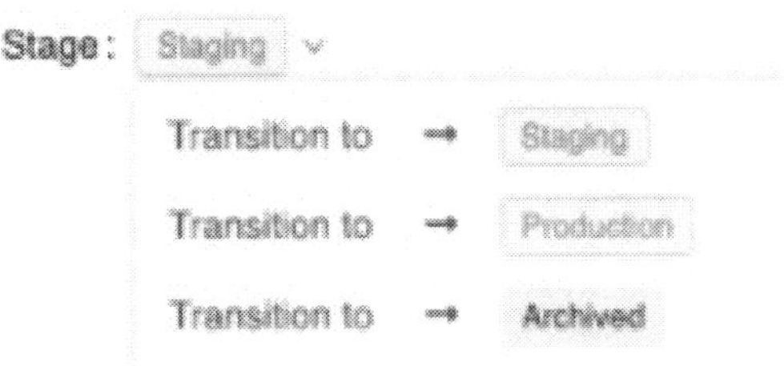

Figure 7.26: *MLflow model stages*

API workflow

Another way to interact with the model registry is using the API workflow with MLflow model flavor or MLflow client tracking API interface.

There are multiple ways to add models to the registry:

1. Using the **`mlflow.<model_flavor>.log_model()`** method:

```
import mlflow
import mlflow.sklearn
with mlflow.start_run(run_name=”RUN_NAME”) as run:
    params = {“n_estimators”: 10, “random_state”: 30}
    # Log parameters and metrics using the MLflow APIs
    mlflow.log_params(params)
    mlflow.log_param(“param_1”, randint(0, 50))
    mlflow.log_metrics({“metric_1”: random(), “metric_2”: random() + 1})
```

2. Using **`mlflow.register_model()`**: Using the code block, we can register the model to MLflow model registry:

```
result = mlflow.register_model(
    "runs:/xxxxxxxxxxxx/sklearn-model",
    "sk-learn-reg"
)
```

   If the registered model with the given name doesn't exist, the preceding method registers the new model and creates **version 1**. If the model already exists, then the method creates a new model version and returns the version object.

3. Using `create_registered_model`: When we use this method, the method will throw an MLflow **exception** if the model name exists because this method requires a unique name:

```
from mlflow.tracking import MlflowClient
client = MlflowClient()
client.create_registered_model("regression-reg-model")
```

Once the MLflow model is registered, we can fetch the model using **`mlflow.<model_flavor>.load_model()`**, or **`using`** `load_model()`.

Let's look at various ways to fetch models from the MLflow model registry:

1. **Fetch specific model version**

   Apply the version number as a part of model URI to fetch the specific model from the MLflow model registry:

```
import mlflow.pyfunc

model_name = "regression-reg-model"
model_version = 1

model = mlflow.pyfunc.load_model(
    model_uri=f"models:/{model_name}/{model_version}" )
model.predict(data)
```

2. **Fetch latest model version for a specific stage**

   In order to fetch the latest model version from a specific stage, we have to provide the model URI that will fetch the most recent version of the model:

```
import mlflow.pyfunc

model_name = "regression-reg-model"

stage = 'Staging'

model = mlflow.pyfunc.load_model(
    model_uri=f"models:/{model_name}/{stage}"
)

model.predict(data)
```

   Once the model is registered in the MLflow model registry, we can serve the MLflow model from the **model** registry, add or update MLflow model descriptions, rename the MLflow model, or transition an MLflow model's stage.

3. **Serve MLflow model from the model registry**

   Once the MLflow model is registered with the model registry, we can serve the model as a service on the host:

```
#!/usr/bin/env sh


# Set environment variable for Model Registry URL

export MLFLOW_TRACKING_URI=http://localhost:5000


# Serve the production model from the model registry

mlflow models serve -m "models:/linear-reg-model/Production"
```

4. **Add/update MLflow model descriptions**

   We can update the model version's description using the **update_model_version()**:

```
client = MlflowClient()

client.update_model_version(
    name="sk-learn-random-forest-reg-model",
```

```
    version=1,
    description="This model version is a linear regression machine learning model"
)
```

5. **Rename MLflow model from the model registry**

   We can use the **`rename_registered_model()`** method to rename the existing MLflow model stored in the MLflow model registry:

```
client = MlflowClient()
client.rename_registered_model(
    name="linear-reg-model",
    new_name="linear-reg-model-100"
)
```

6. **MLflow model stage transition**

   Over time, as the model evolves, the model life cycle also changes. We can transition the registered models to one of these stages: **Staging**, **Production**, or **Archived**:

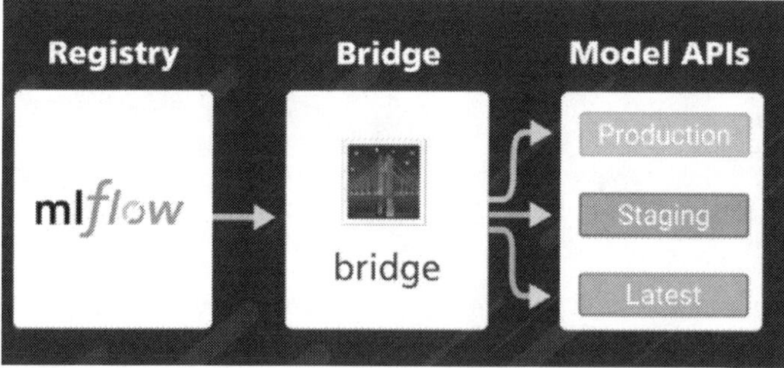

Figure 7.27: ML*flow* *m*odel stages life cycle

7. **Searching MLflow models**

   We can use the following method to search and fetch a list of all registered models in the registry:

```
from pprint import pprint

client = MlflowClient()
for rm in client.registered_models():
    pprint(dict(rm), indent=5)
```

8. **Archive MLflow model**

   If required, we can also move model versions from the production stage to the archive stage:

```
# Archive models version 3 from Production into Archived
            client = MlflowClient()
            client.transition_model_version_stage(
            name="regression-model",
            version=3,
            stage="Archived"
        )
```

9. **Delete MLflow models**

   It is also possible to delete the specific version of the MLflow models or delete the registered models and its version. Once we delete the MLflow model, it is not possible to roll back, so it is better to use this option carefully:

```
# Delete a registered model along with all its versions
client.delete_registered_model(name="binarytree-reg-model")
```

Train and deploy the model

Once the machine learning model is ready, we need to train the machine learning model and then deploy it:

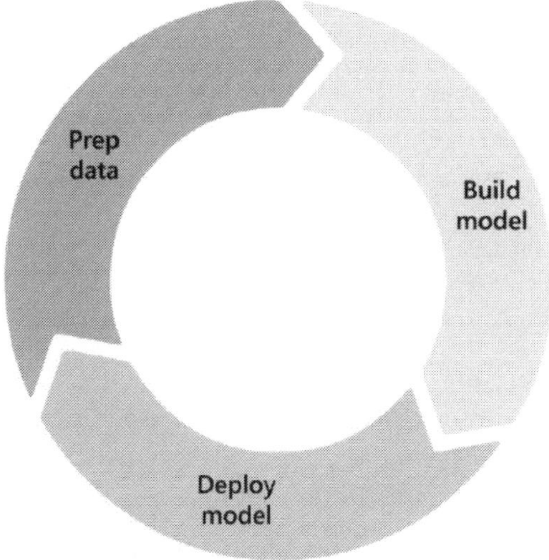

***Figure 7.28**: Machine learning model life cycle*

Training machine learning alone is not a challenge. Similarly, deploying the model alone is not a challenge. However, it is not a simple solution when it comes to the integration of full machine learning life cycle management. MLflow is one of the tools to tackle this kind of a problem.

Let's understand the process of deploying the MLflow model.

MLflow model is a standard format for packaging machine learning model, which can be used in a variety of tools like batch inference on spark or serving real time through REST API. Once the model is ready and registered in the MLflow model registry, we can start deploying the ML model. We can use the MLflow model serving on the Databricks to host the machine learning model from the model registry REST endpoints.

We can also deploy the model using the third-party tools `mlflow.<deploy-type>.deploy()`.

Model deployment can be considered as a process of serving the trained machine learning model in the production environment that can be used by the rest of the world for making inferences:

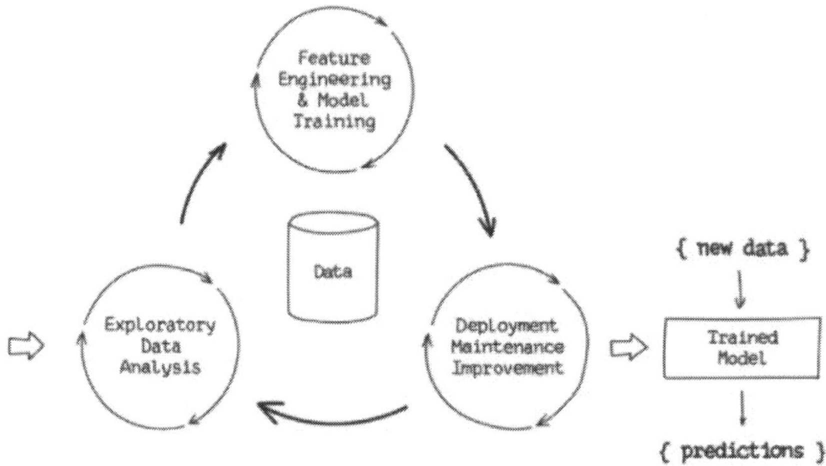

Figure 7.29: *Machine learning model deployment*

There are various ways to deploy and serve machine learning models to production:

1. **Offline prediction**: Offline prediction usually happens on the local machine when the predictions are for a single event and generated directly from the python code. An example of offline prediction is prediction on the test dataset during the hackathon.

2. **Batch prediction**: In batch prediction, we perform the set of predictions by taking file as an input on a periodic basis at a certain frequency:

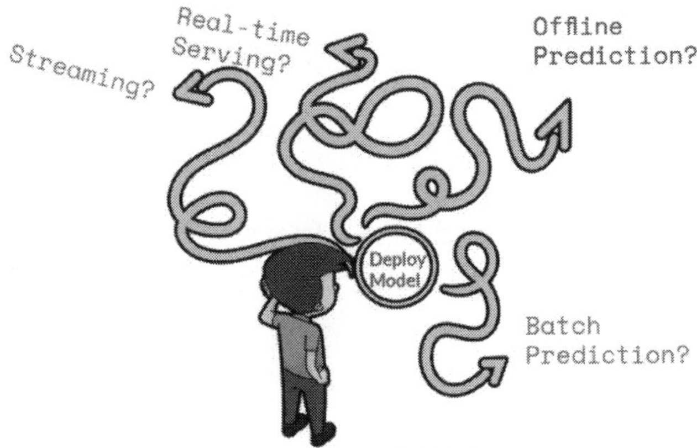

Figure 7.30: Machine learning model deployment types

- **Real-time prediction**: It is also possible to make on-demand predictions using the HTTP calls to a model served in the cloud without any delays. For example, there is a website to detect the object. We have to upload the picture as an input on the website and detect the object as an output:

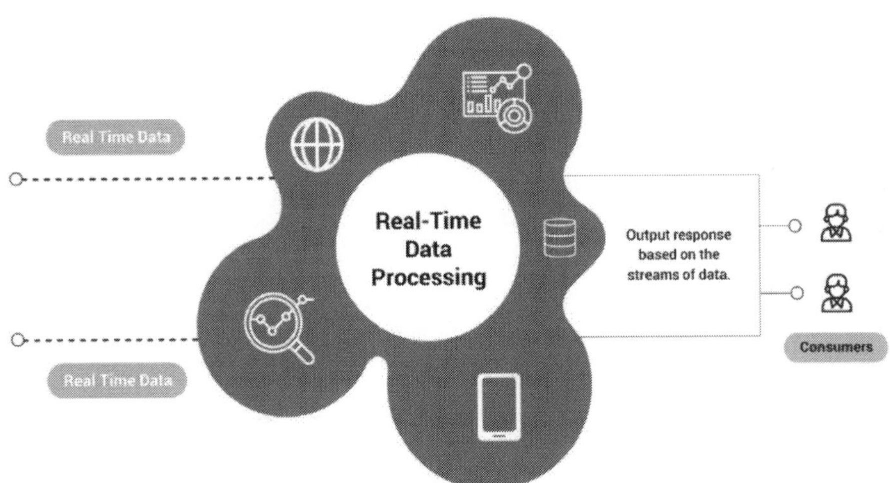

Figure 7.31: Real-time data processing

- **Streaming prediction**: Streaming processing is similar to the batch and reach time processing, but it has an additional queue to handle the volume of data and is able to serve processing rate irrespective of the arrival rate.

Let us take an example of the model deployment on AWS:

```
# Deploy model
deploy_model(
```

```
    model = final_blended,
    model_name = 'logistic_deploy_1',
    platform = 'aws',
    authentication = {'bucket' : 'mlops213001'}
)
# Enter your respective bucket name in place of 'mlops213001'
```

Once the model is deployed, make inferences using our model deployed on AWS:

```
 loaded_model = load_model(
    'lightgbm_deploy_1',
    platform = 'aws',
    authentication = { 'bucket' : 'mlops2345' }
)
predictions = predict_model(loaded_model, data=data_unseen)

# View predictions
predictions.head()
```

Now, using the preceding snippet, our model has been deployed, and it will make batch predictions using the same.

Apart from deploying and serving models using the AWS Cloud, we can perform real-time serving with **Fast API** or **REST API**. Once the model is deployed locally or on cloud, we can use it to make offline or online batch predictions:

Figure 7.32: *REST API working*

Log model metrics

MLflow tracking is an API and UI for logging parameters, code versions, metrics, and output files while running the machine learning code and related visualization. With MLflow tracking, we can log and query experiments using Python, REST API, R, and Java:

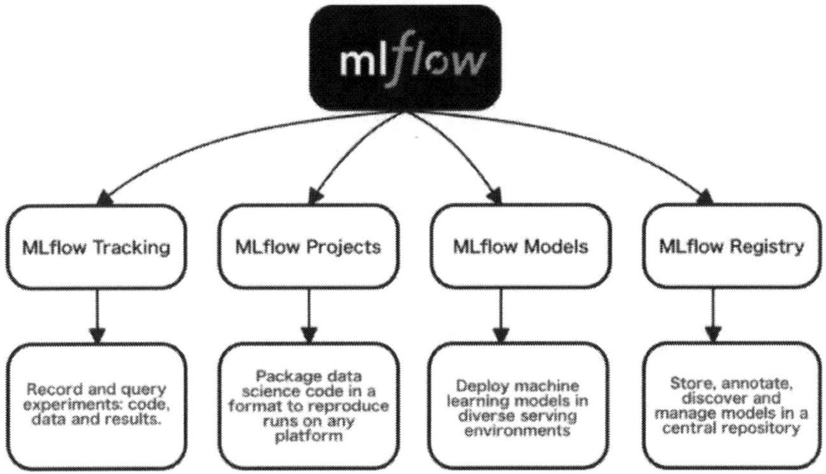

Figure 7.33: *MLflow tracking*

Source: *https://mlflow.org/*

MLflow tracking is organized around the concept of runs, which are the executions of the piece of machine learning/Data Science code. Each piece of code records a piece of information:

- **Code version**: If it was a run from the MLflow project, then the Git commit hash is used.
- **Start and end time**: It displays the start and end time of the MLFlow experiment run.
- **Source**: It is the name of the file that is required to launch the MLflow project. It is, basically, the trigger point to run the MLflow project.
- **Parameters**: Parameters are normally in the form of key-value pairs. Both the key and values are in the form of string.
- **Metrics**: Each defined metric for the MLflow experiment can be updated during the MLflow run, and MLflow records and visualizes the full metric history.
- **Artifacts**: Artifacts from the MLflow run can be in any format.

Conclusion

In this chapter, we explored machine learning model management with Databricks in detail. We took a quick tour of how to implement end-to-end machine learning solutions using Databricks and MLflow. In addition to end-to-end implementation, we covered the basics of MLOps and MLflow. We also went through the concepts of getting started with the MLfLow environment, feature engineering with Databricks, setting up the MLflow project with the model repository, and training and deploying the machine learning model.

Multiple choice questions

1. What are the main components of MLflow?
   a. Tracking
   b. Projects
   c. Models
   d. Model Repository
   e. All of the above
2. How can you install the MLflow package in Databricks?
   a. `pip install mlflow`
   b. `pip install mflw`
3. Can we use MLflow to log the artifacts?
   a. Yes
   b. No
4. Which MLflow component do we use to record the results and model parameters?
   a. Tracking
   b. Projects
5. Which MLflow component do we use to package machine learning models?
   a. Tracking
   b. Models
   c. Projects
   d. All of the above

Answers

1. e
2. a
3. b
4. a
5. c

CHAPTER 8
Continuous Integration and Delivery with Databricks

Continuous Integration and Delivery enables enterprise organizations to swiftly iterate on the software changes while maintaining the overall performance and stability of the platform. Adoption of CI/CD entitles organizations to improve productivity, code quality, and software delivery.

In the previous chapter, we explored machine learning model management with Databricks in detail. We learned about MLOps and MLflow, and we also understood model life cycle management with MLflow. In this chapter, we will explore how to enable continuous integration and delivery with Databricks Lakehouse platform.

Structure

This chapter deals with how to implement DevOps CI/CD with Databricks. Here are the topics that will be covered:

- Repos for Git integration
- Automated multi-environment CI/CD deployment with DevOps

Objectives

After studying this chapter, you should be able to understand the integration of Databricks platform with versioning tools like Git and Azure DevOps. You will also learn how to enable the CI/CD way of working with Databricks deployment and deploy components to all environments in a generic way.

Repos for Git integration

A best practice while working with Data Science and Data Engineering workload is to enable the integration with version controlling tools to maintain code versions as well as history. Databricks Lakehouse platform provides an in-built feature named **Databricks repos** that provides repository-level integration with the Git providers.

With Databricks repos, we can develop the code in the Databricks notebooks and sync it with a remote Git repository. Databricks repos support all the following features of the version controlling Git functionalities:

- Clone remote repos
- Mange branches
- Create push/pull request for code changes
- Visually compare version changes
- Check history of code changes

Databricks repos also have in-built API capabilities to integrate the CI/CD pipelines. With Databricks repos, we can make sure that we can programmatically update the Databricks repos using APIs to always use the most recent version of the code.

Databricks repos also have additional in-built security features, listed as follows, to improve security:

- Control access to the Git repositories only for the whitelisted resources
- Auto detect confidential information in a plain text format in source code

We can also enable audit logging while enabling Databricks repos, which will then log all the audit events when we create, delete, or update the Databricks repos.

Databricks supports the following Git providers for version controlling:

- GitHub
- Bitbucket
- GitLab
- Azure DevOps

In order to integrate version controlling for Databricks platform using the Databricks repos, Git server must be accessible from Databricks. We can't connect to private Git servers from the Databricks platform.

Now, let's understand how to configure Git integration with the Databricks Lakehouse platform:

1. First, go to the **`Settings`** tab on the home page of Databricks UI and click on **`User settings`**:

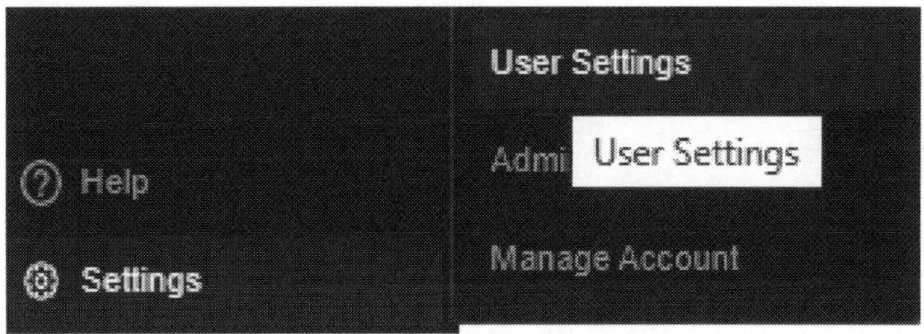

***Figure 8.1**: Databricks user settings*

2. Now, click on the **`User Settings`** option and select the **`Git Integration`** tab:

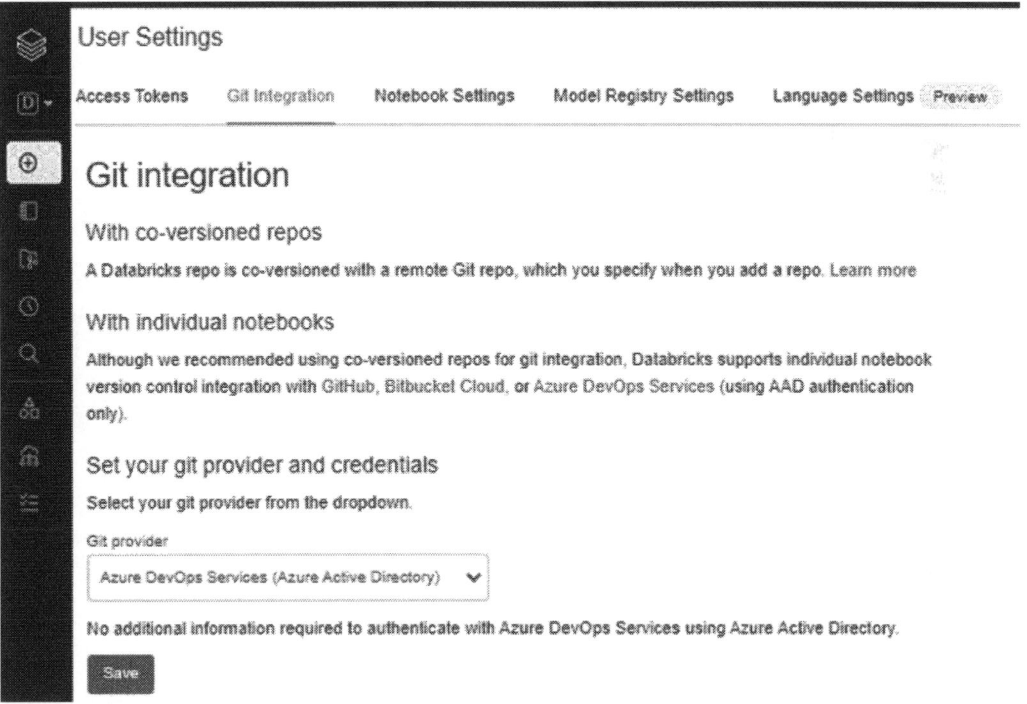

***Figure 8.2**: Databricks repos - Git integration*

3. Select the Git providers as per your convenience: **Azure DevOps**, **GitHub**, **GitLab**, or **Bitbucket**.
4. If the organization has SAML SSO enabled in the GitHub, we should use authorized personal access token for SSO.

Additionally, we can enable the support for configuring arbitrary files in the Databricks repos, including syncing Databricks notebooks with the remote Git repository.

In order to configure non-Databricks notebook files with the Databricks repos, Databricks runtime version should be more than *8.4 or above*.

The steps to enable non-Databricks notebooks files with Databricks repo are as follows:

1. Go to the admin console and click on the **`Workspace settings`**.
2. In the **`Advanced`** section, click on the **`Files in Repos: Disabled`** option:

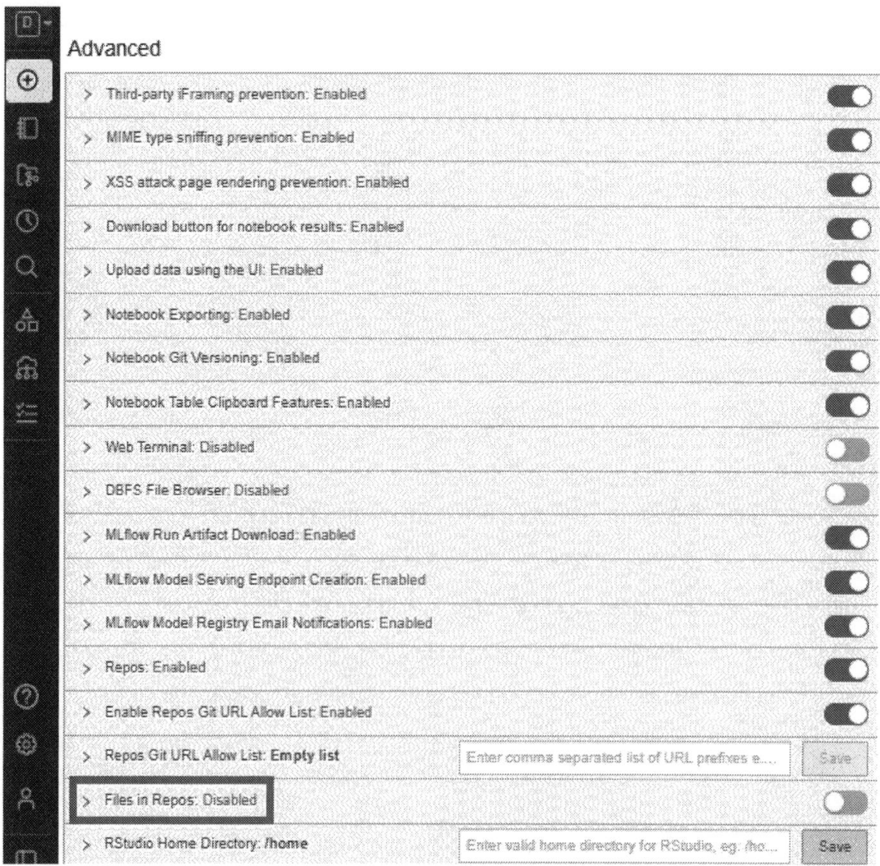

***Figure 8.3**: Databricks repos - Enable files in repos*

3. In order to clone the remote git repository:

   i. Click on the **`Repos`** tab from the menu, provide the remote Git repo URL, and click on the **`Create`** button to save the configurations.

   ii. Once the remote Git repository is cloned, we can create or work with the notebooks in sync with the remote Git repository.

   iii. We can also create different branches for the development work, create pull requests, and resolve conflicts after the integration with remote repos:

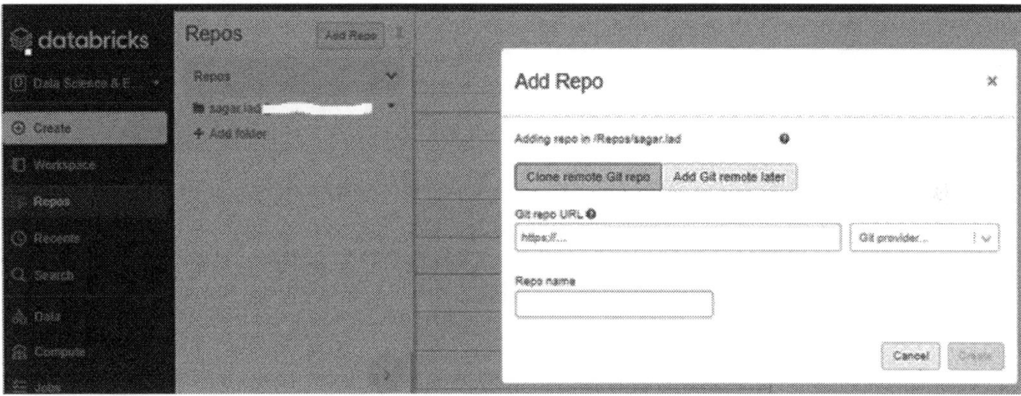

***Figure 8.4**: Databricks repos - Clone remote repo*

4. If you want to move the notebook or folder in the workspace, navigate to the notebook or folder and select **`Move`** from the drop-down menu, as follows:

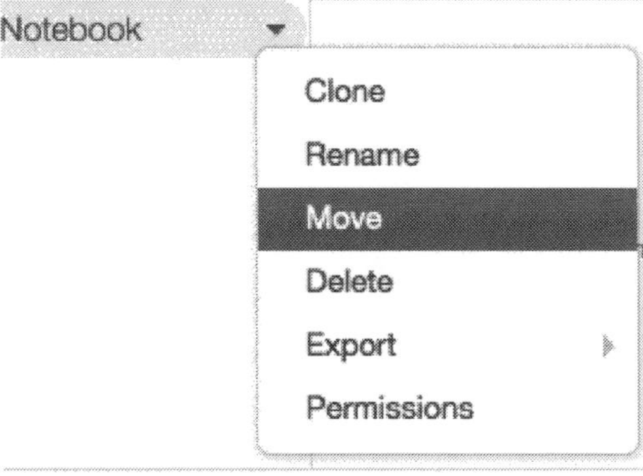

***Figure 8.5**: Databricks repos - Move folder/notebook*

5. Once the branch is created, you can create a new notebook or a folder by clicking on the **Repos** button and clicking on the branch where we want to create notebook or folder:

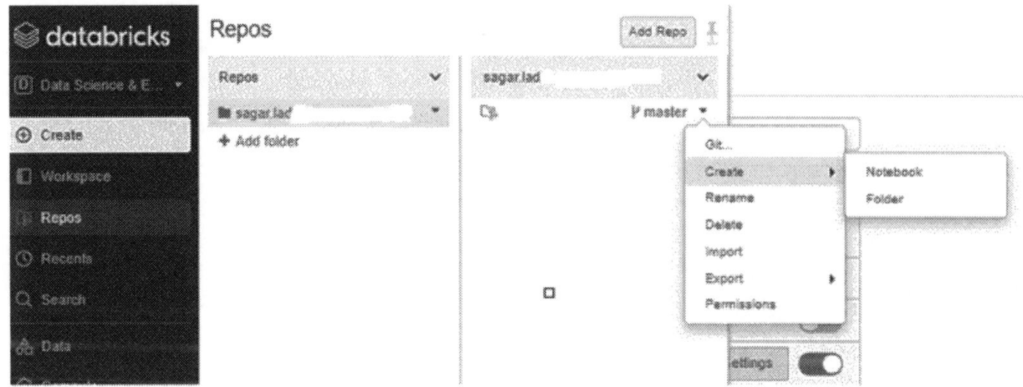

Figure 8.6: Databricks repos - Clone remote repo

We can also import the SQL or Python file in a single cell inside the Databricks notebook:

- Use comment line **- - Databricks notebook source at the top of SQLfile**
- Use comment line # **Databricks notebook source at the top of python file**

As discussed at the beginning of the chapter, we can also work with the non-notebook files with the integration of Databricks repos in the Databricks Lakehouse platform. Right-click on the branch and click on the **File** option to create a new file:

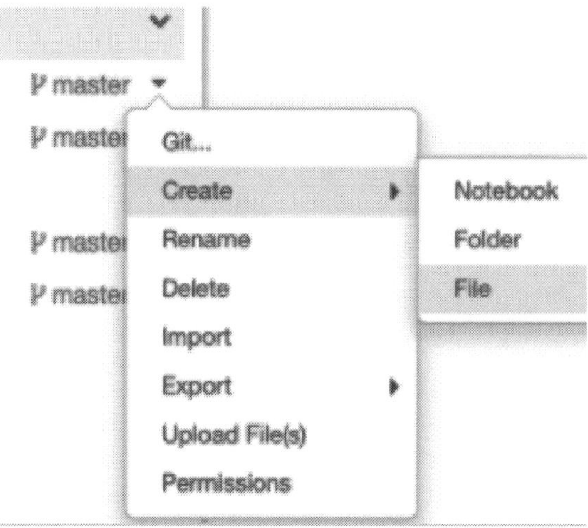

Figure 8.7: Databricks repos - Create new non-Databricks file

In order to upload an existing file, select the branch and click on **`Upload File(s)`**:

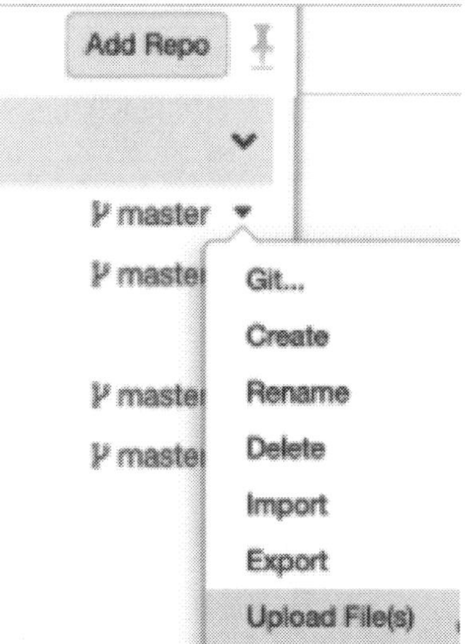

***Figure 8.8**: Databricks repos - Upload new non-Databricks file*

We can also programmatically refer to the files in the repo, such as **`.csv`** or **`.json`** files from the notebook. We can only read the non-Databricks files, but we can't create or edit the files in the notebook:

```
import pandas as pd

df = pd.read_csv(“./sampledata.csv”)
```

We can also use Spark to access the files in the repo. Absolute file path of any file in the repo is: **`/Workspace/Repos/<user_folder>/<repo_name>/file`**.

```
import os

spark.read.format(“csv”).load(f”file:/Workspace/Repos/<user_
folder>/<repo_name>/my_data.csv”)
```

To sync with the remote Git repository, we can use the **`git dialog`**, which will enable you to pull changes from the remote Git repository and commit changes to the remote repos. We can access the Git dialog from the Databricks notebook, as follows:

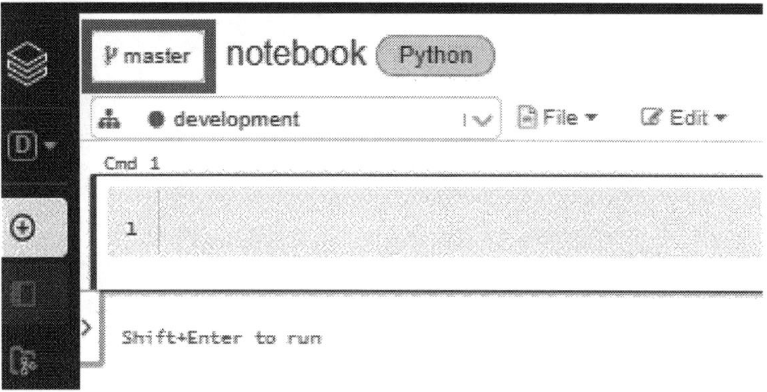

Figure 8.9: Databricks repos - Git dialog

Once you click on the branch, the Git dialog appears, as follows:

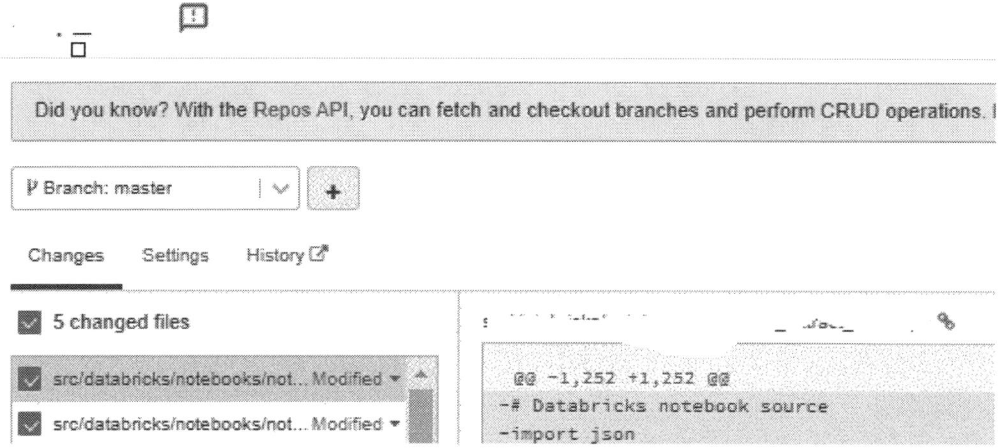

Figure 8.10: Databricks repos - Git dialog commit and push request

Once you are done with the code changes, you can open the Git dialog and commit and push changes to the repo:

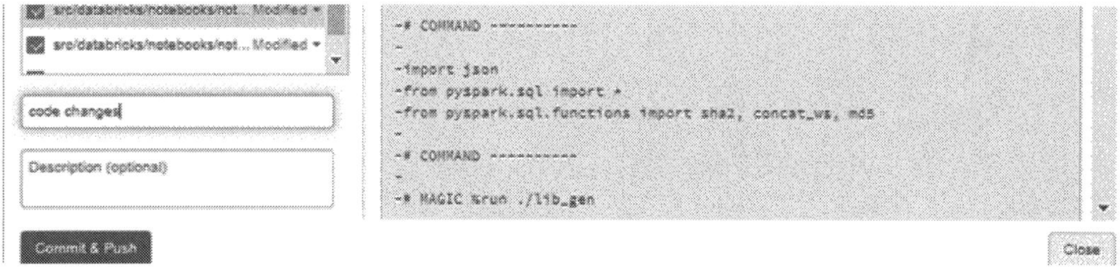

Figure 8.11: Databricks repos - Commit and push changes

If you want to pull the source code content from the remote repo, click on the **Pull button** to pull changes from the remote repo:

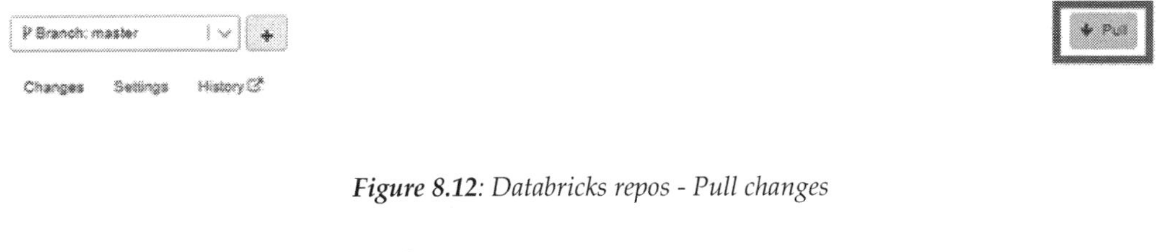

Figure 8.12: Databricks repos - Pull changes

Click on **Confirm** to commit the pull request:

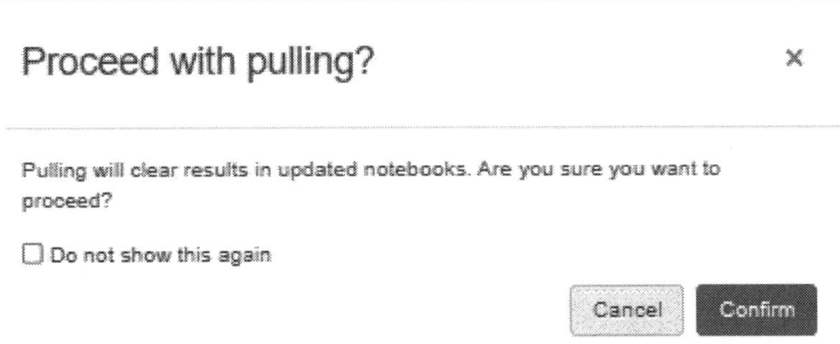

Figure 8.13: Databricks repos - Confirm pull changes

There are various benefits of working with non-Databricks notebook files and its integration with Databricks repos.

Advantages of Git integration for non-Databricks notebook files are as follows.

The following image shows the non-Databricks files for Databricks repos:

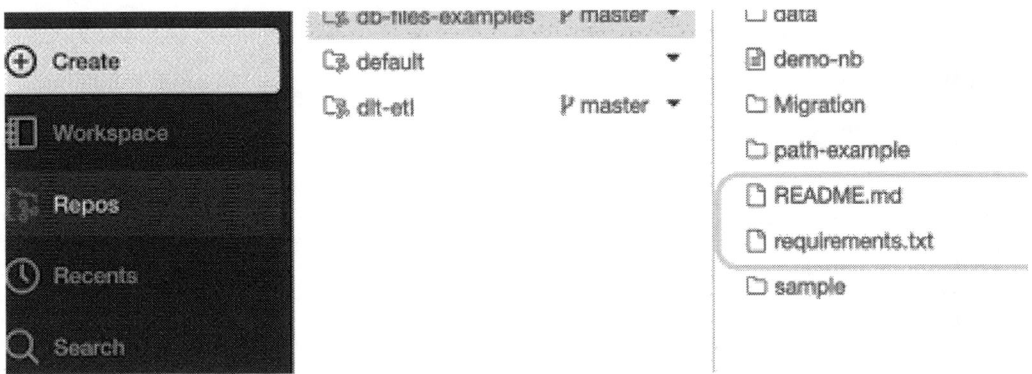

Figure 8.14: Databricks repos - non-Databricks files

- **Code reusability**: Existing Python and R modules can be referenced using the **import** function in the repos as well Databricks notebooks.

- **Store environment specific information with code**:
    - o In order to create a generic code base while working with Databricks notebook, we normally create the configuration files to store environment-specific values as well as **`requirement.txt`** files to install the dependent libraries.
    - o With the introduction of non-Databricks notebooks files, we can reduce the burden of managing the environments manually and eliminating the manual errors.
- **Automate deployments for multiple environments**: We can store environment specific information, such as jobs and clusters, in configuration files, and we can use the configuration files to automate the deployment across multiple environments.

We can also configure and manage the permission to Databricks repos. Admin can manage the allowed list of users to limit which remote users can commit and push the changes in the branch.

Go to **`Settings`**, select the admin **console**, choose the **`Workspace settings`** tab, and **`Enable repos Git URL Allow List`** option.

Users who have permission can commit and push the changes to the Git repositories. Default setting will be empty, and users configured by the admin can commit the changes to the repo:

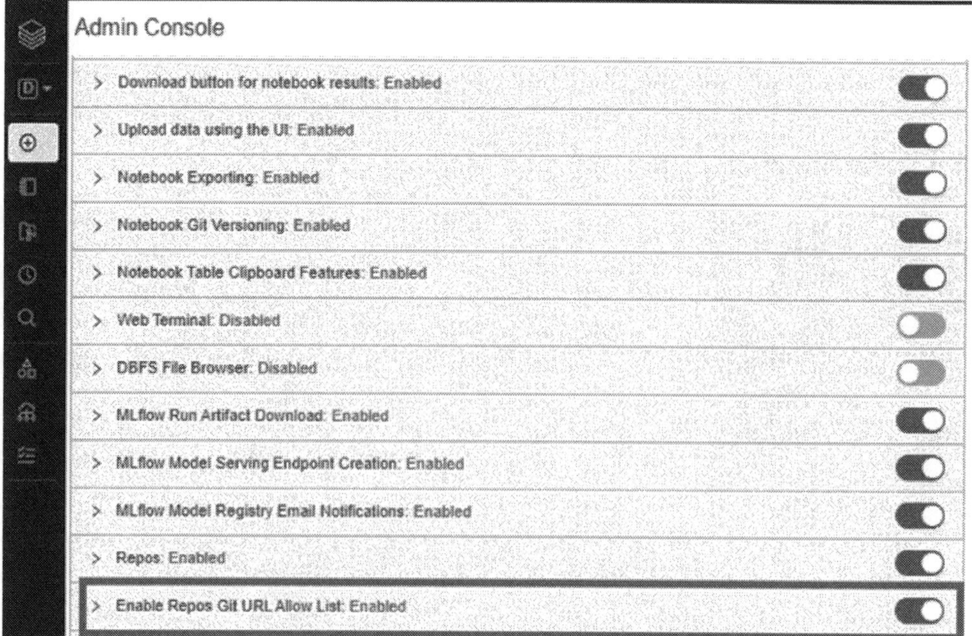

Figure 8.15: Databricks workspace settings - Enable repos Git URL allow list

After understanding different features and ways of configuring various Git tools, let's explore the best practices of working with Databricks repo for Git integration and implementing the end-to-end CI/CD flow for the Databricks workloads.

We will try to understand the best practices of working with Data Lakehouse platform with Databricks repos feature with three different flows:

- Databricks workspace admin
- Data Science/Data Engineering team
- Git integration for Databricks developers

In order to implement the recommended best practices, we have to configure a few settings in Databricks platform itself as well as a few configurations in the Git integrations tools:

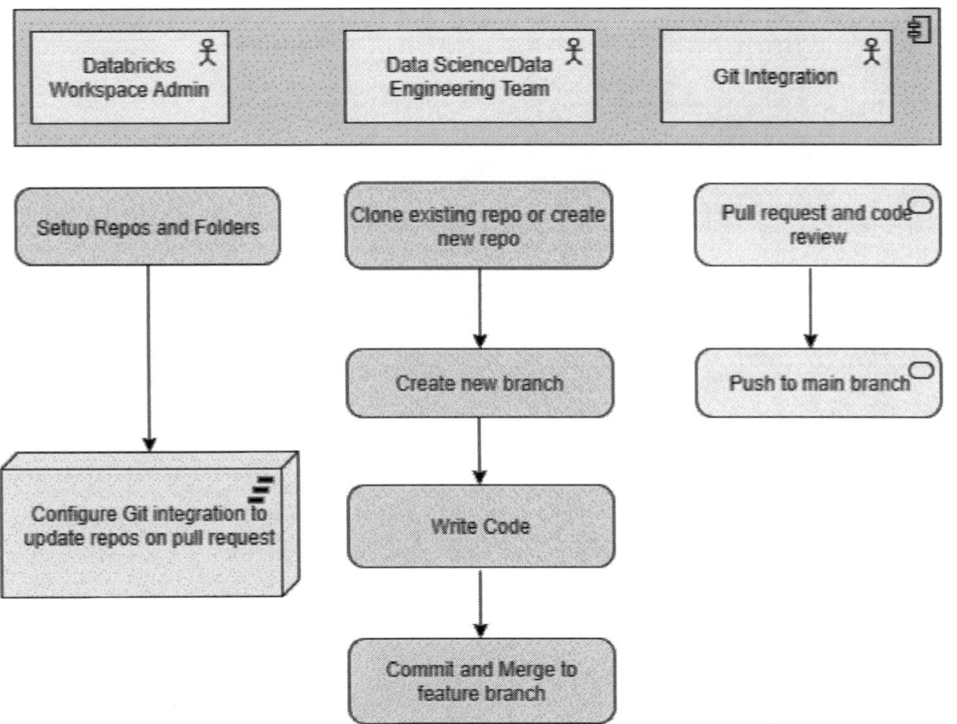

Figure 8.16: Databricks – Best practices for the Git integration

- **Databricks workspace admin**: When we work with Databricks platform, there are two types of folders available on the platform:
- **User level folders**: User-level folders are created automatically for all the users who access the platform during the first-time login.

- **Root folders (non-user level folders)**:
  - o Non-user level folders can only be created by the workspace admin and managed by users who have permission set by the workspace admin.
  - o The most common use case for the top-level folders is to create folders for **`dev`**, **`staging`**, and **`production`** folders, which contain repos for versioning/branching for development, staging, and production environments, respectively:

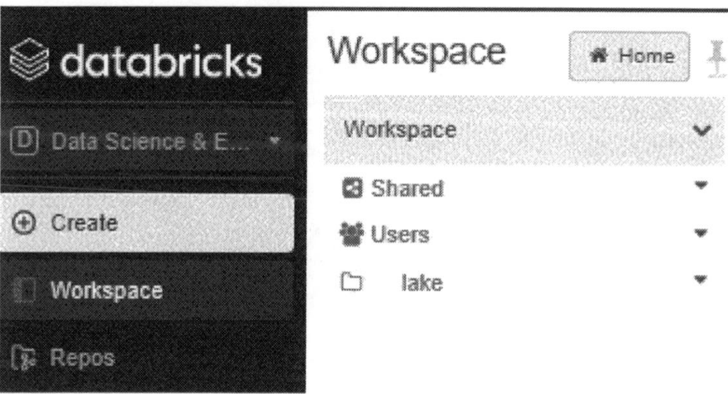

Figure 8.17*: Databricks workspace folders*

In order to make sure that repos always use the latest version, we can set up the Git automation to call the repos API:

- **Data Science and Data Engineering team**: Data Engineers or Data Scientists can start by cloning the repo or creating a new repo using the Databricks repos. The next step is to create a corresponding feature branch or use an existing branch. After selecting the branch, Data Engineers or Data Scientists can make the required changes and commit them to the branch. Once the code is ready, they can create a pull request to review and merge the changes to Git.
- **Git integration**: A recommended practice while working with Databricks for development activity is to enable Git integration using Databricks repos. Start creating feature branches for each new feature and sync it with the remote repository. Create a merge/pull request to the master branch once the code changes are done:

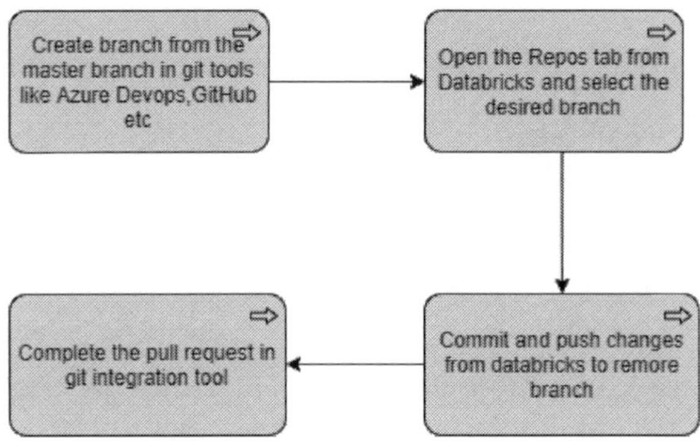

Figure 8.18: Databricks Git integration

There are different ways to integrate the Databricks repos with Git tools:

1. **Using Databricks repos Git integration feature**

   We can configure Databricks repos from the Git versioning tool itself. Let's take an example of configuring Databricks repos from the Azure DevOps tool.

   Go to your Azure DevOps organizations, select the repo that you want to configure, and copy the link to clone the repository.

   Now, go to the **user settings** from the Databricks UI and select the **`Git Integration`** tab, as shown in the following screenshot:

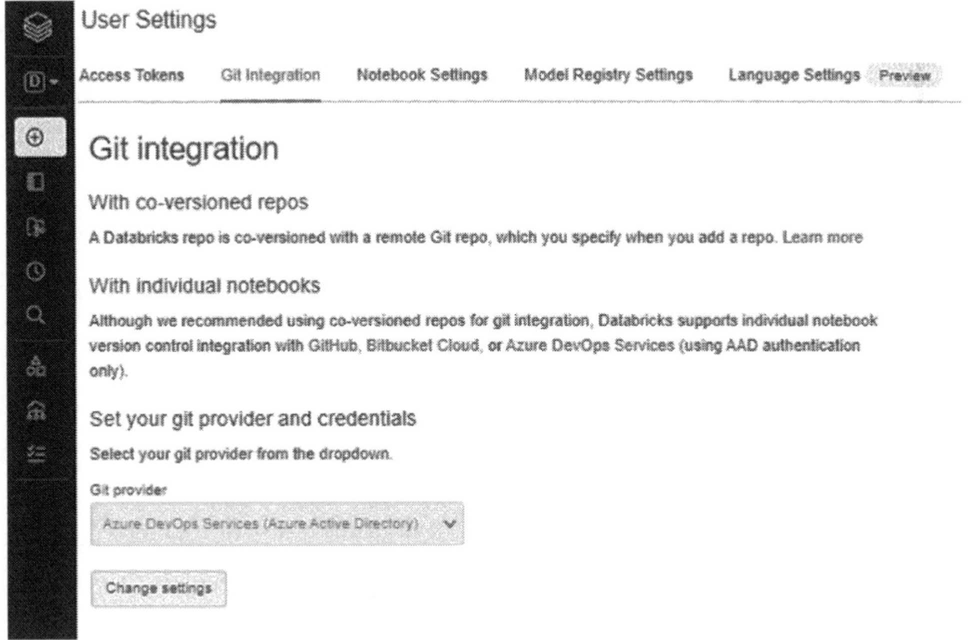

Figure 8.19: Databricks user settings - Git integration

Now, select the notebook, click on **Revision history**, and input the Git repo link, including the branch and input path.

2. **Using Databricks CLI**

   It is a tedious task to manually push the individual notebooks to the remote repository. We can also use the Databricks CLI to download the code onto the local machine and upload it to the repository using the Git command line.

   Once the code is exported to the local machine, use the Git command to check-in the code to the remote Azure DevOps repo:

```
git init
git add *
git commit -m "commit code"
git remote add origin https://<xxxx/yyyy>//_git/SyncDatabricks
git push -u origin master
```

   After understanding the features and best practices of working with Databricks repos, let's also explore the limitations of this feature:

   - **Missing merge functionality with Git dialog**: When the development branch falls behind the master branch from the remote repo, it is not possible to update the branch from the Databricks to avoid the merge conflicts during the pull request.
   - **Syncing of delete branches from the remote repos**: After integrating the repos with Databricks platform, even though the branches are deleted from the remote repos, they won't be deleted from the list of branches with the Databricks repos.

Automated multi environment CI/CD deployment with DevOps

The CI/CD way of working is a modern software development practice that focuses on the frequent incremental code changes with **automated testing, package screening, static code analysis**, and so on to improve the code quality of the deliverables.

Continuous integration pipeline automates build and tests steps to ensure that the request code changes are as per the standard and reliable before merging the changes to the master branch.

Once the continuous integration pipeline is successful, it will trigger the release pipeline to deploy the code/merged changes from the master branch to higher environments:

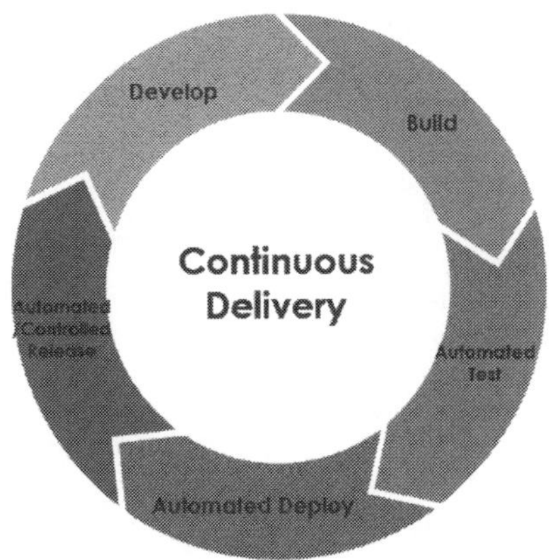

***Figure 8.20**: Continuous integration and deployment*

Let's first understand the high-level steps involved in implementing continuous integration and deployment while working with the Databricks platform:

- **Continuous integration**
  1. **Databricks notebooks and source code interaction**:
     i. Develop the source code and perform tests using Databricks platform or using IDEs
     ii. Perform unit, integration, and regression tests
     iii. Commit the source code and changes to the Git branch
  2. **Build pipeline for continuous integration**:
     i. Pull the new code changes temporarily
     ii. Run automated tests
     iii. Merge the requested changes to the master branch
     iv. Build the package/libraries from the source code
  3. **Create artifacts to trigger the release process:**

     Create artifacts and trigger the release pipeline for the deployment
- **Continuous deployment**
  1. **Deploy Databricks notebooks for continuous deployment**
     i. Deploy the Databricks notebooks to the respective environment, along with the configuration files and related package dependencies
     ii. Deploy libraries for code reusability

2. **Automated testing**

   Run automated tests in respective environments and repost the test results

3. **Operationalize Databricks notebooks**

   Once the notebooks are deployed, schedule the notebooks for your data and AI workload as per the requirements

After understanding the high-level steps of implementing CI/CD pipeline with Databricks, let us understand how to create, build, and release pipeline:

1. **Integration with Git tools**

   The first step is to integrate your Databricks notebooks with the Git tools using the Databricks repos feature. We can sync the work done in Databricks with the remote repos of various Git providers to utilize various features of **version controlling, branch policies**, and so on.

   Refer to the *Repos for Git Integration* section to understand how to configure Databricks repos and best practices to implement the Git integration.

   Once the Git integration is successful, the next step is to create build pipelines:

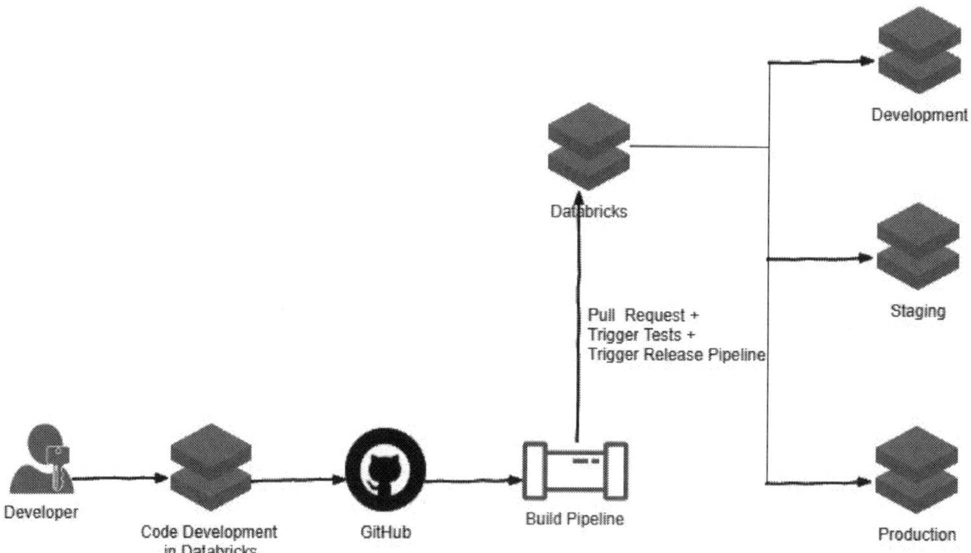

***Figure 8.21**: CI/CD with Databricks*

2. **Build pipeline**

   We need to configure build pipelines to trigger the scanning for the artifacts to be deployed in the higher environments. We can use Azure DevOps, Jenkins, and other such tools to define the build pipelines:

   - **Build pipeline in Azure DevOps**

     Azure DevOps is a cloud-based interface for defining the stages for the CI/CD environments. We can create classic build pipelines or YAML pipelines. Build pipeline runs the automated tests and creates the build pipeline artifacts.

     First, go to Azure DevOps, select **`Pipelines`**, and click on the **`Pipelines`** option:

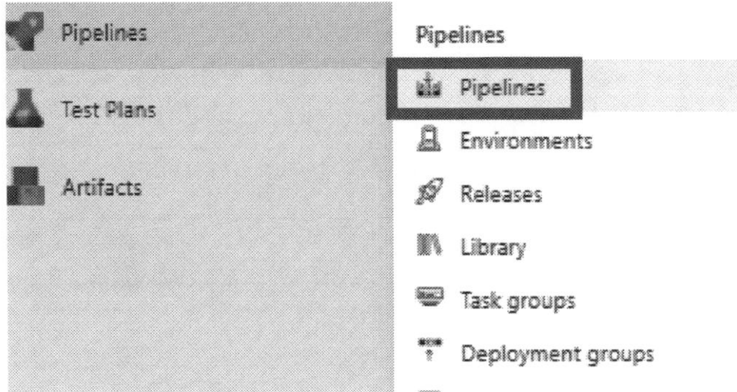

Figure 8.22: Databricks - Azure DevOps build pipeline

     Click on the **`New Pipeline`** button to open the pipeline editor and build the **`azure-pipelines.yml`** file.

     Then, configure the build agent and set up the build pipeline, including downloading the artifacts locally, performing the automation test results, and creating a package to deploy the Databricks notebook changes to higher environments.

   - **Configure build agent**

     o # **Azure Databricks build pipeline - `azure-pipelines.yml`:**

```
trigger:
  - release


pool:
    name: Hosted Ubuntu 1604
```

- **Set up the pipeline to install Python and related packages**:

```
# Install Python
steps:
- task: UsePythonVersion@0
  displayName: 'Use Python 3.7'
  inputs:
    versionSpec: 3.7

# Install required modules including packages required to
execute a unit tests
- script: |
    pip install pytest requests setuptools wheel
    pip install -U databricks-connect==6.4.*
  displayName: 'Install Python Dependencies'

# Use environment variables for Databricks Connect
- script: |
    echo "y
    $(WORKSPACE-REGION-URL)
    $(CSE-DEVELOP-PAT)
    $(EXISTING-CLUSTER-ID)
    $(WORKSPACE-ORG-ID)
    15001" | databricks-connect configure
  displayName: 'Configure Databricks Connect'
```

- **Generate and store deployment artifacts**:

```
- task: ArchiveFiles@2
  inputs:
    rootFolderOrFile: '$(Build.BinariesDirectory)'
    includeRootFolder: false
    archiveType: 'zip'
    archiveFile: '$(Build.
ArtifactStagingDirectory)/$(Build.BuildId).zip'
    replaceExistingArchive: true
```

```
- task: PublishBuildArtifacts@1
  inputs:
    ArtifactName: 'PublishArtifacts'
```

- **Build pipeline using Jenkins**

  Jenkins has different project types to create CI/CD pipelines. First of all, go to the Jenkins UI to define multiple stages in the pipeline:

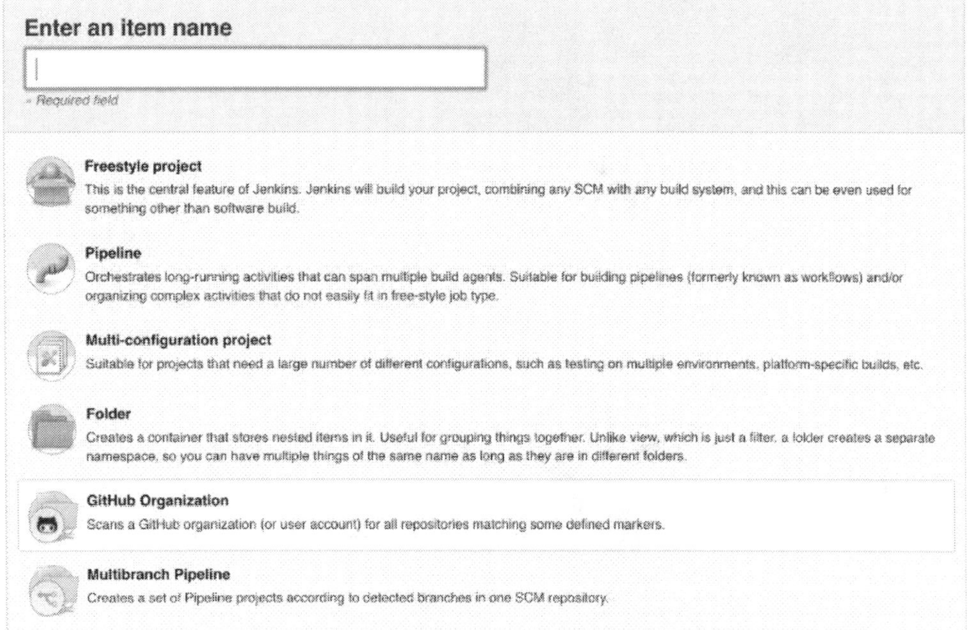

Figure 8.23: *Databricks - Build pipeline in Jenkins*

The next step is to write a pipeline definition in the text file that is checked into the project's source control repository. In the setup stage, configure the Databricks CLI connection with the connection information. Finally, create a stage to generate and store the deployment artifacts to trigger the release pipelines.

- **Create release pipelines for deployment**

  Once the build pipeline is completed and artifacts are ready for the deployment, release pipeline will be triggered to deploy the

Databricks artifacts to all the environments with automated testing stages in between:

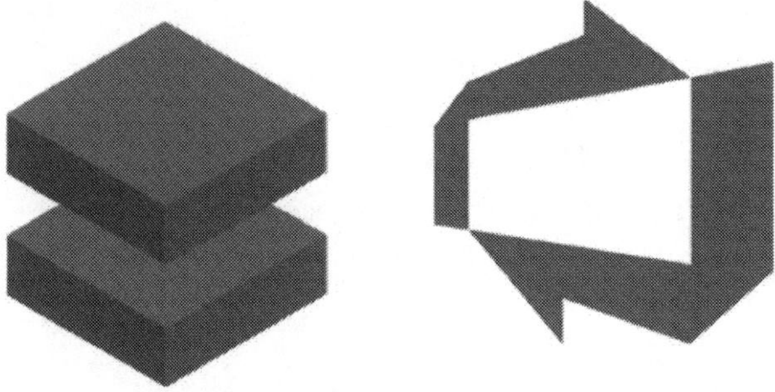

Figure 8.24*: Databricks - Build pipeline in Jenkins*

Based on the choice of deployment tool, we can create release pipelines in either Azure DevOps or Jenkins. We will take an example of Azure DevOps tool to create a release pipeline and understand how we can use it to deploy artifacts across all the environments.

- Create a release pipeline in Azure DevOps with stages for each environment, including the testing stages:

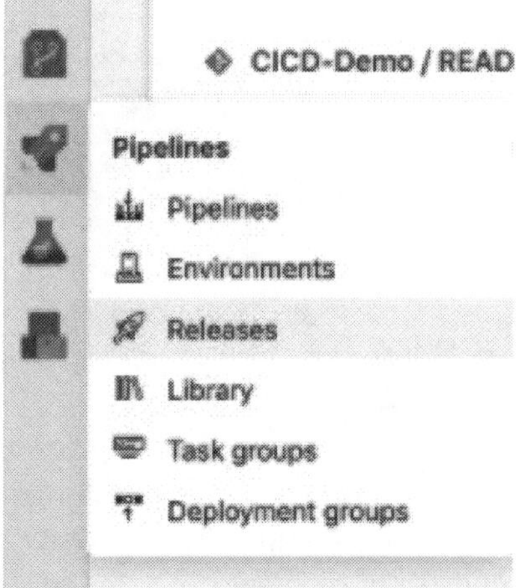

Figure 8.25*: Azure DevOps - Create release pipeline*

- **Add deployment tasks to pipeline stages**

  Once the release pipeline is created, we have to add tasks to the pipeline that will perform the actual deployment of Databricks artifacts to the respective environments.

i. Add **`Use Python Version task`** to make sure that the Python version we are installing the Python version on the pipeline agent with the Python version of the Databricks notebooks:

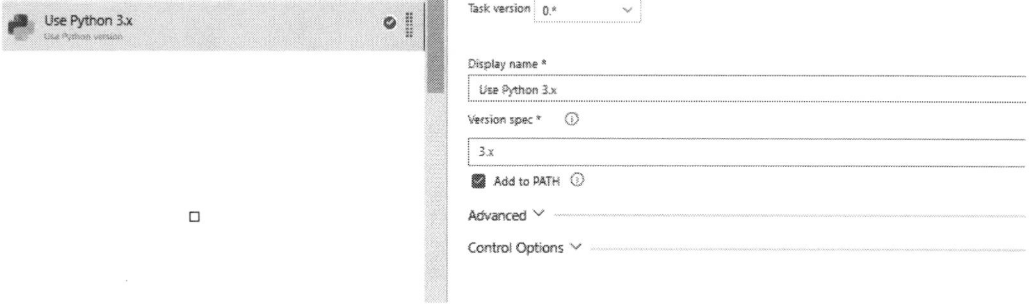

***Figure 8.26**: Azure DevOps - Install Python version*

ii. Add the **`Extract files`** task to extract the Databricks notebooks and related files from the ZIP artifacts files. We have to provide a**rchive file pattern** to **`*zip`** and destination folder name:

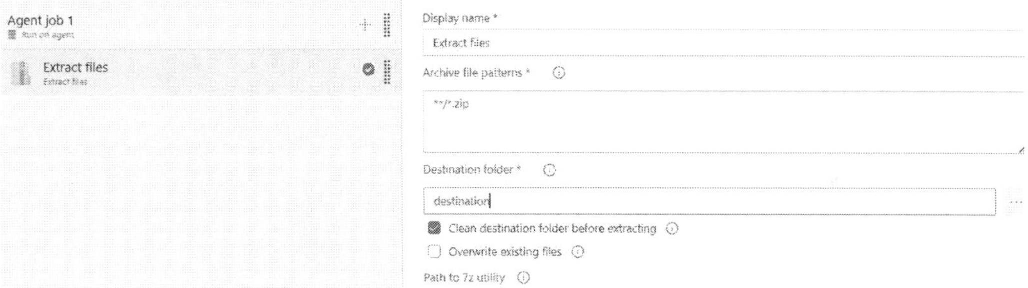

***Figure 8.27**: Azure DevOps Extract file task*

iii. Add the **`Azure PowerShell`** **task** to get the bearer token from the key vault:

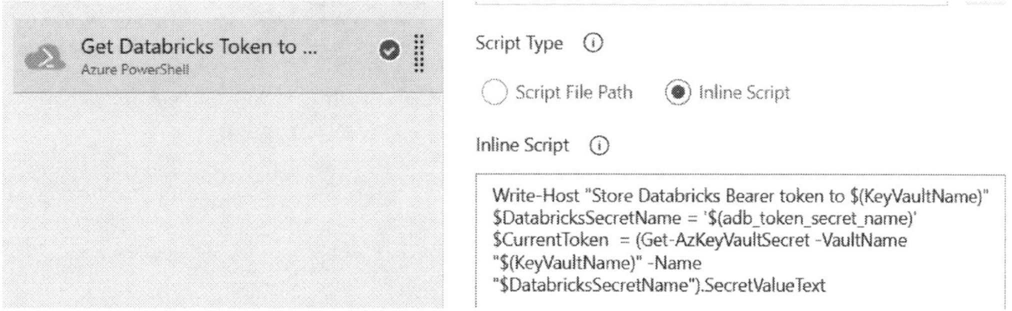

***Figure 8.28**: Azure DevOps Extract file task*

PowerShell script:

```
$BearerToken= (Get-AzKeyVaultSecret -VaultName
"$(KeyVaultName)" -Name "$(adb_token_secret_name)").
SecretValueText
write-host "##vso[task.setvariable
variable=BearerToken]$BearerToken"
```

Here, we have to provide the following details using pipeline variables or initialize these variables during runtime:

`KeyVaultNam`e = Name of the Azure Key Vault

`adb_token_secret_name` = Key vault secret name for Databricks token

iv. Add the **`Databricks Deploy Notebooks`** task to deploy the Databricks notebook. We have to provide **Azure region name** and **Databricks** b**earer token**. Additionally, we have to provide **source file path** that contains the path where Databricks notebook resides in the artifact and the **target file path** that is the desired path within the Azure Databricks workspace directory structure:

Task version 0.*

Display name *
Deploy Data bricks Notebooks

Azure Region *
westeurope

Source files path *
$(System.DefaultWorkingDirectory)\$(Build.DefinitionName)\databricks\notebooks

Target files path *
/$(adb_dbfs_folder_name)

Clean Workspace Folder

Security

Authentication Method *
Bearer Token Service Principal

Databricks bearer token
$(BearerToken)

Control Options

***Figure 8.29**: Azure Databricks: Deploy Databricks notebooks*

- **Deploy configuration files and libraries to Databricks DBFS**

  Add task **Databricks files to DBFS** to deploy the libraries and configuration files to Databricks DBFS. Apart from the **Azure region and Databricks token, we have to provide** a local root folder of the path which contains Python libraries and the target folder that is the path in DBFS where we want to keep libraries and configuration files:

Display name *
Deploy Config file to Databricks
Azure Region *
westeurope
Local Root Folder *
$(System.DefaultWorkingDirectory)/$(Build.DefinitionName)/config/
File Pattern *
.
Target folder in DBFS *
/FileStore/tables
Security
Authentication Method *
Bearer Token
Service Principal
Databricks bearer token
$(BearerToken)

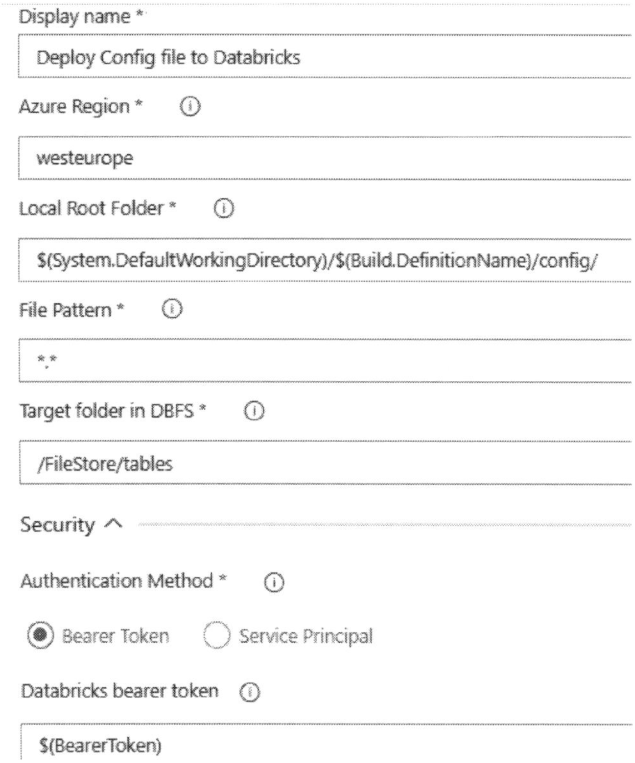

***Figure 8.30**: Azure Databricks: Deploy libraries/config files*

- Finally, add the task **Python script**, which is a custom Python code, to install Python **`wheel/egg`** files to the Databricks cluster:

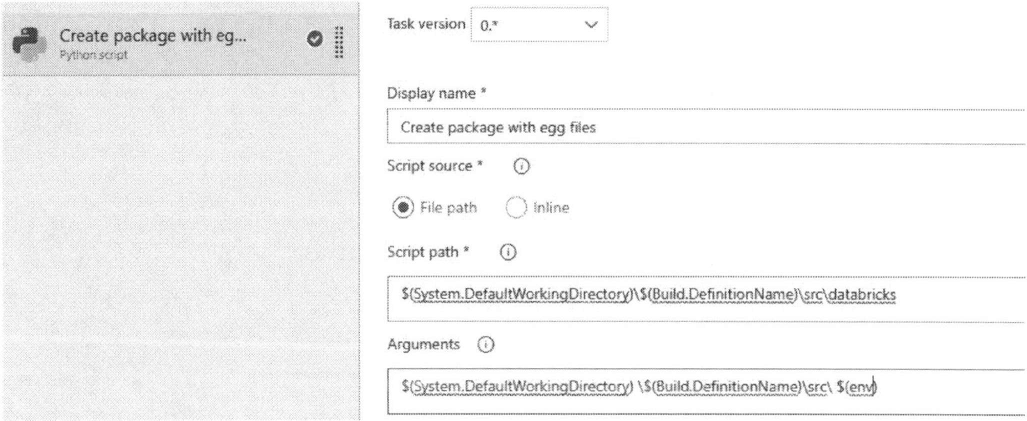

Figure 8.31: Azure Databricks: Deploy libraries/config files

So, we have created an Azure DevOps release pipeline to deploy all Databricks artifacts to all environments with the click of a button. Entire Azure DevOps CD pipeline tasks per environment stage looks as follows:

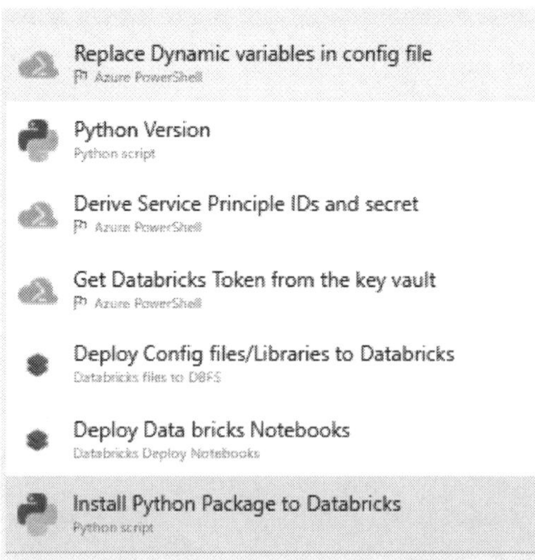

Figure 8.32: Azure Databricks deployment

Once the Databricks artifacts are deployed to the development environment, stages with **integration tests** will be triggered. Integration steps with Azure Databricks notebook can be implemented using Databricks REST API, as follows:

1. **Configure the staging environment**

   Create a command line task to create the directories for the notebook execution logs.

2. **Run the Databricks notebook**

   Add the task **Python script**, which will run the integration test cases for the integration testing. We have to provide a path for the Databricks notebooks and relevant parameters.

3. **Generate test results**

   We have to again add a Python **script** task in the release pipeline, which will generate the relevant test results.

If the test result execution is successful, the release pipeline will proceed with the deployment and will continue to deploy to higher environments using the same tasks we created for the development environment using the task groups.

Overall, Azure DevOps CD pipeline, including all the stages and integration tests, can be visualized as follows:

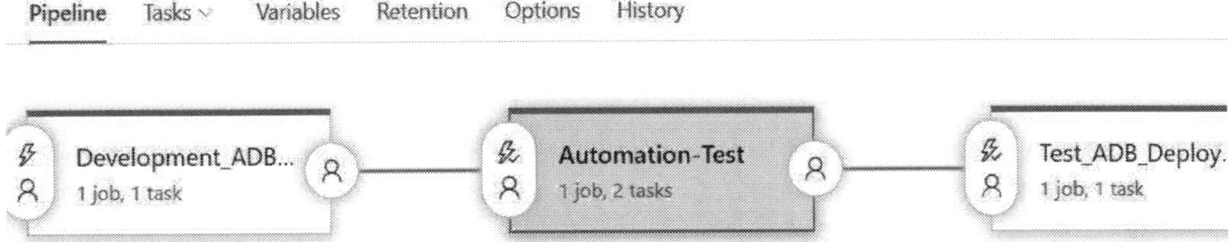

***Figure 8.33**: Azure Databricks deployment pipeline*

It is recommended to use a secret scope to store to manage secrets while working with Azure Databricks. We can create two types of secret scope with Azure Databricks:

a. **Azure Key Vault backed secret scope**

   We can use Azure Key Vault backed secret scope to reference the secrets stored in the Azure Key Vault. We can refer to all the secrets stored in the key vault by the key vault secret name. We can create Azure Key

Vault backed secret scope using this URL: **https://<databricks-instance>#secrets/createScope:**

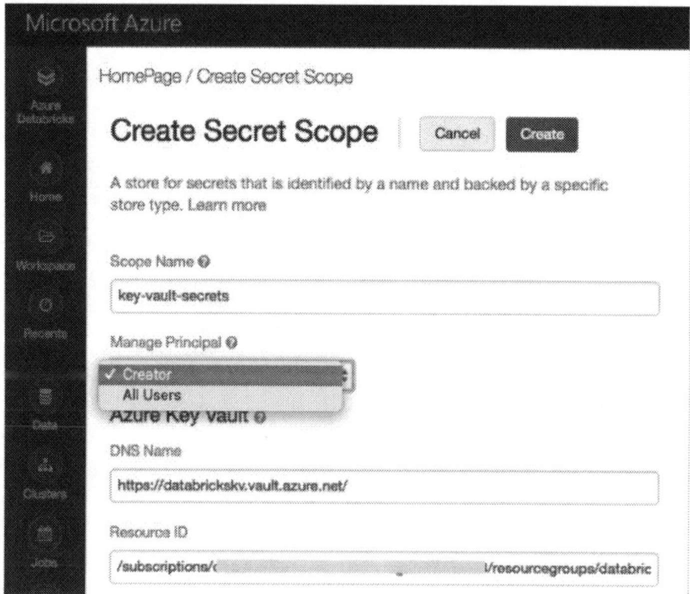

Figure 8.34: Azure Databricks secret scope

Here, we have to fill in the DNS name for the key vault and the resource ID. You can find it by selecting the Azure Key Vault resource from the portal:

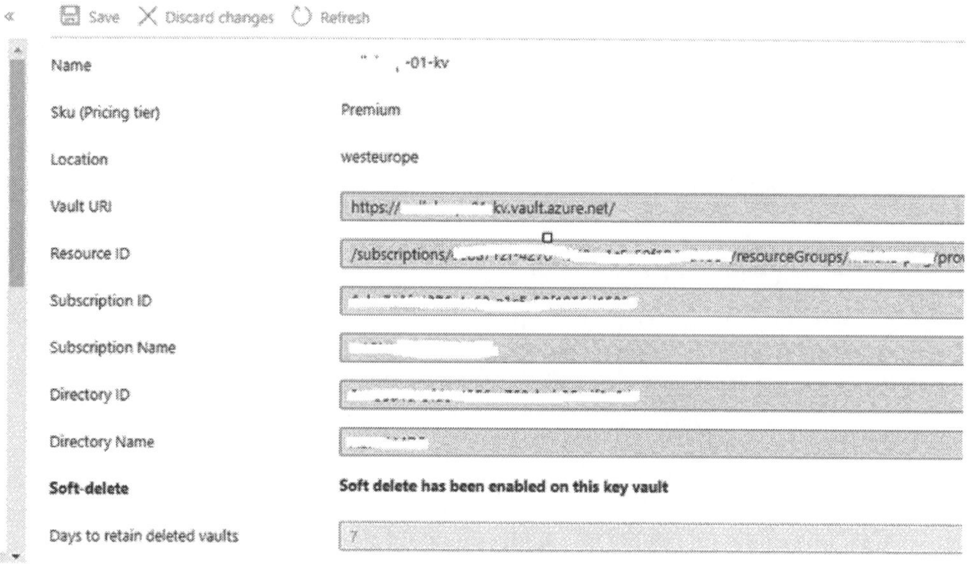

Figure 8.35: Azure Databricks secret scope

Azure Key Vault backed secret scope can also be created using Databricks CLI. You can use this Databricks CLI command:

databricks secrets create-scope --scope <scope-name> --scope-backend-type

AZURE_KEYVAULT --resource-id <azure-keyvault-resource-id> --dns-name <azure-keyvault-dns-name>

b. **Databricks backed secret scope**

Databricks backed secret scope is stored in an encrypted format in the back end by a database in Azure Databricks. Databricks secret scope name should be unique within the Databricks workspace name.

Databricks backed secret scope can be used by the following Databricks CLI command:

```
databricks secrets create-scope --scope <scope-name>
```

So, irrespective of any tools you use, the team can follow the classic Git flow or GitHub flow cycle during the development with Databricks Lakehouse platform:

- Developers can develop individual features using the feature branch.
- Once the local develop is completed, we can commit the changes to the master branch that will trigger the CI/CD pipeline.
- CI/CD pipeline will trigger the Databricks repos APIs to update the project to the latest version.
- CI pipeline downloads the artifacts and performs integration testing.
- Once the testing is successful, the release pipeline will deploy the notebooks and artifacts to higher environments.

Databricks labs continuous integration and deployment templates are the open-source tools that we can use during the software development activity to use the existing CI tooling with Databricks jobs. This open-source tool also has various pipeline templates considering the best practices of working with Databricks Lakehouse platform.

These pipeline templates enable developers to focus on writing the code for the application development on public cloud platforms like AWS, Azure, and so on.

The following are the steps to use Databricks labs CI/CD templates:

1. Install **cookiecutter**:

```
pip install cookiecutter
cookiecutter https://github.com/databrickslabs/cicd-templates.git
```

2. Provide the Databricks token and workspace URL to GitHub secrets and commit the pipeline to the GitHub repo.

   Once we configure the preceding steps, Databricks labs CI/CD pipeline will automatically run the tests for all the Databricks notebooks whenever we commit the code to the repo. Once the code development and testing are done, we can create a GitHub release that will use templates to automatically package and deploy the pipeline as a Databricks job.

   As shown in the following image, Data Scientists and Data Engineers can use Databricks labs CI/CD templates for the testing and deployment of the notebooks. It provides end users with the reusable and generic data project templates to start the development for new use cases.

   At the end of the development life cycle, the whole Databricks project can be deployed to production by creating the releases in GitHub:

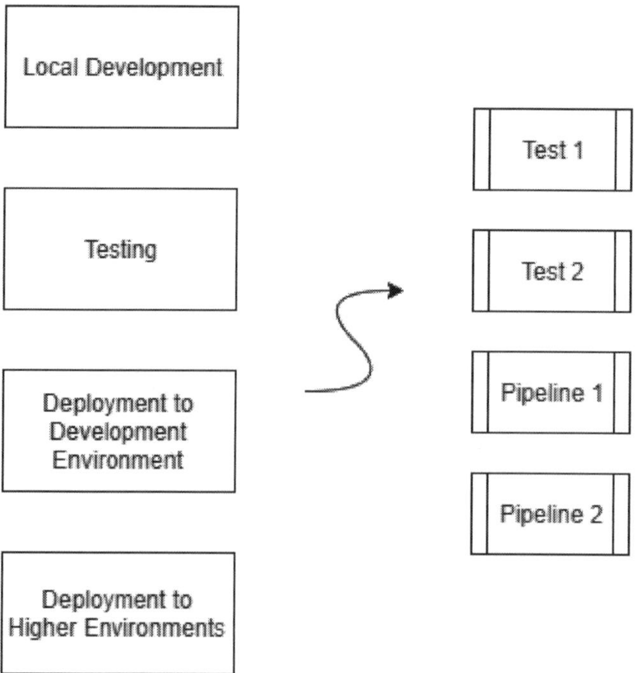

***Figure 8.36**: Databricks deployment lifecycle*

Conclusion

In this chapter, we explored how to use the Databricks repos feature to integrate CI/CD pipelines. It will make sure that we are always using the most recent version of the Databricks code to avoid any discrepancy.

After exploring the Databricks repos for Git integration, we also learned how to create CI/CD pipeline to automated testing and code deployment to development, test, acceptance, and production environments.

Finally, we explored integrating Databricks with various version controlling tools like Azure DevOps, GitLab, Bitbucket, and GitHub.

In the next chapter, we will look at visualizations with the Databricks platform and how various third-party BI tools can be easily integrated with Databricks Lakehouse platform.

Multiple Choice Questions

1. Can we integrate Azure Databricks with Azure Devops?
    a. Yes
    b. No
2. Can we automate Databricks notebook deployment using Azure Devops CI/CD?
    a. Yes
    b. No
3. How can we create secret scope in Databricks?
    a. Key vault backed secret scope
    b. Databricks backed secret scope
    c. Both
4. Can we create non-Databricks files using the Git integration?
    a. Yes
    b. No
5. Can we create Azure Key Vault backed secret scope using Databricks CLI?

a. Yes

b. No

Answers

1. **a**
2. **a**
3. **c**
4. **a**
5. **a**

CHAPTER 9
Visualization with Databricks

Databricks platform has native support of various BI tools like **Power BI**, **Tableau**, **Looker**, **Qlik**, **TIBCO**, **Microstrategy**, **ThoughtSpot**, **Mode**, and **SQL** workbench. We can create interactive visualizations using the data present in the Databricks platform with these BI tools.

In the previous chapter, we explored enabling continuous integration and delivery with Databricks platform. In this chapter, you will learn about visualizations with Databricks Lakehouse platform with various visualization tools, like Power BI and Tableau.

Structure

In this chapter, you will learn the following aspects of visualizations with Databricks Lakehouse Platform:

- Databricks SQL Analytics
- Databricks as a data source with Tableau
- Databricks direct query with Power BI
- Databricks interactive analysis with Qlik

Objectives

After studying this chapter, you should be able to understand the basics of Databricks SQL Analytics. You will also learn about how to create visualizations using Databricks with BI tools.

Databricks SQL Analytics

Databricks also has native support of SQL language, which allows developers to develop SQL applications using the Databricks SQL UI and BI tools.

Let's look at the differences between Databricks SQL UI and BI tools:

Databricks SQL UI	BI tools
Ad hoc analysis of Data Lake using SQL commands	No code interface for data analysis
Create dashboards to corroborate business requirements	Create enterprise-wide reports and dashboards
Monitor dashboards with alerts	Create interrelated dashboards with filtering and advanced customizations

***Table 9.1**: Comparison Databricks SQL and BI tools*

We can use the Data Explorer to access databases and tables in Databricks. Using Data Explorer, we can view schema details and see sample data and table details. Administrators can also change the object-level permission to manage data access in Databricks.

We can access databases from the Data Explorer using these steps:

1. Click on the Data icon from the Databricks UI. which will display a list of databases:

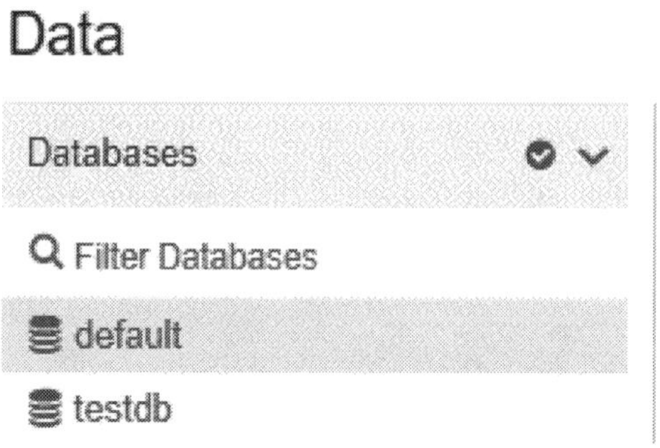

Data

Databases

Filter Databases

default

testdb

***Figure 9.1**: Databricks home page*

2. We can also view table schema with sample data using the Data Explorer. Go to the display **`Databases`** page, as highlighted in the preceding screenshot, and select the table that will display table schema with its properties and a preview of the sample data:

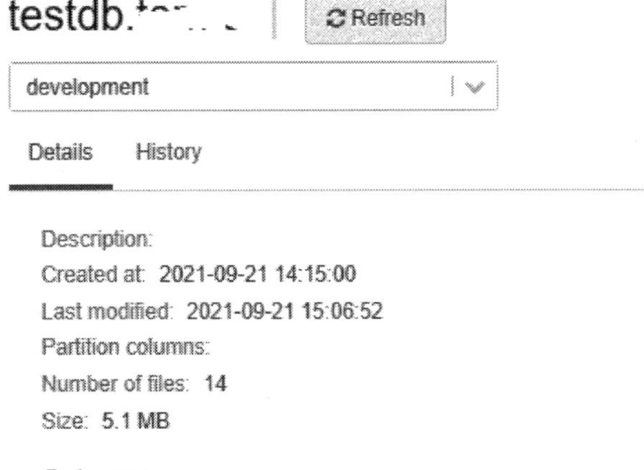

Schema:

	col_name	data_type	comment
1		int	
2		int	
3		string	
4		string	
5		string	
6			
7	# Partitioning		

Showing all 8 rows.

Sample Data:

***Figure 9.2**: Databricks - access database and tables*

3. In order to create visualizations while working with Databricks SQL, you can first open **`SQL query editor`** using the Databricks SQL:

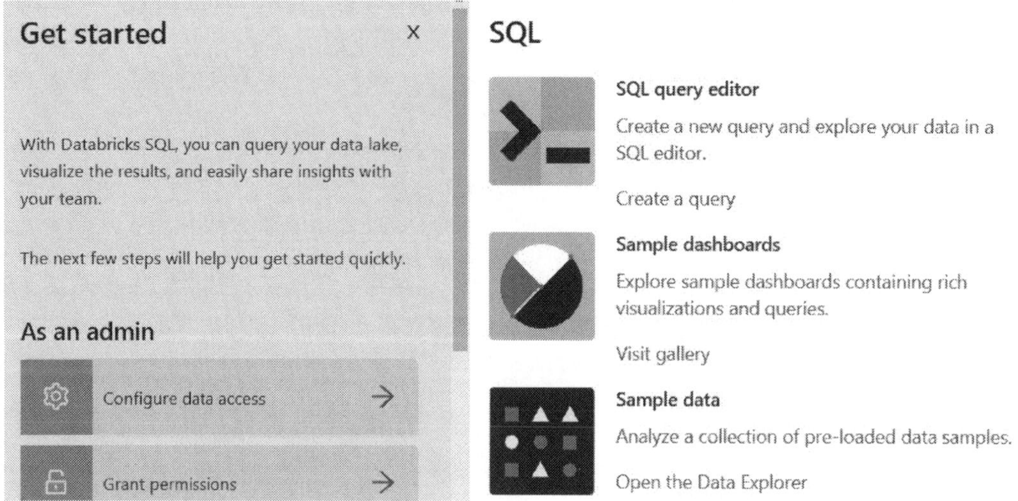

Figure 9.3*: Databricks - SQL query editor*

4. Now, open **`SQL query editor`** and execute the SQL query highlighted in the following screenshot; it will display the result in a tabular format:

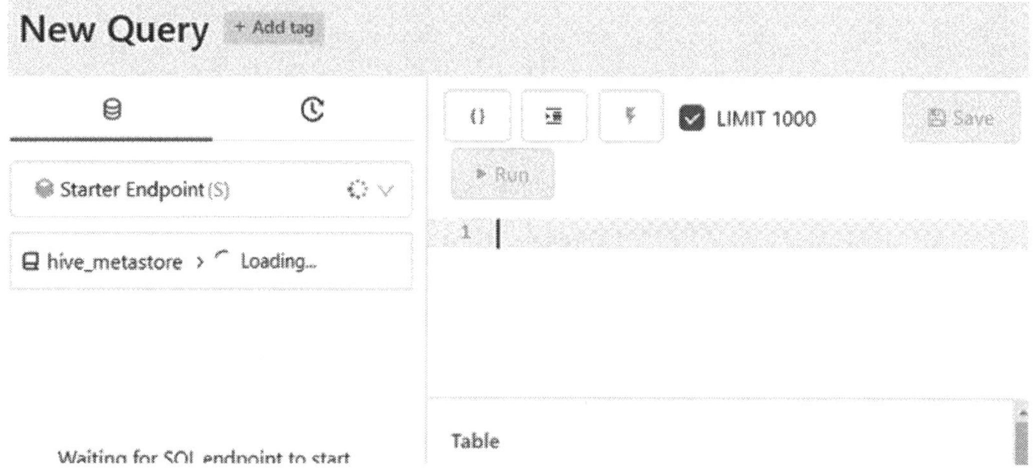

Figure 9.4*: Databricks - execute SQL query*

5. Now, click on the **`Add Visualization`** button to create a visualization. This will open up the **`Visualization Editor`** page, which can be configured according to our requirements:

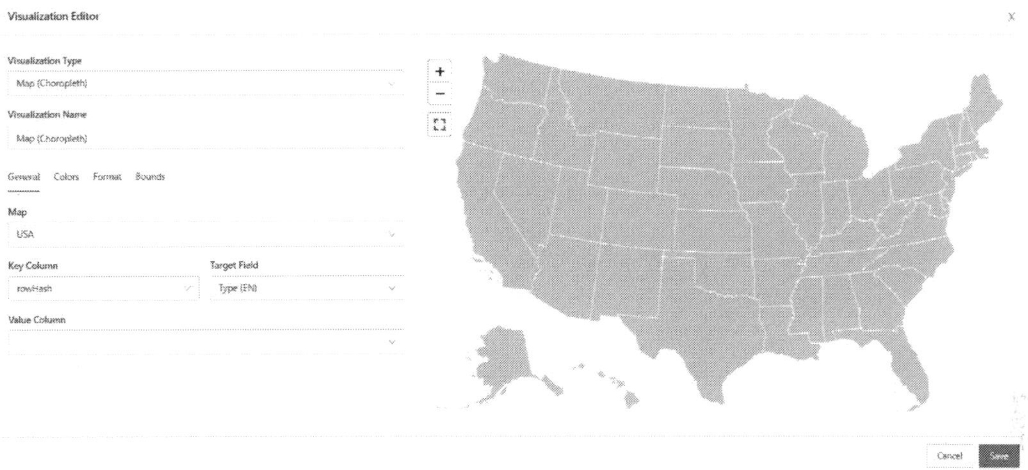

***Figure 9.5**: Databricks SQL - visualization*

We can configure the following properties in the visualization editor:

- **`Visualization Type`**: **`Chart`**, **`Cohort`**, **`Counter`**, **`Details View`**, **`Funnel`**, **`Map`**
- **`Visualization Name`**: Name of the visualization
- **`General`**: **`Chart type`**, **`X/Y Column`**, **`Group By`**, **`Error Column`**
- **`X-Axis`**: Set scale
- **`Y-Axis`**: Set left/right Y-axis
- **`Series`**: Display the data
- **`Color`**: Display the data
- **`Data Labels`**: Show labels with different data/time formats

6. Once you click on the **`Save button`**, visualizations will be saved with the visualization name.

7. We can also add the visualization to the dashboard. Click on the *three vertical dots*, as highlighted in the following screenshot, and select **Add to Dashboard**:

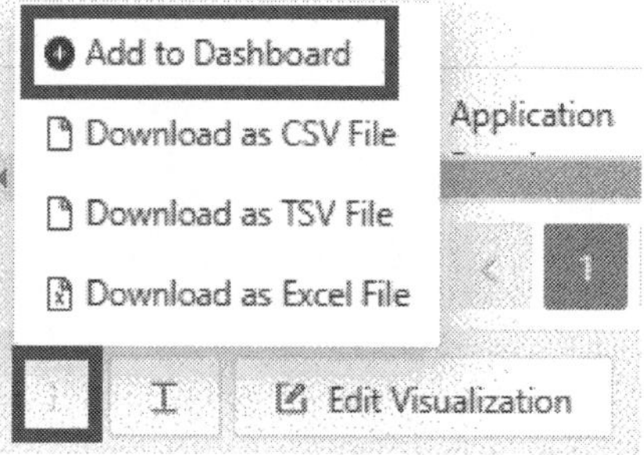

Figure 9.6: Add Databricks SQL Visualization to Dashboard

8. Write the dashboard name and click on **OK**; it will add visualization to a specific dashboard:

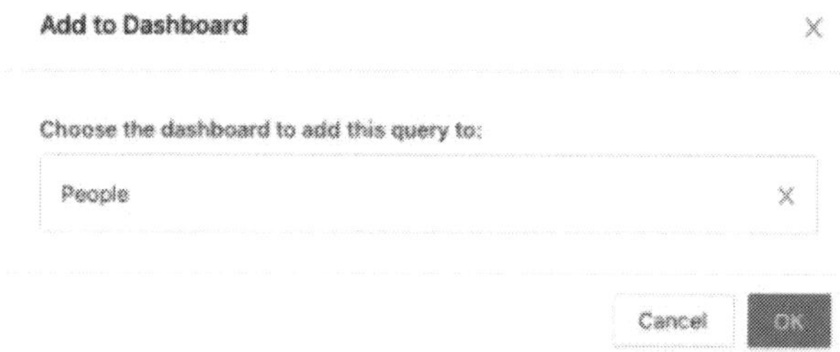

Figure 9.7: Databricks SQL Analytics dashboard

You can also download the chart visualization as an image file.

There are multiple types of visualizations available in Databricks SQL:

- **Boxplot**
- **Charts: bar, area, pie**
- **Cohort**
- **Counter**
- **Funnel**
- **Map**
- **Pivot table**
- **Sankey**
- **Sunburst**
- **Word cloud**

Databricks SQL visualizations that use *X* and *Y axes* are known as **charts**. We can create multiple types of charts in Databricks SQL.

We can combine Databricks visualizations with text boxes to provide explanation about the data. To view the list of available dashboards, click on **dashboards** in the left pane, as highlighted in the following screenshot:

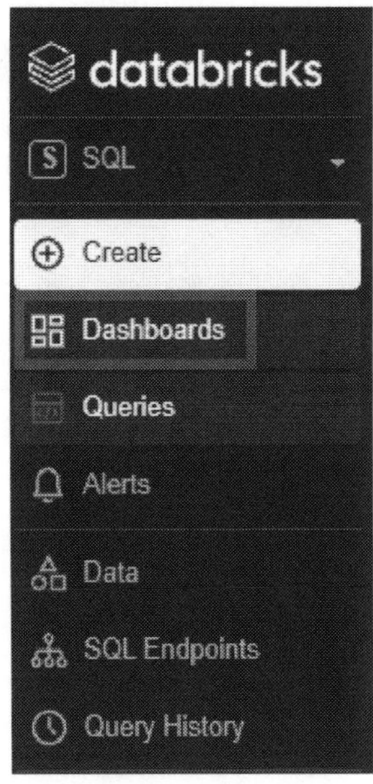

***Figure 9.8**: Databricks dashboards - display list of dashboards*

9. Click on the **`Create Dashboard`** button to create a new dashboard:

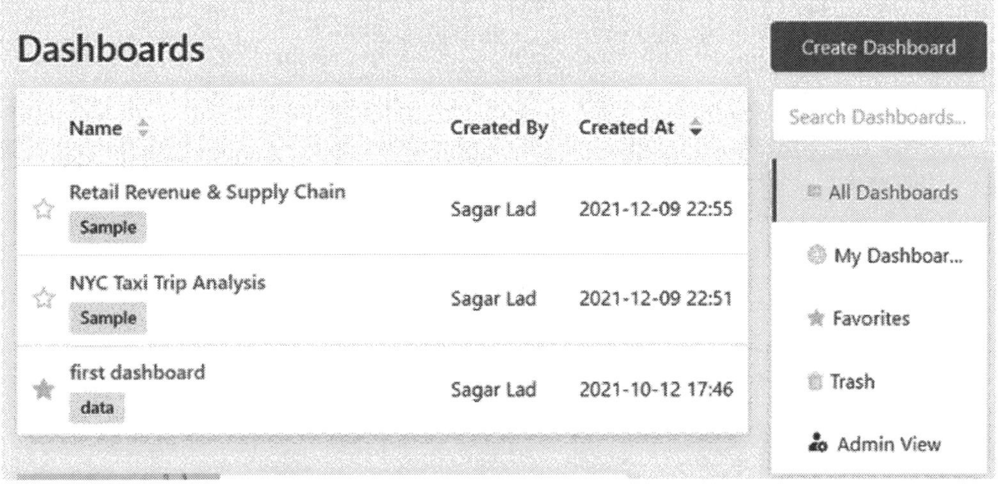

***Figure 9.9**: Databricks dashboards - create dashboards*

10. Once you click on the `Create Dashboard` button, enter the **dashboard name**; it will open the dashboard, as follows:

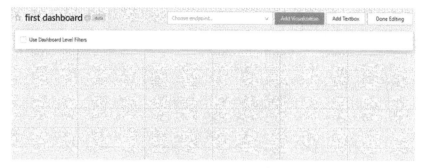

***Figure 9.10**: Databricks dashboards - add visualization and textbox*

11. Once the dashboard is open, you can add visualizations and text as per your requirement. After adding a textbox and visualizations to the sample dashboard, Databricks dashboard looks as follows:

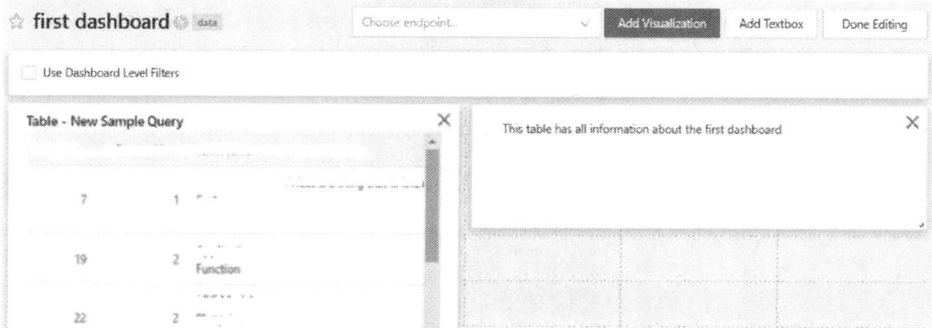

***Figure 9.11**: Databricks sample dashboards*

12. Once you are done with the editing, click on the *three vertical dots*, as highlighted in the following screenshot, to edit, clone, download the dashboard as **PDF** or to delete the dashboard:

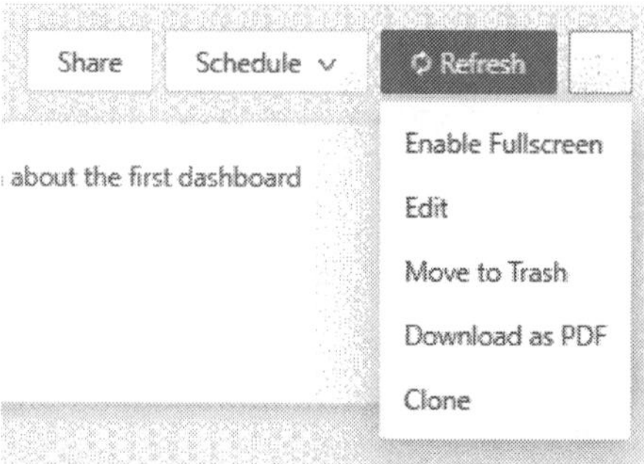

***Figure 9.12**: Databricks sample dashboards*

13. If you want to refresh the dashboard data manually, click on the **`Refresh`** button, and the data will be refreshed.

    We can also automate the data refresh using the **`Schedule`** option. Once you click on the **`Schedule`** button, you have an option to configure the **refresh schedule time, SQL endpoint,** and **subscribers** who will get the report in email. Click on the **Save button** to save these configurations to automate the schedule of refresh data:

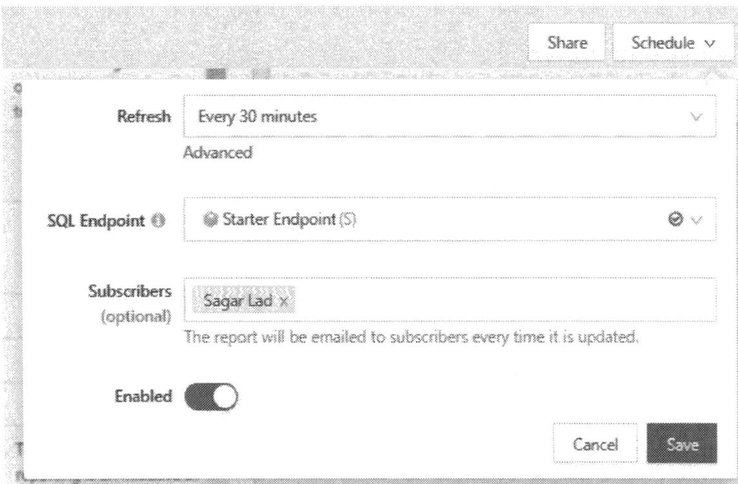

***Figure 9.13**: Databricks data refresh schedule*

If you want to temporarily pause the schedule of refresh data, you can disable the **`Enabled`** button.

As an administrator, you can also delete the dashboard permanently or transfer the ownership of a dashboard if required.

Visualizations and dashboard with Databricks also provide an option to configure alerts to proactively monitor the dashboard for threshold and notification via different modes of communication.

In order to create alerts, we have to create a schedule query. When the schedule query reaches its threshold, alerts will be created based on the notification configuration:

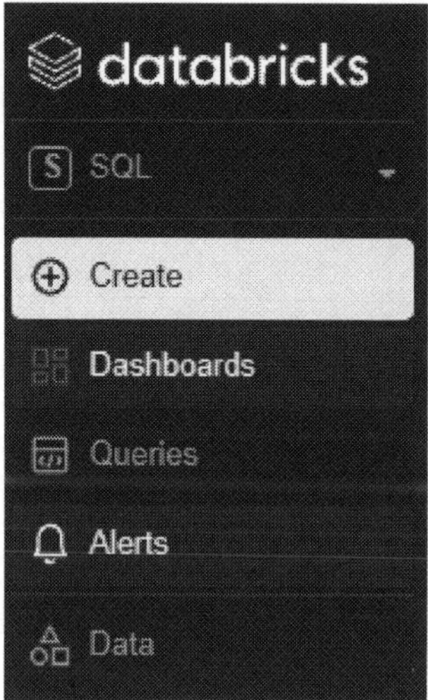

***Figure 9.14**: View alerts*

14. To display the list of existing alerts, select **`Alerts`** from the sidebar:

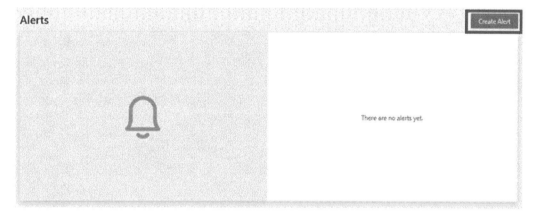

***Figure 9.15**: Display alerts*

15. Now, click on the **`Create Alert`** button to create alerts using the query that will be executed when the specified conditions are met:

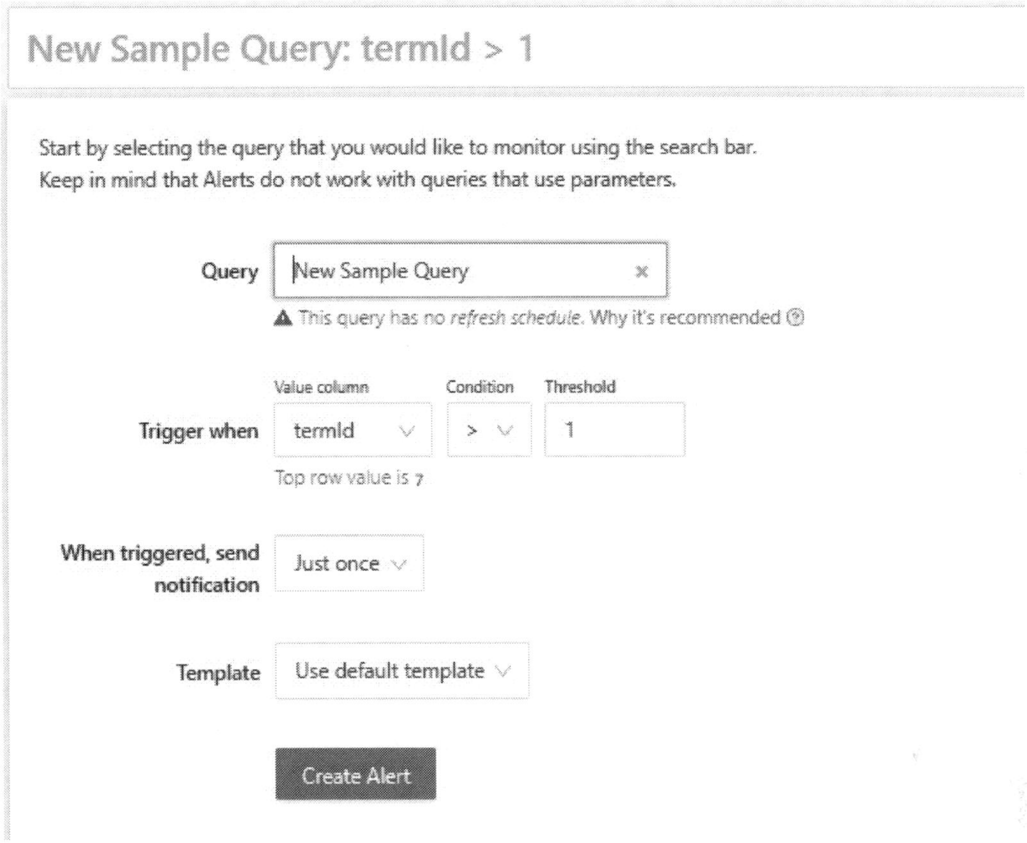

***Figure 9.16**: Create alerts*

There are multiple ways to get alert notifications. In order to configure notification, we have to first create an alert destination. Once you select the **alert type**, we have to configure relevant details to get an email notification. Once a**lert destinations** are created, we can use it to get notifications when the threshold reaches.

We can also set alerts based on the multiple columns of the query using the **`case..when`** statement in the SQL query. When the Databricks SQL sends the notifications to the chosen destinations, it changes the status of alert from

OK to **TRIGGERED**. Based on the frequency of the alert, alert will be set on a specific day:

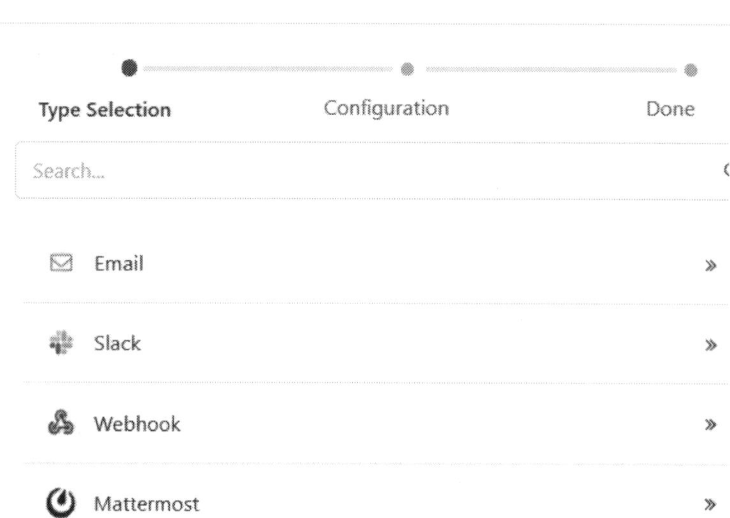

Figure 9.17: Create alert destination

Here, we have to configure alert destination configurations to receive email notifications:

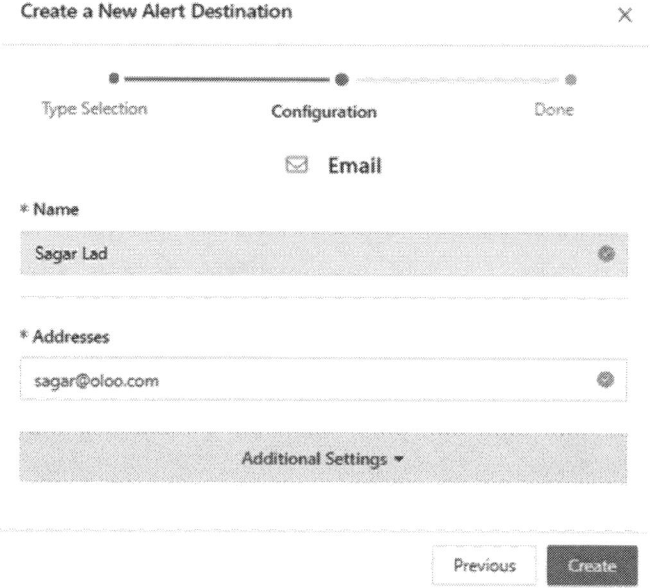

Figure 9.18: Configure alert destination

We can also create favorites and tags to efficiently filter and search queries and dashboards available in the Databricks SQL.

In order to create a favorite query or dashboard, click on the *Star* button to the left of the title in the query and dashboard. Once we click on the *Favorite* button, it will turn *yellow*:

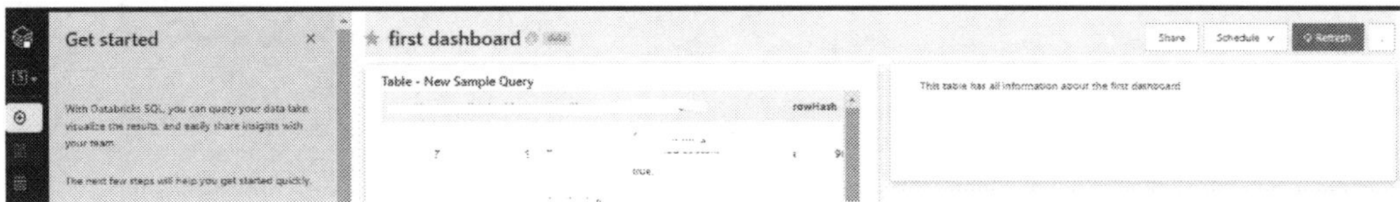

***Figure 9.19**: Databricks SQL - favorite dashboard*

16. We can create meaningful tags to queries and dashboard for our project. Hover over to the dashboard in Databricks SQL, as shown in the following screenshot, and click on the **`+Add tag`** button:

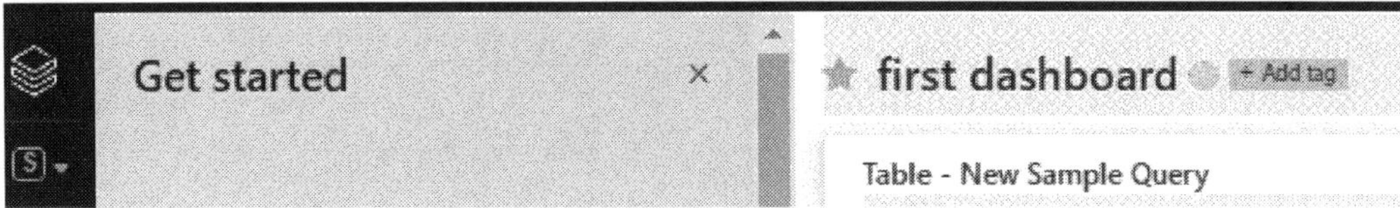

***Figure 9.20**: Databricks SQL - dashboard tags*

This will open the pop-up box, as follows, where we can add new tags or edit the existing ones. Once it is done, click on **`Save`**:

***Figure 9.21**: Databricks SQL - add dashboard tags*

Additionally, Data Explorer in the Databricks SQL enables us to explore and manage permissions on the databases and tables. We can view the schema details, preview the sample data, and see the table details and properties:

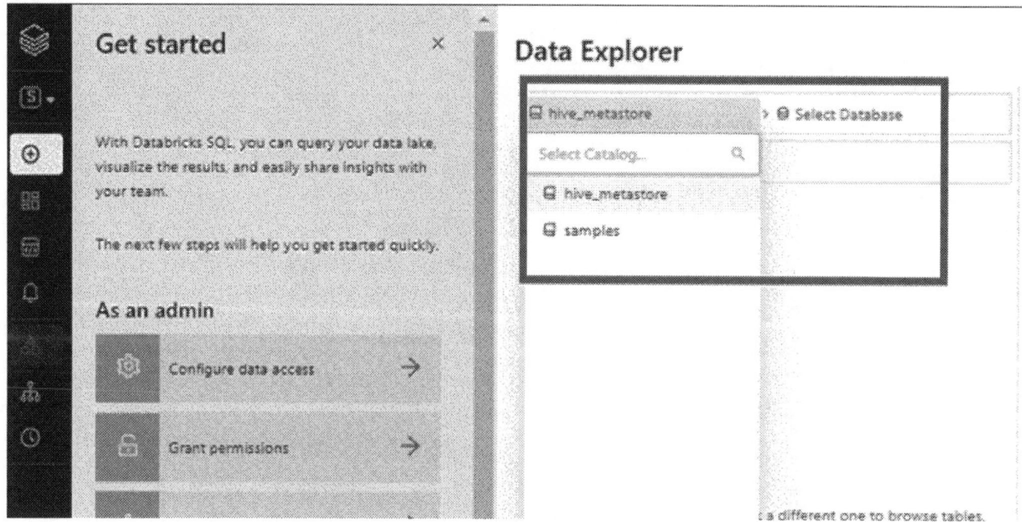

Figure 9.22: Databricks SQL - Data Explorer

As highlighted in the preceding screenshot, once you click on the Data Explorer, it will display the list of available databases.

In the Data Explorer, we can also view the schema of the table, preview the sample data, and table properties:

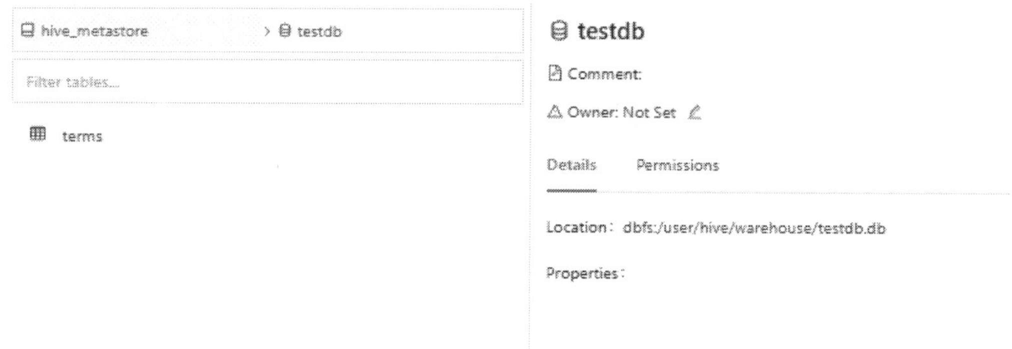

Figure 9.23: Databricks SQL - Data Explorer tables

17. Once you select one of the tables available in the database, it will display the table schema, as follows:

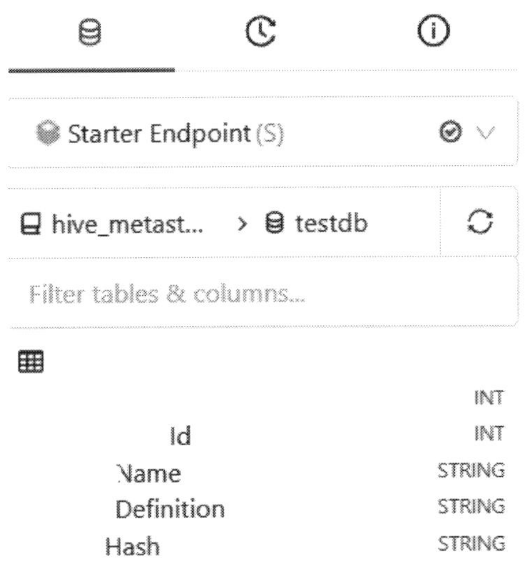

Figure 9.24: *Databricks SQL - table schema preview*

18. Click on **sample data** if you want to preview the sample data. It will display a few sample records for each column of the table:

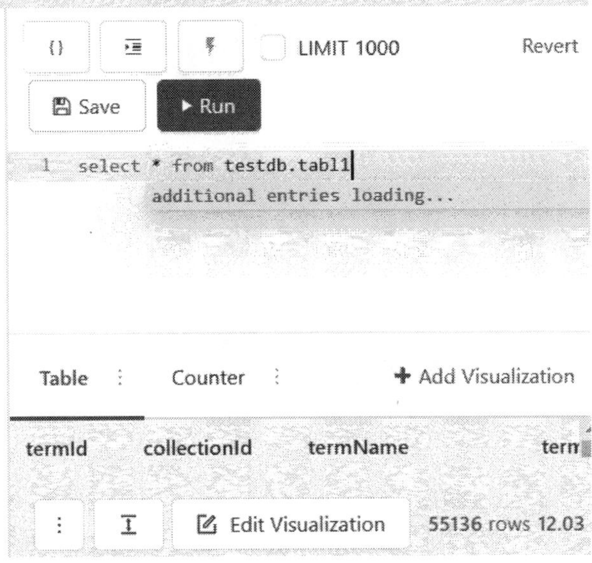

Figure 9.25: *Databricks SQL - table preview*

19. Click on the **`Details`** tab to view the location of the table files, type of the table, and its properties:

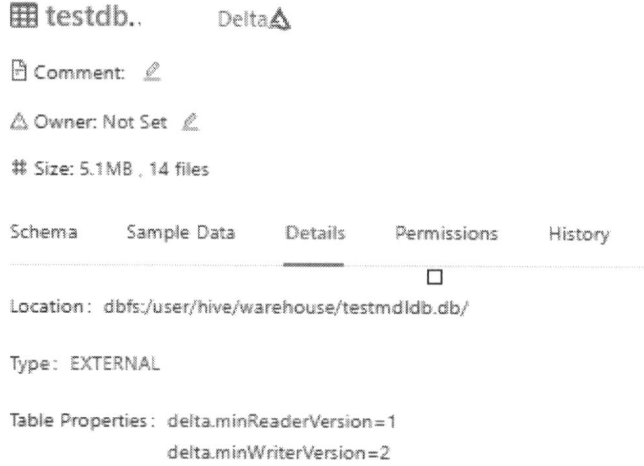

Figure 9.26: Databricks SQL - table details

20. Click on the **`Queries` button** in the left pane to view the list of saved queries:

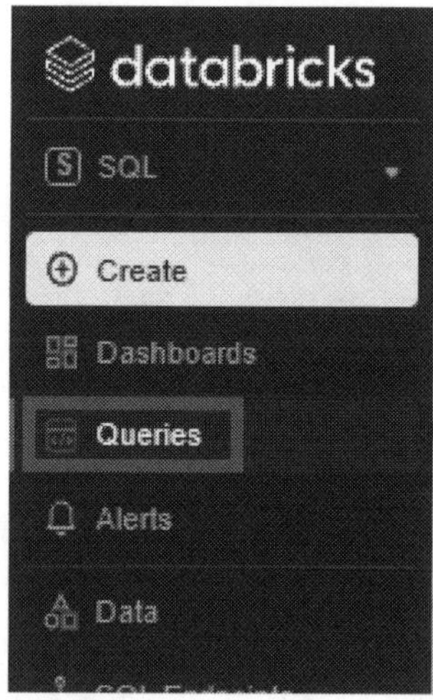

Figure 9.27: Databricks SQL - table queries

As shown in the following screenshot, you can filter the list of queries using different views, like **All Queries**, **My Queries**, **Favorites**, **Trash**, and **Admin View**:

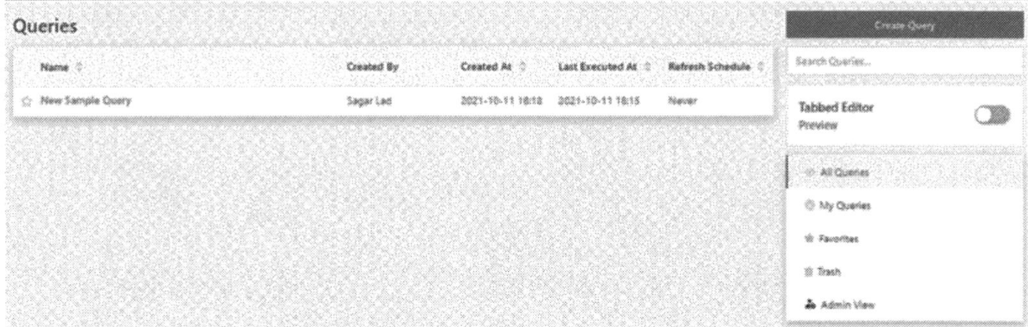

***Figure 9.28**: Databricks SQL - display saved queries*

While writing queries in Databricks SQL, we can also create query parameters whose value can be substituted into the query at any time. Any string between the double curly braces {{ }} is treated as a query parameter.

We can create the following types of query parameters while writing the Databricks SQL queries:

- **Text** (https://docs.databricks.com/sql/user/queries/query-parameters.html#text)
- **Number** (https://docs.databricks.com/sql/user/queries/query-parameters.html#number)
- **Date, Date and Time, Date and Time (with seconds)** (https://docs.databricks.com/sql/user/queries/query-parameters.html#date-date-and-time-date-and-time-with-seconds)
- **DateRange, Date and Time Range, Date and Time Range (with seconds)** (https://docs.databricks.com/sql/user/queries/query-parameters.html#daterange-date-and-time-range-date-and-time-range-with-seconds)
- **Dropdown List** (https://docs.databricks.com/sql/user/queries/query-parameters.html#dropdown-list)
- **Query Based Dropdown List** (https://docs.databricks.com/sql/user/queries/query-parameters.html#query-based-dropdown-list)

For example, to create a text parameter, we can create a query, as follows:

```
SELECT * FROM users WHERE name={{ text_param }}
```

We can also create query snippets to create segments of queries to share and trigger using the auto-complete:

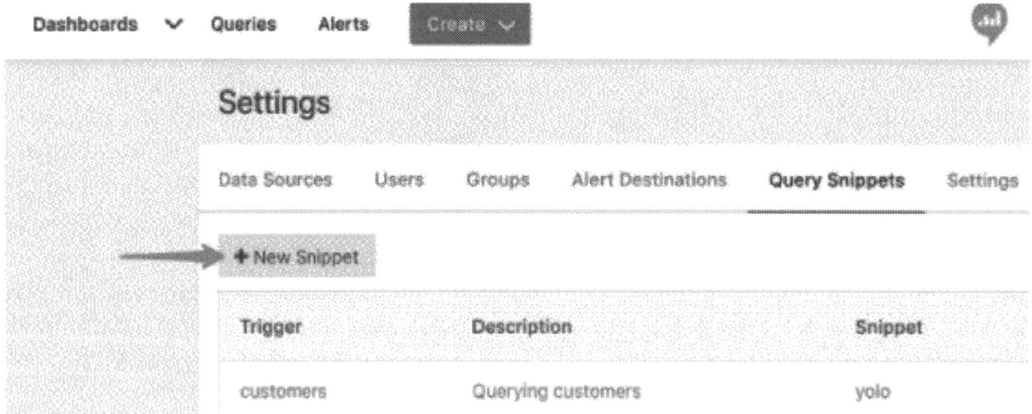

Figure 9.29: Databricks SQL - query snippet

All query history can be visualized from the **`Query History`** section of the Databricks SQL pane:

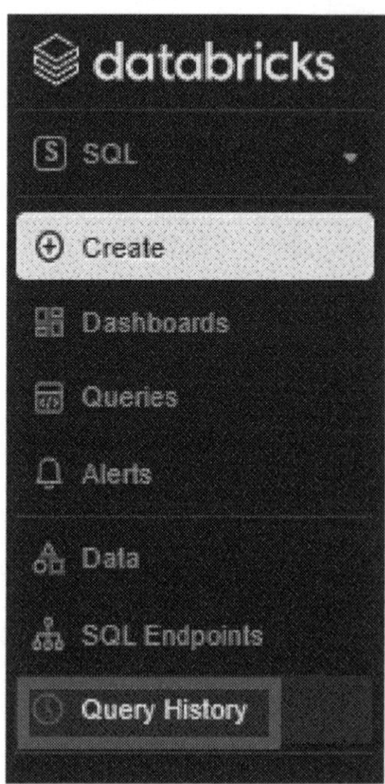

Figure 9.30: Databricks SQL - query snippet

Databricks SQL security model is based on the security model in the SQL database, which can be configured to create fine-grained permissions using the standard SQL statements: **GRANT** and **REVOKE**.

Databricks table access control enables end users to secure various objects in Databricks SQL:

- **CATALOG**: Controls fine-grained access to the data catalog
- **DATABASE**: Controls fine-grained access to a database
- **TABLE**: Controls fine-grained access to a managed/external table
- **VIEW**: Controls access to the SQL views
- **ANY FILE**: Controls access to the underlying file system

Only Databricks administrators and object owners can provide access to the securable objects:

- Databricks administrator can provide access to all the objects and file systems in the catalog.
- Catalog owners can only provide access to all the objects in the catalog.
- Database owners can provide access to all the objects in the database.
- Table owners can only provide access to the tables in Databricks SQL.

Databricks as a data source with Tableau

We can also use Tableau as a data source with Databricks to create persuasive interactive analytics to bring the work of Data Engineering and data scientists to Business Analysts.

Tableau has four tools:

- Tableau Desktop
- Tableau Server
- Tableau Online
- Tableau Prep

We can connect to Databricks from Tableau Desktop and server. We can use a personal access token to authenticate Databricks from tableau. We can also authenticate using the *username* and *password*. It is advised to use a personal access token for authentication.

Now, let us look at every step to connect to Databricks from Tableau:

1. Retrieve Databricks connection details:
    - Databricks server name
    - HTTP path

2. Configure Databricks connection in Tableau.

 Open the **Tableau** application, go to **`Connect`** -> **`To a Server`** and select the **`Databricks`** **connector**:

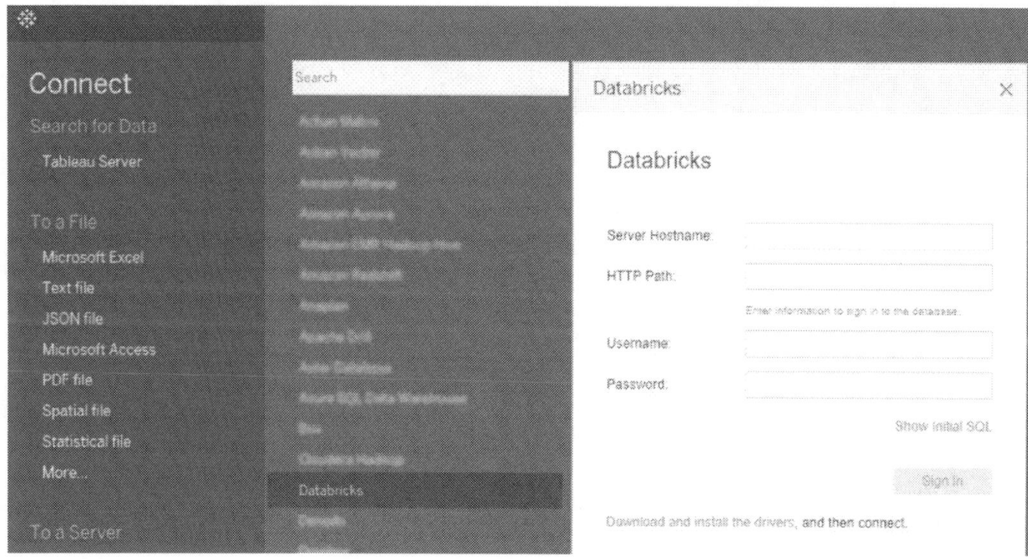

Figure 9.31: Connect Databricks from Tableau

3. Now, in the Databricks dialog, enter the server host name and HTTP path. In the authentication, select the correct authentication method: **`OAuth / Azure AD`**, **`Personal Access Token`**, and **`Username / Password`**:

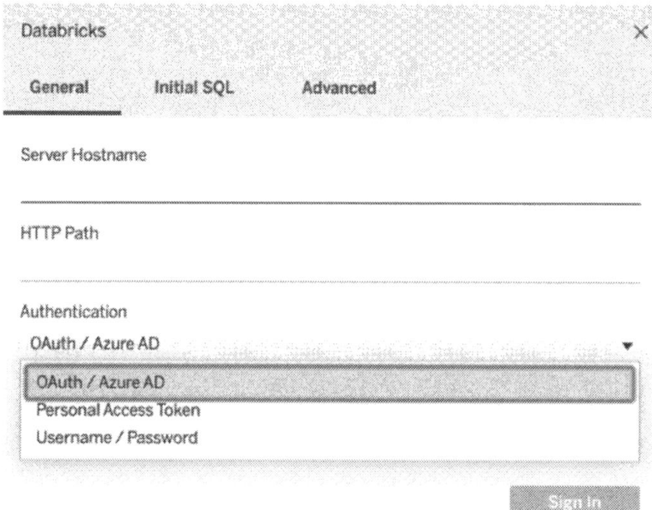

Figure 9.32: Tableau Databricks configuration dialogue

OAuth/Azure authentication is not supported with Azure Databricks.

Based on the selected authentication type, configure appropriate parameters:

- **Personal Access Token**: Enter **Databricks token** in the password field and press *sign in*.
- **Username/Password**: Enter the username and password and click on the *sign in* button.

Once the report is created, we can publish the work to Tableau online. Let's take a quick tour of how to publish reports to Tableau online.

Prerequisite

- Tableau Desktop workbook
- Tableau online account

Steps to publish to Tableau

1. Extract workbook data from Tableau Desktop by clicking on **`Data -> {datasourcename} -> Extract Data`**.
2. Now, browse the location from the local machine to store the extracted data.
3. To publish the workbook data to Tableau online, click on **`Server -> Publish Data Source -> {datasourcename}`**.
4. Sign in to the Tableau server online if not logged in.
5. Now, go to the **`Publish Data Source to Tableau Online`** option and click on the *edit* **link** option.
6. A pop-up box will open; change the *Refresh* **not enabled** to *Allow Refresh* **access**.
7. Select **`Update workbook`** to use the published data source.
8. Click on the **`Publish`** button to publish the workbook using **`Server -> Publish workbook`**.

Tableau online monitors the data source changes as per the configured schedule and updates the workbook if required.

Databricks DirectQuery with Power BI

Microsoft Power BI is a business analytics service to visualize data using the unified, scalable platform for self-service and business intelligence to bring deeper business insights.

We can use the Databricks as a data source with Power BI to use the advantages of Databricks performance and technology for all business users with better visualizations.

Now, let us take a quick tour of connecting Databricks workspace from Power BI.

- **Retrieve Databricks connection information**

  Go to your Databricks workspace and fetch the server hostname, port, HTTP path, and **personal access token** (**PAT**)

- **Configure Databricks connection information in Power BI**

  Open the Power BI desktop, click on the **`File`** menu, and select the **`Get data`** option:

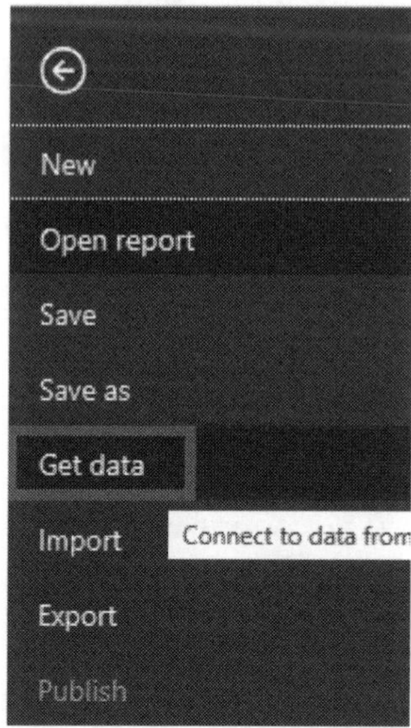

***Figure 9.33**: Power BI desktop - Get data*

After you click on the **`Get data`** option, a pop-up box will open. Select **`Azure`** in the left pane, choose **`Azure Databricks`**, and click on the **`Connect`** button.

Although the preceding screenshot refers to the Azure Databricks workspace, we can also connect AWS Databricks from Power BI.

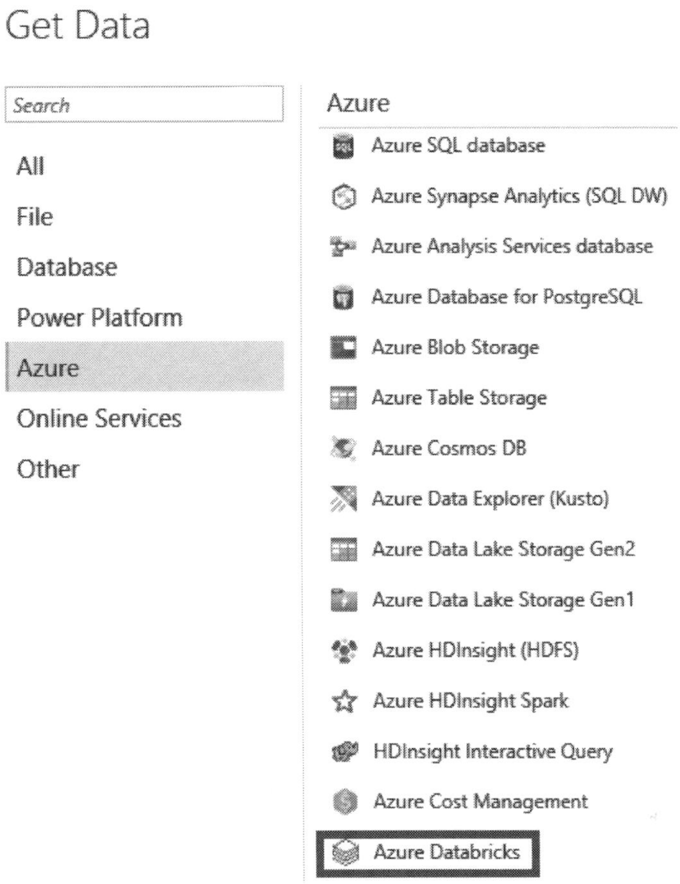

Figure 9.34: *Power BI desktop - Azure Databricks*

Now, enter the **Databricks server hostname and HTTP path**, as shown in the following screenshot. Select the relevant data connectivity mode in the Databricks configuration.

Data connectivity modes

- **Import**: Selected tables and columns will be imported to Power BI desktop.

- **DirectQuery**: Data won't be imported to the Power BI desktop. It will be queried on the fly in Power BI desktop for the underlying data source:

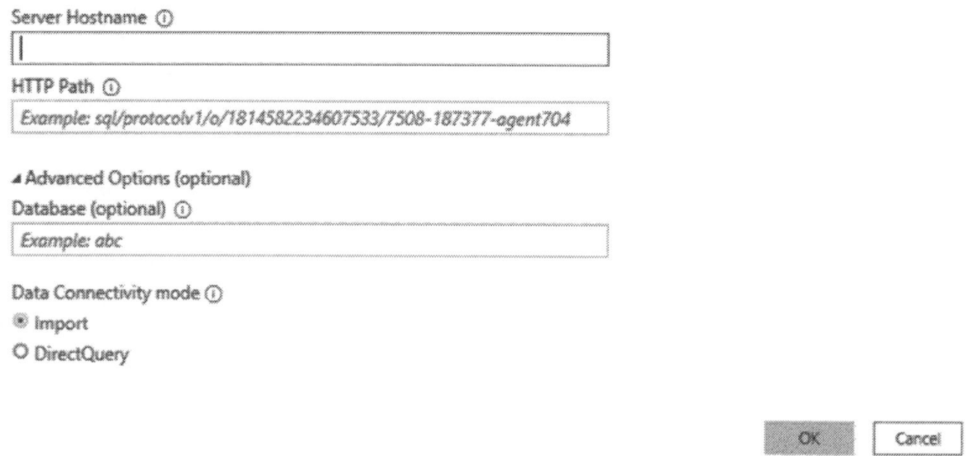

Figure 9.35: Power BI desktop - Azure Databricks configuration

Once you click on **OK**, an authentication prompt will appear. Enter the Databricks username and password, and enter the Databricks PAT token:

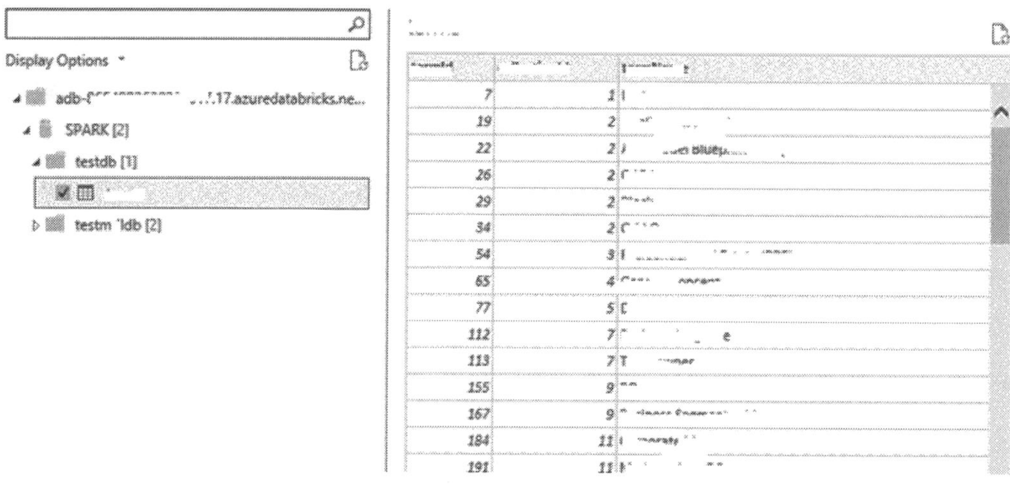

Figure 9.36: Power BI desktop - Azure Databricks tables

There are various benefits of using the DirectQuery in Power BI:

- DirectQuery allows you to build visualizations even with large datasets, where it is impossible to first import the data with pre-aggregation.
- Data we use in Power BI requires data refresh, to reflect the changes to the data. DirectQuery always uses current data and avoids any unnecessary data transfers to display the latest data.
- 1 GB dataset limitation doesn't apply to DirectQuery.

Databricks DirectQuery with Qlik

Qlik is a data analytics and integration solution tool that turns raw data into informed action. Qlik can fetch data from multiple sources like **Oracle**, **Microsoft SQL Server**, **SAP**, **mainframe** into the Databricks delta lake.

Now, let us check how to connect to the Databricks from the Qlik tool:

- Generate the Databricks token as we need Databricks token to authenticate and connect to Qlik.
- Spin up cluster for integration.

When we perform data analytics using Qlik, it will write the data to **S3 bucket**. Databricks cluster will then read the data from the S3 bucket.

In order to access the AWS resources, we have to use the Databricks integration cluster with an instance profile. The **instance profile** will have access to the AWS S3 bucket, where we can write the delta tables.

We can also use IAM credential pass-through, which will enable the user specific access to the AWS S3 data from the shared cluster:

- **Cluster configuration**

  Cluster mode: Standard

  Specify Databricks runtime version

  Enable **Auto Optimize** for Spark configuration using the following properties:

  ```
  spark.databricks.delta.optimizeWrite.enabled true
  ```

  ```
  spark.databricks.delta.autoCompact.enabled true
  ```

- **Connect to the cluster using the JDBC/ODBC connections**: We can use JDBC URL and HTTP path to connect to the Databricks cluster to Qlik using the JDBC/ODBC properties.

- **Configure Qlik with Databricks**: Configure the Qlik with Databricks to connect to the Databricks workspace.

Apart from the preceding tools mentioned, Databricks has integration compatibility with the following partner tools:

Partner
Fivetran
Rivery
Prophecy
Alteryx
dbt labs
Infoworks
Looker
MicroStrategy
Mode
Power BI
Qlik
SQLQ
Stitch
Tableau
StreamSets
Syncsorts
TIBCO
ThoughtSpot

Databricks DirectQuery with TIBCO Spotfire Analyst

TIBCO Spotfire Analyst is an analytical solution to enable users to explore and visualize new data discoveries in the data through the dashboards and advanced analytics.

It can deliver capabilities at scale, including predictive analytics, geo-location analytics, and streaming analytics.

Now, let us explore the step-by-step process to use TIBCO Spotfire with Databricks. You can connect TIBCO Spotfire with Databricks using the **Databricks Cluster** or using the **Databricks SQL endpoint**:

1. First, get the Databricks connection information. Gather Databricks personal access token, server hostname, port, and HTTP path.
2. The second step is to configure the Databricks cluster information into the TIBCO Spotfire tool.
    i. In TIBCO Spotfire Analyst, go to the navigation bar and click on the *plus* button using **`Connect to.`**
    ii. Select the Databricks and click on **`New connection`**.
    iii. In the Apache Spark SQL dialog, enter the server, hostname, and port number.
    iv. Select username and Password for authentication.
    v. In the **`Advanced`** tab, select HTTP and put the HTTP path.

    Once all the configuration details are entered, click on the **`Connect`** button to establish the connection.
3. The next step is to select the Databricks data to start the analysis:

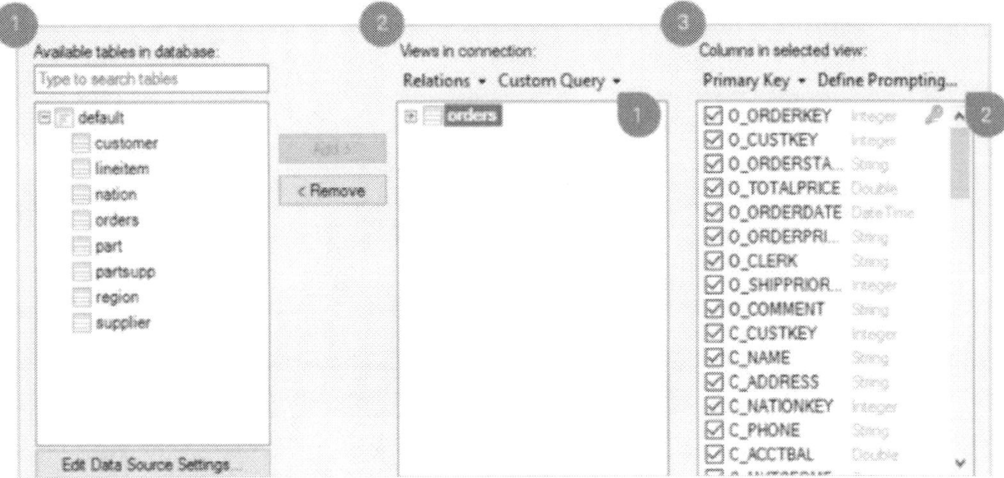

***Figure 9.37**: TIBCO Spotfire - Databricks*

Browse through all the data available in Databricks and select the relevant tables and columns you want to work with for analysis.

4. Once the relevant table data and columns are identified, the next step is to fetch that data from Databricks:

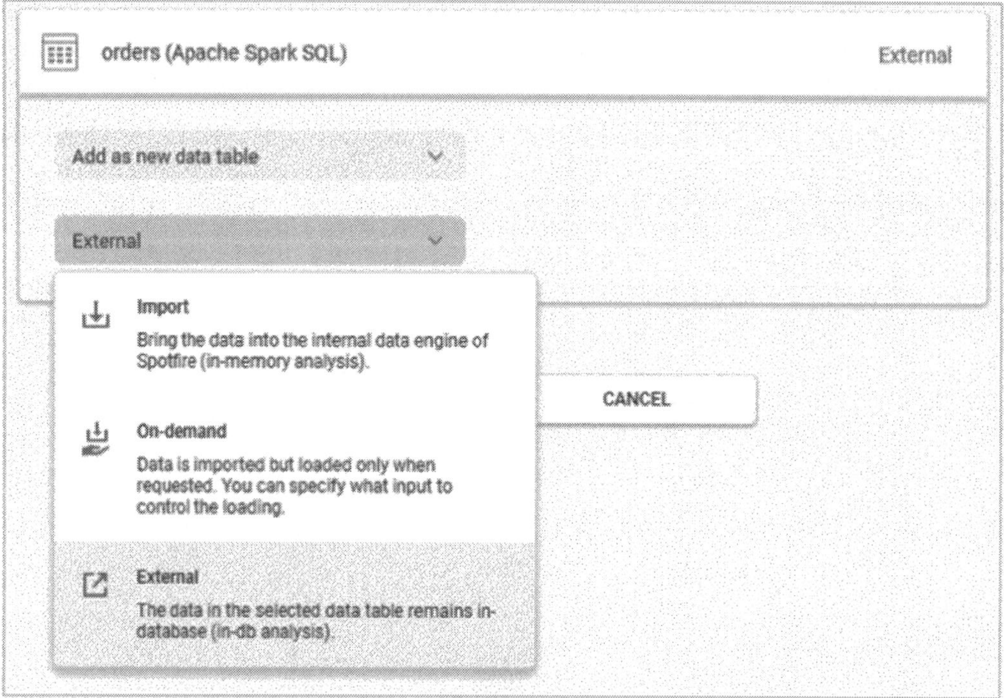

***Figure 9.38**: TIBCO Spotfire - fetch data from Databricks*

The default option to fetch data from the Databricks using TIBCO Spotfire is **`External`**. When we create external tables from Databricks, data will remain in Databricks, but the TIBCO Spotfire tool will push different queries to the dataset to fetch relevant data for the analysis.

It is also an option to use **import**, and TIBCO Spotfire will extract the entire data from the Databricks and load it into the memory for the analysis.

Another option is to use the **`On-demand`** option, in which only the retrieve relevant data from the Databricks required for the analysis.

Conclusion

In this chapter, we explored in detail the Databricks SQL analytics feature to run the ad hoc SQL queries and create interactive visualizations and dashboards. We also explored how to write queries with Databricks SQL and use in-built visualizations to create the dashboards.

After exploring end-to-end query and visualizations with Databricks, we explored how to connect to Databricks from BI visualization tools like Power BI, Qlik, and Tableau.

At the end, we also explored the other partner integrations with Databricks for the visualization.

In the next chapter, you will learn more about how to create secure and governed solutions using the Databricks Lakehouse platform.

Multiple choice questions

1. Can we write SQL queries in Databricks for interactive analysis?
   a. Yes
   b. No
2. Can we download dashboards created in Databricks SQL as CSV files?
   a. Yes
   b. No
3. Which visualizations are available in Databricks SQL?
   a. Box plot
   b. Charts
   c. Map
   d. All of the above
4. Is it possible to create monitoring alerts in Databricks SQL?
   a. Yes
   b. No
5. Can we use oAuth authorization to connect to Databricks from Tableau?
   a. Yes
   b. No

Answers

1. **a**
2. **a**
3. **d**
4. **a**
5. **b**

CHAPTER 10
Best Security and Compliance Practices of Databricks

Not only intruders but even employees within a company can attack enterprise data with the company's system or external private actors. So, whatever solutions enterprise organizations adapt must mitigate the risk to address issues. An application must comply with the best practices of Databricks.

In the previous chapter, we explored the foundation of visualizations with Databricks Lakehouse platform. We also explored in detail how to use external connectors to create dashboards in Databricks. In this chapter, we will understand in detail how to optimize your workload using the Databricks Lakehouse platform, access control, and secret management, and so on.

Structure

In this chapter, we will learn the following aspects of Databricks Lakehouse platform:

- **Delta Lake:** hyperparameter tuning with Hyperopt
- Access control and secret management
- Cluster configuration and policies
- Data governance
- GDPR and CCPA compliance using Delta Lake

Objectives

This chapter is a summary of best security and performance practices while working with Databricks.

Delta Lake: hyperparameter tuning with Hyperopt

Compared to grid and random search, the *Bayesian approach* is more efficient. So, we can explore larger ranges of hyperparameters using the Hyperopt tree of *Parzen estimators*:

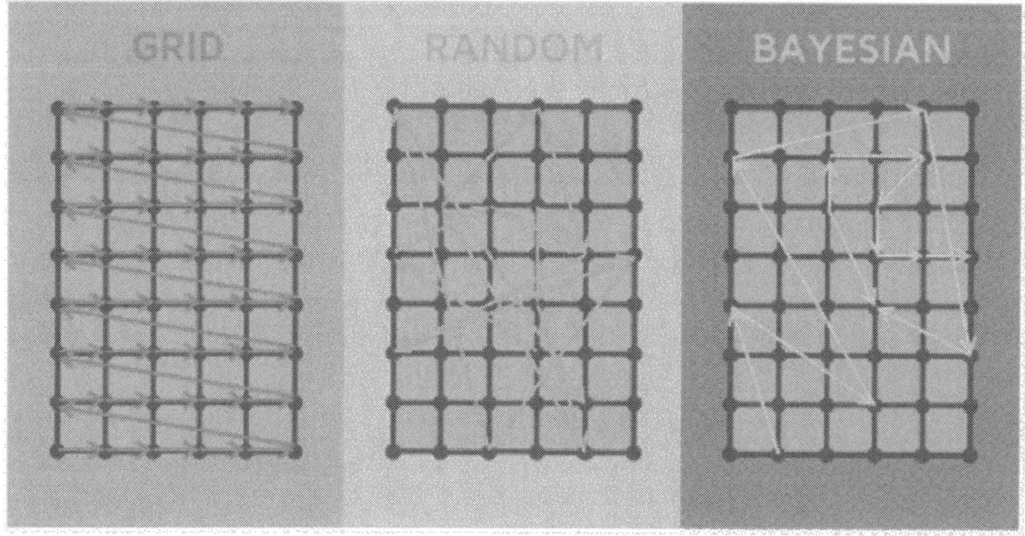

Figure 10.1: *Grid, random, and Bayesian search*

Hyperopt returns the index of the choice list when we use **`hp.choice()`**. So, the parameter logged in MLflow is also the index. We should use **`hyperopt.space_eval()`** to retrieve the parameter values:

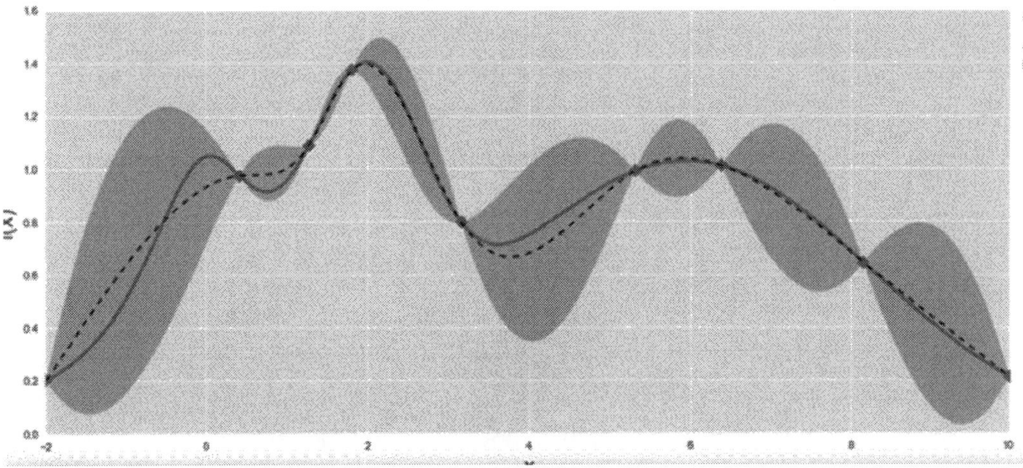

***Figure 10.2**: Automatic hyperparameter optimization with Hyperopt*

It is recommended to start experiments with a small number of datasets and many hyperparameters for a machine learning model, which requires long training time. Once it is done, we can reduce the parameter space as well to identify the best model and evaluate which hyperparameters can be fixed:

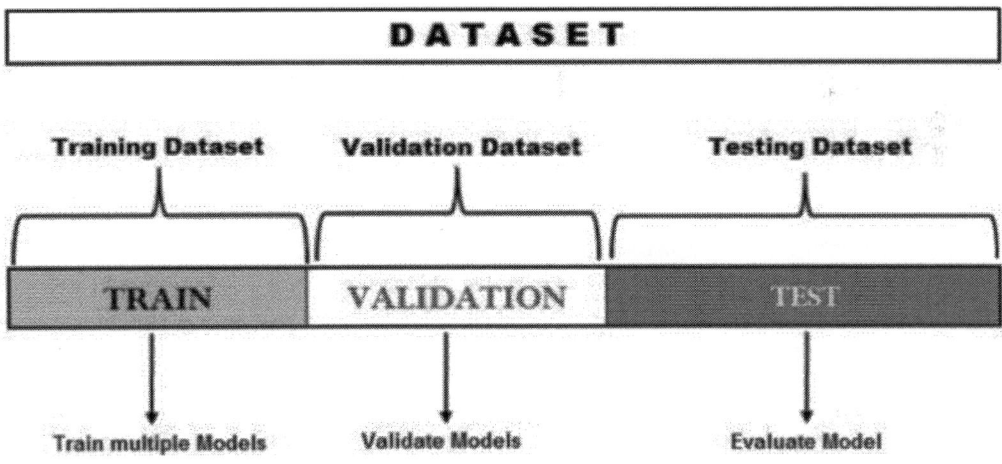

***Figure 10.3**: Training, validation, and test dataset*

CPU and GPU clusters in Databricks use a different number of executor threads for each worker node. In general, CPU clusters use multiple executor threads per node, whereas GPU clusters use one executor thread per node to avoid conflicts among multiple Spark tasks. So, we should take care of how many GPUs each trial can use while selecting the GPU instance types:

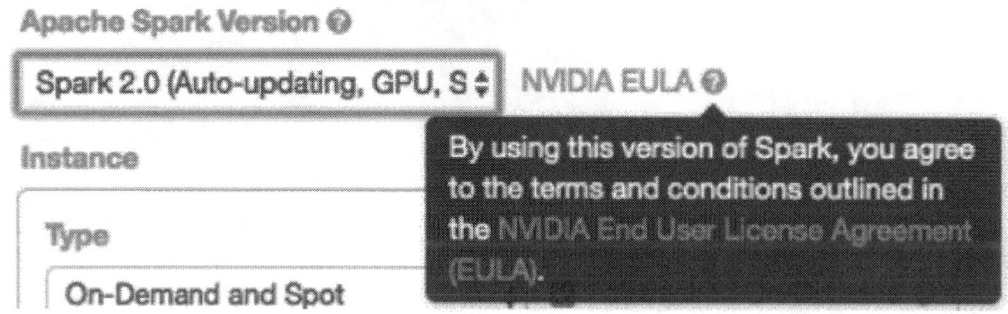

***Figure 10.4**: Databricks GPU Clusters*

Access control and secret management

While working with the Databricks Lakehouse platform, we need to manage access to the data stored as well as the objects.

- **Share data using delta sharing**

  Delta sharing is an open-source protocol developed by Databricks to securely exchange data sharing within the organizations. For Databricks Lakehouse platform, we can share data using the unity catalog:

***Figure 10.5**: Databricks delta sharing protocol*

Reference: **https://databricks.com/blog/2021/05/26/introducing-delta-sharing-an-open-protocol-for-secure-data-sharing.html**

- **Instance profile**

  It is also possible to secure data stored in the Databricks using the instance profile. But one of the preconditions to use the instance profile is that the IAM role must have mandatory permissions to access the S3 bucket. In addition to this, we must add the instance profile to the Databricks workspace:

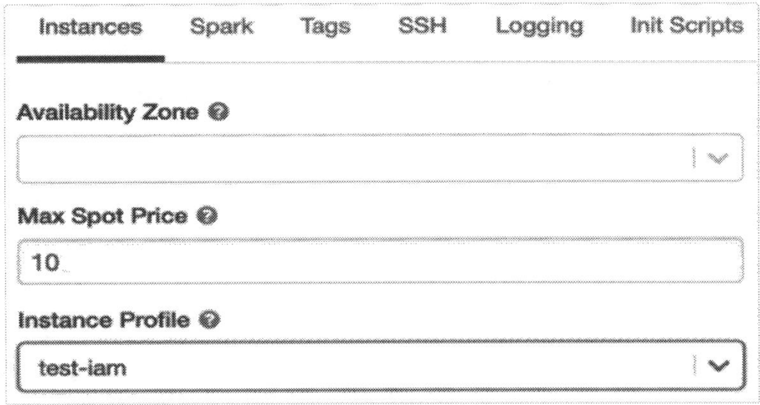

***Figure 10.6**: Databricks instance profile*

Once the cluster is created, we need to make sure that only authorized users have access to the notebook, and unauthorized user access is denied:

Permission Settings for: **New Cluster**

Who has access:

admins (group) — Can Manage

✓ No Permissions
Can Attach To
Can Restart
Can Manage

Add Users and Groups:

Can Attach To — Add

Done

***Figure 10.7**: Databricks cluster permission settings*

- **Credential passthrough**

  Using the Databricks IAM credential passthrough, we can authenticate automatically to S3 buckets from Databricks clusters using the identity to log in to Databricks. When we create a new Databricks cluster, we can enable credential passthrough:

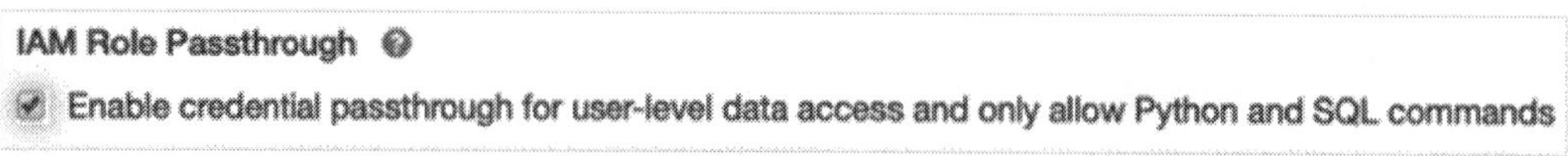

***Figure 10.8**: Databricks credential passthrough - high concurrency cluster*

  In order to enable credential passthrough for standard cluster, use the following option:

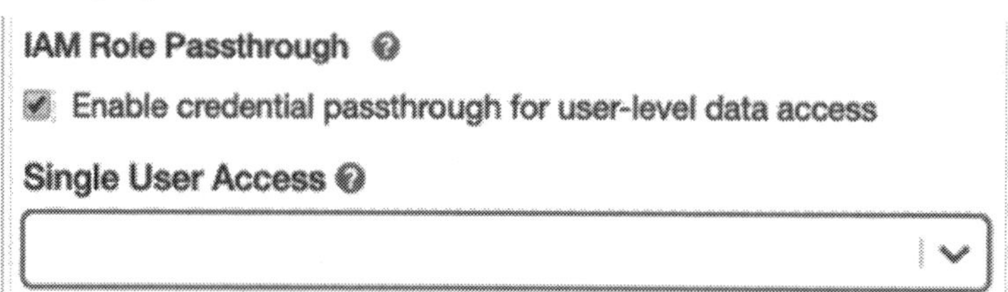

***Figure 10.9**: Databricks credential passthrough - standard cluster*

- **Table access control**

  We can enable table access control in a workspace to programmatically grant, deny, and revoke access to the data from the Spark SQL API. For example, consider an enterprise organization that stores financial data. A company wants analysts to create financial reports using this data. However, data might contain confidential information, which analysts should not access. We can provide the user or group the privileges required to read data from one table but deny all privileges to access the second table.

  In the following illustration, administrator provides **user A**, an **analyst**, with the privileges required to read from **`shared_table`** but denies all privileges to other data.

```
%sql

GRANT Select on Table BFS.shared_table To userA@comp.com
```

  In order to deny access to other data, we can deny privileges:

```
%sql

DENY ALL Privileges on table BFS.private TO userA@comp.com
```

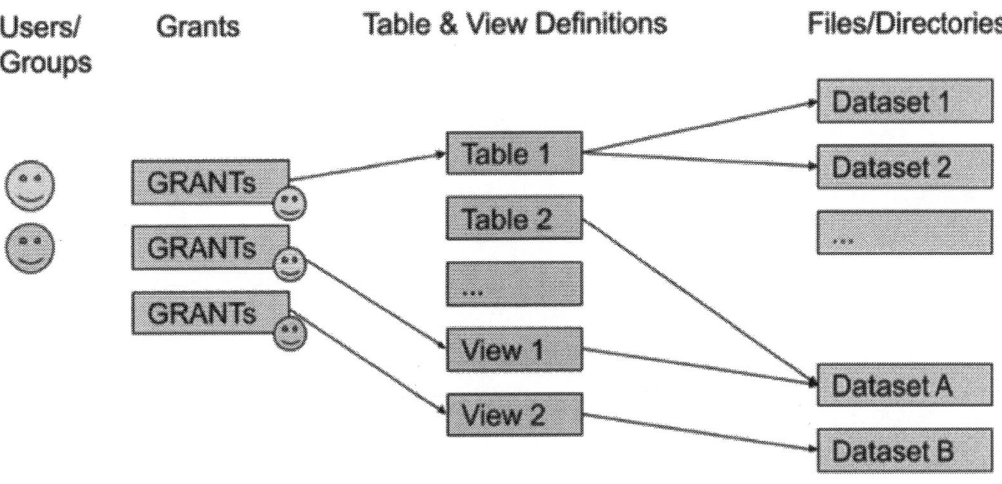

Figure 10.10: Databricks - Table access control

Cluster configuration and policies

In order to manage databases properly, we can use the Databricks cluster policies to provision and manage the clusters with permissions and control the cost. Cluster policies allow the Databricks administrators to create the cluster attributes such as instance type, nodes, and tags. Databricks cluster administrator can create the policy and assign it to the user or group. So, administrators can determine who should have access to the cluster and what type of cluster configurations should be present.

We can define the cluster policies using the JSON files. Once the JSON file is created, cluster policies can be created using the cluster policy UI or cluster policy API:

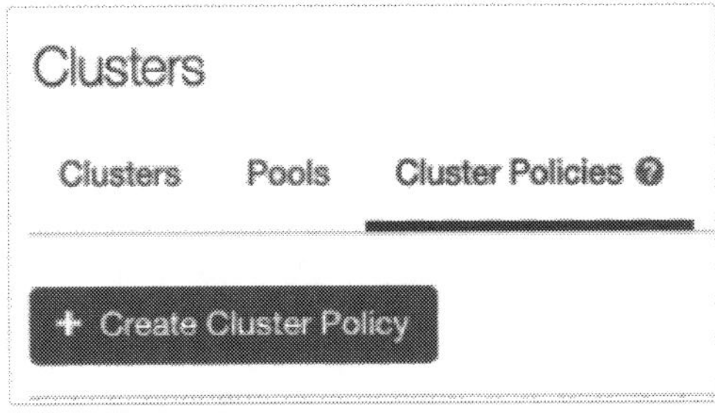

Figure 10.11: Cluster policy UI

We can use the following endpoint API definition to create cluster policies:

Create

Endpoint	HTTP Method
`2.0/policies/clusters/create`	POST

Figure 10.12: *Cluster policy API*

Databricks workspace users can only create a cluster when they have the required permission: `create_cluster` or one of the cluster policies. Workspace administrators can create a required policy and assign it to users so that they can create the cluster.

In the following screenshot, we are creating the cluster policy with the name `Project Team,` creating a cluster based on the policy definition:

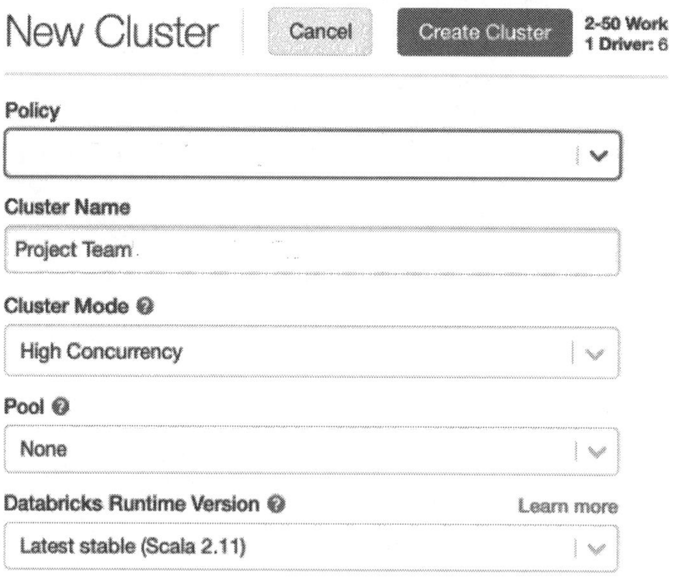

New Cluster
Cancel
Create Cluster
2-50 Work
1 Driver: 6
Policy
Cluster Name
Project Team
Cluster Mode
High Concurrency
Pool
None
Databricks Runtime Version
Learn more
Latest stable (Scala 2.11)

Figure 10.13: *Databricks cluster policy during cluster creation*

It is also possible to automatically provision the cluster and grant permissions to the cluster. Using the REST API for cluster and permissions endpoint, it is easy to provision and grant permission to cluster resources for users and groups. Additionally, we can use an instance profile to the cluster for direct access to any corresponding storage.

The following is an example of a configuration that might be applicable for the new analytics project team.

The requirements are as follows:

- Support the interactive workloads of the team that can work with both SQL and Python.
- Each user will get an equal share of the cluster's resources.
- Provision memory optimized instance types.
- Grant permissions to the cluster so that only limited users can access it.

We can deploy these configurations using the API endpoints in the cluster and permission API. Using the following endpoint, we can create a cluster.

Endpoint: `https://<databricks-instance>/api/2.0/clusters/create`

Here's an **example**:

```
{
    "autoscale": {
   "min_workers": 5,
   "max_workers": 30
     },
   "cluster_name": "project team",
   "spark_version": "latest-stable-scala2.11",
   "spark_conf": {
         "spark.databricks.cluster.profile": "serverless",
         "spark.databricks.repl.allowedLanguages": "sql,python"
    },
  "aws_attributes": {
  "first_on_demand": 1,
  "availability": "SPOT_WITH_FALLBACK",
  "zone_id": "us-youst-2a",
   "instance_profile_arn": "arn:aws:iam::826xxx667205:instan
      ce-profile/test-iam-role",
  "spot_bid_price_percent": 100,
 "ebs_volume_type": "GENERAL_PURPOSE_SSD",
 "ebs_volume_count": 1,
```

```
            "ebs_volume_size": 100
            },
           "node_type_id": "r4.2xlarge",
           "ssh_public_keys": [],
           "custom_tags": {
                   "ResourceClass": "Serverless",
                  "team": "new-project-team"
            },
          "spark_env_vars": {
          "PYSPARK_PYTHON": "/databricks/python3/bin/python3"
          },
        "autotermination_minutes": 60,
       "enable_elastic_disk": "true",
       "init_scripts": []
    }
```

Configuring access control in Databricks and data access and granular access management to data is the first key to creating a data governance solution. But the end-to-end solution requires audit access to the data and creating the monitoring capabilities. Databricks Lakehouse platform has a rich set of audit events to log the activities performed by the Databricks users:

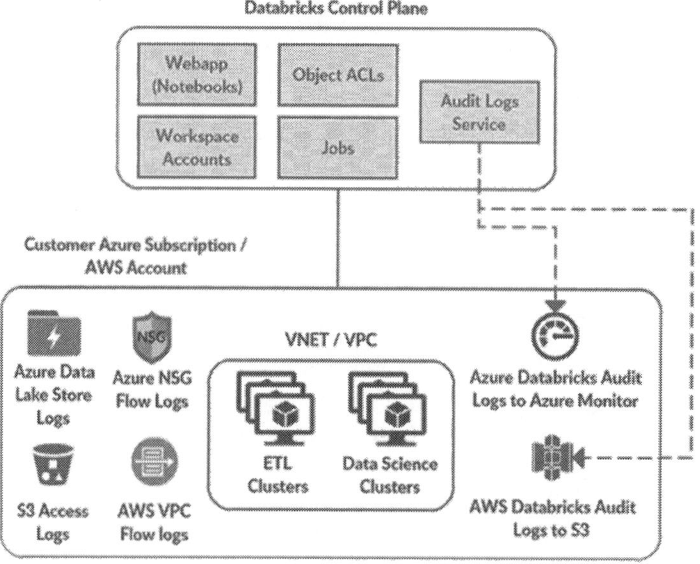

Figure 10.14: *Databricks audit logging*

Reference: **https://databricks.com/blog/2020/03/25/trust-but-verify-with-databricks.html**

In order to configure audit logging, we have to configure the right access policy so that Databricks can deliver audit logs to an S3 bucket. Audit logs are delivered periodically to the S3 bucket and within *72 hours of day close.*

We can configure many types of audit events based on our requirements to track the complete status of audit events, parameters, and audit log schemes.

Data governance

Databricks security and trust center provides information about how to set up security at every layer of the Databricks Lakehouse platform. It enables enterprise organizations to meet the regulatory requirements. This information consists of the following information:

- List of security and governance features into the platform
- Compliance standards required by the platform for each cloud provider
- Package that helps evaluate how Databricks platform is compatible with the for the compliance requirements
- Databricks privacy guidelines

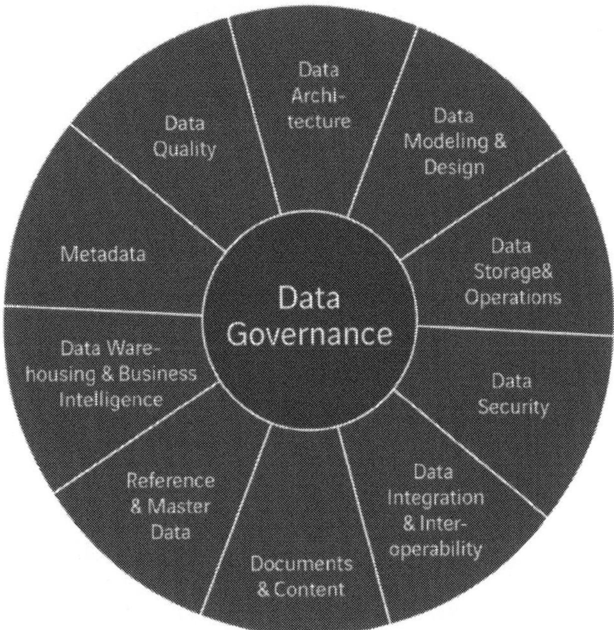

***Figure 10.15**: Data governance framework*

One of the major criteria for successful data governance is to ensure data security across enterprise organizations. Data teams should have visibility of how the data is being accessed by the enterprise organizations. Having a data governance solution in place helps protect the data from unauthorized access and also helps meet regulatory requirements. One of the major challenges faced by enterprise organizations is to secure the data and make sure it is being managed as per the security controls defined within the organizations. Regulatory bodies across the world are changing the way we capture and store data. Typical challenges faced by the enterprise organization are as follows:

- *Do current tools support access controls on the data in the cloud? Do they support inbuilt logging of activities happening on the data?*
- *Will the security and monitoring solution now scale as demand on the data in the Data Lake? It should be easy to provision and monitor data access for a small number of users. What happens when we expose a data lake to large users?*
- *How to proactively monitor data access policies?*
- *How to identify gaps in the existing data security solution?*

Databricks addresses the preceding challenges in multiple ways:

- **Manage access to data and objects**

  Unity Catalog centrally stores data, metadata, and organization's data. Data governance rules scale, regardless of the number of workspaces or the business intelligence tools enterprise organization uses. It grants workspaces access to each metastore and manages access to the data in one place:

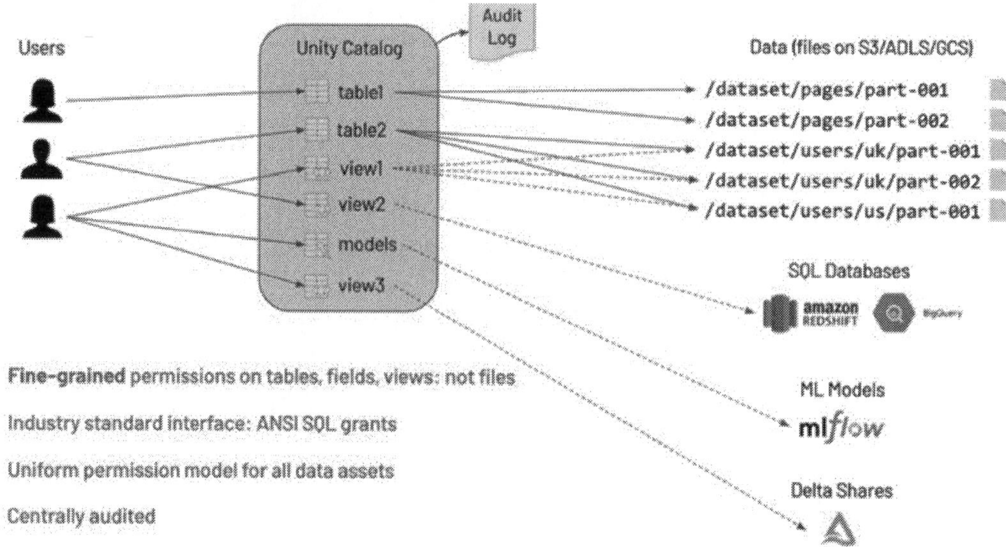

***Figure 10.16**: Data governance framework*

Reference: *https://databricks.com/blog/2021/05/26/introducing-databricks-unity-catalog-fine-grained-governance-for-data-and-ai-on-the-lakehouse.html*

Delta sharing (**https://docs.databricks.com/data-sharing/delta-sharing/index.html**) is an open protocol developed by Databricks to exchange data securely with other organizations, regardless of the computing platforms:

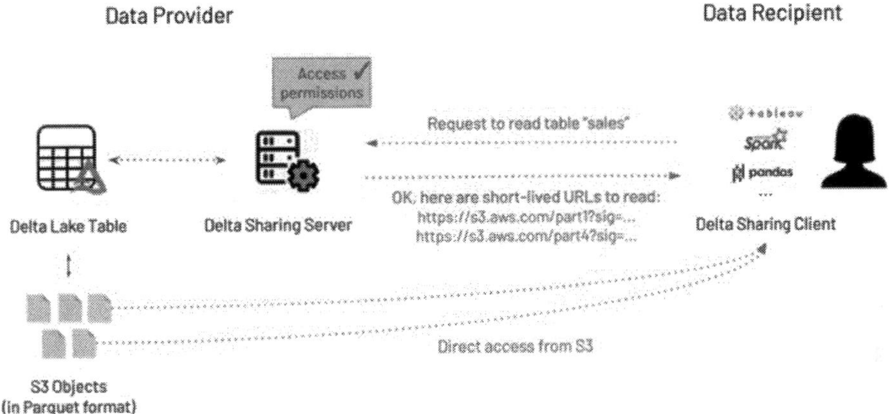

Figure 10.17: *Delta sharing*

Table access control allows end users to apply data governance to control the data. Databricks workspace administrators can only enable ACLs using the **Admin Console** (**https://docs.databricks.com/security/access-control/index.html**) or **Permissions API** (**https://docs.databricks.com/dev-tools/api/latest/permissions.html**).

Credential passthrough feature allows users to authenticate to **S3 buckets** or **Azure Data Lake Storage Gen2** from the Databricks workspace clusters using the identity to log in to the Databricks:

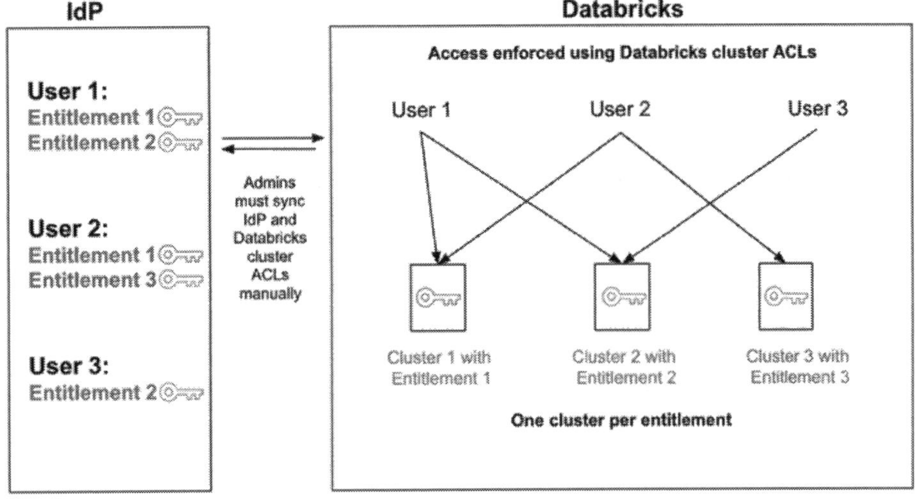

Figure 10.18: *Databricks IAM credential passthrough*

GDPR and CCPA compliance using Delta Lake

With Databricks Delta Lake, enterprise organizations take care of **General Data Protection** (**GDPR**) and CCPA compliance for your Data Lake. Delta Lake simplifies the ability to locate personal data since the Delta Lake has a transactional layer that provides structured data on top of the Data Lake:

***Figure 10.19**: GDPR compliance*

A major challenge faced by enterprise organizations is to manage the big data that has personal information. GDPR and CCPA compliance for this big data set is a humongous task. The major reasons for this are as follows:

- We can store personal information in a distributed manner across multiple datasets. *Ad-hoc* queries to find data are expensive because they require full table scans.
- Data lakes don't have the ability to perform row-level *delete* or *update* operations, so we must rewrite partitions of data. It doesn't provide *ACID* transactional capabilities.

- Data hygiene in the data lake is challenging since Data Lakes, by design, support availability and partition tolerance:

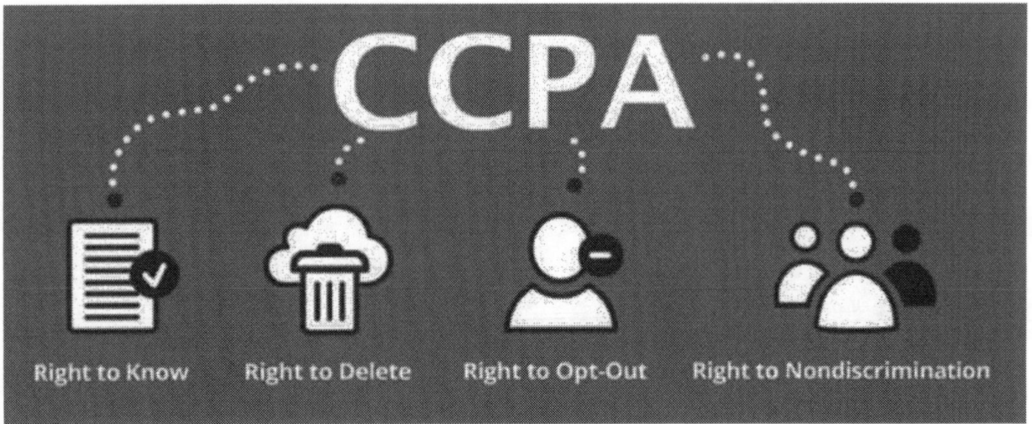

***Figure 10.20**: CCPA compliance*

Databricks Delta Lake addresses the above-mentioned challenges as follows:

- Data anonymization so that personal information can't be tracked back from the data stored in the Data Lake.
- Pipelines and bucket policies to remove raw data, which help comply with the rules.
- Mechanism to locate and remove identifier to destroy the linkage.
- ACID transaction capabilities to prevent end users with access issues when records are being updated or deleted.

Let's consider one use case on how we can delete personal data using the Databricks Delta Lake. Consider a table named **customers** with the following schema:

```
|-- c_customer_id: string (nullable = true)
|-- c_current_addr_sk: integer (nullable = true)
|-- c_first_shipto_date_sk: integer (nullable = true)
|-- c_first_sales_date_sk: integer (nullable = true)
|-- c_first_name: string (nullable = true)
|-- c_last_name: string (nullable = true)
|-- c_birth_day: integer (nullable = true)
|-- c_birth_month: integer (nullable = true)
|-- c_birth_year: integer (nullable = true)
```

```
|-- c_birth_country: string (nullable = true)
|-- c_email_address: string (nullable = true)
```

1. The first step is to convert the tables to the *delta format* using the following command:

   ```
   CONVERT TO DELTA customers
   ```

2. The second step is to delete the personal information of those who requested to remove the PII information:

   ```
   DELETE FROM `customers` AS t1 WHERE EXISTS (SELECT c_customer_id
   FROM cust_dlt_keys WHERE t1.c_customer_id = c_customer_id)
   ```

3. The second last step is to clean up the stale data. Depending on how long a consumer has requested to delete the data from the Data Lake, we need to delete table history and underlying raw data from the Data Lake.

   By default, using the following command, we can remove stale data for *7 days*:

   ```
   VACUUM customers
   ```

4. If we want to remove artifacts younger than *7 days*, use the following command:

   ```
   VACUUM customers RETAIN 100 HOURS
   ```

In addition to this, it is also recommended to set up the retention policy to avoid storing any sensitive personal data that is not intended to be stored.

Conclusion

In this chapter, you learned how to perform hyperparameter tuning with Hyperopt for the Delta Lake. We also understood in detail how to perform access control and secret management. Then, we did a quick tour of cluster configuration and its policies. Then, we also understood in detail the importance of data governance and how Databricks can help us create well governed data solutions using Databricks. At the end, we also explored how Databricks' Delta Lake solution helps enterprise organizations to become GDPR- and CCPA-compliant.

Multiple choice questions

1. Can we authenticate directly to ADLS Gen2 using credential passthrough?
    a. Yes
    b. No
2. Which format is used to store cluster policies?
    a. JSON
    b. CSV
    c. ORC
    d. All of the above
3. Can we enable access control lists for granular access management in Databricks platform?
    a. Yes
    b. No
4. Does Delta Lake support ACID transactions?
    a. Yes
    b. No
5. Can we create Databricks workspace cluster using the API?
    a. Yes
    b. No

Answers

1. **a**
2. **a**
3. **b**
4. **b**
5. **b**

Index

Made in the USA
Columbia, SC
17 October 2023